D1715084

News and Politics
in the Age of
Revolution

Also by Jeremy D. Popkin:

The Right-Wing Press in France, 1792–1800

Press and Politics in Pre-Revolutionary France
(edited with Jack Censer)

NEWS AND POLITICS
IN THE AGE OF
REVOLUTION

Jean Luzac's
Gazette de Leyde

Jeremy D. Popkin

Cornell University Press

Ithaca and London

First published 1989 by Cornell University Press.

International Standard Book Number 0-8014-2301-5
Library of Congress Catalog Card Number 89-31379
Printed in the United States of America
Librarians: Library of Congress cataloging information appears on the last page of the book.

The paper in this book is acid-free and meets the guidelines for permanence and durability of the Committee on Production Guidelines for Book Longevity of the Council on Library Resources.

To Beate

Contents

Preface

This book seeks to establish the importance of the newspaper press in European life in the decades preceding the French Revolution and thereby to illuminate some previously neglected aspects of eighteenth-century life and of the history of journalism. The European newspaper press before 1789 is not a subject that has attracted many scholars of the period. Peter Gay's two-volume survey, *The Enlightenment*, for example, contains only two passing references to newspapers; R. R. Palmer's two-volume work, *The Age of the Democratic Revolution*, has no index entries for either "newspapers" or "press." And yet there is no question that the philosophes who populate Gay's study and the politicians who make a new world in Palmer's were regular newspaper readers. Specialized works on the history of the press do discuss the newspapers of the seventeenth and eighteenth centuries, but those surveys that aim to provide a grand synthesis of the history of journalism, such as Robert Desmond's four-volume work on news reporting and Anthony Smith's short book, *The Newspaper: An International History*, tend to give the subject short shrift. They acknowledge that the first newspapers appeared in Germany and the Netherlands soon after 1600, and they mention the foundation of the *Gazette de France* in 1631, but for all practical purposes the continental European press then disappears from their view until 1789. Historians' neglect of the news journals that brought the thinkers and doers of the eighteenth century their knowledge of what was happening in the political world obscures a vital part of the past; journalism scholars' unfamiliarity with the European press before the French Revolution skews their picture of how the modern news media came to be.

[ix]

At the center of this book stands the story of a great but forgotten newspaper: the *Gazette de Leyde* edited by Jean Luzac. In its day, it was as well known all over Europe as the *New York Times* is to educated and politically concerned individuals throughout the world today. Its editor received mail from Voltaire, from George Washington, and from the ministers of all the crowned heads of Europe. Its readers were scattered from Boston to Calcutta, from Glasgow to Constantinople. Unique among the newspapers of its day because of the respect it commanded, Jean Luzac's *Gazette de Leyde* was the culmination of the first century and a half of European journalism, when the role of the newspaper was to give an impersonal chronicle of ongoing events. But the *Gazette de Leyde* also stood at the threshold of a new era in journalistic history, one in which the newspaper would be called on to represent the force of public opinion and to shape history, as well as to record it. Through this close examination of the environment that produced the *Gazette de Leyde*, how it gathered and printed its reports, its relationship with its readers, and the way it depicted the great events of three critical decades, I hope to contribute both to a better understanding of the age in which the paper appeared and to our grasp of the origins of one of the great forces that shape our world today, the news media.

When I first began to consider working on the history of newspapers and journalism during my years of graduate study, many of my professors did their best to discourage me. They were persuaded, as many historians still are, that such work all too often produces only pedestrian conclusions about what second-rate minds wrote about secondary issues. There were, of course, some exceptions: Hans Rosenberg, one of my teachers at Berkeley, took a strong interest in my first efforts to show that journalism history could make a significant contribution to social and political history. Martin Malia consented to direct my dissertation on right-wing newspapers in revolutionary Paris. And I well remember the inspiration I derived from Robert Darnton's presentation of his work on the publication of the *Encyclopédie:* he demonstrated that the social history of ideas could be not only significant but exciting.

My fascination with newspapers, however, was already too strong for my well-meaning teachers to discourage it. When this interest first developed I cannot say: I only know that when my classmates were dreaming of growing up to be quarterbacks or millionaires, I was already determined to be a great press baron. I had an early interest in history, too, and the two interests came together when my father, trying to help a thirteen-year-old with a term paper project on the origins of World War I, took me to the dusty attic of the Claremont Colleges' Honnold Library and showed me the yellowed, crumbling volumes of the *New York Times* from 1914. I found them irresistible. They brought home to me for the first time the fact that history is something that people make without knowing how it will come out, and I was fascinated by the difference between the medley of stories in the *Times* of 28 June 1914 and the orderly arrangement of facts recorded in the history books.

At about the same time my grandmother, Zelda Popkin, a novelist and sometime reporter, gave me a book that has had far greater impact on my thinking about newspapers than almost any of the weighty academic works I have read since. It was A. J. Liebling's *The Press*, a collection of essays about American journalism in the 1940s and 1950s. An unlikely work to interest an American teenager of the 1960s, perhaps, but Liebling's sense of the complexity behind even the simplest newspaper story and his implicit message about the importance of honest journalism in a free society made an indelible impression on me.

With such a background, it would have been natural for me to become a journalist myself. During my student days, I worked on several newspapers. Reporting on the student riots of the 1960s for the Berkeley *Daily Californian*, I learned firsthand the thrill of being in the center of the action and of seeing one's words in print the day after they were written. A great deal of what I learned from those experiences has gone into my subsequent academic work. But I also learned the limitations of journalism: the impossibility of ever thinking a subject through as fully and completely as one would like before setting one's thoughts down on paper, the constant pressure and tension of a journalist's life, the inevitable recognition that what one has written will be quickly forgotten. When my friends from the *Daily Californian* went off to start their apprenticeships at newspapers around the country, I went off to Paris and sublimated my passion for newspapers by burying myself in the old journals in the Bibliothèque nationale. It was there, many years later, that I first read a copy of the prerevolutionary *Gazette de Leyde*. I recognized in it the qualities that had fascinated me about newspapers from my childhood, and out of that encounter has come this book. The late A. J. Liebling, war reporter, boxing fan, gourmet, and anything but academic in his inclinations, might have scratched his head at the idea of such a project. But I like to hope that some of his spirited enthusiasm for the press has passed into these scholarly pages.

In the course of my research and writing, I have incurred many obligations. I thank the National Endowment for the Humanities, the Newberry Library, the American Philosophical Society, the American Council of Learned Societies, and the University of Kentucky Research Foundation for fellowship support in connection with this project. The Newberry Library in Chicago and the Max-Planck-Institut für Geschichte in Göttingen provided supportive environments for the de-

velopment of the ideas incorporated in this book. I am grateful to the
staffs of many libraries and archives for their assistance, particularly the
Regenstein Library of the University of Chicago, the Leiden University
Library, the Leiden Gemeentearchief, the Algemeen Rijksarchief of
The Hague, the Rijksarchief en Zuid-Holland, the Koninklijk Bibli-
otheek, the Bibliothèque nationale, the Archives nationales, the New-
berry Library, the Library of Congress, the Archive de la Ministère des
Affaires étrangères, the Huntington Library, the Massachusetts Histor-
ical Society, the Folger Library, the Margaret I. King Library of the
University of Kentucky, and the university libraries of Amsterdam,
Göttingen, Wisconsin, and Indiana. I thank the University of California
Press for permission to use some material from my contribution to Jack
R. Censer and Jeremy D. Popkin, eds., *Press and Politics in Pre-
Revolutionary France,* published in 1987.

For more than a decade, my friend Jack Censer has shared with me his
enthusiasm and his extensive knowledge of the forgotten newspapers of
the eighteenth century. His incisive critiques have saved me from many
an error. Martin Welke of the Deutsches Zeitungsmuseum in Meers-
burg, West Germany, has been equally generous in allowing me to
benefit from his unrivaled knowledge of the world of eighteenth-century journalism. I am also grateful to Raymond Birn, Harold Ellis, and
my colleague Mark Summers for their careful reading of the entire
manuscript, and to Jan De Vries, Herbert Rowen, and Wayne te Brake
for their advice to a historian of France adrift in the unfamiliar world of
the Dutch Republic. My friend Judy Hansburg Woodward donated her
time to give me my first information about the Luzac papers in Leiden,
and Jan Van den Berg, Ivo Schöffer, Ernestine Van der Wall, Anita van
Bokhoven of the Rijksarchief en Zuid-Holland, and Josien Huizinga of
the Nederlands Persmuseum in Amsterdam have been helpful in locat-
ing other archival information on the subject. Keith Baker and Pierre
Rétat have given much valued encouragement and inspiration over the
years. Robert Hodges and Andy McIntire made the index. Like the
editor of the *Gazette de Leyde,* Jean Luzac, the central figure in my story, I
am acutely aware of how difficult it is to obtain the truth about events far
away and long ago: I can only say, as he did, that I have tried to keep my
errors to a minimum and that it is I, not my friends, who must bear the
responsibility for them.

Unless otherwise indicated, all translations in the text are my own.

JEREMY D. POPKIN

Lexington, Kentucky

Abbreviations

AN	Archives nationales (Paris)
AR	Algemeen Rijksarchief (The Hague)
BN	Bibliothèque nationale (Paris)
DP	Dumont-Pigalle papers
Dumas	Charles Dumas papers
GL	*Gazette de Leyde*
KB	Koninklijk Bibliotheek (The Hague)
LC	Library of Congress (Washington, D.C.)
LGA	Leiden Gemeentearchief
LGA-VH	Van Heukelom Family Archive
LUL	Leiden University Library
Luzac	Luzac Family Archive
MAE	Archives de la Ministère des Affaires étrangères (Paris)

News and Politics
in the Age of
Revolution

[1]

News and European
Culture in the
Eighteenth Century

"Newspapers. I set this word down with a feeling of deep respect. Newspapers are one of the great instruments of culture through which we Europeans have become what we are."[1] So wrote the German journalist August Ludwig von Schlözer, one of the founders of modern social science, in 1804. He had just lived through the period of the French Revolution, when the newspaper press had become a political force impossible to ignore, but there is no doubt that Schlözer meant his comment to apply as well to the prerevolutionary era, when he himself had been one of the continent's leading newsmen, editor of the celebrated German political magazine known as the *Stats-Anzeigen*. Indeed, long before 1789, the political newspaper had become one of the most widespread of European cultural institutions, and its ubiquity was, as Schlözer noted, one of the distinctive characteristics of European civilization. No other major world civilization had developed any comparable medium for the dissemination of information, not only to government officials, but to a general public limited only by the ability to pay the modest price of a subscription or of admission to a coffeehouse or tavern where newspapers were available.[2]

1. August Ludwig von Schlözer, *Theorie der Statistik* (Göttingen: Vandenhoeck and Ruprecht, 1804), 78.
2. The Chinese may have been the first to have periodical newssheets, perhaps as early as the eighth or tenth centuries, but "these gazettes . . . should be considered a press service exclusively for the benefit of the official bureaucrats rather than of the people at large." Lin Yutang, *A History of the Press and Public Opinion in China* (New York: Greenwood, 1968 rpt. ed.), 12. In the Ottoman Empire, printing in Turkish or Arabic was banned altogether until 1727 and the single printing establishment created then was suppressed in 1742, not to be reopened until 1784. Bernard Lewis, *The Emergence of Modern Turkey* (London: Oxford University Press, 1961), 51. News periodicals first appeared in Japan in the 1860s,

By the second half of the eighteenth century, newspapers were printed in numerous European cities and towns that had no other major intellectual institutions: no universities, no academies, no book publishers. There were at least 93 newspapers published in German-speaking Europe in 1750, and 151 by 1785. In Britain, 28 provincial cities had one or more local newspapers by 1758, in addition to the dozen or more London papers that circulated nationally. In France, where the official *Gazette de France* had a monopoly on the publication of news, there were authorized reprints of that paper in 28 cities in 1749, and 44 cities had a local newspaper by 1784. Although newspapers were most numerous in western and central Europe, the institution had taken root even in those countries with the lowest literacy rates and the most autocratic governments. The first Spanish newspaper had appeared in 1641, the first Russian one in 1702.[3] Wherever Europeans settled in the world, they created newspapers modeled after those at home. There were 22 in Britain's North American colonies by 1760, and others appeared in the European colonies in the West Indies and in India.[4] A map showing where newspapers were published would be impressive enough by the 1770s, but newspapers were for sale in many other communities as well: indeed, there was probably no permanent European settlement anywhere in the world where printed newssheets did not eventually make their way.

Newspapers also had a very wide readership, larger perhaps than that of any other genre of printed material except popular almanacs and devotional works. Martin Welke, the leading expert on the German-language newspaper press before 1800, has estimated the total press run of all German-language newspapers in the eighteenth century at about 300,000 copies a week, with each copy reaching at least several readers.[5]

under the influence of Western models; the extensive broadsheet and pamphlet press of the Tokugawa period had been largely apolitical and subject to strict censorship. Albert Altman, "'Shimbunshi': The Early Meiji Adaptation of the Western-style Newspaper," in William G. Beasley, ed., *Modern Japan: Aspects of History, Literature and Society* (Berkeley: University of California Press, 1975), 52, 56.

3. Paul-J. Guinard, *La presse espagnole de 1737 à 1791* (Paris: Centre de recherches hispaniques, 1973), 111; Gary Marker, *Publishing, Printing, and the Origins of Intellectual Life in Russia, 1700–1800* (Princeton, N.J.: Princeton University Press, 1985).

4. Figures from Martin Welke, "Die Legende vom 'unpolitischen Deutschen.' Zeitungslesen im 18. Jahrhundert als Spiegel des politischen Interesses," *Jahrbuch der Wittheit zu Bremen* 25 (1981), 183; Roy Wiles, *Freshest Advices: Early Provincial Newspapers in England* (Columbus: Ohio State University Press, 1965), 28; Gilles Feyel, *La "Gazette" en province à travers ses réimpressions, 1631–1752* (Amsterdam and Maarssen: APA-Holland University Press, 1982), 20–22; Feyel, "La presse provinciale au XVIIIe siècle: Géographie d'un reseau," *Revue historique*, no. 552 (1984), 353–74; Stephen Botein, "'Meer Mechanics' and an Open Press: The Business and Political Strategies of Colonial American Printers," *Perspectives in American History* 9 (1975), 150; Joachim von Schwarzkopf, "Von Kolonial-Zeitungen," *Allgemeiner Litterarischer Anzeiger*, 5 Mar. 1801, 337–42.

5. "Gemeinsame Lektüre und frühe Formen von Gruppenbildungen im 17. und 18. Jahrhundert: Zeitungslesen in Deutschland," in Otto Dann, ed., *Lesegesellschaften und bürgerliche Emanzipation* (Munich: Beck, 1981), 30.

The German states were undoubtedly the area with the largest news-paper-reading audience, but in England, France, the Netherlands, and northern Italy, newspapers were available to most literate adults. The late-eighteenth-century newspaper was far from being a genuine mass medium—the persistence of adult illiteracy was enough to prevent it from achieving that status—but it was the one genre of printed material that reached an audience extending from the wealthy elites to a consid-erable portion of the urban lower classes and even some of the peas-antry.[6]

Yet despite its broad audience, the news press of the seventeenth and eighteenth centuries has received little scholarly attention. Too dry and limited in content to interest intellectual historians, the newspapers of the early modern world have been considered to be too much a product of governing elites to interest researchers looking for evidence of popu-lar *mentalités*. Historians of the English-speaking world, where formal precensorship was abolished at the end of the seventeenth century, have been more attentive to the news press than their colleagues concerned with other areas: the modern Anglo-American concept of press freedom has clear roots in the early modern period, and the importance of the press's role in both English domestic politics and the coming of the American Revolution is too obvious to have been overlooked.[7] The history of newspapers in continental Europe has remained isolated from the mainstream of historical research, despite the publication of several recent multivolume national press histories;[8] general historians of those countries have not seen the early modern press as a significant aspect of their culture or politics, and historians of the press have not viewed the newspapers published before 1800 as important forerunners of the nineteenth- and twentieth-century press.

The purpose of this book is to challenge these assumptions and to show that the continental European news press before the French Revo-lution was indeed consequential both in the life of its own day and in the making of modern journalism. The journalism historian James W. Carey has justifiably asserted that the study of the newspapers of the past reveals "the story of the growth and transformation of the human mind as formed and expressed by one of the most significant forms in

6. For the most recent survey of literacy in Europe at the end of the eighteenth century, see Harvey J. Graff, *The Legacies of Literacy* (Bloomington: Indiana University Press, 1987), 173–259.

7. On the evolution of press freedom in Britain and the United States, see Leonard Levy, *Emergence of a Free Press* (New York: Oxford University Press, 1985). On England, see Jeremy Black, *The English Press in the Eighteenth Century* (Philadelphia: University of Pennsylvania Press, 1987).

8. See particularly Claude Bellanger et al., *Histoire générale de la presse française*, vol. 1 (Paris: Presses universitaires de France, 1969); and Valerio Castronovo et al., *La stampa italiana dal cinquecento all'ottocento* (Bari: Laterza, 1976), the first volume of the *Storia della stampa italiana*. Margot Lindemann, *Deutsche Presse bis 1815* (Berlin: Colloquium, 1969), is less satisfactory.

which the mind has conceived and expressed itself during the last three hundred years—the journalistic report."[9] In exploring the largely neglected world of the eighteenth-century news press, this book aims to add a new dimension to the understanding of politics in what historian R. R. Palmer has labeled "the age of the democratic revolution," and to show that the European newspapers of that era made a substantial contribution to defining the possibilities of journalism in modern societies.

The typical eighteenth-century newspaper would probably repel the modern reader. When one opens a bound volume of such a publication, one confronts columns of crowded type, unrelieved by such modern journalistic inventions as headlines, subheads, and illustrations, recounting long-forgotten events in the style of a dull student research paper. But to contemporaries, these were passionately exciting reports of the world they lived in; they reached for these texts more avidly than many of the other eighteenth-century works we now find more fascinating. The words on paper in newspapers were words that made a difference: they were an important aspect of eighteenth-century reality itself, affecting the functioning of its political institutions and the outcome of movements as momentous as the major revolutions of the time. They are, furthermore, valuable clues to some much-neglected aspects of eighteenth-century mentality, particularly to its sense of time and of historical change. This book will attempt to demonstrate, then, that our picture of the eighteenth-century world is as incomplete without an awareness of its newspapers as a picture of our own society would be without reference to its most important news sources.

Newspapers mattered to their eighteenth-century readers because they were the best source of information about contemporary events. Unlike modern historians, who enjoy a vast array of other sources of information about this period, people of those times found it difficult to find out what was taking place beyond the range of their own eyes and ears. The dry and fragmentary news bulletins and the now nearly incomprehensible documents published in eighteenth-century newspapers were the fruits of a major effort of information gathering in a world that lacked the resources for that task which modern men and women take for granted.

It is true that eighteenth-century Europe had a fairly extensive system of communications. Since the beginning of the seventeenth century, regular postal systems had existed in most of western and central Europe. The quality of road networks varied greatly from region to region, but passable routes linked all parts of the continent during most of the

9. James W. Carey, "The Problem of Journalism History," *Journalism History* 1 (1974), 27.

year. Roads and postal systems permitted the dissemination of ideas and information, but they did not make the process automatic. Mail was expensive and slow, and only a few exceptional individuals, such as Voltaire and Horace Walpole, could afford the time and money to maintain a correspondence network that kept them informed regularly about major events all over the continent. Travel, too, was costly and time-consuming. A spontaneous journey to the scene of some interesting event was an extraordinary undertaking, characteristic of such adventurers of dubious reputation as the future French revolutionary Jacques-Pierre Brissot but not of those who had steady careers and responsibilities.

It was the printing press that enabled European civilization to overcome these barriers. But the printing press also had severe limitations. The wooden hand press, scarcely improved since Gutenberg's day, lacked the technical capacity to transmit anything like the volume of information that the power-driven printing machinery of the nineteenth century would be able to handle. For cultural and political reasons, moreover, even the existing printing technology was not used to its full capacity. Governments did not systematically publicize their acts; in most states, the prevailing assumption was that the subjects had no right or need to know what their rulers were doing or even what the laws of their country were. When they did set out to broadcast a particular item of information to the entire literate population, rulers found themselves largely unprepared for the task. Thus the French government had to rely on a haphazard network of individual printers to circulate the edicts of convocation for the Estates-General of 1789: there was no established machinery of public information to carry out the job.[10]

If it was difficult to obtain the latest government edicts and regulations, it was equally difficult to obtain older ones. Vital public documents were often maintained only in manuscript form, in inaccessible archives. Information from other countries was also in short supply. Travelers arrived irregularly, and their qualifications as observers naturally varied tremendously. The eighteenth-century vogue for travel books is testimony to the interest in information about distant places, but also to the difficulty in obtaining it. Even basic facts about major European countries remained in dispute. There were no reliable population figures: "We poor Germans still do not know how many of us there are," Schlözer complained in one of the statistics-filled articles he published in his journal.[11] There were few accurate economic statistics, and sometimes

10. There is extensive documentation on the difficulties of publicizing the instructions for the convocation of the Estates-General in AN, V(1), 549, e.g., documents no. 31 and 449.

11. Schlözer, *Briefwechsel meist historischen und politischen Inhalts* v. 3, no. 13, 18n. (Jan. 1778).

no accepted data on the sizes of long-established territories. Compared with the world that came into existence in the nineteenth century, held together by the telegraph and the railroad, and kept informed by daily newspapers capable of transmitting far more information than their forerunners, the eighteenth century lived in a perpetual fog of uncertainty about distant events.

The periodical newspaper was the early modern European world's most ambitious attempt to remedy this situation. The newspaper was part of that broad drive for systematic, rational control over the environment which has characterized European civilization since the Renaissance. The printing press made the newspaper possible; dependable postal systems made it practical. The regular, periodic transmission of messages meant one could produce a regular printed version of those messages, and improved systems of mail and transport made it possible to market such printed products widely enough to make them profitable. A regular, comprehensive survey of major world events, previously available only to rulers via their diplomatic networks and to businessmen as wealthy as the Fuggers, now became available to a much broader public. The progress of the newspaper closely paralleled that of the private timepiece, as described in David Landes's *Revolution in Time:*[12] both served to orient the actions of individuals in time, the personal watch by allowing users to time and control their own activities, the newspaper by giving them a sense of the movement of the wider world.

Like the pocket watch, the newspaper was perfected and improved throughout the seventeenth and eighteenth centuries, but without any revolutionary technological transformation. There was a steady movement toward more frequent publication and toward the delivery of a larger total amount of content in a given period. Newspaper publishers achieved these gains by increasing the size of the paper used, employing smaller type, and printing more pages. Most of the early seventeenth-century papers appeared at most once a week; by the end of the century, 64 percent of German newspapers were issued biweekly and an additional 7 percent had three or more issues per week.[13] This increase in the information-carrying capacity of individual newspapers paralleled a steady growth in the number of papers throughout the period.

What these newspapers had to offer was a skeletal narrative of major public events: wars, diplomatic negotiations, and major political occurrences within states, ranging from royal edicts to constitutional conflicts. These newspaper accounts were soon superseded even in their own day

12. David Landes, *Revolution in Time* (Cambridge, Mass.: Harvard University Press, 1983).

13. Jürgen Wilke, *Nachrichtenauswahl und Medienrealität in vier Jahrhunderten* (Berlin: De Gruyter, 1984), 40.

by other forms of narrative and polemic, from ephemeral pamphlets to the "histories" of significant happenings which writers of the time produced as speedily as the journalistic historians of today. But the very process by which newspaper accounts were replaced by other forms of journalistic literature points to the unique characteristics of the newspaper text which made it so important in its own time: its timeliness and its regular, predictable publication.

Otto Groth, the leading student of the genre, has defined periodic publication as one of the essential attributes of all newspapers.[14] By providing a regular account of events and arriving at a predictable time, the newspaper sets itself off from other kinds of journalism such as pamphlets and books. Periodicity allows readers to anticipate the arrival of their newspaper and structures their reactions to the changes in the world its text reports. The newspaper's periodicity was also a mechanism for structuring the flow of time, which thus became broken into predictable segments. Within those segments, events, no matter how unsettling, would be promptly and dependably named, recorded, and put into the comforting framework of journalistic stereotypes. What was new and threatening in the world would thus be made more manageable.

Another specific feature of newspapers is timeliness. As Groth puts it, the purpose of the newspaper is to print up-to-date information: "The means by which newspapers first win over and then maintain their audience . . . is the satisfaction of a common desire for what is new."[15] Although the newspaper's account of events could soon be supplanted by accounts in other media, its special claim was that it gave the first report. The arrival of the newspaper set off the first reactions to the news it contained, whether idle conversations among its readers or concrete actions, ranging from changes in the bids on stock exchanges to outbreaks of popular violence. The newspaper was the first point of contact between its readers and new events occurring at a distance from them.

To attempt to describe and analyze the content of all the surviving European newspapers of the eighteenth century would be a monumental undertaking. My approach is rather to focus on one particular publication, a newspaper that contemporaries recognized as the finest exemplar of the genre, and to examine its history during the years of its greatest glory, just before the French Revolution. We can then follow its struggle to survive in the new political climate that the Revolution created. The years running from just after 1770 to just before 1800 were crucial: the American and French Revolutions, the diplomatic earth-

---

14. Otto Groth, *Die Zeitung* (Mannheim: Bensheimer, 1928), 1:22.
15. Ibid., 1:50.

quake resulting in the partitions of Poland and rise of the great powers who would dominate European affairs until the First World War, and domestic political crises in almost every country occurred in this period. The development of modern journalism coincided with these events. In the revolutionary upheavals of the time, the press became not only a medium for the communication of information but also a force in shaping public opinion. The achievements and limitations of Europe's most respected newspaper in covering dramatic news events and coping with the changing nature of journalism illustrate most facets of the functioning of the eighteenth-century news press as a whole. The successes and failures of this one publication show how the news system of the European old regime functioned and what happened when that world was suddenly transformed. Happily, we can follow the fortunes of this newspaper during these dramatic years through a range of archival materials more extensive than any yet discovered for other newspapers before the modern era.

The method I follow is to analyze this newspaper as a coherent text, that is, as a representation of the world in words, chosen and arranged in accordance with certain specific rules. To be sure, such a text can be fully understood only with reference to a number of contexts that framed it. I argue that this particular newspaper fully qualifies as one of those complex texts for which, as Dominick LaCapra has written, "one has [a] set of interacting contexts whose relations to one another are variable and problematic and whose relation to the text being investigated raises difficult issues of interpretation."[16] Among the key contexts that conditioned this eighteenth-century newspaper were the conscious and unconscious intentions of its editor, the traditions of journalistic discourse within which it operated, the rival publications against which it competed, and the nature of the European society in which it circulated.

The *Gazette de Leyde*

Among the several hundred news publications available to European readers in the 1770s and 1780s, one title stood out. Thomas Jefferson called it simply "the best in Europe" and "the only one in Europe worth reading."[17] According to a French source, Louis XVI "respected it, and

16. Dominick LaCapra, "Rethinking Intellectual History and Reading Texts," in LaCapra and Steven L. Kaplan, eds., *Modern European Intellectual History* (Ithaca, N.Y.: Cornell University Press, 1982), 57.

17. Jefferson to John Jay, 17 June 1785, and Jefferson to C. F. Dumas, 31 July 1788, in Julian Boyd, ed., *The Papers of Thomas Jefferson* (Princeton, N.J.: Princeton University Press, 1950–), 8:226, 13:438–39.

it was said to be the only one he read."[18] Joachim von Schwarzkopf, a German diplomat who wrote the first international survey of the newspaper press in the 1790s, gave the paper a detailed encomium: "By water and land it was sent to the most distant countries; it was read with the same intense interest at the gates of the Seraglio and on the banks of the Ganges, and copied from by almost all other newspaper editors. . . . In exactitude on diplomatic matters, in completeness and impartiality, and in conciseness and elegance of expression, it was unmatched by any other newspaper."[19]

The publication to which Jefferson and Schwarzkopf referred bore the unwieldy title of *Nouvelles extraordinaires de Divers Endroits*, but it was universally referred to simply as the *Gazette de Leyde*. One of several gazettes published in the Netherlands but printed in French, it had appeared continuously since 1677, but it acquired its almost unquestioned position as Europe's newspaper of record only in the latter half of the eighteenth century, first under the ownership of Etienne Luzac, editor and publisher from 1739 to the early 1770s, and then even more strikingly under his nephew Jean Luzac, from 1772 until 1798. During this period, the *Gazette de Leyde* clearly outdid all other journals in providing a detailed chronicle of ongoing political events in Europe as a whole and within the major countries of the continent. Even when the French Revolution had utterly transformed Europe's journalistic landscape, a set of back volumes of the *Gazette de Leyde* remained indispensable for those who wanted a comprehensive record of the history of their own times. No less a personage than Louis Bonaparte, installed by his brother as king of the Netherlands after 1806, contacted the paper's owner in quest of such a collection.[20]

The *Gazette de Leyde* in the years of Jean Luzac's editorship was the culmination of a long history of French-language news reporting in the Netherlands.[21] Indeed, the earliest known gazette published in the

18. [Pidansat de Mairobert, attrib.], *Mémoires secrets pour servir à l'histoire de la république des lettres en France, depuis MDCCLXII jusqu'à nos jours* (London: John Adamson, 1777–89), 28:166 (8 Mar. 1785).

19. *Allgemeiner Literarische Anzeiger*, 23 Sept. 1800. On Schwarzkopf's life and his pioneering comparative survey of world newspapers, see Otto Groth, *Geschichte der deutschen Zeitungswissenschaft* (Munich: Weinmayer, 1948), 68–81. Schwarzkopf published the results of his country-by-country survey in a series of articles in the *Allgemeiner Literarische Anzeiger* in 1800–1801.

20. Letter signed Briatte, to Etienne Luzac, 13 April 1809, in LGA-VH, Z(2), no. 121.

21. The most comprehensive existing study of the Dutch French-language gazettes as a whole is Eugène Hatin, *Les gazettes de Hollande et la presse clandestine aux XVIIe et XVIIIe siècles* (Paris: Pincebourde, 1865). The publication of this work inspired a nineteenth-century Dutch scholar, Willem Pieter Sautijn Kluit, to compile a series of monographs on the Dutch papers based on scrupulous archival research but consisting of little more than excerpts of the documents he found. A bibliography of his numerous articles is in *Docu-*

French language, the *Courant d'Italie et d'Almaigne*, appeared in Amsterdam in 1620, eleven years before the founding of the first newspaper on French soil.[22] In the first half of the seventeenth century, Amsterdam was the only source of French-language gazettes in the Netherlands, but a similar paper may have appeared in Leiden in the 1660s, since the city issued a ban against such publications in 1669.[23] This initial French gazette does not seem to have been the direct ancestor of Luzac's paper, however. The history of the *Gazette de Leyde* began in 1677, when Jean Alexandre de la Font, a French Huguenot, began to publish a newssheet under the title of *Traduction libre des Gazettes flamandes et autres*.[24] The title indicated that the paper began as a by-product of the flourishing Dutch-language news industry, like the Amsterdam *Courant d'Italie et d'Almaigne* a half-century earlier. By 1679, however, the paper had adopted a new title that suggested a bid to be taken seriously as a news source in its own right: *Nouvelles extraordinaires de Divers Endroits*.[25] This formula, typical of the seventeenth-century European press, remained the paper's official name until 1798, long after most other European newspapers had gone over to shorter titles; in this, as in many other respects, the Leiden paper remained rooted in the journalistic conventions developed in the late seventeenth century.

The *Gazette de Leyde* had come on the scene at an auspicious moment: the increasing stream of French Huguenot refugees arriving in the Netherlands guaranteed an easily accessible audience, and the wars of Louis XIV guaranteed a steady flow of news to print. Repeated bans against the publication of such gazettes issued by the the Estates of Holland had no effect.[26] In the 1680s and 1690s, the *Gazette de Leyde*

---

mentatieblad Werkgroep Achttiende Eeuw, no. 39 (May 1978), 15–22, and a short summary of his main points is in Graham C. Gibbs, "The Role of the Dutch Republic as the Intellectual Entrepôt of Europe in the 17th and 18th centuries," in *Bijdragen en Mededelingen betreffende de Geschiedenis den Nederlanden* 86 (1971), 323–49. The most complete listing of these and similar papers published elsewhere in Europe is in Jerzy Lojek, "Gazettes internationales de langue française dans la seconde moitié du XVIIIe siècle," in *Modèles et moyens de la réflexion politique au XVIIIe siècle* (Lille: Presses universitaires de Lille, 1977), 1:369–82.

22. The paper was a translation of the Dutch-language *Courante uyt Italien en Duytslandt*, founded in 1618. Four numbers of the *Courant d'Italie et d'Almaigne* from 1620–21 are reproduced in Folke Dahl, *Dutch Corantos 1618–1650* (The Hague: Nijhoff, 1946).

23. Willem Pieter Sautijn Kluit, "Geschiedenis der Nederlandsche Dagbladpers tot 1813," in *Bijdragen tot de Geschiedenis van den Nederlandschen Boekhandel* 7 (1896), 114.

24. Willem P. Sautijn Kluit. "De Fransche Leidsche Courant," in *Handelingen en Mededeelingen van de Maatschappij der Nederlandsche Letterkunde te Leiden*, (1869–70), 3–13. An early number of this publication, dated 31 August 1677, is reproduced in W. P. van Stockum, *La librairie, l'imprimerie et la presse en Hollande à travers quatre siècles* (The Hague: Mouton, 1910), 82–84. Publication apparently had begun in March 1677.

25. The issue for 16 November 1679, in the Bibliothèque Mazarine (Paris), is the earliest known copy with the new title.

26. J. T. Bodel Nyenhuis, *De Wetgeving op de drukpers en boekhandel in de Nederlanden tot in het begin van de 19e eeuw* (Amsterdam: Van Kampen, 1892), 135–44, lists edicts against the

seems to have enjoyed success. Its four-page biweekly issues were re-issued in several counterfeit editions, a sure sign of a good journalistic reputation.[27] Despite the ongoing wars between France and the Nether-lands, the paper circulated in Louis XIV's kingdom; it was publicly advertised in Grenoble in 1697–98.[28]

Jean Alexandre de la Font had died in 1685. The paper evidently was taken over by his son, Anthony de la Font, born, like his father, in Languedoc; they were among the many Huguenot refugees who made a new life in the United Provinces of the Netherlands. Little evidence exists about the condition of the paper in the early eighteenth century, other than the Leiden city fathers' renewal of its privilege in 1706.[29] It continued to print news that was kept out of the domestic press in the major European states: in 1716, it published secret summaries of the proceedings against an English peer implicated in the Jacobite rebellion of 1715.[30] In 1723, the de la Fonts took an action that determined the history of the paper for the rest of the century: they engaged the teenaged son of another Huguenot refugee, one Etienne Luzac, to assist in the editing of their journal.[31] Anthony de la Font continued to be listed as publisher until his death in 1738. During the 1720s and 1730s, the paper remained important enough for several foreign governments to lodge protests with the Dutch government about its reports, but these complaints seem to have had no serious consequences.[32]

---

publication of French-language papers in the province of Holland in 1679, 1686, and 1691. The latter measure was later extended to cover all Dutch provinces.

27. Given the scarcity of issues from this period, it is not easy to distinguish counterfeit from genuine copies. The Lilly Library at Indiana University, Bloomington, has several issues from 1690 bearing an imprint at the bottom of p. 4 reading "A LEIDE Chez De la Font," with printed area measuring 18.8 cm by 12.3 cm and catchwords at the bottom of the right-hand columns on pp. 1–3. If this edition is authentic, then de la Font had slightly altered the paper's format by 1698, when the series of copies now in the Folger Library in Washington, D.C., were produced. Their imprint reads "Leide, Chez de La Font, Avec privilège des Etats de Hollande et de West-Frise." The printed area measures 19.4 cm by 11.6 cm, and there are no catchwords. The high quality of the printing and the use of the minute *brevier* or *petit texte* letters—a Dutch printing specialty—make it probable that these copies represent the authentic edition. The Folger and Lilly libraries both possess a few numbers of a version of the paper that has no imprint and whose printed area measures 18 cm by 13 cm, the Folger's numbers dating from 1687 and the Lilly's from 1688. These are more crudely printed and use the slightly larger type size known as *petit romain* in France. They probably represent an unauthorized reprint of the paper.

28. Feyel, La "Gazette" en province, 150.

29. Kluit, "Fransche Leidsche Courant," 19.

30. An English political figure, John Oldmixon, was accused of having tried to arrange for an English translation of the documents printed in French in the newspaper. Jeremy Black and Pat Rogers, "Oldmixon Incurs 'The Displeasure of the Most Honourable House of Peers,'" in *Factotum* (Newsletter of the Eighteenth-Century Short Title Catalogue), no. 24 (Aug. 1987), 4.

31. Kluit, "Fransche Leidsche Courant," 21.

32. Protest letters in LGA-VH, Z(1), include documents no. 7 (complaint from Hanau, 1737), and no. 20 (complaint from Poland, 1741).

The event that cleared the way for the *Gazette de Leyde*'s eventual rise to the status of Europe's most trusted newspaper occurred in 1738, when Anthony de la Font died. Ownership of the paper, whose privilege had just been renewed in 1736,[33] passed to his daughter Aletta Maria and her husband Johannes de Graaff, a lawyer in The Hague. The pair had no interest in running a newspaper themselves; after complex negotiations with several would-be purchasers, they finally made a contract with Etienne Luzac, under which he agreed to take over the enterprise and to pay the de Graaffs a yearly sum of 1,500 gulden, of which 300 represented the yearly payment owed to the city of Leiden for the paper's privilege.[34] From 1738 onward, the paper bore the imprint "A Leide, par Etienne Luzac." The actual printing of the paper was handled by Etienne Luzac's brother Jean Luzac, who had been admitted to the city's printers' guild in December 1735.[35]

Little is known about the personalities of Etienne Luzac or his brother. Both were sons of the second marriage of one Jean Luzac, a Huguenot refugee originally from Bergerac in the Dordogne, who settled in Franeker in the Dutch province of Friesland, and whose other descendants included the writer, bookseller, and polemicist Elie Luzac, known for his works against French materialism.[36] John Adams, American representative in the Netherlands during the early 1780s, remembered them as two "venerable sages" who "entertained me with the controversies . . . between the Maritime Provinces and the Inland." Clearly they were well versed in the details of Dutch politics.[37]

Etienne, the younger of the two brothers who took over the *Gazette de Leyde*, left Franeker at an early age and, as we have seen, joined the editorial staff of de la Font's paper in 1723, when he was just seventeen. The rest of his life seems to have been devoted almost exclusively to the paper. He took great pride in his high journalistic principles, returning a proffered gratuity to one overzealous agent for a foreign government with a letter stating that "in order to preserve my quality as a true historian, I accept neither payments nor pensions, so that if I happen to

33. Ibid., no. 6.
34. Contract in ibid., no. 11.
35. LGA, Gildenboek 83, vol. 3, p. 36.
36. Elie Luzac was a descendant of the elder Jean Luzac's first marriage, and thus a half-cousin of Etienne and Jean Luzac. See the family tree in L. Knappert, "Een gedenksteen voor Professor Jean Luzac," in *Leidse Jaarbookje* 7 (1910), 112–22.
37. Adams to F. A. Van der Kemp, n.d. but 1807, cited in Helen Lincklaen Fairchild, ed., *Francis Adrian van der Kemp, 1752–1829. An Autobiography* (New York: Putnam, 1903), 68n. Adams mentions that the elder Luzacs discussed "Addresses to the Prince of Orange in their youth," which suggests the possibility that the Luzac brothers had participated in the radical *Doelisten* movement which sought to use the restoration of the House of Orange as an opportunity to reform the oligarchical town government of Leiden in 1748. On the Leiden *Doelisten*, see Maarten Prak, *Gezeten Burgers. De Elite in een Hollandse Stad. Leiden 1700–1780* (The Hague: Hollandse Historische Reeks, 1985), 94.

err, I do so in good faith."[38] He never married, but he acted as a second father to the four children of his brother Jean; on his death, his niece Emilie recalled his "entirely admirable and lovable character."[39] His personal papers include drafts of some poems directed against the Orangist supporters of the stadholder, the principal magistrate in the complex Dutch government, but he does not seem to have been particularly active in Leiden politics. At his death in 1787, he left a respectable inheritance of 41,010 gulden to his heirs, including half-ownership of a house on the fashionable Steenschuur which he had shared with his brother.[40] Even less is known about his brother Jean, father of the younger Jean Luzac who edited the *Gazette de Leyde* after 1772. The elder Jean Luzac lived from 1702 to 1783 and was active as a printer and bookseller, but his main business seems to have been the publication of the *Gazette de Leyde*. It paid him well: at the time of his death, he had accumulated an estate of 64,000 gulden.[41] But there is nothing to indicate that he ever had any influence on the contents of the newspaper, the legal control of which was entirely in his brother's hands.

When Etienne Luzac took over the direction of the *Gazette de Leyde*, nothing particularly distinguished its news coverage. Its news from France was hardly more exciting than that published in the *Gazette de France*. But the new publisher soon altered that situation. The paper's French coverage underwent a startling change by the early 1750s, with the eruption in France of a lengthy dispute over the Catholic hierarchy's attempt to suppress Jansenist dissent by refusing last rites to individuals who could not prove that they had abjured the propositions condemned in the famous papal bull *Unigenitus*. Together with the other *gazettes de Hollande*, the *Gazette de Leyde* became a main vehicle for the French law courts, the parlements, in their noisy campaign against these refusals of sacraments. French officials quite plainly regarded this avalanche of documentation about their domestic problems as a new departure in the behavior of the Dutch papers. Chrétien Lamoignon de Malesherbes, the friend of the philosophes who was then *directeur-général de la librairie*, referred to it as "this newly introduced practice of receiving false or exaggerated documents from all the ill-intentioned people in the kingdom and spreading them all over Europe."[42] Although several of the foreign-based French-language papers participated in this campaign,

38. Etienne Luzac to Charles Bressanelli, representative of King Stanislas-August of Poland in Amsterdam, 31 Jan. 1770, in LGA-VH, P(4).
39. Emilie Luzac to Jean Luzac, 30 Jan. 1787, in LUL, Luzac, carton 29.
40. Documents in LGA-VH, P(4). In a pattern characteristic of wealthy Leiden residents of the period, his fortune consisted almost entirely of bonds issued by various Dutch and foreign governments. See Prak, *Gezeten Burgers*, 131.
41. LGA-VH, P(8), documentation of division of estate, 10 Aug. 1783.
42. "Mémoire sur la gazette d'Hollande donné à M. le Chancelier au mois de mars," n.d. but 1759, in BN, Anisson-Duperron collection, Ms. fr. 22134, ff. 227–31.

the *Gazette de Leyde* distinguished itself by the amount of space it devoted to documents such as the remonstrances issued by the parlements and by its soft-spoken but unmistakable support for the parlementary and Jansenist cause. A recent analysis of the paper's role in the refusal-of-sacraments controvery has shown that reports and reprinted documents on this one issue often filled more than half the paper's news space in the mid-1750s.[43] Alone among the foreign papers, the *Gazette de Leyde* explicitly linked Robert-François Damiens's attempt to assassinate Louis XV in 1757 to the king's bungling efforts to settle the controversy. At a moment when even the foreign-based papers had been enlisted to affirm the French people's love of their king, only Etienne Luzac's journal came forward, in Pierre Rétat's words, "to contest the unanimity and the filial devotion that the press and all the texts about the event exalted, to dissipate the official pretenses and illusions, and to stress the actual conditions, troubling and unhealthy, under which the trial took place."[44]

Etienne Luzac's success in stamping the paper with a pronounced character was due in part to his having achieved firm personal control over it. In 1751, the privilege he had purchased from de la Font's heirs expired, and he was able to obtain a new authorization from the city fathers in his own name, at the higher price of 600 gulden a year. The greatly increased royalty of 3,000 gulden a year that Luzac agreed to pay to the city when he obtained a subsequent renewal in 1766 is eloquent testimony to the paper's success under his direction.[45] Luzac had clear authority to proceed as he chose, and it may well be that the paper's more partisan coverage of French affairs starting in 1752 was connected with the editor's confidence that the paper was now his property.

The refusal-of-sacraments controversy was only the first of a long series of French domestic issues that the *Gazette de Leyde* reported much more fully than any native French publication. The Seven Years' War, which lasted from 1756 to 1763, also gave the paper ample material. The war's end may have caused some dip in circulation, but there was still no lack of news. Etienne Luzac filled his columns with stories about English political and social disputes, the beginnings of agitation in the American colonies, troubles in Poland and Sweden, and the never-ending succession of domestic political crises in Louis XV's France.

The paper had found its niche in the European press market. At a time when many of its older competitors were floundering under incompetent editors, the *Gazette de Leyde* established itself as a sober, depend-

43. Carroll Joynes, "The *Gazette de Leyde:* The Opposition Press and French Politics, 1750–1757," in Jack R. Censer and Jeremy D. Popkin, eds., *Press and Politics in Pre-Revolutionary France* (Berkeley: University of California Press, 1987), 133–69.
44. Pierre Rétat, in Pierre Rétat, ed., *L'attentat de Damiens* (Paris: Centre national de la recherche scientifique, 1979), 88.
45. Copies of the privileges are in LGA-VH, Z(1), no. 31 (1751) and 32 (1766).

able source of information. It firmly eschewed spicy anecdotes, which the manuscript newsletters retailed and in which some of its competitors such as the *Gazette d'Utrecht* dabbled. The *Gazette de Leyde* also rejected humble subservience to governments in whose territories it hoped to circulate and calmly pursued its course of documenting public criticism of established governments without necessarily endorsing it. Despite its quiet tone, the *Gazette de Leyde* made no effort to conceal its sympathy with the French parlements' long-drawn-out resistance to Louis XV's ministers' efforts to enforce extensive claims for royal authority. It publicized domestic and colonial complaints about George III's policies in the 1760s, but expressed strong dislike for John Wilkes's agitation for radical reforms in England. Luzac was similarly unsympathetic with radical protest in Geneva in the late 1760s. By the time the young Jean Luzac joined his uncle in editing the paper in 1772, its format, its news policies, and its editorial tone had been firmly set for a decade and a half.

Jean Luzac and the *Gazette de Leyde*

It was under the editorship of Jean Luzac that the *Gazette de Leyde* obtained a genuinely unique position in the world of the European press. This success owed something to the younger man's distinctive personal qualities, which won him the friendship of such personalities of the revolutionary era as John Adams and Filippo Mazzei, but it was due more to the continuation of editorial policies laid down by Etienne Luzac and to the changing circumstances in Europe. The period of Etienne Luzac's full control over the paper, 1751 to 1772, had been a time of relative calm in European politics. The Seven Years' War had been a major news story, of course, but it had not led to revolutionary upheavals in any of the countries involved. French politics had generated much sound and fury, but no decisive explosion. The Netherlands themselves, after the Orangist restoration in 1747, had enjoyed two decades of domestic tranquillity. Jean Luzac's tenure as editor, 1772 to 1798, saw far more dramatic events: the partitions of Poland, the American Revolution, the Dutch Patriot movement, and finally the French Revolution and the wars resulting from it. No doubt Etienne Luzac possessed the journalistic skills to have profited from public interest in these events, but he was an old man by 1772, and he had been going through the routine of editing the paper twice a week for forty-nine years. He was to live until 1787, but the paper was fortunate to be in younger, more vigorous hands when the drama of the age of revolutions opened. Jean Luzac, on the other hand, benefited from the reputation his uncle had earned for the paper: it gave him a competitive edge in obtaining the news he needed to make it the best-informed journal in Europe.

The young man who returned to his native Leiden in 1772 to assist his elderly uncle looks out at us in two surviving portraits. A drawing in chalk by A. Delfos, the basis for the Lucas Portman engraving of Luzac reproduced in this book, shows a round-faced man with fine features and lively eyes, who looks more French than Dutch.[46] A posthumous medallion for Luzac's monument in the Pieterskerk in Leiden is recognizably the same man, but here the eyes gaze into the distance and an unseen breeze ruffles the subject's hair, giving Luzac a touch of the romantic spirit, which had arisen by the Napoleonic period. Neither portrayal really suggests the personality that emerges from the *Gazette de Leyde*'s editor's letters or from the recollections of those who knew him. Luzac may have favored his French ancestors in physical appearance, but he was every inch a sober, serious Dutchman, a "genuine Batave," as one American friend called him, rather than a lively, animated Latin.[47] Nor was he the romantic hero his friends had commissioned to be sculpted for his funerary monument: his was a life of principles and duties, always concerned with issues close at hand, not with distant horizons.

Born in 1746, Luzac belonged to the third generation of his Huguenot family to live on Dutch soil. By the time of his birth, the descendants of the Huguenot refugees had given up any hope of returning to France and had accepted the permanence of their situation in the Republic. Jean Luzac's father, settled in Leiden as a printer, married a native Dutchwoman, Anna Valckenaer, the daughter of a schoolteacher. Dutch was the younger Jean Luzac's first language; it was the language in which he carried on most of his family correspondence all his life. He remained linked to the Huguenot tradition through his religious affiliation: Jean Luzac was a member of Leiden's French (Waalse) Calvinist congregation.[48] The characterizations of his personality offered by both friends and enemies strongly suggest that he had inherited the energy and the self-righteousness so often associated with the Calvinist faith.

46. The Delfos drawing is reproduced in Ivo Schöffer, "Een Leids Hoogleraar in politieke moeilijkheden. Het ontslag van Johan Luzac in 1796," in J. F. Heijbroek, A. Lammers, and A. P. G. Jos van der Linde, eds., *Geen Schepsel Wordt Vergeten* (Amsterdam and Zutphen: Trouw, 1985), 62.

47. William Vans Murray, diary entry, 19 Oct. 1798, in LC, William Vans Murray papers.

48. Luzac's friend, the nineteenth-century Dutch philologist Matthias Siegenbeek, maintained that Jean Luzac was a pious Christian all his life, but there is no trace of more than a conventional adherence to the Reformed church in any of Luzac's surviving papers. Siegenbeek's claim probably reflects the more intense religiosity of the nineteenth-century Netherlands. Willem Bilderdijk and Matthijs Siegenbeek, *Leidens Ramp* (Amsterdam: Allart and Ruis, 1838), 154.

Jean Luzac, 1747–1807. Engraving by Lucas Portman.
Courtesy of Prof. J. W. Schulte Nordholt.

Both his strong sense of responsibility and a certain moral pessimism in his outlook were also strengthened when he inherited a heavy load of family obligations after the death of his mother while he was still in his teens. The stiff and formal tone of the *Gazette de Leyde* and its rigid devotion to principles, though determined to some extent by journalistic conventions, undoubtedly mirrored aspects of Luzac's personality.

Luzac's social position in Dutch society and his other professional activities also affected his newspaper. Paradoxically, this man, who came closer than any other newsman of the period to embodying the qualities considered ideal in a journalist of his era, was not at all typical of the newspapermen of his time. He was able to live up to the professed ideals of his trade in many ways only because he was not fully a professional: it was his firm place in Dutch society, his multiple sources of income, and his personal political involvements that enabled him to eschew the compromises other gazetteers had to make to succeed. His contemporaries among the editors of French-language international gazettes were usually adventurers who turned to journalism, like Charles Théveneau de Morande, who had been trained as a French lawyer but had to start a new life in London when he was forced to flee France because of various scrapes with the authorities, or Jean Manzon, Piedmontese by origin, who ended up settling in Prussian territory.[49] Cut off from their native milieu, such emigrés were totally dependent on their journalistic enterprises and had to purchase the political favors that gave them access to information and opportunities to circulate their papers.

Jean Luzac's situation was completely different. He was deeply rooted in his Dutch environment; indeed, he was even more provincial than most educated Dutchmen of his day. Except for the four years immediately following his university studies, when he moved to The Hague, about ten miles away, Luzac spent his entire life in his native Leiden. He had undoubtedly traveled to some of the other major Dutch cities, but the only documented occasion on which he left the Netherlands was a brief trip to Brussels in 1798, after he had been forced to give up his editorial control of the paper.[50] Luzac's assimilated Huguenot family was able to provide him with the qualifications to ascend almost as high in Leiden society as its complex structure allowed. Unlike the members of such non-Calvinist religious minorities as the Catholics and the Baptists, the members of the Huguenot congregations were not subject to any religious barriers: the only positions closed to them were those monopolized by the oligarchy of regent families that dominated the city's political system. Luzac's father Jean and his uncle Etienne had not taken full advantage of the opportunities offered by assimilation. Both had devoted themselves to the French-language newspaper, a typical enterprise for immigrants whose linguistic abilities gave them an edge in this particular field.[51] The members of the next generation, such as the younger Jean Luzac, had a much broader involvement with Dutch society and greater aspirations. According to one of their employees, the elder Jean Luzac had been "a man without vanity, without ostentation,

49. Paul Robiquet, *Théveneau de Morande* (Paris: Quantin, 1882); François Moureau, "Jean Manzon," in Jean Sgard, ed., *Dictionnaire des journalistes. Supplement I* (Grenoble: Centre d'Etudes des Sensibilités, 1980), 107–10.

50. Luzac to [Baudus], n.d. but probably 1800, in LUL, Luzac, carton 28, no. 54.

51. Hans Bots and René Bastiaanse, "Die Hugenotten und die niederländischen Generalstaaten," in Rudolf von Thadden and Michelle Magdeleine, eds., *Die Hugenotten* (Munich: Beck, 1985), 68–70.

without pretentions," but the younger Luzacs, despite being raised "in their father's messy shop," had "all the self-importance of parvenus."[52]

The urban community that shaped so much of Jean Luzac's life was a virtually autonomous city-republic. Since the Dutch revolt against Spain, Leiden, like the other Dutch cities, had been governed by its own city council, which chose the city's representatives to the Estates of the province of Holland, which in turn sent deputies to the national States-General in The Hague. The provincial assembly and the States-General, chosen mostly by the town councils, had very limited powers over the city governments, and Luzac grew up in a political environment that fostered devotion to traditional local institutions. Those institutions were formally republican, shaped by the long European tradition of municipal self-government and the distrust of hereditary executive authority that has come to be known as civic humanism.[53] The civic-humanist paradigm stressed the value of political liberty and made sovereignty in the city an emanation from the people, but it did not require representative democracy. It pointed toward the establishment of a mixed government dominated by an aristocracy made up of the "best citizens," what the French-born Dutch republican publicist and sometime associate of Luzac, Antoine-Marie Cerisier, described as "a popular aristocracy" in which "the magistrates select themselves, but no native of the country is excluded because of his birth."[54] Even more than his identification with his Dutch homeland and his Calvinist religious affiliations, Jean Luzac was shaped by this municipal republicanism.

Jean Luzac was not brought up with a journalistic career in mind. He received the rather old-fashioned humanistic education favored by the Dutch upper classes at the Leiden Latin school. He had a gift for languages, which was stimulated by his maternal uncle Lodewijk Caspar Valckenaer, professor at Leiden University and one of the most distinguished classicists of his day. Luzac learned French by the age of seven and Latin soon after; the earliest of his surviving letters, written when he was fourteen, is a Latin missive.[55] This background seemed to destine

52. AR, DP, note in carton 59, "Contre Luzac."
53. On the ideological origins of the civic-humanist tradition in early modern Europe, see J. G. A. Pocock, *The Machiavellian Moment* (Princeton, N.J.: Princeton University Press, 1975), esp. 66–80. On the emergence of Dutch republican thought after the revolt against Spain, see E. H. Kossmann, *Politieke Theorie in het zeventiende-eeuwse Nederland* (Amsterdam: N. V. Noord-Hollandsche Uitgevers, 1960), and on developments in the eighteenth century, I. Leonard Leeb, *Ideological Origins of the Batavian Revolution* (The Hague: Nijhoff, 1973), both of which focus on discussions of the Dutch national constitution.
54. Antoine-Marie Cerisier, *Tableau de l'histoire générale des Provinces unies* (Utrecht: Schoonhoven and Wild, 1777–84), 10:471.
55. Jean Luzac to Jacob Valckenaer, 7 Dec. 1760, in LUL, Luzac, carton 29. The letter was no mere scholastic exercise: it describes Luzac's determination to return to his studies in spite of his grief over the death of his mother.

him for an academic career, but Luzac initially wanted to be a lawyer, and he graduated from Leiden University with a degree in that field in 1768, having written a dissertation on Cicero and Roman law.[56] He was offered teaching positions at two Dutch universities, but turned down these opportunities and went into legal practice in The Hague, where he "soon obtained a brilliant reputation," according to one biographer.[57]

Had Jean Luzac stuck to the law, and merely hired an employee to edit the family newspaper when he became responsible for it, he would have followed the pattern of the other holders of privileges for French-language gazettes in the country in the later eighteenth century. In contrast to the editors and publishers of French-language gazettes outside of the United Provinces, the owners of the Dutch papers tended to become rentiers, exploiting their local monopolies—each city allowed the publication of only one such gazette—while leaving the actual editorial work to a hired hand. Instead, in 1772, Luzac returned to Leiden and reluctantly bowed to family pressures to join his uncle in the actual running of the *Gazette de Leyde*, and by 1775 he had become the paper's working editor.[58] The paper's archives give graphic evidence of the process by which Luzac assumed responsibility from his uncle: month by month, the younger man's handwriting appears on more and more of the documents, even though the correspondence that he drafted continued to be sent out over Etienne Luzac's signature. In 1783, the elder Etienne Luzac formally handed over ownership of the newspaper enterprise to Jean and his brother Etienne, who became the paper's printer. With their uncle's death in 1787, the two brothers became the sole legal owners of the *Gazette de Leyde*.[59]

Although Luzac joined his uncle in putting out the paper, he never committed himself exclusively to journalism. He remained active as a lawyer, participating in several cases that drew national attention in the early 1780s. Largely as a result of this, he also became an important figure in Leiden city politics, serving briefly as the city council's attorney during the crisis year of 1785, when radical and moderate factions struggled for power. That was also the year in which he became a

---

56. Johan Luzac, *Specimen Academicum, exhibens observationes nonnullas apologeticas pro Jurisconsultis Romanis, ad locum Ciceronis in Oratione pro Murena Capp. XI–XIII princ.* (Leiden: Luzac, 1768).

57. "Jean Luzac," in *Galerie historique des contemporains ou nouvelle biographie* (Brussels: Aug. Wahlen et Comp., 1817–20), 6:345.

58. On Jean Luzac's reluctance to abandon his promising legal career, see [Jean Baudus], "Notice sur M. Luzac, mort au désastre de Leyde," *Journal de l'Empire*, 22 Dec. 1807. Baudus, one-time Hamburg correspondent of the *Gazette de Leyde*, identified himself as the author of this obituary in a letter to Jean Luzac's brother Etienne, 23 Dec. 1807, in Amsterdam University Library, Ms. G.G. III.

59. Contract between Etienne Luzac senior and Jean and Etienne Luzac, 18 Feb. 1783, in LGA-VH, Z(2), no. 51.

professor at Leiden University, which led him to reduce his connection with the newspaper by hiring an editor. Academic life was anything but an ivory-tower retreat for Luzac. His initial plan to leave the day-to-day running of the newspaper to an employee never worked satisfactorily, and for most of the period from 1785 to 1796, he combined both jobs, even though his professorial status involved him in controversies which became as time- and energy-consuming as his activities in Leiden city politics. Although he never held a major municipal office after 1785 and never obtained a seat in the *Vroedschap* or city council, Luzac's political influence, his professorial status, and his solid personal fortune made him a major figure in Leiden's affairs.

As if Luzac's involvements with legal proceedings, city politics, and academic affairs were not enough to distract him from the running of the *Gazette de Leyde*, he was also preoccupied with family matters throughout most of the years of his editorship. His mother's early death left him the eldest of four children, and his extensive family correspondence, particularly with his sister Emilie, testifies to the degree of his involvement with his siblings. His own marriage in 1784 seems to have been a happy one, and he and his wife had six children. The fact that his sister Emilie was married to Wybo Fijnje, one of the leading radical Patriots, and that his brother Etienne's wife, Johanna Suzanne Valckenaer, was the sister of Johan Valckenaer, a cousin of the Luzacs and another of the radical Patriot leaders, ensured that the complex family affairs of the Luzacs were inextricably linked with larger political issues that ultimately affected the ownership of the *Gazette de Leyde*. Particularly during the years of the French and Batavian revolutions, family life was no refuge from the world for Jean Luzac, but rather the arena in which great political conflicts were fought out.

The calm tone of the *Gazette de Leyde* thus in no way reflected the reality of its editor's hectic life. Nor did it reflect his personality. Filippo Mazzei, the peripatetic apostle of eighteenth-century revolutionism, spent a few weeks in Leiden and ever after recalled Luzac's "sweetness of character and perfect kindness of heart."[60] But Matthias Siegenbeek, who later became a Leiden University professor, knew Luzac much better. He recalled the older man as a true and loyal friend, always ready to help others and chronically overworked because of the many commitments he took on. "The main feature of his character . . . the source of his many praiseworthy qualities and at the same time of his minor defects and weaknesses . . . is a strong measure of feeling and a lively sensitivity," Siegenbeek wrote, and he recognized that these traits often

60. Philip Mazzei, *Memoirs of the Life and Peregrinations of the Florentine Philip Mazzei 1730–1816*, Howard R. Marraro, trans. (New York: Columbia University Press, 1942), 265.

led Luzac into bitter quarrels.[61] Punctilious in carrying out his promises, Luzac was often irritated when others failed to appreciate what he had done for them. After the Prussian intervention that suppressed the Dutch Patriot movement in 1787 had forced his sister Emilie and her husband to flee the country, Luzac made great efforts to help them salvage their property.[62] But he apparently could not help reminding them that their political views, which he did not share, were the reason for their troubles. According to a mutual acquaintance, he drove his sister to the point where "she confessed that she would be more easily able to endure the loss of her business and everything she possessed, than his continual and inhuman reproaches."[63]

Luzac himself, in one of his earliest published writings, acknowledged that he was always frank about his feelings, even at the risk of offending others. "Whenever I have truth and right . . . I am not in the habit of sacrificing them to anyone," he proclaimed.[64] Proud and self-righteous, he frequently became embroiled in controversies in which personal animosities became combined with the defense of principles. An angry exchange of pamphlets over a local legal case in 1775 led his opponent, his half-cousin Elie Luzac, to complain that when he met opposition, Jean Luzac "called the defense of one's own rights or the refusal to yield blindly to the wishes or ideas of another, one-sidedness or stubbornness."[65] After he was appointed to the Leiden University faculty in 1785, he conducted a long-running feud with his colleague Adriaan Kluit about the boundary lines of their respective disciplines, a dispute embittered by the two men's political differences—Kluit was an Orangist, Luzac a Patriot—and their disagreements about academic procedures. Luzac waged war on his colleague both by advancing high-minded arguments based on academic precedents in the university senate and by trying to lure students away from Kluit's classes into his own. Even when the two were persecuted together during the period of the Batavian Republic, Luzac remained hostile to his former rival.[66] The same combativeness eventually led him to break off contact with his brother and partner in running the *Gazette de Leyde*: in 1798, Etienne wrote to his brother-in-law Johan Valckenaer, "for more than a year I have neither

61. Bilderdijk and Siegenbeek, *Leidens Ramp*, 152–53.
62. Christine Kroes-Ligtenberg, *Dr. Wybo Fijnje* (Assen: Van Gorcum, 1957), 107–9, 164.
63. AR, DP, note in carton 59, "Contre Luzac."
64. [Johan Luzac], *Aantwoord van Mr. Johan Luzac, aan den Wel. Ed. Heer Mr. Elias Luzac* (Leiden: n.p., 1775), 22.
65. Elie Luzac, *Aantekeningen op het Antwoord van Mr. Johan Luzac, aan den Wel.-Ed. Heer mr. Elias Luzac* (Leiden: n.p., 1775), n.p.
66. E. J. Vrij, "Het collegegeschil tussen de hoogleraaren Adriaan Kluit en Jean Luzac," *Jaarboekje voor geschiedenis en oudheidkunde van Leiden en omstreken* 63 (1971), 121–42.

seen him nor talked to him except on the street."[67] The editor of the soft-spoken *Gazette de Leyde* was a man of strong passions.

His newspaper was one of those passions. He often referred to journalism in a deprecating fashion, and in the first stages of his battle to regain his professorship in 1796, he even denied that he had had anything to do with the editing of the paper in the years from 1789 up to the French occupation of the Netherlands.[68] In fact, however, there is ample evidence to demonstrate that the *Gazette de Leyde* played an important part in Luzac's life and that it was only with great reluctance that he finally severed his connection with his beloved journal. Throughout the period of his active involvement with the paper, he devoted himself to its affairs. He personally corresponded with people who could provide it with essential information, chiding the American representative in the Netherlands, John Adams, for instance, when the latter began to give the latest news to a rival paper before passing it to Luzac.[69] Even in the two-year period when he had hired Antoine-Marie Cerisier to edit the paper, Luzac remained actively involved in determining its policy.[70] When he finally gave up his links with the *Gazette de Leyde* in 1798, Luzac complained to his brother about his exclusion from "an establishment made great and famous through hard work, to which I devoted myself body and soul for nearly thirty years."[71]

From 1772 to 1798, then, the editorial direction of the *Gazette de Leyde* was in the hands of a dedicated journalist who was also deeply involved in the great political controversies of his age. Determined to uphold the journalistic tradition established by his uncle, Jean Luzac was equally determined to promote the political ideals he espoused in his own life. Under his leadership, the paper was no mere passive observer of events but a participant in the dramas of the American Revolution, the Dutch Patriot movement, and the French Revolution.

67. Etienne Luzac to Valckenaer, 17 Mar. 1798, in LUL, Ms. BPL 1036X.

68. Jean Luzac, ed., *Verzameling van Stukken, betreffende het gedrag der Curateuren van Holland's Universiteit te Leyden, in den jaaren 1796. en 1797. Bijzonder in de zaak van Mr. Johan Luzac* (Leiden: Honkoop, 1797), 12.

69. Luzac to John Adams, 10 Dec. 1781, in Adams Papers microfilms, r. 355.

70. The Patriot organizer P. A. Dumont-Pigalle, who was well-informed about the internal politics of the *Gazette de Leyde* during 1785 to 1787, repeatedly referred to Luzac, rather than Cerisier, as the man who decided what the paper would print. Dumont-Pigalle, letter to Coste, secretary at the French Embassy in The Hague, 21 Aug. 1786, in AR, DP, carton 1. Dumont-Pigalle's notes concerning Luzac include a copy of one of the paper's crucial articles about Dutch affairs from August 1786, when Cerisier was supposedly in control of it, in Luzac's handwriting, strongly suggesting that he himself had written it. Article of 15 Aug. 1786, in ibid., carton 59, "Contre Luzac."

71. Jean Luzac to Etienne Luzac, 14 June 1799, in LGA-VH, Z(2), no. 109.

The Environments of
an Eighteenth-Century
Newspaper

Newspapers are bound to be conditioned by the society surrounding them. But in the case of the *Gazette de Leyde*, the elucidation of the links between press and society is unusually complicated. This paper was enmeshed in two quite different societies: the Dutch world in which its editor lived and in which the paper was produced, and the wider European world from which its information came and to which it was addressed. The Dutch world was one of small, self-contained city-republics, of a certain intellectual stagnation, of a rather rigid bourgeois oligarchy, but also one in which a certain amount of public participation in politics existed. The wider European world was dominated by great monarchies, and it was open to a variety of new ideological and political currents, but it remained in many ways an aristocratic society without participatory political institutions. The concerns of these two societies were quite different, and it is remarkable that an institution so rooted in the special circumstances of Dutch life could play such a large role in the cosmopolitan European world of its day.

The Dutch Milieu

The United Provinces of the Netherlands in the late eighteenth century differed considerably from most other European societies, both in its social structure and in its political institutions. In the aftermath of its successful revolt against the Habsburgs and its subsequent rise to economic leadership in Europe, Dutch society had come to be dominated not by titled aristocrats, as most of its neighbors were, but by an urban, bourgeois elite, drawn originally from the merchant class but composed by the eighteenth century primarily of wealthy rentiers. Over the years, this regent oligarchy had perfected a system of control maintained through carefully arranged marriages, but it had not simply adopted the values of the European aristocracy. In politics, the regent-governed Dutch towns and provinces successfully obstructed the development of any strong central governing institutions: their outlook was antibureaucratic and their concern was to keep power dispersed in the councils of the fifty-odd cities represented in the States-General and the Estates of the seven independent provinces. In view of this wide dispersal of political authority, the Netherlands had an early need for a news press: the interconnections, commercial and otherwise, between its different cities required that residents of each community know what was happening elsewhere. By the eighteenth century, this need was met by publications such as the remarkable *Nederlandsche Jaarboek*, which collected city council and provincial estate resolutions, appointments to offices, and other politically relevant information from the entire country in a systematic form and on a massive scale: the volume for 1785 contains 1,780 pages.

In some respects, then, the Netherlands seemed more modern than its continental neighbors: the bourgeoisie had triumphed over the landed aristocracy, obtaining the lion's share of both wealth and political power, and there was an extensive system of political communications. But this modernity was only partial. The Dutch bourgeoisie's precocious triumph meant that the country's ruling elite in the eighteenth century was not a forward-looking group open to the opportunities of a rapidly growing economy, but a "bourgeoisie d'ancien régime" produced by the growth of international trade in the sixteenth and seventeenth centuries and concerned primarily to convert its wealth into prestigious political titles and sinecures in the eighteenth century.[1] It was not modernity alone that accounted for the rise of an institution such as the *Gazette de Leyde* within the Netherlands, and indeed the *Gazette de Leyde*, like the country as a whole, was in some ways a seventeenth-century innovation that had become rather old-fashioned by the time of the French Revolution.

The main ways in which this idiosyncratic society fostered a publication such as the *Gazette de Leyde* are obvious. The Dutch Republic exercised a good deal more tolerance toward the press than most other European states. It had a well-developed printing industry, which had long concentrated on producing for export. And the Republic occupied a central position in the European networks of communications and

1. Heinz Schilling, "Die Geschichte der nordlichen Niederlände und die Modernisierungstheorie," *Geschichte und Gesellschaft* 8 (1982), 505.

transport, making it easy for gazetteers to acquire news and send it to their customers. The *Gazette de Leyde*'s Dutch location does pose some significant questions, however. Although the Netherlands had long been the home of a French-language press, the majority of the Dutch-based publications had declined into insignificance by the time the *Gazette de Leyde* achieved its greatest importance. Throughout the entire period of Jean Luzac's editorship, his main rivals appeared in other states: the Rhineland, England, and the Austrian Netherlands, and, after 1789, France. The French Revolution, which suddenly transformed Paris into the center for newspaper publication in Europe, simply completed a process that had begun much earlier.[2] The Dutch newspaper industry had followed a pattern common to many other Dutch commercial and industrial enterprises during the period: without shrinking in absolute terms, it lost ground relative to more dynamic enterprises in neighboring countries, which often benefited from more aggressive state support.[3] The question to be resolved, then, is twofold: what qualities of Dutch society and of the city of Leiden had allowed the *Gazette de Leyde* to establish itself there, and what qualities of that particular paper enabled it to maintain itself in the midst of the general decline of the Dutch French-language press?

The essential reason why French-language publications established themselves in the Netherlands was already clear to the great French press historian Eugène Hatin, writing in 1865. It was not the existence of legally guaranteed press freedom, but rather the absence of a strong central government capable of controlling the press.[4] The Dutch Republic had inherited from the Habsburgs the assumption that the sovereign had the right to censor the content of publications and control the industry that manufactured them. In the wake of the revolt against Spain, however, these sovereign powers became dispersed among a host of quasi-independent authorities. Edicts attempting to regulate printing and the press emanated from the States-General, the Estates of the various provinces, and the councils of the different cities represented in those Estates. None of these authorities, however, had any effective machinery to enforce their regulations. The result was a system of de facto press freedom, disturbed but never seriously threatened by peri-

2. Jean Sgard's survey of the eighteenth-century French-language periodical press shows that the phenomenon was not simply confined to newspapers. The proportion of French-language journals published in the Netherlands declined markedly after 1750, although the total number of titles was growing rapidly. Jean Sgard, "Journale und Journalisten im Zeitalter der Aufklärung," in Hans-Ulrich Gumbrecht, Rolf Reichardt, and Thomas Schleich, eds., *Sozialgeschichte der Aufklärung in Frankreich* (Munich: R. Oldenbourg, 1981), 2:32.

3. Johan De Vries, *De economische Achteruitgang der Republiek in de Achttiende Eeuw*, 2d ed. (Leiden: Stenfert Kroese, 1968), 29, 172.

4. Hatin, *Gazettes de Hollande*, 93.

odic fulminations, ranging from the blanket ban on French-language newspapers in 1691 (which was never enforced) to the notorious condemnation of Rousseau's *Emile* in 1762.[5] In contrast to the Anglo-American situation in the same period, the Dutch situation did not lead to any philosophical campaign for legal guarantees of press freedom. Since the laws could be evaded so easily, printers and authors had little reason to demand their repeal.

Given the absence of effective government regulation, newspapers were able to spring up in the Netherlands to serve a French-speaking market well beyond the country's borders. The major Dutch international gazettes were products of the flow of Huguenot refugees into the Low Countries, which had begun some time before the revocation of the Edict of Nantes in 1685. For Dutch publishers, gazettes were a logical complement to the other French-language publishing activities that developed in the Republic, which included books of all sorts and learned periodicals such as those of Pierre Bayle and Jean Le Clerc. All these enterprises benefited not only from the absence of effective restrictions but from the Dutch preeminence in international trade at the end of the seventeenth century. Despite the lack of a home market for these products, Dutch entrepreneurs, accustomed to exporting goods of all kinds, had the skills necessary to sell them. The publishing industry also enjoyed an ample supply of cheap paper and a considerable fund of printing expertise: as is well known, in the seventeenth century, Dutch printers such as the Elseviers had been at the forefront of the book industry, perfecting methods for printing inexpensive but high-quality editions.[6]

The French-language press originally flourished in the Netherlands also because of the lively intellectual atmosphere fostered by the Huguenot refugees and by native Dutchmen at the end of the seventeenth and the beginning of the eighteenth centuries. By the middle of the eighteenth century, however, the major centers of intellectual creativity in Europe were elsewhere. The reputation of the Dutch universities had declined, and conditions for intellectual activity in the Netherlands during this period were not particularly good. J. Grabner, a German observer whose *Briefe über die vereinigten Niederlände* is among the most extensive and interesting descriptions of the country from this period,

5. On the general subject of Dutch press freedom in the period of the Enlightenment, see H. H. Zwager, *Nederland en de Verlichting*, 2d ed. (Haarlem: Fibula-Van Dishoeck, 1980), 54–74. The various edicts affecting the press and printing in the Republic are described in Bodel Nyenhuis, *Wetgeving*. For the ban on newspapers, which extended an earlier enactment by the Estates of Holland in 1686, see 135–44; for the condemnation of *Emile*, 163.

6. S. H. Steinberg, *Five Hundred Years of Printing* (New York: Penguin, 1979 [orig. 1955]), 183–85.

noted that the opportunities for those who sought to live by their pen were very limited. "The best thinker will not obtain the smallest position on the basis of his literary activities, and if he did not have so many ways to make a reasonable income by other means, he could, in spite of all possible talents, die of hunger."[7] Literary life remained relatively backward, the number of critical journals was small, and even the university professors seemed to have little desire to publish. The Dutch publishing industry had maintained its international dominance for a while even after the decline of the country's general economic standing by putting out the works of major writers from other countries, such as Voltaire, Montesquieu, and Rousseau, but even this business fell off after 1760 as more dynamic firms elsewhere, like the Société Typographique de Neuchâtel, captured the trade.[8]

In view of the declining importance of intellectual life and the printing industry in Holland in the second half of the eighteenth century, the fact that the *Gazette de Leyde* reached its zenith between 1770 and 1795 cannot be explained by reference to the general characteristics that had made the Netherlands a center of French-language publishing around 1700. When it had been founded in 1677 by the Huguenot refugee de la Font, the paper had been just one of the many intellectual products of a period fertile in enterprises of all sorts. By the time Jean Luzac became editor in 1772, however, the *Gazette de Leyde* was the last of the Dutch French-language gazettes to have maintained itself in the first rank of the European press, and it was probably the last intellectual enterprise in the Netherlands to remain significant on a continental scale. Not the least intriguing aspect of its success was this ability to swim against the current that had swept away every other vestige of the Netherlands' intellectual supremacy.

The paper's location in Leiden provides a few clues to the reasons for its survival. French-language papers in some other Dutch cities suffered from handicaps that the *Gazette de Leyde* did not have to face. In The Hague, the presence of the stadholder's court after 1748 made the city's papers obvious tools of a clearly identifiable faction, especially after the Orangist court printer, Pierre Gosse, Junior, obtained the privilege for both the Dutch-language and French-language gazettes in 1770.[9] Even the fact that Gosse and his son, Pierre Frédéric Gosse, were the most aggressive and competitive publishers in the Netherlands in the 1770s and 1780s was not enough to make their French-language gazette a success. Amsterdam also turned out to be a less than ideal location for newspapers, even though it came closest to providing the hustle and

7. J. Grabner, *Briefe über die vereinigten Niederlände* (Gotha: Ettinger, 1792), 401–4.
8. Yves-Z. Dubosq, *Le livre français et son commerce en Hollande de 1750 à 1780* (Amsterdam: H. J. Paris, 1925).
9. W. P. Sautijn Kluit, *De s'Gravenhaagsche Courant* (Leiden: Brill, 1875), 59.

bustle that is normally assumed to be essential for journalistic excellence. It seemed superficially to have much in common with the other European cities that housed the most flourishing and varied news press, London and Hamburg. The presence of the Amsterdam Bourse, the great banking houses, and the other appurtenances of a world economic center should have given the Amsterdam gazetteers an edge over their rivals elsewhere in the country. But the city had so many foreign interests that its government in effect conducted a foreign policy of its own, frequently in conflict with that of the stadholder's court in The Hague. The result was interference with the local gazettes, whose contents always had the potential for causing diplomatic problems. The Amsterdam city council was sufficiently concerned about the press to keep the operation of its Dutch-language newspaper, the *Amsterdamsche Courant*, directly under its own control, naming the editor and publishing the paper in a city-owned printing shop, a procedure that does not seem to have been imitated anywhere else in the Republic.[10] As a result, the country's major Dutch-language paper was published in Haarlem, not in Amsterdam. The French-language gazette had suffered less from city government interference in the first half of the eighteenth century and enjoyed a good reputation, but the urban vitality of Amsterdam and even the large French-speaking population there, which supported cultural institutions such as a French theater, were not sufficient to keep the paper operating at a high level after 1760. City government interference also played a role in the final demise of the *Gazette d'Utrecht* in 1787, as the privilege was granted and then withdrawn from a succession of publishers for political reasons.[11]

The genealogical accident of the Luzac family's two generations of talented, dedicated, and long-lived journalists who maintained a personal interest in the paper had much to do with the success of the Leiden paper. In the other major Dutch cities with French-language papers, the families that owned the hereditary exclusive privileges for such publications generally became rentiers, farming out the actual running of the papers to hired underlings. Because of the licensing system, newcomers could not compete with these privileged enterprises. The Amsterdam gazette was the most extreme case: a descendant of Jean Tronchin Dubreuil, that paper's publisher in 1686, was still the paper's owner in 1795, but the paper's editorship had passed from one hired editor to another after 1750, none of whom had managed to forge a reputation for journalistic quality.[12] The French journalists who edited the Amster-

10. Isabella van Eeghen, "De Amsterdamsche Courant in de Achttiende Eeuw," *Jaarboek Amstelodamum* 44 (1950), 31–58.
11. W. P. Sautijn Kluit, "Hollandsche en Fransche Utrechtsche Couranten," *Bijdragen en Mededeelingen van het Historisch Genootschap, gevestigd te Utrecht* 1 (1878), 113–14.
12. M. M. Kleerkooper and W. P. van Stockum, Jr., *De Boekhandel te Amsterdam voornamelijk in de 17e eeuw* (The Hague: Nijhoff, 1914–16), 840–45.

dam paper for its rentier owners in the 1780s complained repeatedly about their incompetent interference with it.[13] In the period from 1751 to its demise in 1787, the *Gazette d'Utrecht's* privilege was held by seven different people; during the same period, the *Gazette de Leyde* remained the property of a single owner. This continuity of ownership by a family dedicated to journalistic excellence seems to be characteristic of many outstanding newspapers—the four generations of the Walter family played a crucial role in maintaining the standing of the London *Times* in the nineteenth century, and the Ochs-Sulzberger dynasty has performed a similar function for the modern *New York Times*. Had Etienne Luzac not lived long enough to turn the paper over to a blood relative, or had he given up personal control of the paper and lived off the royalties from its privilege, the *Gazette de Leyde* might have followed the other Dutch French-language gazettes into oblivion, particularly in the face of aggressive competition from such newly founded titles as the *Courier du Bas-Rhin* and the *Courrier de l'Europe*, whose editors were unprotected by privileges and therefore were forced to work very hard to make their papers succeed.

Etienne's and Jean Luzac's personal devotion to the paper probably had the most to do with the *Gazette de Leyde*'s eventual triumph over the other gazettes. Nevertheless, Leiden was in many ways a favorable environment for such an enterprise, even though it had few of the characteristics of the great metropolises that have generated internationally significant newspapers either in the eighteenth century or in more modern times. The Rapenburg, a beautiful tree-lined canal with old houses on both sides, on which Jean Luzac lived before his marriage and again at the end of his life, was even then "very noble," according to the English traveler Joseph Marshall, although he added, "but not, as the inhabitants assured me, the finest in Europe."[14] But the quiet Rapenburg was certainly no Fleet Street. Leiden had been one of the great centers of textile manufacturing in seventeenth-century Holland, and it remained primarily a manufacturing city in Luzac's day, but by then it was not a very prosperous one: the population, which had reached a peak of perhaps 70,000 in the 1600s, had declined to a mere 28,000 by 1793, and Jean Luzac himself commented to his foreign visitors on the city's decline.[15] Of the 4,772 households in the city in 1793, only 795 included servants, indicating that the majority of the population were relatively poor artisans and workers.

13. François Bernard to Dumont-Pigalle, 17 Feb. 1786, 25 Oct. 1786, in AR, DP, carton A.

14. Joseph Marshall, *Travels Through Holland, Flanders, Germany, Denmark, Sweden, Lapland, Russia, the Ukraine and Poland, in the Years 1768, 1769, and 1770* (London: J. Almon, 1772), 1:34.

15. Petrus F. Blok, *Geschiedenis eener Hollandsche Stad* (The Hague: Nijhoff, 1910–18), 3:7; Elkanah Watson, *Tour in Holland in 1784* (Worcester, Mass.: Thomas, 1790), 104–5.

Although the news press is often seen as a modern institution, the *Gazette de Leyde* was rooted in an archaic urban milieu. The city almanac for 1790 listed seventy-three guilds, each with its own officers.[16] The city had the same hierarchical social structure as most other Dutch towns of the period. Political power was in the hands of a small and fairly stable elite of regent families who dominated the city council and the dozens of urban offices.[17] Despite the presence of the famous university, members of the learned professions, among whom a sophisticated journalist would have found the greatest moral support, were few: in addition to the twenty professors, there were only eighteen lawyers in 1790, twenty-five doctors, and three professional translators. The university itself was a mere shadow of what it had been early in the eighteenth century. The enrollment in the 1780s was about 400, and none of the faculty ranked among the leading European intellectual figures of the time. The library remained famous for its extensive holdings, but a German visitor complained that the books were jumbled together so that they could not be located and that it was only open for a few hours two days a week.[18]

The university was still considered the best in the United Provinces, however, and it did attract a steady stream of foreign visitors and students from abroad, from whom an enterprising newspaper editor could recruit valuable contacts in other lands. Alongside the university, there were some signs of independent intellectual life in the city. It was the center of a revival of interest in Dutch literature in the 1760s, marked by the creation of the Maatschappij der Nederlandsche Letterkunde in 1766; the group, which Jean Luzac presided over in the 1790s, took as its goal the purification of the Dutch language through the compilation of a dictionary and the translation of highly regarded books from other languages, and promoted an appreciation for Dutch writers as opposed to a slavish imitation of foreign models.[19] On the whole, then, Leiden still provided a certain amount of intellectual stimulation, perhaps more than Amsterdam where commerce absorbed so much more energy.

Leiden's provinciality was offset to some degree by its place in a well-developed system of communications and transportation. Since the mid-1660s, a unique system of regular passenger barges or *trekschuiten* linked the major urban centers of Holland. Although Amsterdam enjoyed the best communications links through this system, statistical measurements show that Leiden ranked a close second.[20] In addition to the

16. *Naemwijzer waer in gevonden worden de Naemen van de Ed. Groot Achtb. Heeren, Regenten der Stad Leyden* (Leyden: A. and J. Honkoop, 1790).

17. On Leiden's eighteenth-century regents, see Prak, *Gezeten Burgers*.

18. Grabner, *Briefe*, 426.

19. Blok, *Geschiedenis*, 3:283–84.

20. Jan de Vries, "Barges and Capitalism: Passenger Transportation in the Dutch Economy, 1632–1839," *Afdeling Agrarische Geschiedenis Landbouwhogeschool Waginengen* 21 (1978), 46, 72.

trekschuit network, the Netherlands had an excellent system of postal couriers. Leiden was on many of the main postal routes, including those linking London and Paris with Amsterdam.[21] Compared with the Amsterdam gazette, the *Gazette de Leyde* was farther from the Amsterdam Bourse, an important communications nexus, but the *Gazette de Leyde* was closer to the foreign embassies in The Hague, a mere three-and-a-half hours away by *trekschuit*. For a publication concerned with events outside the Netherlands, that diplomatic milieu was a more important source of information than the commercial center of Amsterdam.[22]

Leiden also was home to several important publishers, including the internationally known Luchtmans firm.[23] A list of Dutch booksellers from 1778 names twenty-six enterprises in the city, making it the second busiest center for the book trade in the Republic after Amsterdam.[24] Although Leiden was not a major center of news-periodical publishing on the scale of Hamburg in Germany (which had two major political newspapers, one commercial paper, and several newsmagazines in the late 1780s), it supported not only the *Gazette de Leyde* and the monthly *Mercure historique et politique* throughout most of the eighteenth century but also a prosperous Dutch-language paper of no particular distinction, the *Leidsche Courant*, which probably earned far more money than Luzac's enterprise.[25] The *Gazette de Leyde* was thus published in an urban setting in which the "black art" was sufficiently developed to provide the manpower and skills necessary for its production, although the example of the French-language printing enterprises established in such isolated spots as Bouillon and Neuwied in the same period showed that a periodical could survive quite well without such a thriving publishing milieu.

The pocket principalities of Bouillon and Neuwied could not provide a newspaper's editor with the firsthand political education that Leiden did, however. The internal life of this Dutch city-republic was anything

21. J. C. Overvoorde, *Geschiedenis van het postwezen in Nederland vòòr 1795* (Leiden: Sijthoff, 1902).

22. A German observer of the period noted that the English ambassador actually opened and decoded many of the secret dispatches addressed to London, so that the information they contained was potentially available in The Hague even before it crossed the Channel. K. G. Küttner, *Beyträge zur Kenntniss vorzüglich des gegenwärtigen Zustandes von Frankreich und Holland* (Leipzig: Dyckischen Buchhandlung, 1792), 303–4.

23. Arie C. Kruseman, *Aantekeningen betreffende den Boekhandel van Noord-Nederland, in de 17de en 18de Eeuw* (Amsterdam: Van Kampen, 1893), 625. The Luchtmans house later became the well-known academic publishing house of Brill, which still flourishes today.

24. "Alphabetische Naamlijst der Boekverkoopers, met Hunne Woonplaatsen, in de Zeven Provincien, Opgemaakt, in den Jaare 1778," ms. in Amsterdam University Library, collection of the Vereeniging ter Bevordering van de Belangen des Boekhandels.

25. W. P. Sautijn Kluit, "De Hollandsche Leidsche Courant," *Mededelingen gedaan in de Vergadering van de Maatschappij der Nederlandsche Letterkunde te Leiden* (1870–71), 3–86. In 1772, the *Leidsche Courant* contracted to pay the city an annual royalty of 8,375 gulden, a staggering sum compared to what the French-language paper paid.

but placid. During the period of Jean Luzac's tenure as publisher, Leiden was in an almost continual state of uproar. It experienced seven years of constant local politicking during the *Patriottentijd*, the period of protest against established institutions, from 1780 to 1787, including a major street riot in 1784, and was the site where the "Leidse Ontwerp," the most important of the Patriot manifestoes of the period, was drawn up in 1785.[26] If the city lacked intellectual figures of international standing, it nonetheless included among its population eloquent spokesmen of all political persuasions, ranging from Elie Luzac and the poet, pamphleteer, and natural scientist Johannes Le Francq van Berkhey on the Orangist side to Patriot radical Pieter Vreede, the poet laureate of the *Vrijcorps* movement. During the Patriotic years, the city saw the rise of several new forms of political organization, including the citizen militia or *Vrijcorps* and what amounted to political parties. After experiencing a year-long battle for control of the city council in 1785, the city underwent Prussian military occupation and a conservative purge in 1787, followed by French military occupation and a radical takeover in 1795, and then by the intense political excitement of the period of the Batavian Republic. Citizens of Leiden experienced all these tumults not as passive victims but as active participants. If Leiden never obtained as much international publicity for its domestic disputes as Geneva, a city not much larger, it can nevertheless be said that its inhabitants were just as passionately involved in the debates over the great issues of the "democratic revolution." Leiden, for all its provinciality, was a microcosm of the world of its day. This constant political tempest kept Luzac alert to the significance of the great issues in other lands that his paper covered. Yet political conflict in Leiden always remained within certain bounds, in contrast to what happened in other Dutch cities such as Utrecht and Amsterdam. The triumphant radicals in 1785, the vindictive Orangists in 1787, and the French-backed Batavian republicans in 1795 never carried out a violent purge of their opponents, which would have involved the suppression of independent voices like that of the *Gazette de Leyde*.

The milieu of the Netherlands and of the city of Leiden thus nourished the *Gazette de Leyde* by providing a tolerant political climate, the necessary economic opportunities, and a political culture in which the issues that affected the greater world presented themselves clearly, even if in miniature. Indeed, when one compares Leiden with other cities

26. Cornelius De Wit, *De Nederlandse Revolutie van de Achttiende Eeuw 1780–1787* (Oirsbeek: n.p., 1974), 66. The text of the "Leydse Ontwerp" is in *Verzameling van Placaaten, Resolutien en andere authenthyke Stukken enz. betr. de gewigtige gebeurtnissen, in de maand Sept. 1787 en vervolgens in de vereenigde Nederlanden,* 50 vols. (Campen: J. A. de Chalmot, 1789–93) 50:185–244.

where international French-language gazettes appeared in Luzac's day, one may conclude that although many types of urban community could generate such newspapers, Leiden was one of the few in which a politically independent paper could survive. With its population of 28,000, Leiden was large enough to have some serious political life of its own, and the owner and editor of the *Gazette de Leyde* was active in that political life. This experience in making political decisions carried over into his editorial activities. In the two great metropolises with French-language gazettes, London and Amsterdam, this was not the case. In both cities, the ruling elite was far wealthier than the French-language newspaper publishers, who were left to exploit their enterprises in whatever fashion they pleased. On the other hand, in small cities with similar papers—Cleves with 4,243 inhabitants, for example, and Neuwied with even fewer—or in medium-sized cities such as Avignon and Cologne, comparable in size to Leiden but without local institutions of self-government, newspaper publishers were constantly reminded of their dependence on authorities whose actions they could not control. Lacking any experience of political responsibility, they, like the publishers and editors in the big cities, were also more likely to lack journalistic independence.

The European Environment

The urban milieu of Leiden shaped Jean Luzac's political awareness and responsibility. But it was the larger society of continental Europe that shaped his newspaper and the European newspaper press in general. In the broadest sense, newspapers became possible earlier in Europe than elsewhere thanks to the long-standing European penchant for technological tinkering that led to the invention of the printing press in the fifteenth century.[27] Gutenberg's invention was applied to the dissemination of political news almost immediately, but before the periodical newspaper could replace the pamphlet and the broadsheet, other developments had to occur as well. As noted earlier, periodicity was only practical when dependable postal services developed in the late sixteenth and early seventeenth centuries.[28] Newspapers also depended on a sufficiently large literate audience, with a strong interest in current affairs and the economic means to pay for the information it wanted. A

27. David S. Landes, *The Unbound Prometheus* (Cambridge: Cambridge University Press, 1969), 21–32. On the development of printing, see Lucien Febvre and Henri-Jean Martin, *L'avènement du livre* (Paris: Albin Michel, 1958).

28. On the French postal system, see Eugène Vaillé, *Histoire générale des postes françaises* (Paris: Presses universitaires de France, 1952–55). A regular postal system covering the whole of the United Provinces existed by 1680. Overvoorde, *Postwezen in Nederland,* 83.

general reading public began to emerge in the Middle Ages;[29] the quick success of the newspaper formula after its introduction in about 1600 demonstrates that the public audience was already at hand.

Besides technological innovation, an extensive communications system, and a large reading public, certain features of the European political system also nurtured the press. Both the structure of international relations and the changing relationship between state and society within individual polities helped create an environment for the development of the press before 1789. The European state system was a patchwork of independent political sovereignties of very different sorts. By the late nineteenth century the sovereign nation-state became the dominant form; the map of eighteenth-century Europe was far more varied. As Albert Sorel has noted, "Every form of government existed in Europe, and all were considered equally legitimate."[30] States differed enormously in size and power, from the great monarchies of France and Russia with vast populations and powerful military resources, to the pocket principalities of Anhalt-Zerbst and Massa-Carrara. Absolute monarchies coexisted with limited monarchies in which the monarch shared authority with various estates and republics, each organized in its own way and ranging in size from the United Provinces and the Swiss Federation to the city-states of Venice, Geneva, and Germany.

The hundreds of differing governments in eighteenth-century Europe had few interests in common, and their relative independence of one another made it impossible for the stronger to coerce the weaker in a consistent way. As Sorel put it in the introduction to his *L'Europe et la Révolution française*, the international order of the old regime was not a "society of states constituted in an orderly fashion, in which each member followed generally recognized principles in his conduct . . . [and] in which the conviction of a solidarity among monarchies assured the maintenance of public order."[31]

The significance of this situation for the development of journalism was that no state could entirely control the flow of news within its own borders, because none could count on other states to police information about their neighbors with genuine severity. Before the French Revolution, the major powers were never willing to work together to achieve effective regulation of the press; they therefore had to live with the consequences of allowing each sovereign state, no matter how small, to set its own rules. And even though no state other than England offered any real legal protection to the news press before 1789, there were always enough rulers willing to tolerate news publication to ensure the

29. Graff, *The Legacies of Literacy*, 75–107.
30. Albert Sorel, *L'Europe et la Révolution française*, 8 vols. (Paris: Plon, 1908), 1:15.
31. Sorel, *L'Europe*, 1:9.

availability of newspapers. These states fell into two categories: some were republics, like the Netherlands, or limited monarchies, like Great Britain, which for their own internal reasons permitted a greater degree of press freedom than other countries. This tolerance was often annoying to neighboring monarchies, but even the relatively weak United Provinces was still too large to be easily intimidated. On the other hand, a number of small and completely defenseless territories, such as the principality of Neuwied on the Rhine, the papal enclave of Avignon in southern France, and the duchy of Bouillon along France's northern border, also permitted a high degree of press freedom.[32] In these cases, there was no question of internal press freedom: the local authorities permitted news publication for external consumption only. They calculated that the profits to be made from permitting periodicals to be published in their territories outweighed the risks of foreign invasion: they assumed that, in the general web of politics, they were too insignificant to be punished for their transgressions. And, indeed, as the major powers learned that they had to live with such unlicensed publications, their governments found various ways of arriving at a modus vivendi with publishers in these pocket territories.

By the eighteenth century the vast majority of governments had not only realized that the political diversity of the continent made it impossible to control the publication of news but had come to see that it was in their own best interests to facilitate the flow of a considerable volume of information, rather than to obstruct it. From the time of the invention of printing, numerous rulers had seen the value of publicizing their own views of international issues, if not to their own populations, at least to those of other states. Through printed propaganda, one government could expose the bad faith of another and assert the purity of its own motives.[33] Over the centuries, printed propaganda concerning international disputes became increasingly elaborate. Richelieu patronized Théophraste Renaudot's *Gazette de France*, founded in 1631, because he saw the value of presenting both the French and international public with a regular account of events from a point of view favorable to his government. By the end of the seventeenth century, Louis XIV was sponsoring a complex propaganda machine involving not only the *Ga-*

32. On Neuwied, see Karl d'Ester, *Das politische Elysium oder die Gespräche der Todten am Rhein* (Neuwied am Rhein: Strüdersche Buchdruckerei, 1936–37), 39–49. This tiny principality's economy depended almost entirely on producing to meet the demands of France's prerevolutionary elite: in addition to publishing, it housed several major furniture-making enterprises serving Versailles and Paris. On Avignon, René Moulinas, *L'imprimerie, la librairie et la presse à Avignon au XVIIIe siècle* (Grenoble: Presses universitaires de Grenoble, 1974), 72–107; on Bouillon, Raymond F. Birn, *Pierre Rousseau and the "Philosophes" of Bouillon* (Geneva: Institut Voltaire, 1964), 74–75.

33. Erich Everth, *Die Oeffentlichkeit in der Aussenpolitik von Karl V. bis Napoleon* (Jena: Fischer, 1931), 2.

zette but a variety of pamphlets, magazines, and manifestoes specifically prepared for varying audiences.[34] Even if it was difficult to specify exactly what tangible results governments expected from this investment in paper and ink, rulers were convinced of its necessity. Theorists writing about international relations agreed that the image a country projected abroad, the "opinion" it managed to propagate, was a fundamental aspect of its power. "The state which has *opinion* in its favor is always, even if it has inferior physical forces, the stronger in political relations," asserted the editor of the late-eighteenth-century *Encyclopédie méthodique*'s section on diplomacy.[35]

The circulation of news and propaganda to boost one's country's image was, of course, a game that any number could play: it was inherently impossible for any one state to compel all the others to silence except by conquering them all. Hence the European public grew accustomed to hearing the arguments of all parties to each major dispute. And in this situation, it would have taken an exceedingly obtuse propagandist not to realize that he had to frame his works in the expectation that many readers would compare them critically with what his opponents were saying. The best propaganda, at least for an educated and sophisticated audience, would be propaganda that openly invited comparison with opposing views. Efforts to suppress information and the rival parties' statements were likely to backfire by inviting suspicion. By at least the mid-seventeenth century, the European state system had come to accommodate publications that served no other purpose than to collect the news and arguments put forward by the major powers so that those interested could weigh all sides to a dispute and come to a rational conclusion. In the German world, one such collection, the *Acta publica*, began as early as 1621.[36]

Most European states ceased to make any special effort to prevent the circulation of official announcements and manifestoes from their rivals; they resigned themselves to a virtually free flow of such information in exchange for the right to circulate their own pronouncements as freely as possible. In a private memorandum to the French ministry in 1759, Chrétien Lamoignon de Malesherbes, then *directeur-général de la librairie*, wrote that the international gazettes "have since time immemorial had the practice of receiving news, statements and justifications from all the princes, so that a gazette is a sort of tribune from which each power has

34. Howard M. Solomon, *Public Welfare, Science, and Propaganda in Seventeenth-Century France* (Princeton, N.J.: Princeton University Press, 1972), 108–10; Joseph Klaits, *Printed Propaganda under Louis XIV* (Princeton, N.J.: Princeton University Press, 1976).

35. Jean-Nicolas Démeunier, *Encyclopédie méthodique: Economie politique et diplomatique* (Paris: Panckoucke, 1784–1788), 1:457.

36. Everth, *Oeffentlichkeit*, 155.

its turn to plead its case before the public."[37] As editor of the *Gazette de Leyde*, Etienne Luzac echoed those words in 1772 when he reminded a French diplomat that "periodical authors have had the right to publish . . . documents relative to politics for more than a century (you can verify it in all the collections)."[38] With respect to international disputes, one can say that there was a tacitly accepted "public space," in Jürgen Habermas's term, by the middle of the seventeenth century.[39] Since the existence of competing independent states made the publication of some news and opinion about international affairs inevitable, the question for each power was how to manipulate the process of publication in its own favor. And among the best strategies for accomplishing this was the insertion of items in ostensibly independent periodicals outside the borders of the state providing the information. There were practical advantages to all governments in encouraging a limited number of respected press organs that could be counted on to publish all their public statements fairly. Such enterprises simplified the publicizing of propaganda claims and guaranteed to each government that readers would see not only the accusations made against it in international disputes but also its own replies. Thus even governments that banned any publication of political news in their own territories colluded in furnishing information to publications such as the *Gazette de Leyde*. "The views and designs, the intrigues and projects, of courts are let out by insensible degrees and with infinite art and delicacy in the gazettes," a disabused John Adams reported to the American Continental Congress in 1783; he feared the impact of these "great engines of fraud and imposture" on "the good people of America" who did not understand how the European journalistic system functioned.[40]

The question of how best to manage these extraterritorial newspapers, indispensable for spreading propaganda against rivals but annoying when they turned their attention to domestic affairs, troubled governments throughout the eighteenth century, but none found it possible to eliminate their influence altogether. Malesherbes, one of the most enlightened French officials of the century, canvassed almost all of the approaches available to an absolutist government in his lengthy memorandum of 1759. He had been asked to recommend policy in response to a French printer's request for permission to reprint one of

37. "Mémoire sur la gazette d'Hollande," BN, Ms. fr. 22134, ff. 227–31.

38. Etienne Luzac to Desnoyers, secretary of the French Embassy in The Hague, 5 July 1772, in LGA-VH, Z(I), no. 34.

39. For Jürgen Habermas's definition of *bürgerliche Oeffentlichkeit* (which might be translated as the realm of public discourse in civil society), see *Strukturwandel der Oeffentlichkeit* (Berlin: Luchterhand, 1962), 13–41.

40. Adams to president of Congress, 8 Sept. 1783, and to Livingston, 24 June 1783, in Francis Wharton, ed., *The Revolutionary Diplomatic Correspondence of the United States* (Washington, D.C.: Government Printing Office, 1889), 6:682 and 6:504.

the Dutch gazettes for circulation. Malesherbes was no great champion of censorship: in another private memorandum, he had actually recommended the abolition of precensorship of political news, arguing that free discussion would help correct policy errors.[41] But faced directly with independent newspapers, he produced a long complaint about their subversive effect in French affairs. He was especially concerned about the Dutch papers' habit of publishing the manifestoes of the parlements and other groups that were in the habit of obstructing the crown's policies, and he admitted that the wide circulation of these papers in France had complicated the task of governing. "The gazettes of Amsterdam and Utrecht circulate all over Europe, set fire to the kingdom, and are constantly giving foreigners an impression of our difficulties that can only be disadvantageous to the state. One could add that this is the means that the inciters of disorder often use to put forward and gain favor with the public for ideas that they would not dare pronounce themselves," he wrote.[42]

But Malesherbes doubted that an attempt to ban these publications would have any real result. Even if the government were to adopt the double policy of banning the import of foreign gazettes and of publishing a reprint edition of one of them with only the articles about internal French affairs removed, such "cut-up gazettes would only be purchased by those who could not obtain the real ones and there are a thousand ways to smuggle in a printed sheet . . . and the editor, irritated by a prohibition that would certainly reduced his sales, would allow himself even more freedom." The French government could make diplomatic protests to the Dutch about the gazettes, but Malesherbes termed this "always an unfortunate resource," since it lowered the king's ministers' dignity to make repeated complaints about "a miserable libel" and also offered Their High Mightinesses a chance to make embarrassing countercomplaints on other issues. The most practical recommendation was simply "to show the gazetteers that it would be in their personal interest to be more reserved about the domestic affairs of the kingdom"—in other words, to bribe them. Thus Malesherbes recognized that the existence of sovereign states outside of France's borders which did not follow a restrictive press policy made it impossible to maintain a rigid system of press controls inside France's borders.[43]

The various alternatives that Malesherbes considered were actually tried at one time or another by different European governments. Diplomatic representatives in The Hague remained convinced that, although

41. Chrétien Lamoignon de Malesherbes, *Mémoires sur la librairie et sur la liberté de la presse* (Paris: Agasse, 1809), 77–78, 85.
42. Malesherbes, "Mémoire sur la gazette d'Hollande."
43. Ibid.

the gazetteers could not be eliminated, they would prove to be "govern-able . . . by fear aided by reason."[44] Virtually every state in Europe made angry representations to the Dutch States-General about the French-language gazettes at one time or another during the eighteenth century, but the usual outcome was that Their High Mightinesses in The Hague referred the complaint to the appropriate provincial Estates, which in turn passed it along to the city council of the locality where the paper was published, which, after properly deliberate Dutch consideration of the matter, might summon the editor and urge him to be more cautious. Because diplomatic complaints had little chance of success, govern-ments frequently did resort to bribery or the extension of special favors to editors. Some journalists, for example Jean Manzon, editor of the important *Courier du Bas-Rhin*, were quite amenable to such methods, but not all of Manzon's colleagues shared his flexibility: there is no evidence that either Etienne Luzac or his nephew Jean ever allowed such favors to influence the *Gazette de Leyde*.

Malesherbes had also considered the possibility of allowing the do-mestic publication of a paper that would give the same or better foreign news as the imported gazettes, in the hope of cutting into their sales. During the most vigorous of the several attempts made in France to bring the parlements and their supporters to heel, the Maupeou "coup" of 1771–74, such a project was actually tried. René Maupeou and the duc d'Aiguillon, the hard-line ministers appointed in 1770 to tame the opposition, had already replaced the editor of the *Gazette de France* with one of their henchmen, but the traditional constraints on that paper made it unsuitable as a replacement for the foreign gazettes. According to a source hostile to the ministers, they had therefore decided to back a new trimonthly, the *Journal historique et politique*, which was intended to "eliminate the foreign gazettes." But this critical observer claimed that the project was doomed because the news reports the new journal published were "visibly mutilated, and, by the clever choice of only those facts that favor despotism, exalting it and putting it above all other governments, the aim is to condition the people for servitude."[45] The journal, put out by the famous publisher Charles-Joseph Panckoucke and edited at first by Simon-Nicolas-Henri Linguet, succeeded in spite of this negative reception, but it did not make much of a dent in the sales of the foreign gazettes and eventually ended up being incorporated as a

44. Abbé Desnoyers, French representative in The Hague, to the duc d'Aiguillon, 10 July 1772, in MAE, Corr. Pol.—Hollande, 524.

45. [Pidansat de Mairobert, attrib.], *Journal historique de la Révolution opérée dans la Constitution de la Monarchie françoise, par M. de Maupeou, Chancelier de France* (London: John Adamson, 1776), 3:285 (report dated 16 Oct. 1772).

news supplement in Panckoucke's literary magazine, the *Mercure de France*.[46]

The experiment of an officially inspired rival to the Dutch gazettes was only a partial success under Maupeou, but this did not keep either the French or other governments from experimenting with the idea of permitting competition to the established international papers under overt or covert patronage. The French government, which had complete control over the *Courrier d'Avignon* after it ended a six-year military occupation of the papal enclave in 1774, also subsidized the London-based *Courrier de l'Europe* after 1777, and permitted publication of a sanitized edition of it in Boulogne during the American War of Independence.[47] The Prussian government had permitted the establishment of the *Courier du Bas-Rhin* in Cleves in 1767. But if such secretly managed international gazettes were to have any impact, they had to be allowed to publish the same sort of news as such genuinely independent international papers as the *Gazette de Leyde*. As the publisher of the government-subsidized *Courrier de l'Europe* protested when it was suggested that the paper be put out in Paris, under the eyes of French censors, "What importance would a journal reviewed, corrected, and castrated by the Paris censors have? . . . In that case, the *Courrier de l'Europe* would be regarded as an ordinary newspaper."[48]

In his memorandum, Malesherbes had also considered the policy of simply allowing the offending paper to be reprinted inside the country, thus allowing readers to have the independent news they wanted but depriving the offending publisher of his profits. The Austrian emperor Joseph II actually employed this policy against the *Gazette de Leyde* from 1786 to 1792: angered by the paper's hostility to his project for reopening the Scheldt River to trade, he granted the Viennese journalist Charles Grandménil a privilege to reprint the entire text of the Dutch paper and sell it in the Habsburg lands for less than the price of the original.[49] There is no evidence, however, that this effort to punish the paper had any effect on its editorial policy. In short, despite many efforts, European governments throughout the eighteenth century had

46. Suzanne Tucoo-Chala, *Charles-Joseph Panckoucke et la librairie française* (Pau: Marrimpouey, 1977), 194–202.

47. On the *Courrier d'Avignon*, Moulinas, *L'imprimerie*, 324–37; for the French government's relations with the *Courrier de l'Europe*, see Hélène Maspéro-Clerc, "Une 'gazette anglo-française' pendant la guerre d'Amérique: le 'Courrier de l'Europe' (1776–1788)," *Annales historiques de la Révolution française*, no. 227 (1976), 572–94.

48. Swinton to Beaumarchais, 10 Apr. 1778, in Pierre Augustin Caron de Beaumarchais, *Correspondance*, Brian M. Morton, ed. (Paris: Nizet, 1969–78), 4:102–3.

49. Etienne Luzac to Dutch States-General, 1786, in LGA-VH, Z(2), no. 77; Kurt Strasser, *Die Wiener Presse in der josephinischen Zeit* (Vienna: Notring, 1962), 39–40. I would like to thank Helmut Lang of the Oesterreichischen Nationalbibliothek, Vienna, for

to concede the truth of Malesherbes's conclusion that the international gazettes were an unavoidable evil.

Malesherbes had recognized that newspapers carrying news about France's internal affairs existed not only because there were foreign states prepared to harbor them but because there was a strong market for them within the country. "There is not a single lackey fond of news in Paris who doesn't read them regularly," he complained, and he couched many of his conclusions about the difficulties of suppressing the foreign papers in terms of his assumptions about how their readers would react.[50] The problem he confronted arose from a new force in eighteenth-century life: public opinion. Everywhere on the continent, a growing number of subjects had the education, the wealth, and the experience to believe that they had a right to make independent judgments about political affairs, and this educated public insisted on its right to relevant political information. Nor could even supposedly absolutist rulers ignore this demand. Despite the rhetoric they resorted to on ceremonial occasions, Louis XV and other rulers were acutely conscious of the fact that they did not possess absolute power over their subjects. Both in theory and in practice, public opinion had come to be a major factor in political life.

At the level of ideas, all those active in public life during the 1700s had become increasingly aware of the need to invoke the "tribunal of the public" to justify their political claims. Just as public reaction rather than conformity to traditional artistic rules had become the measure of an actor's or a painter's success,[51] so "ministers have become the most carefully observed actors on the stage of the great world, and their performance is the most severely judged," the French minister Jacques Necker observed.[52] The concept of "public opinion" as the rational consensus of the private members of society had crystallized in the eighteenth century, as Jürgen Habermas has shown in his *Strukturwandel der Oeffentlichkeit*. Rulers and rebels alike increasingly sought legitimacy for their claims not by referring to divine authority or to the weight of tradition but by asserting that they represented this intangible but powerful force.[53] And, of course, recognition of public opinion as the

letting me consult a copy of the *Gazette de Leyde* for 13 July 1792, from his private collection which appears to be an example of this licensed pirate edition. It can be distinguished from the original because its columns of type are somewhat wider: 67 mm instead of the original's 61 mm.

50. Malesherbes, "Mémoire sur la gazette d'Hollande."

51. See particularly the analysis in Thomas Crow, "The 'Oath of the Horatii' in 1785: Painting and Pre-Revolutionary Radicalism in France," *Art History* 1 (1978), 426–71.

52. Jacques Necker, *De l'administration des finances de la France* (N.p., 1785) 1:6.

53. On the development of public opinion as a political concept in eighteenth-century France, see Keith Baker, "Politics and Public Opinion Under the Old Regime: Some Reflections," in Censer and Popkin, eds., *Press and Politics in Pre-Revolutionary France*, 204–

source of political legitimacy implied recognition of the public's right to relevant political information to form its opinion. According to one writer, the publication of an official gazette that "informs the Nation about current events, from the government's point of view," was one of the characteristics that distinguished European states from such despotic states as Turkey, whose principle was "to keep the people ignorant."[54]

At the level of political practice, the recognition of the importance of courting public opinion was a result of the limits of the state's power. By modern standards, even the king of France, ruler of the most powerful of eighteenth-century states, possessed only a weak and clumsy set of administrative tools for implementing his will. He did not need to stand for election or share his powers with an elected representative body, but he did need to persuade his people as well as command them. This required that the subjects be given some sense of what the state was doing and why. Even the French bureaucracy was not always responsive to the ruler unless the population at large was prepared to accept royal policies: many officials had purchased or inherited their offices and could not be removed for refusing to obey. During Louis XV's endless quarrels with his sovereign law courts, the parlements, he repeatedly found that his own officers, the intendants, were often afraid to antagonize the powerful aristocratic families that made up the courts by enforcing the king's edicts. Another sphere in which the monarchy needed the subjects' trust was in marketing the bonds which enabled it to survive until the final crisis of 1788. Here, too, it was essential that the population be told of the government's actions and given some reason to believe that royal obligations would be a prudent investment, because the king could not simply compel them to give him their money.

It is clear that the independent gazettes played a crucial role in this process. Even if the *Gazette de France* had been wheeled into the unbecoming role of bond salesman, its credibility would have been nil. The French situation was not unique; in Tuscany after 1743, for example, an enlightened, reforming administration actively promoted the publication of newspapers and journals that sometimes exceeded the government's own intentions in pushing for changes.[55]

For its own political purposes, then, an absolute monarchy often needed an at least apparently independent news press. Moreover, eighteenth-century governments lacked any institutional means of uni-

---

45; and Mona Ozouf, "L'Opinion publique," in Keith Baker, ed., *The French Revolution and the Creation of Modern Political Culture*, 3 vols. (Oxford: Pergamon, 1987–89), 1:419–34.

54. *GL*, 5 Oct. 1784 (Constantinople, 27 Aug.).

55. Castronovo, Ricuperati, and Capra, *La stampa italiana dal cinquecento all'ottocento*, 237–39.

fying and directing public opinion. Religion had long since ceased to play such a role, at least among the educated classes, and political parties, which had begun to serve this function in England, did not exist in the continental states. The press, particularly the uncensored foreign press, offered a partial substitute. By giving a fairly broad elite the feeling that they were in the know about important political decisions, these more or less independent newspapers served to legitimate absolutist policies. In the absence of other bonds between the state and society, the press offered at least one way in which governments could appeal to the most influential elites among their subjects.

The newspapers that filled the need for at least ostensibly independent news reporting during the seventeenth and eighteenth centuries differed from the elite press of modern times in that they were obliged to seek an international readership. If they circulated only in a single state, their economic survival became dependent on their free access to that one market, giving the government of the state effective control over their contents and vitiating even the pretense of independence. But the ability to reach a multinational audience depended on the existence of a common language read by at least a significant sector of the population in several states. Fortunately for eighteenth-century journalists, there was such a language: French. The adoption of French as the preferred language of nobles, thinkers, and political elites throughout the continent created "a kind of intellectual aristocracy, a cosmopolitan patriciate, an oligarchic republic of liberated spirits," who provided the audience for a variety of sophisticated texts in many genres, including political newspapers.[56] This audience was not confined to members of the titled nobility, however; as the publisher of one short-lived French-language gazette pointed out in his prospectus, French "can be called the language of all nations, equally useful to the nobility, to merchants, and above all to people traveling for business or pleasure."[57] This international audience permitted the development of a high-quality international press, including over a dozen competing titles in the late 1700s. Through their ability to find subscribers in so many countries, the French-language papers obtained greater room to maneuver than their rivals in other languages. There were other practical advantages to publishing in French: the fact that French was the language of international diplomacy, for example, meant that the raw material for their most important category of news came to the French gazettes in the language in which they printed it, whereas competitors in other languages had to have their news translated.

Because Europe was divided into rival states, a sphere for the public

56. Louis Réau, *L'Europe française au siècle des lumières* (Paris: Albin Michel, 1938), 5.

57. Cited in Maria Augusta Morelli Timpanaro, "Persone e Momenti del giornalismo politico a Firenze dal 1766 al 1799," *Rassegna degli archivi di stato* 31 (1971), 463.

discussion of political affairs could survive, even though none of these countries guaranteed legal freedom of the press. The fact that even supposedly absolutist governments needed to inform and persuade their subjects as well as command them enabled newspapers that covered domestic politics to circulate in most European states, even if they could not be published there. The unique role of the French language during this period made it possible for publications in that language to reach a truly international audience and thereby to achieve a degree of independence that would not have been possible had language frontiers corresponded to political boundaries. To be sure, this press had to accept the basic framework of the European order within which it operated. The time when some European countries would offer constitutional protection even to periodicals that openly sought the overthrow of the society in which they appeared, such as the socialist and anarchist journals of the nineteenth century, was still far off. But, despite tough-sounding censorship laws in most continental countries, the reading public of the late eighteenth century had access to a significant political news press that did much more than merely transmit what governments wanted their subjects to know.

[3]

The Eighteenth-Century
European Press

The nature of Dutch society and the characteristics of the European state system made the appearance of such newspapers as Jean Luzac's *Gazette de Leyde* possible, but they did not guarantee the success of his particular publication. To assure its survival and prosperity, Jean Luzac had to find a special place for his journal in the highly competitive international commercial market for political news. In 1772, the prospectus for a new French-language newspaper promised readers that the editors would digest information from more than 200 other European periodicals.[1] Clearly, late-eighteenth-century readers had a wide choice of newspapers and journals; they usually read several titles to keep up with events. Many readers could compare one newspaper to another more easily than they can today, because they read their papers in a coffeehouse or some other public gathering place, where a large selection of the available news media would be within easy reach.

Jean Luzac had to bear in mind rival newspapers and a variety of other channels through which political news was disseminated. Some of these, such as magazines, which were becoming an important feature of the journalistic scene, had a great future ahead of them; others, such as manuscript newsletters and political pamphlets, were products of the special conditions of the early modern world. Altogether, these media constituted a system of journalistic communication unique to the eighteenth century. The *Gazette de Leyde*'s success depended on carving out a unique niche for itself amid this crowd of competitors.

1. Cited in [Pidansat de Mairobert, attrib.], *Journal historique*, 3:285 (16 Oct. 1772).

The European Newspaper Market

By the 1770s, several hundred newspapers were published in Europe. The majority were either government-sponsored or government-controlled court gazettes, which were precensored and required to devote a good deal of space to the court that sponsored them, or censored provincial papers, which, like the numerous French *Affiches*, were devoted primarily to advertisments supplemented by literary and political items. The journalistic quality of these periodicals varied tremendously. A court gazette might be censored so closely that it was virtually useless as a guide to events both inside and outside its country of publication: the *Gazzetta di Parma*, a fairly respectable Italian newspaper, got through the entire year of 1789 with only one accidental reference to the occurrence of a revolution in Europe's most powerful monarchy, and the *Gaçeta de Madrid* seems to have managed to ignore the event altogether.[2] But this degree of pusillanimity was unusual. Most court gazettes offered a fair amount of news about states other than their own. The carefully controlled *Berlinische Nachrichten*, for example, gave an explicit summary of the demands the French Third Estate was raising at the beginning of 1789, remarking admiringly, "The spirit of the free people of America prevails in their petitions."[3] Even the *Gazette de France*, the model of the genre, routinely drew on dispatches from the French diplomatic corps to give a reasonably full account of ongoing wars and major public events in foreign capitals.

Like most court gazettes, the *Gazette de France* couched its account of its sponsoring court in elaborate formal language, referring to all local personnages by their full titles. Whereas news from foreign capitals was edited to concentrate primarily on events of definite political significance—English parliamentary debates, the appointment and dismissal of ministers, the outcome of battles—the domestic news consisted primarily of the round of court ceremonial. As a contemporary critic put it, "This paper says the least about what happens in France, except to report the days when the Royal Family has been to Mass or heard a sermon, the presentations at Court, the marriage contracts the king has approved, etc."[4]

2. The *Gazzetta di Parma* covered the convening of the Estates-General and occasionally referred to speeches by the king's ministers, but the only hint that anything extraordinary was occurring in Paris and Versailles during the year was a sentence slipped into a story about the revolution in Liège, remarking that "the energetic example of the French Nation in demanding its natural rights cannot fail to stimulate similar desires among her neighbors." *Gazzetta di Parma*, 25 Sept. 1789 (Liège, 20 Aug. and 4 Sept.).

3. *Berlinische Nachrichten*, 15 Jan. 1789 (Paris, 1 Jan.).

4. [Pidansat de Mairobert, attrib.], *L'espion anglois* (London: John Adamson, 1777–84), 1:6–7, (1 Dec. 1775).

In the *Gazette de France*, the French king appeared not as a political figure but as the symbolic center of the country's existence. He paid his respects to a higher sovereignty on Sundays and holidays; he approved the marriages of his noble subjects; he granted audiences to the representatives of the various corporate bodies of his realm. Political decisions, such as the issuing of edicts and the appointment of ministers, were only some of the many ways in which the king publicly exhibited his sovereignty, and not necessarily the most important. Such actions were never explained, nor were the other public functions the king performed. The purpose of this kind of journalism was not to make the king's actions rationally comprehensible but simply to render them visible. In this respect, the court gazette was entirely different from the official press of modern totalitarian countries, which aims at inculcating ideological attitudes and refuting opposing views, even if those views are never allowed direct expression. The court gazette was not an ideological distortion of the world for political purposes: it was a vehicle for what Jürgen Habermas has called *repräsentative Oeffentlichkeit*, that is, for the representation of the ruler to the world as though he himself constituted the public dimension of the polity over which he ruled.[5] Political conflict within the realm was depicted as nonexistent and the king's will as omnipotent. The very real political conflicts occurring in other states could be reported in more or less neutral terms: their outcome could in no way affect the king's exercise of his sovereignty at home. Hence the court gazettes characteristically combined relatively objective foreign reports with highly stylized representations of court ceremonial.

However insipid they may appear to modern eyes, however, these gazettes were taken seriously as news sources by eighteenth-century readers. Their coverage of international events was usually the first word readers in their country received about such matters, and the court gazettes were not necessarily suspected of distorting the events they covered. It was only when it came to reporting the domestic events of the country where the gazette originated that an outside newspaper enjoyed a distinct advantage. On the other hand, the court gazette was invariably cheaper and reached its audience more quickly, and in its native language. Consequently, it is not surprising that court gazettes normally had higher circulations than their outside competitors in their home states. Sales of the *Gazette de France* exceeded 12,000 in 1781 and 6,000 in 1787, whereas the total press run of the *Gazette de Leyde* was just over 4,000 in 1785, and not all of those copies were destined for France. The continent's newspaper-reading public had by no means rejected the officially sponsored periodical at the time of the French Revolution.

5. Habermas, *Strukturwandel*, 19–25.

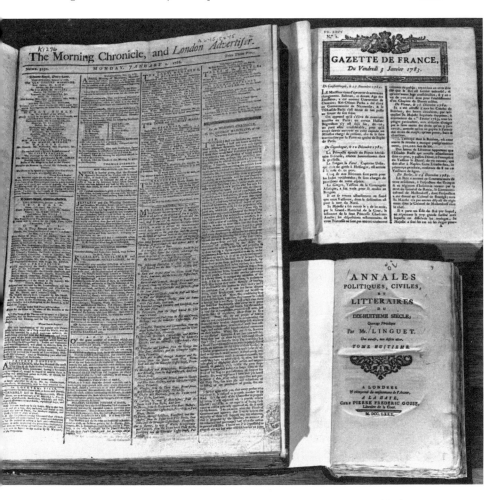

The *Gazette de Leyde*'s competition: the London *Morning Chronicle* (folio format), the *Gazette de France* (quarto format) and Simon-Nicolas-Henri Linguet's *Annales politiques* (octavo format). Courtesy of the Newberry Library.

Other publications thus had to constantly demonstrate that they had something to offer that the court gazettes could not provide.

There were only two major European countries where newspapers were not in theory subject to formal precensorship by their governments: Great Britain and the Netherlands. In both cases, however, the language these countries' domestic newspapers were printed in and their style of journalism prevented them from finding a broad readership outside their home countries. Sophisticated readers across the continent recognized the uniqueness of England's uncensored papers, but only a minority even of the educated elites in continental countries could read English. Furthermore, though the English papers were free, they were also notoriously corrupt. It was common knowledge that all the London papers of the 1770s and 1780s received subsidies from either the Ministry or the Opposition, and that they routinely accepted paid "paragraphs" attacking private individuals from interested parties.[6] A French visitor in 1777 wrote that "the sixty papers are seasoned with wild stories of all sorts—the most absurd and untrue reports, the most virulent satires, the most offensive personal attacks are offered in quantities with a persistence that may amuse the most reasonable and taciturn Englishman but which charm and delight the *canaille*."[7] In any event, until the revolutionary period none of the London papers distinguished itself by its coverage of affairs outside the island, except for stories directly involving British interests, such as the American war. And, as a final handicap to establishing circulation on the continent, the British papers, particularly the large-format London dailies, were extravagantly expensive. According to the American agent in The Hague during the American war for independence, the *London Evening Post* cost four times as much there as the *Gazette de Leyde*.[8]

The Dutch-language press was even less of a potential rival to the French-language international papers. The Dutch papers occasionally circulated in Germany, but elsewhere the language barrier prevented them from developing foreign markets. Like the English papers, the Dutch gazettes concentrated heavily on advertising, which was not of interest to most readers abroad. Except during the Patriot troubles of the 1780s, they carried less news about their own country than the English press, but their foreign news was generally limited. In 1789, for example, the Dutch-language Leiden paper normally carried only a few paragraphs in each issue about the French Revolution.

Newspapers published in German and Italian, even though they rarely enjoyed the freedom from control characteristic of the English and Dutch press, did compete successfully with the French-language gazettes in some areas. Indeed, the most reputable of the German papers, the four-day-a-week *Hamburg Correspondent*, had a circulation of over 20,000 at the time of the French Revolution, dwarfing that of all other papers of the time,[9] and Joachim von Schwarzkopf did not hesitate to compare its news coverage to that of the best French-language

6. Lucyle Werkmeister, *The London Daily Press 1772–1792* (Lincoln: University of Nebraska Press, 1963), 4–5.

7. François Lacombe, *Observations sur Londres* (1777), cited in Josephine Grieder, *Anglomania in France (1740–1789)* (Geneva: Droz, 1985), 50.

8. Charles Dumas to Congress, 12 April 1777, in AR, Dumas, carton I.

9. Lindemann, *Deutsche Presse*, 162–65.

papers. The Italian papers were often the best in reporting events in the Mediterranean and the Near East. Regardless of the quality of papers printed in these regions, however, language barriers prevented them from achieving the cosmpolitan status of the French-language gazettes.

The most direct competition for the *Gazette de Leyde* came, then, from the other gazettes that sought to perform the same function as it did. In France itself, one newspaper had managed to avoid censorship and circulate a great deal of news unfavorable to the government during much of the eighteenth century. This was the Jansenist *Nouvelles ecclésiastiques*, first published in 1728 and continued into the Napoleonic period.[10] In the 1750s and 1760s, this remarkable weekly gave extensive coverage to the confrontations between the parlements and the crown that were also the main subject of the *Gazette de Leyde*'s French reports. By the 1770s, however, the Jansenist paper had changed character, possibly as a result of a secret accommodation with the government, and essentially became a single-issue journal for readers concerned about the theological and canon-law complexities of the religious issues affecting this sect. Throughout the period of Jean Luzac's editorship, there was little overlap between the *Gazette de Leyde* and the *Nouvelles ecclésiastiques*.

The same could certainly not be said of the other French-language international gazettes. Collectively, these papers made up the "elite press." They were aimed at readers who wanted the fullest available political information as quickly as possible, those who would not settle for the watered-down information carried in the censored court gazettes.[11] These rival texts competed with the *Gazette de Leyde* for the same news and for the same readership, and they tended to resemble it closely in format and appearance. Indeed, readers often did not distinguish between the different papers, referring to them all, even those published in other countries, as "la gazette de Hollande." The Leiden paper had been founded roughly contemporaneously with similar publications in several other Dutch cities, and throughout its life it coexisted with many similar gazettes. There is no evidence that the *Gazette de Leyde* enjoyed any superiority over its Dutch rivals in the years before 1770. In the first half of the century, the *Gazette d'Amsterdam* seems to have been a more important paper. The Amsterdam and Utrecht papers joined the Leiden gazette in publicizing the conflict between the French crown and the parlements in the 1750s, and little distinguished them in reputation during that period.

10. Michel Albaric, "Un page d'histoire de la presse clandestine: 'Les Nouvelles Ecclésiastiques,' 1728–1803," *Revue française d'histoire du livre* 10 (1980), 319–32.
11. On the concept of the "elite press," see John C. Merrill, *The Elite Press* (New York: Pitman, 1968), 3–17.

In the period of Jean Luzac's editorship, however, the *Gazette de Leyde*
did manage to elevate itself above its Dutch rivals. During the 1770s and
1780s, the Amsterdam and Utrecht papers were in sharp decline. A
comparison of the number of collections of the other Dutch French-
language gazettes preserved in major libraries today with those of the
Gazette de Leyde leaves no doubt that the latter was the most influential of
the group in this period.[12] The Utrecht paper was not able to fill as many
pages as its Leiden rival; it normally delivered only six pages per issue, as
opposed to Luzac's eight. These two old rivals both saw several changes
of editorship, particularly in the stormy 1780s, and both suffered as a
result of the political repression following the collapse of the Dutch
Patriot movement in September 1787. In its last years, the *Gazette
d'Utrecht* adopted the classic journalistic underdog's strategy of printing
salacious material the more successful papers eschewed. In 1782, the
paper's editor told his Paris correspondent to ignore official warnings to
be more restrained, saying that he was "determined to keep for his paper
the advantage of *making noise*."[13] The Prussian occupation of the
Netherlands marked the end of the Utrecht gazette; the Amsterdam
paper continued to appear but had lost all impact on European affairs.
At the other end of the Dutch political spectrum, the *Gazette de La Haye*
suffered from its status as a thinly disguised court gazette loyal to the
stadholder. The *Gazette de Leyde* thus emerged as the only important
international gazette still published in the Netherlands by the end of the
1780s.

This supremacy in the Dutch market did not mean that the Luzacs'
paper lacked competition, however. As the Dutch international press
gradually declined new rivals had sprung up in other states. The oldest
of these dated to the 1730s: the *Gazette de Cologne* had been founded in
1733, the *Courrier d'Avignon* in 1734. Both were published in small
Catholic territories and had a reputation for Ultramontane loyalties. By
the 1770s, neither was a formidable rival in quality to the *Gazette de Leyde*.
The *Gazette de Cologne* was poorly edited, and its French news usually
lagged behind the *Gazette de Leyde*'s; indeed, its reports often seem to
have been copied directly out of that paper or the *Courier du Bas-Rhin*.

12. Comparison based on holdings listed in the following catalogues: *National Union List
of Serials* (United States), *Catalogue collectif des périodiques* (France), *Catalogo dei periodici delle
biblioteche lombarde* (Italy), *British Union Catalogue of Periodicals*, *Standortskatalog wichtiger
Zeitungsbestände in deutschen Bibliotheken* (Germany; holdings as of 1933), *Centrale catalogus
van periodieken en seriewerken in nederlandse bibliotheken* (Netherlands). All of these catalogues are incomplete, but there is no reason to believe that their listings reflect a bias that
would overstate the number of preserved copies of the *Gazette de Leyde* compared with
those of other titles.
13. Cited in Kluit, "Hollandsche en Fransche Utrechtsche Couranten," 106. Kluit gives
considerable documentary information about the decline of the paper, whose sales in 1783
were only about 300 copies.

The Cologne gazette retained a certain importance in French affairs during the 1780s by publishing critical reports and the more established papers sometimes felt compelled to respond to them. For example, it published accusations that one of Marie-Antoinette's favorites was involved in a complex financial scandal; these stories evoked a denial, undoubtedly supplied from Versailles, in the columns of the *Gazette de Leyde*.[14] The Cologne paper also played a definite role in the Catholic-inspired unrest in the Austrian Netherlands during the same years, which provoked the authorities there to plant replies to it in the *Gazette de Leyde*. Despite its outspokenness, however, there is no evidence that the *Gazette de Cologne* actually had much impact on European politics on the eve of the French Revolution.

The *Courrier d'Avignon* was a different case, even though it was less independent than any of the other major international papers. Located in the papal enclave of Avignon, it enjoyed relative freedom from political control, but it could only circulate with the connivance of the French authorities through whose territories all copies had to pass. After the end of the direct French occupation of Avignon in 1774, when the paper's editor had relocated to the principality of Monaco for several years, the paper passed under virtually total French control. The French government appointed its editor, and the paper certainly printed nothing that was likely to cause offense in Versailles.[15] The *Courrier d'Avignon* did print the first report on the *journée des Tuiles* in Grenoble in June 1788, an important prerevolutionary incident, but it carefully avoided mentioning that blood had been shed and that the royal troops had lost control of the city.[16] The paper's distinction came from its geographic location: as the only French-language international paper printed south of the Alps, it had a large captive market in southern France, northern Italy, and the Iberian peninsula. As it was only half the size of the *Gazette de Leyde* (two four-page issues a week), it also cost much less than its northern rival. Evidence suggests that this paper accepted a minor role on the international scene in exchange for the opportunity to exploit a very lucrative monopoly over its regional market.

14. The stories involved the "affaire des alluvions," a dispute over royal claims to the new soil deposited along the banks of the Gironde River in the Bordeaux region, which came to a head in 1786. The *Gazette de Cologne*'s story accusing Marie-Antoinette's favorite the duc de Polignac of trying to profit from his position at the expense of local noble landowners appeared in the issue of 15 June 1786 (Paris, 10 June). There was an editorial note in the *Gazette de Leyde* of 14 July (Leiden, 12 July) stating that the paper had been informed that the duc de Polignac was not involved in the affair. On the details of the affair, see William Doyle, *The Parlement of Bordeaux and the End of the Old Regime* (New York: St. Martin's Press, 1974), 250–58.

15. Moulinas, *L'imprimerie*, 328–30; Charles F. Hinds, "The *Courrier d'Avignon* in the Reign of Louis XVI" (M.A. thesis, University of Kentucky, 1958).

16. Jean Sgard, *Les trente récits de la journée des Tuiles* (Grenoble: Presses universitaires de Grenoble, 1988), 41.

Despite the continued existence of similar long-established papers in the Netherlands, Avignon, and elsewhere, the rival gazettes that provided the Leiden paper with its most serious competition were newer titles that had sprung up after the Seven Years' War. Two of the most important of these, the *Courier du Bas-Rhin* and the *Courrier de l'Europe*, were located in the territories of major powers, rather than in small states in the interstices of the European state system. The *Courier du Bas-Rhin* appeared in the Prussian garrison town of Cleves, the *Courrier de l'Europe* in London. The *Courrier de l'Europe*, founded in 1776, enjoyed a privileged location in the British capital, but rather than being able to take advantage of the famous English freedom of the press, this publication ended up being tightly controlled by both the British and French governments at a time when they were in open conflict with one another. As the American diplomat and future president John Adams explained to the Continental Congress, "if it should offend the English essentially, the ministry would prevent its publication; if it should sin against the French unpardonably, the ministry would instantly stop its circulation."[17] The *Courrier de l'Europe* thus deserved its reputation of servility, but this did not prevent it from being a highly successful business enterprise: the French government subsidized it lavishly, taking a bulk order of 4,800 subscriptions—almost equal to the entire press run of the *Gazette de Leyde*—and intervened to protect it against unwanted competition, while the British government secretly paid its publisher to spy on his French patrons.[18]

Its London location did give the *Courrier de l'Europe* an advantage in covering the American war, because most information about the hostilities passed through London. (During the war, the paper published a bowdlerized edition for continental distribution in Boulogne-sur-Mer.) But the paper's coverage of French affairs had no credibility within the country, and the paper's main selling point was its reporting of the British Parliament's debates; indeed, it claimed that it brought together in one place information on British politics that could otherwise be found only by reading the full range of the British press.[19] Its French news was invariably pro-ministerial and often very incomplete: it made no mention of Necker's dismissal in 1781, said nothing about the arrest of Cardinal de Rohan when the Diamond Necklace scandal broke in 1785, and castigated all opponents of Calonne's and Brienne's at-

17. Adams to president of Congress, 8 Sept. 1783, cited in Wharton, ed., *Revolutionary Diplomatic Correspondence*, 6:682.

18. *Correspondance politique et anecdotique sur les affaires de l'Europe* (N.p., 1789–90), 1:92–93, Maastricht, 21 Nov. 1780; Hélène Maspéro-Clerc, "Samuel Swinton, éditeur du Courier de l'Europe à Boulogne-sur-Mer (1778–1783) et agent secret du gouvernement britannique," *Annales historiques de la Révolution française*, no. 262 (1985), 527–31.

19. *Courrier de l'Europe*, 19 Jan. 1781.

tempted reform measures in 1787 and 1788. Certainly more informative than the *Gazette de France*, the *Courrier de l'Europe* was nevertheless far from being an independent account of French political life.

The *Courier du Bas-Rhin*, like the *Courrier de l'Europe*, was widely known to be under the thumb of its host government. But its editor, Jean Manzon, was a genuinely talented journalist who succeeded in making his paper a major presence on the European journalistic scene. His was the only other international gazette that the *Gazette de Leyde* felt compelled to treat, albeit reluctantly, as something of an equal. In international affairs, the *Courier du Bas-Rhin* was frequently labeled "l'oracle de Berlin" because of its understandable adherence to a pro-Prussian line, but this restraint did not hinder the paper in its coverage of domestic disputes in other states. Manzon sold his services freely and engaged in various blackmailing schemes—in other words, his ethics resembled those of the leading English journalists of the period—but he wrote in a lively style and produced a highly readable paper. His paper had more intellectual content than the other gazettes. He flirted with the philosophes, and allied himself with the most original political journalist of the prerevolutionary years, Simon-Nicolas-Henri Linguet. Like Luzac, Manzon had unmistakable political biases, but his were nearly always in direct opposition to those of the *Gazette de Leyde*. Whereas the Leiden paper was normally the organ of constituted bodies struggling against real or imagined threats of despotism, Manzon was the habitual advocate of strong central authority. He was for the French crown against the parlements and for the Dutch stadholder against the Patriots. When the French prerevolutionary crisis generated demands for greater public involvement in politics, the *Courier du Bas-Rhin* commented sarcastically, "There is no doubt that we will soon have in France some of this ingredient called *patriotism*, which has been sown so plentifully in the disunited provinces of the Low Countries." Later in the year, the paper dismissed the general proposition that rulers were bound to respect their country's traditional institutions with the remark that "the constitution of any state can be completely transformed, without any infringement on the privileges of a nation."[20]

Of all the other gazettes it had to compete with, the *Courier du Bas-Rhin* was the only one that the *Gazette de Leyde* ever felt compelled to respond to directly. The *Courier du Bas-Rhin* regularly provoked such a dialogue in its own columns, particularly during the years of the Dutch Patriot movement in the 1780s, when it frequently attacked Luzac and his paper for their opposition to the House of Orange. Luzac's circle of French-speaking Patriot acquaintances responded with pamphlets

20. *Courier du Bas-Rhin*, 18 July 1787 (Paris, 10 July); and 11 Aug. 1787 (Brussels, 5 Aug.).

aimed at the rival paper—such as Dumont-Pigalle's *The Dinner at the Golden Lion, or the Singular Adventures that happened in July 1783 to Mr. Manzon, alias, Loud-Mouth, editor of the gazette called the 'Courier du Bas-Rhin'*—and Luzac's correspondence proves that he paid close attention to this annoying rival.

In the face of this rigorous competition, the *Gazette de Leyde* sought to distinguish itself by a sober tone and cautious reporting. To be sure, Luzac's paper was not a colorless chronicle, but more than his rivals, Luzac insinuated his political opinions into his paper indirectly. He wrote no sarcastic footnotes commenting on the dispatches he printed, as Jean Manzon often did in the *Courier du Bas-Rhin*. Luzac's paper was not always first with the news, and indeed it sometimes held back reports that appeared in rival papers, but when it did so, the avowed reason was always to confirm stories that seemed confusing or hard to believe. But the *Gazette de Leyde* never passed over significant events in silence, as the *Courrier de l'Europe* or the *Courrier d'Avignon* sometimes did. Luzac's journalistic formula was not the only one that led to success at the end of the Old Regime, but it had the unique quality of combining a strong attraction for the general public with a strong appeal to governing elites. According to a French source from the 1780s, the Leiden paper was "the most sought after in recent years, because it sometimes contained fresher and more detailed political news than the others." In this way, it satisfied the reading public, but it also pleased the French authorities, because "it was ordinarily very circumspect and extremely quiet about sensitive issues."[21] Ministers recognized that material published in the *Gazette de Leyde* had more credibility than what was inserted in its rivals: as John Adams reported, the ministers favored Luzac for items concerning "the more grave and solid objects," reserving for less distinguished papers items designed to affect "the small talk of coffee-houses, and still smaller and lower circles."[22] Other papers, such as the *Courier du Bas-Rhin*, might on occasion be more titillating or provocative, but the *Gazette de Leyde* had succeeded in carving out a niche in the market for international gazettes by winning the trust of readers and rulers alike.

Alternatives to the Newspapers

Besides other newspapers, the *Gazette de Leyde* had to compete with manuscript newsletters or *nouvelles à la main*. These handwritten bul-

21. [Pidansat de Mairobert, attrib.] *Mémoires secrets*, 28:166 (8 March 1785).
22. Adams to president of Congress, 8 Sept. 1783, in Wharton, ed., *Revolutionary Diplomatic Correspondence*, 6:682. Adams said that the *Gazette d'Amsterdam* was also employed in this regard, but there is little evidence that it was actually taken seriously by most European governments by this time.

letins had flourished since the sixteenth century and the Fugger newsletters of that time. The composers of these *nouvelles* were engaged in exactly the same enterprise as the correspondents of the international newspapers, and in fact they were often the same people. For example, the Paris correspondence printed in the *Courier du Bas-Rhin* during the late 1760s later appeared as part of the printed version of an extensive set of *nouvelles à la main*, the so-called *Mémoires secrets de Bachaumont*.[23]

Compared to the international newspapers, these newsletters offered the attraction of quicker delivery, as they did not have to be sent to a distant location to be printed and then mailed to subscribers who were often closer to the source of the news than their newspaper was. The newsletters also had the lure of being apparently completely free of censorship, although the example of the Paris newsletter enterprises of the 1770s and 1780s shows that this notion was misleading: the police had their ways of tracing and pressuring the manuscript *nouvellistes* just as they did the printed newspapers. Louis-Sébastien Mercier claimed that the manuscript *nouvellistes* operated with the knowledge and approval of the ministers, and the German journalist Schlözer asserted that the French ministers secretly paid the author of one of the main Paris newsletters to avoid being attacked in it.[24] The authors of these manuscript news services certainly tried to stress the superiority of their products to the printed gazettes. The author of one set of bulletins, later published under the title of the *Espion anglois*, prefaced his work with a stinging critique of his printed rivals. "Aside from the fact that they have to divide their attention among the various states they report on," he wrote, "they are desperate to be allowed to circulate in Paris, and as a result they are reduced to silence or flattery on a multitude of topics, to avoid being banned."[25]

While Jean Luzac was editing the *Gazette de Leyde*, two great manuscript news bulletins emanated from Paris, and similar enterprises existed in other major European capitals. One of the Parisian bulletins was the "Bachaumont" operation, whose manuscripts eventually provided most of the material published as the *Mémoires secrets* in the 1780s;[26] the

23. François Moureau, "Les mémoires secrets de Bachaumont, le Courier du Bas-Rhin et les 'bulletinistes' parisiens," in Jean Varloot and Paule Jansen, eds., *L'année 1768 à travers la presse traitée par ordinateur* (Paris: Centre national de la recherche scientifique, 1981), 58–79.

24. Louis-Sébastien Mercier, *Tableau de Paris*, "nouvelle édition," 10 vols. (Amsterdam, 1782–88), 7:18; Schlözer, *Briefwechsel meist historischen und politischen Inhalts*, vol. 6, no. 41, 271–72 (25 Oct. 1780).

25. [Pidansat de Mairobert, attrib.], *L'espion anglois*, 1:7 (1 Dec. 1775).

26. The only comprehensive work on the eighteenth-century manuscript newsletters remains Frantz Funck-Brentano, *Figaro et ses devanciers* (Paris: Hachette, 1909). On the Bachaumont enterprise, see also Robert S. Tate, Jr., "Petit de Bachaumont: His Circle and the *Mémoires secrets*," (Geneva: Institut Voltaire, 1968). Corrections to it are in Louis

other, known as the "Métra," combined a manuscript news service with a printed bulletin devoted to literature known as the *Correspondance secrète*.[27] An example from central Europe is the manuscript later published under the title *Correspondance politique et anecdotique sur les affaires de l'Europe*, devoted primarily to Austrian affairs but with some coverage of other German capitals.[28]

These manuscript bulletins contained a certain amount of material that did not appear even in the best-informed printed news media. In particular, the *nouvelles* included many personal anecdotes about public personalities which never appeared in the gazettes, and their authors allowed themselves a freedom in commenting on their news reports that their printing-press rivals did not enjoy. "They are particularly hard on private individuals; silent vengeance insinuates itself in these almost invisible canals, which carry poisonous malignity everywhere," Mercier wrote.[29] The newsletters' gossipy tone resembled the scandalous "paragraphs" of the London press more than the sober content of the continental gazettes. Thus both the international gazettes and the newsletters gave extensive space to a series of sensational Paris court cases in the mid-1770s, but whereas the papers simply summarized the juicier testimony, the Métra *bulletiniste* felt free to add, "You will have remarked that when the judgments have been handed down, the credit of the well-connected party has always enabled him to triumph over the weaker one."[30] Even crowned heads were not safe from the manuscript journalists. The *Correspondance politique et anecdotique*, based somewhere in central Europe, allowed itself to retail an item about counterfeit French coins supposedly circulating in Frankfurt, with the portrait of Louis XVI "decorated with the headdress that the Eternal gave to Moses," and its first report on Frederic the Great's successor on the Prussian throne in 1786 praised him because "he hasn't had anything like an orgy, hasn't touched a woman's breast since he ascended the throne."[31]

Olivier, "Bachaumont the Chronicler: A Doubtful Renown," *Studies on Voltaire and the Eighteenth Century* 143 (1975), 161–79; and Moureau, "Les mémoires secrets."

27. The Métra enterprise operated out of the small German principality of Neuwied, on the Rhine near Frankfurt. The manuscript news bulletins it sent out were first published in A. Lescure, ed., *Correspondance secrète inédite sur Louis XVI, Marie-Antoinette, la cour et la ville de 1777 à 1792* (Paris: Plon, 1866). One manuscript set of the news bulletins is now in the Lilly Library, Indiana University. On the Métra news service, see, in addition to Funck-Brentano, Martin Fontius, "Mettra und seine Korrespondenzen," *Romanische Forschungen* 76 (1964), 405–21; and Cécile Douxchamps-Lefèvre, "Un magazine de la Cour de France au début du règne de Louis XVI," *Revue historique*, no. 549 (1984), 95–108.

28. Unlike the "Bachaumont" and "Métra" correspondences, this interesting set of news bulletins has not been employed much by scholars working on the period. There is a copy in the Göttingen University library.

29. Mercier, *Tableau*, 7:18.

30. Lescure, ed., *Correspondance inédite*, 1:54 (9 May 1777).

31. *Correspondance politique et anecdotique*, 4:48 (Frankfurt, 17 May 1786); 4:93 (Berlin, 29 Aug. 1786).

In these manuscript newsletters, the *Gazette de Leyde* faced a rival that could provide a more comprehensive picture of the same political events, but although they certainly enriched the picture of events that readers received, they tended to merely embroider the hard news the printed gazettes carried. Mercier pointed out that the *nouvelles à la main* never succeeded in giving advance notice of genuinely important political events.[32] The censored gazettes of the continent might be ordered to pass over a significant occurrence in total silence, as the *Gazzetta di Parma* did during the French Revolution, but the *Gazette de Leyde* and other international gazettes could not be controlled the same way. A comparison of the Luzac paper with the two main French newsletters of the period shows that no crucial French political event of the period went unmentioned in the Leiden paper, and that the information about France the paper printed was as up to date as that of its manuscript rivals. The difference was in the wealth of "human interest" anecdotes and snide comments that "Métra" and "Bachaumont" could offer their subscribers. When it came to the great public events, the stuff of history, the Leiden paper was comprehensive.

Moreover, the hand-copied *nouvelles* could not reach as broad an audience as the printed newspapers. These manuscript news services were costly, and even on the most generous estimates they could not produce as many copies as the printed journals. As the preface to a subsequent printed version of the "Métra" literary bulletins noted, "The high cost of this sheet and the discretion with which it has had to be distributed have prevented it from being very widely read."[33] In addition, most such services covered news from only a single capital. These gossipy bulletins went primarily to rulers and wealthy noblemen. Eventually, versions of these manuscripts made their way into print; for example, the published works derived from the "Bachaumont" bulletins nearly achieved the regularity of a periodical publication by the early 1780s, in the form of the *Mémoires secrets*. But by the time they did appear in print, the gossip had lost its freshness: these bulletins were contemporary history, not journalism.

Another reason why the *Gazette de Leyde* did not suffer unduly from the competition of the manuscript newsletters had to do with its status as a public institution. Once news was published in the paper's columns, it was known in principle to the entire world, and actors on the public stage had to conduct themselves accordingly. Furthermore, the paper had a definite reputation for reliability; its reports carried a certain credibility. In contrast, the information in the manuscript newsletters,

---

32. Mercier, *Tableau*, 7:19.

33. *Correspondance secrète, politique et littéraire, ou Mémoires pour servir à l'Histoire des Cours, des Sociétés & de la littérature en France, depuis la mort de Louis XV*. (London: John Adamson, 1787), 1:preface.

although they undoubtedly circulated widely among political insiders, was not public. Indeed, their great attraction was their promise to provide *secret* information that would be known only to their subscribers. Because an item was ostensibly secret, however, public figures could afford to ignore it if they wished. Certainly they could not be compelled to respond to it, as they might have to in the case of published reports. And the manuscript services had none of the cachet of credibility that the *Gazette de Leyde* enjoyed. Their reports were not subject to critical examination and possible correction. By their very nature, they carried a great deal of information that could never be verified—rumors, supposed transcripts of conversations, stories about the sexual lives of prominent people.

The journalist and polemicist Simon-Nicolas-Henri Linguet, himself a frequent target of attacks in the *Mémoires secrets*, was telling the truth when he asserted that everyone in Paris knew how unreliable the gossip that ended up in the newsletters was; consequently readers gave only "partial credence to these fleeting slanders." He dismissed the Bachaumont memoirs as "a collection of these respectable fables."[34] However plausible the stories they recounted, the manuscript newsletters' powers of persuasion depended on their readers' willingness to suspend their critical faculties to a certain degree, whereas the *Gazette de Leyde*'s proudest claim was that the material it printed could be verified. The two genres of reporting were thus very different forms of journalism, fulfilling two different functions. The "Bachaumont" newsletters certainly have great interest as sources for historians today, but it is by no means evident that their contemporary impact was more significant than that of the duller but more reliable *Gazette de Leyde*.

Like the newsletters, political magazines shared some of the functions of the international gazettes. In fact, a number of magazines included a political news section that was in effect simply a gazette. The *Journal de Bruxelles*, a news supplement included with the popular literary journal *Mercure de France*, was a good example. This periodical, published in France with an official privilege, included nothing controversial, but its content differed considerably from the *Gazette de France* in being much less court-centered. It omitted all reference to political controversy, such as the quarrels between crown and parlements, but gave full coverage to such events as natural disasters: in 1788, it provided the most comprehensive reporting to be found in the European press on the terrible hailstorm of 13 July, which led to the high grain prices that helped spark unrest in France in 1789.

In the German-speaking world, magazines actually came closer to performing the functions of the elite political press than did the news-

34. *Annales politiques*, 1:496–97 (1777).

papers. During Luzac's day, August Ludwig von Schlözer's *Stats-Anzeigen* and Gottlob Benedikt von Schirach's *Politische Journal* dominated the German political press. The *Stats-Anzeigen*, a quarterly, combined a certain amount of current news with a variety of reprinted documents and pamphlets, all enlivened by its editor's often caustic critical footnotes. Schlözer's journalistic formula was less wedded to the news of the moment and more determined to give readers the perspective they needed to understand events. Even more successful in terms of circulation than the *Stats-Anzeigen* was the Altona journalist Schirach's *Politische Journal*. This monthly magazine printed almost exclusively current news, rather than combining journalism with historical interests as Schlözer did. It gave readers a streamlined summary of recent events, easier to follow than the stories in newspapers, and it had the advantage of being able to omit all the commercial advertising that took up half the space in the best German newspaper of the period, the *Hamburg Correspondent*. As a central locus for political news about the German states, the *Politische Journal* actually performed much the same function as the *Gazette de Leyde* did for the French political world; it benefited from the fact that newspapers had a more commercial role in the German-speaking world than they did in the French-speaking regions.

The French-speaking world also had a variety of news periodicals that were more like modern magazines than newspapers. There was no direct equivalent to the *Stats-Anzeigen* in terms of quality, and the demise of the Leiden-based *Mercure historique et politique* in 1773 marked the disappearance of publications similar to the *Politsche Journal*. Luzac had to bear in mind journals such as the *Affaires de l'Angleterre et l'Amérique*, a "single-issue" periodical devoted to the American war, which appeared from 1776 to 1779 with covert backing from the French government, and the *Politique hollandois*, a similar publication intended to acquaint the European public with the later stages of the American war and then with the issues in the Dutch Patriot period. Both journals printed documents and ideological commentary. An even more overtly ideological news publication appeared in the Belgian provinces in 1785: the *Journal général de l'Europe*, tolerated by Joseph II because of its outspoken support for his controversial reform program. In its openly committed tone, it foreshadowed the revolutionary press that developed in France in 1789.

The most striking success in employing the magazine medium for political purposes before the French Revolution, however, was Linguet's *Annales politiques*, a venture in which news reporting gave way to political commentary.[35] Linguet's endless embroilments with the French and

35. On Linguet's life and his journal, see Darline Gay Levy, *The Ideas and Careers of Simon-Nicolas-Henri Linguet* (Urbana: University of Illinois Press, 1980).

other governments and his irregular work habits kept his journal from ever achieving regular periodicity. It appeared erratically even at the best of times and was repeatedly interrupted, particularly by the author's two-year stay in the Bastille in 1780–82. When it did appear, however, it offered a dynamic model of journalism very different from the Luzacs' style. Linguet was less concerned with providing a chronicle of events than with delivering his personal opinion about their meaning. Whereas the *Gazette de Leyde* accepted the structure of the world it reported on as a given, Linguet constantly called it into question. He argued that force was the basis of social relations and of the right of property, that slavery was more humane than the modern wage system, and that both the French and British constitutions were fundamentally vicious.

Linguet delivered his controversial opinions in highly colored prose, far removed from the stilted tone of the international gazettes. His intention was to overwhelm his readers emotionally, rather than to convince them by a sober appeal to their reason. Though he was often dismissed by contemporaries for his "paradoxes," he was a great success with the European reading public. "Even if Linguet was not the founder of an already existing genre," remarks an Italian scholar, "he was certainly its most original and intelligent practitioner, the only one able to turn it into an effective instrument of political criticism and of the diffusion of ideas."[36]

Linguet's journal was extensively counterfeited all over the continent and may well have had the largest circulation of any French-language political periodical issued before the French Revolution.[37] Furthermore, Linguet's techniques clearly foreshadowed those of the French revolutionary press. The highly charged rhetoric of his articles, the direct attacks on political figures he disliked, and his overt determination to change government policies rather than merely to describe them were all completely antithetical to the formal rules adhered to by the international gazettes. These features signaled the arrival of a new spirit on the journalistic scene. The fact that Linguet's journal prospered because of secret arrangements with the French Foreign Ministry in no way diminishes its revolutionary impact: the minister (the unimaginative comte de Vergennes) and his underlings, who carefully controlled the letter of Linguet's text, simply failed to comprehend its spirit.

For all his success in demonstrating the new possibilities of individualistic political journalism, however, Linguet seems to have had little immediate impact on the traditional political journalism of the interna-

36. Ginevra Conti Odorisio, *S. N. H. Linguet dall'ancien regime alla rivoluzione* (Rome: Giuffrè, 1976), 201.

37. Jeremy D. Popkin, "Un journaliste face au marche des périodiques," in Hans Bots, ed., *La diffusion et la lecture des journaux de langue française sous l'ancien régime* (Amsterdam and Maarssen: APA-Holland University Press, 1988), 11–19.

tional gazettes. Linguet had no intention of competing with them directly and often referred readers to them for the bare details of the news. "I leave it to the gazettes to risk the succession of contradictory reports that fill their columns, and keep their readers in suspense," he wrote in one of his early issues, "That is not my object. Minor or uncertain reports are not . . . what you expect from me."[38] The total circulation of the *Annales politiques* was far above that of any of the international gazettes, but it by no means diminished their appeal. Readers still wanted a steady, dependable flow of news, as well as the combination of information, entertainment, and provocation that Linguet delivered. Although his success anticipated the evolution of opinion journalism and the eventual decline of the "impartial narrator" whose voice the international gazettes claimed to embody, Linguet's achievement was essentially the creation of a unique form of journalism and a new market for it.

The court gazettes and other newspapers of the continent, the manuscript newsletters, and the magazines that appeared contemporaneously with the *Gazette de Leyde* all shared the general characteristic of periodicity—even if some of them, like Linguet's *Annales*, honored that principle only in the breach. But another genre of nonperiodic publication was also fundamental to eighteenth-century political discourse: the pamphlet. The political pamphlet had come into existence more than a century before the newspaper, and it was important well into the nineteenth century, before being displaced by its periodical rival.[39] During the eighteenth century, pamphlets were still at least as influential as periodicals. But there was no basic incompatibility between the functions of newspapers and those of pamphlets in this period. In fact, many pamphleteers referred to the international press to provide readers with the factual background they needed to understand the pamphlets. And many a pamphleteer was spurred to action by an article in an international paper, as was the author of a pamphlet on the rights of Jews in France who began his work, "My attention was recently caught by an article in the *gazette de Hollande*."[40] Newspapers frequently referred their readers to relevant pamphlets, or even published their texts in their own columns. The *Gazette de Leyde* mentioned more than fifty French political pamphlets in the two years before the convening of the Estates-General in 1789.

38. *Annales politiques*, 2:22.

39. Unlike periodical publications, pamphlets as a genre have received little systematic study, although specific corpuses of texts, such as the pamphlets of the Protestant Reformation, have been analyzed. For an introduction to the existing literature, see Lester Condit, *A Pamphlet about Pamphlets* (Chicago: University of Chicago Press, 1939).

40. [Bernard de Valabrègue], *Lettre ou réflexions d'un Milord à son Correspondant à Paris; Au sujet de la Requête des Marchands des Six-Corps, contre l'admission des Juifs aux Brevets, etc.* (London: n.p., 1768), p. 6.

Because pamphlets did not rely on subscription sales for their diffusion, they could more easily evade censorship regulations. They did not
require a specially organized printingshop permanently committed to
their production, so they could be turned out close to the scene of
events. The production of occasional pamphlets did not require the
same sort of all-absorbing professional commitment that periodical
journalism demanded: the authors of pamphlet texts often included
major actors in events, and first-rate writers and thinkers such as Voltaire or Condorcet who would not have tied themselves down to the
routines of regular publication. In a world in which political events
occurred irregularly, the flexible pamphlet was in some senses better
adapted to serve as a vehicle of political opinion than the newspaper or
magazine.

It has sometimes been asserted that the distinction between pamphlets and newspapers before the French Revolution was that the former conveyed opinions and the latter were restricted to providing information. This distinction is not entirely valid: some newspapers, like the
Gazette de Leyde, had unmistakable political viewpoints, whereas pamphlet journalism could be informative as well as polemical. Nor is it true
that pamphlets could completely escape censorship and other political
controls to which periodicals were subject: in France, for example, most
political pamphlets in fact circulated with a *permission tacite*, an oral
permit from the police.

The main advantage of the pamphlet was its flexibility: a pamphlet
could be of any length, from a single page to over a thousand; it could be
in any style, serious and factual, satirical, or emotional; and it could deal
with any topic, whether it fitted into the gazettes' rather stereotyped
categories for news or not. Thus a collection of pamphlets against the
French minister Necker issued at the time of his disgrace in 1781 includes dialogues, diatribes, collections of statistics, even suppositious
speeches by Necker himself. Many of these pieces had clear political
motivations, but some also constituted genuine investigative reporting
of a sort never engaged in by the eighteenth-century periodical press.
For example, a work titled *Seconde Suite des observations du citoyen* gave a
detailed if hostile summary of Necker's career from his humble origins
to his rise to wealth during the Seven Years' War and his involvement in
the complex affairs of the French India Company—all relevant information for anyone seriously interested in understanding Necker's role
in French public life. Other pamphlets provided serious if critical discussions of the implications and probable consequences of Necker's policies.[41]

41. *Collection complette [sic] de tous les ouvrages pour et contre M. Necker, avec des notes critiques,
politiques et secrètes* (Utrecht: n.p., 1781).

Taken as a whole, the dozen or more pamphlets issued against Necker in 1779–81 fulfilled most of the functions that were to be taken on by the periodical newspaper press in France after the Revolution. Their authors demonstrated all the abilities that would be required of postrevolutionary journalists, both in their ability to investigate and provide relevant facts and in their ability to marshal those facts for polemical purposes. Contemporaries had no doubt that the pamphlets had a very real effect on events, and that they contributed considerably to the pressures leading to Necker's dismissal in 1781. Like the newspapers during and after the French Revolution, the anti-Necker pamphlets emanated from the minister's personal and political enemies and represented alternative ideas about how policy should be conducted.[42]

What the pamphleteers lacked, of course, was the ability to issue their journalism in periodical form. The French pamphlets against Necker and other similar *libelles* of the period, both in France and elsewhere, circulated semiclandestinely, even though their authors and distributors were rarely subject to serious penalties. An organized public dialogue between Necker's supporters and opponents was out of the question, although pamphlets frequently were written explicitly to answer other pamphlets: in the Necker collection just cited, a work titled *Les comments* was a response and commentary to Necker's own *Compte rendu*. But the sporadic and irregular way in which pamphlets appeared and circulated saddled the genre with certain weaknesses. If the pamphlet's irregular appearance allowed it to mold itself more closely to the episodic nature of eighteenth-century political life, it also made it impossible for pamphleteers to establish a durable bond with their readership. They had no chance to build up a track record of credibility that would extend from one issue to another. As it happens, the author of several of the major pamphlets against Necker was also the anonymous author of the most successful pamphlet series against Maupeou published during the crisis of 1771–74: J. M. Augéard had produced the celebrated *Correspondance secrète et familière de M. de Maupeou avec M. de Sor*** Conseiller du nouveau Parlement*, a heavy-handed satire which had kept the Maupeou regime's police busy and resulted in the largest trial for press offenses in eighteenth-century France.[43] But Augéard conducted his offensive against Necker as an entirely separate project, with no reference to his earlier

42. On the background of the most effective anti-Necker pamphlets, see J. M. Augéard, *Mémoires secrets de J. M. Augéard*, Evariste Bavoux, ed. (Paris: H. Plon, 1866), 98–107. See also Jeremy D. Popkin, "Pamphlet Journalism at the End of the Old Regime," in *Eighteenth-Century Studies* (forthcoming 1989).

43. Augéard, *Mémoires*, 45, 65. In January 1774, the "reformed" Parlement de Paris, loyal to Maupeou, condemned no less than forty-nine individuals for complicity in writing and distributing the *Correspondance* and another serial pamphlet against the embattled chancellor.

publications. Only the arrest of his faithful collaborator Pierre-Jacques Le Maitre in 1786 exposed the workings of a pamphleteering operation that had extended over fifteen years.[44]

This absence of continuity made the pamphlet press a weak tool for the organization and coordination of public response to the news. A successful pamphlet might have great impact, but, as one of the most thoughtful journalists of the revolutionary period noted, the periodical could reach more readers "every day, at the same moment . . . in all classes of society . . . ; being the almost indispensable basis for each day's conversation, not only do they affect a larger body of people, but their impact is stronger than that of any other type of printed matter."[45] The pamphlet was quickly outdistanced by the movement of events, whereas the newspaper could react, adjust its position, or shift its attention to new issues. Furthermore, the periodical had the chance to make its point more powerfully, thanks to the effect of repetition. Linguet, the master polemicist of the prerevolutionary period, underlined this in his response to a reader who complained that he returned to the same subject too often. Referring to his long campaign against the philosophe d'Alembert, Linguet asserted that "this success has been due to continual repetition: a moment of silence [from me] would put M. d'Alembert back on his pedestal, and the public would relapse into veneration, or at least into uncertainty."[46] The strength of the periodical was the fact that its influence continued over time. In this way, it also provided a bond among its readers, who regularly received the same message at the same time, and whose reactions were thus coordinated.

These distinctions, and the advantages they gave to periodicals over irregular pamphlet publications, became obvious in France during the revolutionary era, but the same processes were at work even before 1789. They account for the durable influence of even soft-spoken periodicals, such as the *Gazette de Leyde*, despite the fact that on every issue that the paper covered, pamphlets circulated that were more outspoken, more completely informed, and frequently more interesting. For all its importance in eighteenth-century public life, the pamphlet press did not render the gazettes superfluous, nor did it necessarily exercise greater influence over events.

44. On the Le Maitre case, which rivaled the trial of Cardinal de Rohan in the French press for several months in early 1786, see André Doyon, *Un agent royaliste pendant la Révolution: Pierre-Jacques Le Maitre (1790–1795)* (Paris: Société des études robespierristes, 1969), and contemporary newsletters and newspapers, particularly Nicolas Hardy, "Mes Loisirs," BN, Ms. fr. 6685, entries for 14 Dec. 1785, 19 Dec. 1785, 30 Dec. 1785, and 15 Jan. 1786.

45. Pierre-Louis Roederer, "Essai analytique sur les diverses moyens établis pour la communication des pensées, entre les hommes en société," *Journal d'economie publique*, 30 brumaire, An V (1796), 429.

46. *Annales politiques*, 6:391.

When one takes into account the full range of written media that carried political news in the last decades of the Old Regime, it becomes clear that the international gazettes occupied a liminal position between the official press and the newsletters and pamphlets that were normally tolerated but not officially acknowledged. State authorities were willing to acknowledge the existence of such papers as the *Gazette de Leyde* and they even referred to them as legitimate sources of information, which was not the case for the secret correspondences and *libelles*, even though both genres circulated freely among political elites. The international gazettes could publish some news and documents that exceeded the officially sanctioned picture of political reality, because what they printed did not officially commit the governments that allowed them to circulate. They could leave the safe shore of official reality, but they could not venture into the deep waters that only the semiclandestine media could explore. Newspaper editors were aware of those boundaries. They were among the people most likely to have access to even the most seditious pamphlet publications, even though they knew they could rarely make use of that material. Etienne Luzac, during his struggle with the authoritarian Maupeou-d'Aiguillon government in France in the early 1770s, sought to defend his right to print news that went beyond what was in the official French newspapers by listing the clandestine antiministerial pamphlets that he had received but had been careful not to mention in his gazette.[47] The significance of the international gazettes, and especially of the most distinguished representative of the genre, the *Gazette de Leyde*, was that its content marked the exact limit to which the pressure of reader demand and political necessity had been able to extend the official picture of reality. The gap between the news that appeared in the *Gazette de France* and what appeared in the *Gazette de Leyde* was the measure of the success of public opinion in wresting control over political information from Europe's governments.

47. Etienne Luzac to Desnoyers, 5 July 1772, in LGA-VH, Z(1), no. 34.

[4]

Making News in the
Eighteenth Century

An eighteenth-century Italian engraving shows the offices of a Florentine gazette contemporary with the *Gazette de Leyde*, the *Notizie del mondo*. Dressed in wigs and knee-breeches, going over their copy with quill pens, the editors seem to have little in common with their twentieth-century journalistic descendants. But the excitement with which the two men on the left are perusing the bulletins that have just come in and the evident haste with which the seated editors are marking up copy for the printers in the background indicate that some aspects of the news business have not changed. Twice a week, for almost thirty years, Jean Luzac sat at his desk in Leiden and, like his contemporaries in Florence, selected the news reports and documents to make up the next issue of his *Gazette de Leyde*. As he sorted through the manuscript bulletins from his correspondents and the newspapers and pamphlets he collected from all over the world, he was composing a picture of political reality for his readers. It had to be a picture comprehensive and convincing enough to maintain his niche in the highly competitive European news market. That picture also had to be acceptable to the governments that controlled the flow of news and the distribution of newspapers on the continent, to ensure that the *Gazette de Leyde* would be able to circulate freely.

Luzac's choice of news items was influenced not only by commercial and political concerns function but also by his own background and character. He brought the same seriousness of purpose and passionate commitment to his journalistic work that he did to every other aspect of his life. In a letter to a friend who had praised his paper, Luzac expressed his feelings about the importance of what he did:

[68]

No one perceives better than I the shortcomings of this genre of publication—defects, unfortunately, that cannot be remedied, in part because of
the necessity of appearing at fixed intervals, and limiting oneself to a fixed
amount of space, [and] in part because of the public's demand to always
have something new, however uncertain and unconfirmed it may be,
rather than to allow one to use such a collection to insert items and
documents worthy of being preserved that one did not have place for at
the proper time. But after all, finding myself called to this task, I have
done what I could to lift it above the contempt to which the bad taste, the
ignorance, and the bad behavior of so many chroniclers have condemned
it, in order to make it as useful as possible to my contemporaries.[1]

For Luzac, the journalistic profession was a moral calling. In accomplishing what modern sociologists would call his "news work," he strove
to satisfy two imperatives.[2] One was to give the news as fully as possible,
without favoring any one party, thereby fulfilling his function as a "mere
reporter."[3] Luzac took pains to underline the fact that he invariably
documented both sides of controversial issues, even when he had good
reason to believe that his readers were largely of one opinion. Public
reference to his professional obligation of impartiality protected him
against complaints from both subscribers and authorities. But Luzac
also selected his news in accordance with a second moral principle,
articulated in one of his many letters responding to diplomatic complaints about his paper's content. As he so often said in the paper itself,
Luzac asserted that he tried to be impartial. "But I do not at all believe,"
he continued, "that this impartiality consists of a cold indifference between good and evil. My idea of impartiality is that it means to judge
without personal motives, unaffected by either friendship or enmity,
and to acknowledge one's position. If one had to speak of good and evil,
of vice and virtue, in the same tone, the profession of reporter, as well as
that of historian, would be very difficult . . . for a frank and honest
writer."[4] Confident that he was not swayed by selfish private motives,
and that he rigorously followed his journalistic obligation to present the
public statements of all parties in the controversies he reported, Luzac
was untroubled by the doubts that have assailed modern journalists who
have come to question the possibility of eliminating subjective biases

1. Luzac to unidentified correspondent, probably A. Caillard, n.d. but 1785–87, in
LUL, Luzac, carton 28, no. 69.
2. Two particularly influential studies employing this concept are Gaye Tuchman,
Making News (New York: Free Press, 1978), and Mark Fishman, *Manufacturing the News*
(Austin: University of Texas Press, 1980).
3. *GL*, 17 Mar. 1789 (Hamburg, 6 Mar.).
4. Luzac to Hertzberg, Prussian foreign minister, 21 Mar. 1783, in LGA-VH, Z(2), no.
54.

The editorial office and printing shop of the *Notizie del mondo*, Florence, 1769.
Courtesy of Prof. Franco Venturi and Giulio Einaudi Editore.

from the news.[5] He saw no contradiction between objective news coverage and strong personal commitment.

Collecting the News

The first task of the eighteenth-century newsman was to collect a variety of information about potentially newsworthy events in the world around him. Jean Luzac had access to professional correspondents and newsletters, material from diplomatic and political contacts, items from other newspapers, and stories sent in by interested private parties. His paper's reputation as Europe's premier source of news depended on his success in using these sources. Because of slow communications, Luzac had far fewer information-gathering possibilities than his modern successors. Nor could he verify the information he received by cross-checking with other observers at the scene of distant happenings. And the scanty financial resources available to a publication whose printing technology limited its circulation and therefore its overall income prevented him from guaranteeing the authenticity of his reports by relying solely on employees paid primarily for their services to his paper. This reliance on its own paid correspondents was the basis of the nineteenth-century London *Times*'s superiority, but it was able to adopt such a policy because it had mechanized printing presses that allowed a circulation and therefore an income several orders of magnitude higher than that of any eighteenth-century news publication.[6] By comparison with "newspapers of record" in the nineteenth and twentieth centuries, the *Gazette de Leyde*'s news-gathering operation was modest in size and held together by the journalistic equivalent of spit and baling wire, but it was the best that could be done in Luzac's day.

An eighteenth-century newspaper's reputation depended above all on the quality of its network of paid correspondents. Unlike modern professional reporters, the *Gazette de Leyde*'s correspondents were not full-time paid members of the paper's staff. They were often engaged in other activities as well, and were paid a regular sum in exchange for providing a dependable account of news in their vicinity. Even though his correspondents were rarely full-time newsmen, they were still expensive, and Luzac could only afford to hire permanent correspondents in locations where he could be sure there would be a regular flow of news. How many of these Luzac employed at any one time is not known. He probably had at least as many as the best Dutch-language news gazette,

5. See the discussion in Michael Schudson, *Discovering the News* (New York: Basic Books, 1978), esp. 159.
6. Stanley Morison et al., *History of the "Times"* (New York: Macmillan, 1935–53), 2:89.

the *Oprechte Haarlemsche Courant*, which had employed eight foreign correspondents in 1738–42, several of whom worked simultaneously for Luzac's uncle Etienne, then the editor of the *Gazette de Leyde*.[7] During the 1770s and 1780s, the content of the gazette makes it clear that it received regular information from London, Paris, Brussels, Hamburg, Cologne, Frankfurt, Vienna, Berlin, St. Petersburg, and Constantinople. When circumstances required, Luzac employed temporary correspondents elsewhere. But the paper could not afford to expand its payroll indefinitely, particularly because the limitations imposed by the printing process made it impossible to use lengthy news bulletins from more than two or three locations in each issue.

Only a handful of the paper's correspondents can be identified. The best documented of the paper's paid correspondents was its man in Paris from 1781 to 1789, Pascal Boyer, a good example of the eighteenth-century reporter or *bulletiniste*. "A big, husky fellow," according to a French revolutionary police report, Boyer had been born in Tarascon in southern France in 1741 or 1742.[8] By the 1770s, he was part of the milieu of diplomatic agents and gossip-collectors on the fringe of French politics,[9] and in 1776 he became the Paris correspondent of the newly established *Courrier de l'Europe*. In 1780, however, the *Courrier de l'Europe* dismissed him; soon afterward he was arrested in a roundup of *bulletinistes* in January 1781, and spent ten days in the Bastille. After Boyer was released, however, a period source tells us that the comte de Vergennes "sought to console him for this mistake, by giving him the greatest opportunities to increase the distribution of his correspondence and his contacts abroad."[10] Among those opportunities, apparently, was the job of Paris correspondent for the *Gazette de Leyde*.

Boyer obviously had promised that the government would have no reason to worry about his newsletters, and Vergennes, for his part, had pursued a policy of tolerating the activities of known *bulletinistes* rather than having to chase down newcomers who might be even less amenable to reasonable persuasion.[11] According to the *Mémoires secrets*, Boyer also

7. D. H. Couvée, "The Administration of the 'Oprechte Haarlemse Courant' 1738–42" *Gazette* 4 (1958), 103–4.

8. Dossier in AN, F^7 4615, d. 2. At the time of his arrest in 1794, Boyer was married and had two adult children.

9. The classic description of this milieu remains Frantz Funck-Brentano, *Les nouvellistes*, 2d ed. (Paris: Hachette, 1905).

10. Frantz Funck-Brentano, *Lettres de Cachet* (Paris: Imprimerie nationale, 1903), 406. Vergennes's role in freeing Boyer is confirmed in the minister's letter of 8 Feb. 1781, to La Vauguyon, the French ambassador in The Hague, in MAE, Corr. Pol.—Hollande, 543.

11. In 1782, Vergennes ordered the lieutenant of police Jean-Charles-Pierre Le Noir to release a certain Charles Fouilhoux, Paris correspondent of the *Gazette d'Utrecht* and the Brussels French-language paper, on these grounds. Vergennes added that "his confession, . . . and the appearance of his having acted more from imprudence than from evil intent, have led us to treat him with indulgence." Cited in W. P. Sautijn Kluit, "Hollandsche en Fransche Utrechtse Couranten," 106.

tried to supplement his income as a *nouvelliste* by setting up "a political Museum, or club in the English manner" in 1782. His intended clientele consisted of rich gentlemen who wanted a place to read the newspapers and discuss politics without having to rub elbows with the *hoi polloi* in the cafés or the reading rooms of the Palais-Royal. Boyer had supposedly obtained government approval for his enterprise "on condition that there will be no discussion of government or religion, and that women will not be admitted." The *Gazette de Leyde*'s correspondent was thus an experienced newsman, with good social contacts, but he was also a man whose enterprises were dependent on the favor of the French government. Boyer's subservience to the French authorities did not bother Jean Luzac; when his shipments to France were temporarily blocked in 1785, Luzac reminded the French ambassador in the Hague that he "employed only correspondents who are not without the approval of the government," and "kept out of our papers all articles that reach us from more suspect sources."[12]

Despite this dependence on the French authorities, Boyer proved himself to be an extremely able reporter. He provided the paper with a full and accurate narrative of the major events of Calonne's ministry, the sensational Diamond Necklace affair, the convening of the first Assembly of Notables in 1787, and all the other events leading up to the summoning of the Estates-General. Comparison with other press organs of the period establishes without any doubt that Boyer's reports in the *Gazette de Leyde* were the best publicly published reporting on French affairs available at the time. Boyer produced a lengthy newsletter in time for the mail coach twice a week; many of his dispatches recount events that occurred the afternoon before they were written, so we know that he often worked late into the night. During the day, he may occasionally have participated in the regular exchanges among *nouvellistes* that took place in various cafés and public parks,[13] but it would be a mistake to imagine that Boyer relied very heavily on this kind of political gossip in drafting his newsletters. His employer in Leiden wanted verifiable facts, not free-floating rumors, and his mentors in the Foreign Ministry would not have tolerated his forwarding a mass of information, accurate or not, from uncontrolled sources. His life had its dangers: when the French government was aroused, it could ensure that "nothing is harder and more dangerous than to report political news and novelties from here, notwithstanding the fact that one can easily hear them being discussed in all coffeehouses, societies and public places," as the correspondent of

12. [Pidansat de Mairobert, attrib.] *Mémoires secrets*, 20:154, 156 (1 and 4 Apr. 1782); Jean and Etienne Luzac to marquis de Vérac, French ambassador to the Netherlands, 10 Mar. 1785, in MAE, Corr. Pol.—Hollande, 562.

13. He figures as a participant in the fictional dialogues about the Anglo-French naval conflict after 1778 that appear in volumes 9 and 10 of [Pidansat de Mairobert, attrib.], *L'espion anglois*.

a German periodical noted in 1781.[14] Despite these perils, however, Boyer was not a scribbler scrambling to survive. He moved easily among the powerful whose activities he chronicled.

Boyer's main sources were undoubtedly members of the royal bureaucracy and of certain key political institutions who furnished him with news on a regular basis; like modern reporters, he frequented government institutions that generated news themselves and also assembled information from scattered sources for their own benefit.[15] There is no other way he could have obtained and continued to publish his detailed internal reports on the Parlement de Paris, for example, unless he had been in touch with a member of that body. And it was certainly a high-ranking court figure who gave him and other European journalists the ostensible transcript of the conversation in which Louis XVI and Marie-Antoinette accused Cardinal de Rohan in the Diamond Necklace affair—a conversation heard by only "six persons in all, constituting the highest council in the land."[16]

From Luzac's point of view, the only drawback was that Boyer's correspondence was not exclusive: his newsletters also appeared regularly in the Leiden paper's archrival, the *Courier du Bas-Rhin*.[17] How Boyer managed to make the two hostile editors, Jean Luzac and Jean Manzon, accept this situation is not clear: perhaps the French government facilitated the circulation of these two papers and offered them a wider range of information from official sources in exchange for their agreeing to share the Foreign Ministry's preferred *bulletiniste*, or it may be that Luzac and Manzon tacitly agreed to use the same correspondent because they could share the cost of paying him and thereby save money.

The activities of newspaper correspondents outside of the great capitals took a somewhat different form. Many of them were stationed not at the scene of major events but at a key crossroads where travelers from capitals or battlefronts would pass through; their function was to collect

14. *Politische Journal*, Apr. 1781, 391–92. The article refers specifically to the arrest of Boyer, at that point still working for the *Courrier de l'Europe*.

15. See the analysis of American reporters' news-gathering practices in Fishman, *Manufacturing the News*, 45–51, and the general discussion in Bernard Roshco, *Newsmaking* (Chicago: University of Chicago Press, 1975), 23, 116.

16. Frances Mossiker, *The Queen's Necklace* (New York: Simon and Schuster, 1961), 272. This text appeared in numerous European newspapers, including the *Gazette de Cologne*, 2 Sept. 1785, and the *Hamburg Correspondent*, 31 Aug. 1785.

17. This fact makes it possible to be certain that the texts on France published in the *Gazette de Leyde* were composed primarily in Paris and not in Leiden. Neither paper was simply copying from the other, because in some instances each had a given story before the other printed it. I have verified regular duplication of material in the two papers from January 1786 to July 1789, but there is no reason to doubt that the practice had begun earlier. Some attentive readers were aware of the duplication at the time; Dumont-Pigalle mentioned it in his notes on Manzon (AR, DP, carton 48). On the basis of a few random comparisons, it seems possible that the French news in the leading German newspaper of the period, the *Hamburg Correspondent*, also came from this source, but the fact that its stories appeared in German makes it more difficult to establish precise duplication.

information about events from elsewhere and forward it to Leiden. Hamburg was a key listening post for news from the Baltic states; in the mid-1790s, Luzac paid his correspondent there between 150 and 250 gulden every three months for his services.[18] The correspondent Luzac engaged in Boston in 1782 was to gather news from the whole of the North American continent, largely by reading the American newspapers.[19]

Professional correspondents were vital to the *Gazette de Leyde*'s newsgathering activities, and they produced a substantial portion of the paper's content: the unidentified London correspondent and Boyer together furnished close to half the paper's news for most of the 1780s. But correspondents of this sort were not able to satisfy the paper's need for information by themselves. Almost equally important to Luzac were the sources of information he was able to cultivate among the continent's diplomatic agents, military officers, and major political figures. Governments maintained information-gathering networks vastly larger than what any private journalistic enterprise could afford.[20] Journalists naturally sought to take advantage of these networks, either by covertly obtaining information from embassy staffs and army officers eager to supplement their often meager stipends—sometimes by furnishing information their governments would have preferred to keep secret—or by cultivating contacts with officials who were willing to share such information to further their government's policies. Indeed, journalists expected governments to supply them with information about wars and other public affairs: when the Russian government refused to give out bulletins about the campaign against Turkey in 1788, the *Mercure de France* made a public complaint.[21]

One of the most important of these liaisons was the paper's "Polish connection." In the two periods when the *Gazette de Leyde* distinguished itself by detailed coverage of affairs in the Polish kingdom, it apparently did not have a paid correspondent chosen by the editor: the best part of its information came through intermediaries chosen by those participants in Polish politics, most notably King Stanislas-August, who wanted to see their views supported in the paper.[22] For news from America,

18. Jean Luzac to Baudus, Hamburg correspondent, n.d. but 1795, in LUL, Luzac, carton 28, no. 41.

19. [Benjamin Gerrish] to Jean Luzac, Boston, 23 Nov. 1782, in Huntington Library (San Marino, Calif.), Rufus King collection, RK 485.

20. On the French diplomatic information network, see *Les affaires étrangères et le corps diplomatique français*, 2 vols. (Paris: Centre national de la recherche scientifique, 1984), 1:204–14.

21. *Journal de Bruxelles* (news supplement of *Mercure de France*), 19 July 1788 (Frankfurt, 5 July).

22. Jerzy Lojek, "International French Newspapers and Their Role in Polish Affairs during the Second Half of the Eighteenth Century," *East Central Europe* (1974), 58–59, 61. It is not always clear that Luzac knew the identity of his Polish sources. One letter from

Luzac depended heavily on the American representatives in Europe. Early in the course of the colonies' struggle, Luzac came in contact with Charles Dumas, the dedicated Dutch representative of the American cause in The Hague, who told Benjamin Franklin and Silas Deane in early 1777 that Luzac had "inserted in his papers several small articles that I sent him, and he would print more if I could furnish them . . . I would strongly advise you, Gentlemen, to take advantage of his good will, in giving me what he needs (but more facts than political arguments)."[23] Dumas continued to send Luzac information until at least 1791, including such important pieces as the official text of the treaty between the United States and France. During this period, Luzac also received materials directly from such distinguished sources as John Adams and Thomas Jefferson.

Luzac also received official information directly from the French government before the Revolution. His personal papers contain an extensive series of letters from Antoine-Bernard Caillard, the secretary of the French embassy in the Hague from 1786 to 1789. The two men were friends and Luzac did various small favors for Caillard in Leiden, such as examining copies of rare books that the French representative, an ardent bibliophile, was considering buying. From time to time, Caillard forwarded short notes concerning French foreign policy, which Luzac invariably transcribed into the paper. In March 1787, for example, Caillard asked Luzac to reassure the public that the death of the comte de Vergennes would not mean any change in French policy. The requested article appeared just four days after Caillard wrote his letter.[24]

By successful recruitment of able correspondents and personal contacts with soldiers and diplomats, Luzac was often able to obtain information in advance of other news publications. But he could not afford to keep correspondents everywhere, nor could he depend on friendly diplomats and government officials to make keeping him informed their top priority. He therefore had to rely extensively on other newspapers, public sources that were equally available to his competitors. Eighteenth-century newspaper editors used each other's products as a form of news service, copying freely to fill up their own columns, and many of

Stanislas-August to an intermediary who forwarded materials to the *Gazette de Leyde* specifically instructs the king's agent to conceal the source of his information. Stanislas-August to Filippo Mazzei, 4 Apr. 1789, in *Lettres de Philippe Mazzei et du roi Stanislas-August de Pologne* (Rome: Istituto storico italiano, 1982), 222.

23. Dumas to Franklin and Deane, 11 March 1777, in AR, Dumas, carton I.

24. Caillard to Luzac, 23 Mar. 1787, in LUL, Luzac, carton 29; article in *GL*, 27 Mar. 1787. Caillard, born in France in 1737, had begun his bureaucratic career as an assistant of Turgot's during the latter's intendance in Limoges. He subsequently held a number of diplomatic posts before and during the Revolution. J. Balteau, M. Barroux, and M. Prevost, eds., *Dictionnaire de biographie française* (Paris: Letouzey and Ane, 1933–).

them, particularly the editors of provincial papers, had no other sources for distant news at all. The *Gazette de Leyde* relied much less on scissors and paste than these lesser journals: it could hardly fulfill its claim to special status as Europe's best-informed journal on the basis of articles that had appeared first in other publications. But these reports were often the first indication the paper received of events in distant places. Responding to a diplomatic complaint from Copenhagen, Etienne Luzac asserted that his first reports on the overthrow of the Danish minister Johann Friedrich Struensee in 1772 had been constructed entirely from materials already published in the Dutch-language gazettes, because he had been unable to obtain any information directly.[25] Newspapers from distant locations were often the Leiden paper's source for documents of political importance, such as many of the materials about American affairs Jean Luzac inserted during the War of Independence.

Many eighteenth-century newspapers also relied heavily on letters volunteered by amateur correspondents in whose vicinity something newsworthy had happened. These correspondents were the lifeblood of the English provincial papers: a printer could easily fill his columns with their colorful accounts of local festivals, crimes, and hangings. But Jean Luzac made little use of such unsolicited information, because his "newspaper of record" could not afford to vouch for the authenticity of such reports. Of the major stories the paper dealt with during Luzac's editorship, the only one for which he appears to have relied primarily on such volunteered letters was the Geneva revolt of 1781–82. Luzac mentioned in the paper the extraordinary volume of mail he had received concerning this outbreak of dissension.[26] He printed a number of sharply conflicting accounts reflecting the different viewpoints of the contending parties, although he made his own distaste for the rebels quite clear. His difficulty was that he could not secure a Genevan news source equivalent to those he had found for the affairs of other countries: a small city-state did not have the bureaucratic machine of the French or even the fledgling American government. In general, the *Gazette de Leyde* seems to have avoided relying on ordinary readers' letters as sources of news. Its notion of journalistic responsibility did not yet require that it print only information obtained and verified by its own personnel, but it did rule out reports from individuals without some sort of "public character" that the paper could verify. Luzac did, of course, borrow from other newspapers, but when he had doubts about their information, he satisfied himself by indicating his source and thus transferring the responsibility for the report's accuracy.

25. Letter of March 1772, in LGA-VH, Z(1), no. 33.
26. *GL*, 5 July 1782 (Leiden, 4 July).

News Categories

As he sorted through the correspondents' letters, insiders' information, and out-of-town newspapers that arrived with each mail coach,
Jean Luzac looked for news that fitted into specific categories. The types
of events that he found newsworthy were the classic categories of public
information of all major European newspapers of the period: wars,
diplomatic negotiations, domestic high politics in major states, constitutional crises—in the eighteenth-century sense of the term—and major
outbreaks of social violence. Notably absent from the *Gazette de Leyde* was
any trace of the "human interest" story so characteristic of modern
journalism, as well as the variety of essays, literary news, poems, theater
reviews, sports reports, and miscellaneous items common in the London
dailies, the magazines, and some provincial newspapers. There was a
lively interest in such subjects on the continent, as the success of such
publications as the *Mémoires secrets* and the *Causes célèbres*, a publication
devoted to sensational trials, demonstrated, but the *Gazette de Leyde*
consciously chose to ignore them.[27] As the editors of the *Mémoires secrets*
commented, "The gazettes . . . are strictly the theater of sovereigns,"
from which the history of the private individuals who made up civil
society was excluded.[28] If one of the characteristics of the elite press in
general is a concentration on international relations and politics, then
the *Gazette de Leyde* carried this tendency to an extreme, even compared
with the other newspapers of its time.

Wars were Jean Luzac's most urgent concern. Wherever armies
marched and warships set sail, he scrambled to record their activities.
The priority the paper assigned to this task was shared by most of the
other newspapers of the period.[29] Luzac tried to obtain news from all
the belligerent powers in any conflict, including Spain and other states
that were otherwise rarely mentioned in the paper. War news took
precedence over all other matters: as the paper's Paris correspondent
wrote after the French declaration of war in April 1792, "From now until
the peace, the operations of the National Assembly will receive much
less attention than those of the army."[30] This war news was not organized in an attempt to reconcile the different versions of events obtained
from the combatants: readers were left to puzzle out the truth for
themselves from the welter of conflicting reports.

Although the paper's coverage of military events was usually even-

27. On the various eighteenth-century publications of this genre, see Hans-Jürgen
Lüsebrink, *Kriminalität und Literatur im Frankreich des 18. Jahrhunderts* (Munich and Vienna:
R. Oldenbourg, 1983), 104–72.
28. [Pidansat de Mairobert, attrib.], *Mémoires secrets*, 25:6.
29. See the articles on war news in Paule Jansen et al., *L'année 1778 à travers la presse
traitée par ordinateur* (Paris: Presses universitaires de France, 1982).
30. *GL*, 1 May 1792 (Paris, 22 April).

handed, Luzac never restricted himself entirely to official sources if he could help it. As he explained in answering Russian complaints about his use of unofficial sources during the Russo-Turkish war in 1788, official bulletins often arrived too late: he could not make his impatient readers wait that long for information.[31] Furthermore, unofficial reports often supplied much interesting information that the official bulletins omitted. The disastrous opening of the Austrian army's campaign against the Turks in 1787 was an extreme example: the Viennese court refused to issue any official acknowledgment of the humiliating failure of its attack on Belgrade, forcing the paper's Vienna correspondent to choose among competing unauthorized versions furnished by officers in the Austrian army.[32]

The paper's war stories, often written by military professionals, were addressed to an audience with some sophistication in military matters. A lengthy article on George Washington's defeat at Kingsbridge in 1776, based on two letters from English officers and a variety of English press accounts, gave a careful technical reconstruction of the action, with many references to what one could learn by plotting the events on a map;[33] indeed, the paper often advertised special maps for readers who wanted to follow war news.[34] When there was no real action to report, the paper risked losing its readers. An editorial comment on the stalemated War of the Bavarian Succession in 1778 tried to mollify the public by claiming that "connoisseurs" would admire "the art with which the talented generals on both sides seek to gain advantages of terrain, while avoiding exposing themselves to a battle whose success could not be assured."[35] The battle reports for which readers waited so eagerly tended to be extremely dry catalogues of the units involved and the posts taken. This was particularly true of the wars fought before 1792, when armed combat was essentially an affair for professionals and when the only wars on the continent were taking place in central and eastern Europe, hindering the paper's news gathering. The outbreak of the war between revolutionary France and the other European powers in that year gave rise to war coverage of a new sort: it was more voluminous and often more emotional, as Luzac sought to describe "a war that the most violent, we may even say the most atrocious, passions on both sides have set off."[36]

31. Ibid., 29 July 1788 (Leiden, 29 July).
32. Ibid., 1 Jan. 1788 (Vienna, 15 Dec. 1787). When the Austrian government finally cracked down on these unauthorized correspondents, the paper had virtually to abandon the story. Ibid., 23 Sept. 1788 (Vienna, 6 Sept.).
33. Ibid., 3 Jan. 1777 (Leiden, n.d.).
34. The issue of 12 Aug. 1788 contains a typical example of this sort of advertising. It offered a map of the Crimea and surrounding territories in which the Russo-Turkish war was being fought.
35. GL, 15 Sept. 1778 (Leiden, 13 Sept.).
36. Ibid., 9 Oct. 1792 (Leiden, 7 Oct.).

The paper also concerned itself with major diplomatic negotiations. Unlike the beginning of the 1700s or the period after Napoleon's defeat, the late eighteenth century was not an age of great diplomatic congresses in which the fate of the continent was decided, and at which journalists could obtain a rich harvest of rumors and leaks for their papers. The negotiations Luzac had to record were normally bilateral, but their consequences often affected all of Europe. As in the case of wars, the paper usually succeeded in obtaining information from both sides. Whereas military operations were essentially public events that might be witnessed by outsiders, diplomatic negotiations generally took place in secrecy, and the *Gazette de Leyde* was dependent on what informed participants chose to tell it. In no other aspect of its news coverage did it have so much difficulty in establishing the reliability of the information it published. Luzac solicited news by keeping up close contacts with the diplomatic corps in The Hague.[37] He followed a consistent policy to confirm the accuracy of the unauthenticated diplomatic documents he published: he normally announced the impending publication of major documents one issue in advance, as he told one complaining ambassador, "with the intention of discovering whether there is any objection to their insertion." If none of the foreign envoys in The Hague complained, he considered himself entitled to proceed.[38]

The public signs of diplomatic activity that the paper's correspondents were able to observe were usually limited to the arrival and departure of representatives and to public ceremonies; beyond that, their dispatches consisted of a swirl of rumors and deductions. Verification came from the course of events unless the paper could obtain the actual texts of treaties, documents that it generally succeeded in publishing thanks to leaks from one party or another, usually long after the event. Thus the paper correctly reported the existence of a Franco-American treaty, signed in December 1777, on 17 March 1778,[39] but was unable to give the text of the agreement until it obtained it from an American source nearly a year later.[40] In the meantime, of course, the outbreak of hostilities between England and France had served to confirm the paper's initial report.

The paper was well aware that most of the information it received about diplomatic negotiations was leaked by parties who believed that it

---

37. In 1789, he was able to supply a Paris correspondent with detailed notes about each of the nine accredited ambassadors in residence there. Jean Luzac to Johan Valckenaer, 7 July 1789, in LUL, Ms. BPL 1030. The notes on the ambassadors were for transmission to an unnamed French official, possibly a prospective French ambassador to the Netherlands.

38. Jean Luzac to Baron de Reischack, n.d. but 1774, in LGA-VH, Z(1), no. 36.

39. *GL*, 17 Mar. 1778 (Paris, 9 Mar.).

40. Ibid., 19 Feb. 1779 (n.d., but crediting the *Providence* [R.I.] *Gazette* of 19 Dec. 1778).

was to their advantage to publicize something. After giving readers two different versions of the Russo-Turkish peace agreement of 1790, neither of which it could confirm, Luzac noted, "It appears that there are Courts, which, having obtained details of this treaty, have hastened to make them public, in order to damage the interests of one of the contracting parties."[41] But readers' interest in the outcome of negotiations and the paper's obligation to keep up with developing stories compelled the *Gazette de Leyde* to publish even uncertain information in this domain. As a result, the columns of the paper were a favored site for the release of trial balloons and the elaboration of diplomatic smokescreens. The paper's record of prophecy was hardly outstanding: if it correctly predicted French involvement in the American war as early as August 1777—admittedly after having dismissed the possibility in April[42]—it had overoptimistically reported a peaceful settlement of the Austro-Prussian dispute over Bavaria, a story disproved when war broke out.[43] Readers were subsequently able to verify that Joseph II and Catherine II's conference at Cherson in 1787 did lead to both countries' attacking Turkey, as the paper had inferred at the time,[44] but Luzac was reluctant to believe that Austria would come into open conflict with revolutionary France until just shortly before the war started in April 1792. The fault on all these occasions, however, lay not in any lack of foresight on Luzac's part, but in the nature of the diplomatic process. It was frequently to the participants' advantage to circulate misleading reports.

Besides war and diplomacy, the *Gazette de Leyde* was concerned with certain kinds of domestic occurrences within European states. It faithfully recorded all changes in the political leadership of European powers, but with a keen sense of the relative importance of different categories of such shifts. More or less normal and predictable changes, such as the death of a monarch and the succession of an heir, were noticed but not dwelled on, even when the change of a ruler foreshadowed a significant change in policy. The paper disposed of the death of Louis XV, fraught with significance for the outcome of the Maupeou experiment in taming the parlements in France, in two successive issues. Frederic II's death in 1786 was the occasion for one of the paper's coups—it obtained the news before the French court did—but Frederic had been ill for some time and the paper did not linger over an event that it evidently regarded as being part of the ordinary course of things.[45]

41. *GL*, 4 May 1790 (Leiden, 2 May).
42. Ibid., 18 Apr. 1777 (Paris, 11 Apr.); 1 Aug. 1777 (Leiden, 30 July).
43. Ibid., 30 Jan. 1778 (Leiden, 28 Jan.).
44. Ibid., 3 Apr. 1787 (Leiden, 1 Apr. 1787).
45. Ibid., 25 Aug. 1786 (Leiden, 24 Aug.). Luzac had been informed by a Hanoverian diplomat who had traveled directly from Berlin to the Netherlands.

Changes in royal ministries often occupied the paper more than changes in rulers. Results of political decisions rather than of the accidents of human mortality, these shifts were less predictable and often generated considerable speculation and anticipation before they happened. By concentrating on ministers instead of monarchs, the the *Gazette de Leyde* portrayed even the politics of absolutist states such as France as though such countries had a constitutional system in which the ministers mattered much more than the king. In general, the *Gazette de Leyde* treated the professional politicians and administrators who held ministerial rank as the prime movers in politics, and gave them the publicity that the court gazettes reserved for monarchs.

Although ministers were unquestionably important people in the *Gazette de Leyde*'s scheme of news values, the domestic political stories it reported at greatest length were those involving political assemblies of various sorts. These bodies generated extensive amounts of copy on a predictable basis. Britain was, of course, the model case, and reports of Parliament's debates were a staple of the paper's content for the half of every year during which that body was in session. In France, the paper treated the most important judicial body, the Parlement de Paris, as a Gallic equivalent to Westminster, thereby bolstering the judges' pretentions to be regarded as spokesmen for the French nation.[46] The paper, and the European press in general, gave extensive and regular summaries of the speeches in the Polish Diet during the two crisis periods of 1772 to 1774 and 1788 to 1792. As in its coverage of the British Parliament, the *Gazette de Leyde* identified parties and factions within the Diet, discussed their views, and indicated which side it favored. The paper's coverage of the revolutionary movements in the United Provinces and in the Austrian Netherlands in the 1780s also involved extensive coverage of proceedings in a variety of provincial Estates and municipal councils in both countries. Even before the French Revolution, the *Gazette de Leyde* had made a clear decision to treat parliamentary talk about politics as newsworthy, and to elevate the status of assemblies at the expense of monarchs.

The convening of the Estates-General in France in 1789 compelled the *Gazette de Leyde* to devote a major share of its attention to a new locus of parlementary activity. Here, even more clearly than in the case of the British Parliament, was a talking shop that made news, and the National Assembly and its successors quickly outstripped all other assemblies in the space they received in the paper's columns. Whatever Luzac's reaction to their doings, the French assemblies were in many respects a

46. In 1786, when the Paris Parlement voted to acquit Cardinal de Rohan of charges stemming from the Diamond Necklace affair, the *Gazette de Leyde* even gave the roll call of the judges' votes. *GL*, 13 June 1786 (Paris, 5 June).

journalist's dream: continuously in session, unlike the British Parliament with its annual recesses, and almost continuously undertaking important acts, they provided a most dependable stream of copy. The difficulty was, however, that the French press quickly took over the function of publicizing these debates. The *Gazette de Leyde*, which had flourished by giving the most comprehensive French-language versions of the proceedings of assemblies all over the continent, could not maintain its monopoly over the French revolutionary legislatures, but neither could it afford to ignore them and thus throw the readers it was able to retain after 1789 into the arms of its new Paris-based rivals. The result was an untenable journalistic situation for the paper. In this way as in so many others, the French Revolution brought changes that made the decline of the Leiden paper inevitable.

In many cases, coverage of assemblies shaded over into coverage of another category of domestic political news: constitutional crises. These events captured the paper's earnest attention even more than the ministerial politics and the regular assembly proceedings already discussed. As in the case of wars, the paper was careful to cover all the significant disputes about constitutional authority that occurred in this period, ranging from the American Revolution to the disputes in Geneva. It rarely took sides explicitly, but it served the interests of the American colonists, the Irish Volunteers, the Dutch Patriots, and many other movements by publishing their manifestoes. From 1751 on, the paper was one of the normal publicity outlets for the French parlements' remonstrances, ostensibly secret petitions to the king but in fact veritable political declarations. Luzac justified his publication of material about such domestic controversies, often technically clandestine, on the grounds of his duty to provide objective information. Where there was a dispute about political legitimacy, it was not his duty to take sides: "All that [a newspaper editor] can do in such cases is to report the news for and against [the government], insofar as he can obtain it," he told the Leiden city council in response to one foreign complaint.[47] The *Gazette de Leyde*'s attention to this sort of news left readers in no doubt that the paper viewed the fundamental constitution of any polity as the legitimate concern of all of its citizens, not the exclusive property of its nominal sovereign.

The *Gazette de Leyde*'s coverage of popular violence constituted something of an exception to the usual run of its reportage. This was its only category of news in which the lower classes played a prominent role; it was also the category in which the paper went furthest in covering events that the controlled media within the major continental countries passed

47. Etienne and Jean Luzac to Leiden city council, response to Polish complaint, 25 Oct. 1774, in LGA-VH, Z(1), no. 35.

over in silence. Curiously, however, the paper's often detailed reporting of outbreaks of social violence was actually less subversive of the established order in which the *Gazette de Leyde* operated than its extensive coverage of political crises or "revolutions" within established political institutions.

The *Gazette de Leyde* was not in the least squeamish about covering these stories. Like the outbreak of wars or the occurrence of floods, popular uprisings were part of the natural history of society, and the paper covered them in a matter-of-fact tone devoid of panic or moral condemnation. To be sure, it was often unable to obtain prompt and reliable information. The great Pugachev insurrection in the distant interior of Russia reached the paper only in the form of terse and confusing summaries of rumors circulating in St. Petersburg. On 21 June 1774, readers learned of the rebellion in a short paragraph included in a story on the war in the Crimea, together with a later dispatch reporting the public celebration in Moscow of a victory over Pugachev's followers. A week later they discovered that Emelian Pugachev was still at large; on 9 September 1774 the paper suddenly informed them that the rebels were threatening Moscow and Nizhni-Novgorod; and on 8 November 1774 came the news that Pugachev was finally defeated.[48] Needless to say, the paper had no direct contact with the rebels and printed no news about them that had not been filtered through Russian government and military sources; its ability to depict this greatest of eighteenth-century peasant rebellions was limited because of the remoteness of the events and the Russian government's restrictive information policy.

That the *Gazette de Leyde*'s minimal coverage of the Pugachev rebellion was not a result of any general policy of suppressing news about such events is clear from its treatment of other episodes of the time. The paper provided much more extensive coverage of another major peasant uprising, the Horea revolt in Transylvania at the end of 1785, coverage that was possible because there was a newspaper published even in that remote part of the world and because considerable information filtered back via the Austrian government.[49] This coverage could hardly be called objective: one story from Hermanstadt remarked, "If

48. This final report was datelined Moscow, 22 Sept. 1774, just one week after Pugachev's capture and the end of the rebellion, so that the paper's information was as up to date as the slowness of communications with Moscow permitted. The fluctuations in the paper's evaluations of the rebellion's seriousness reflected the Russian government's own confusion. See Isabel de Madariaga, *Russia in the Age of Catherine the Great* (New Haven, Conn.: Yale University Press, 1981), 249–55.

49. On the events of the Horea uprising, see Katherine Verdery, *Transylvanian Villagers* (Berkeley: University of California Press, 1983), 94–104. For a recent comparative study of the coverage of the rebellion in the European press of the day, see Nicolai Edroiu, *Horea's Uprising: European Echoes* (Bucharest: Academiei Republicii Socialiste Romania, 1984).

one considers that the Wallachian Nation . . . consists of about 600,000 souls, and that they are almost entirely stupid and ignorant people, who have little or nothing to lose, one can easily understand how easily the spirit of sedition and pillage can spread, and, once it has been set in motion, how it can lead to the worst excesses."[50] But its series of reports from Hermanstadt and Vienna gave a detailed account of the campaign against the rebels and pulled no punches in depicting the Austrian army's difficulties in putting them down.

Of all the incidents of urban violence the paper described in the years before the French Revolution, the two that received the most extensive coverage were the Gordon Riots in London in 1780 and the Lyon silkworkers' insurrection of 1786. Both events took place in countries of interest to the paper, and it had little trouble obtaining information. In the case of the London outbreak, information was freely available from the London papers themselves. As in the case of the Horea rebels, the paper's coverage showed no sympathy with the rioters. According to one article, "The revolt . . . caused disorders and destruction which it would be difficult to match in the annals of civilized nations: But, having only the most vile class of the people for partisans, [who were] acting . . . on a pretext whose frivolity was acknowledged by the better part of the citizens," and lacking a real leader, "this revolt was no more than a straw fire, blazing up with the most extreme violence in order to extinguish itself quickly."[51] This dismissive attitude toward the significance of the largest outbreak of urban violence in eighteenth-century England did not lead the paper to ignore the details of the event: the same issue recapitulated the entire story at much greater length than had been possible in previous issues. But Luzac and his correspondents saw the riot, for all its violence, as a meaningless incident in the larger context of English politics.[52]

Although the paper's treatment of the Horea rebellion and the Gordon Riots were typical of the way it normally stereotyped stories involving popular violence, its coverage of the Lyon silkworkers' revolt in 1786 had quite a different tone.[53] The significance of the paper's extensive reporting on this episode was considerable, because there was no cover-

50. *GL*, 18 Jan. 1785 (Hermanstadt, 25 Dec. 1784).
51. Ibid., 20 June 1780 (London, 9 and 13 June).
52. This attitude toward popular insurrections was a common one in eighteenth-century thought: it resembles Voltaire's comment, in his *Philosophical Dictionary*, that the people might indeed revolt from time to time, but that "these wars all end sooner or later with the subjection of the people, because the rich have the money." Article "Egalité," in *Dictionnaire philosophique* (Paris: Garnier, 1964), 172. The passage is a paraphrase of a text of John Locke, cited in C. B. Macpherson, *The Political Theory of Possessive Individualism* (Oxford: Oxford University Press, 1962), 223, and reflects a deeply rooted Enlightenment attitude.
53. On the Lyon uprising, see the detailed account in Louis Trénard, "La crise sociale lyonnaise à la veille de la Révolution," *Revue d'histoire moderne et contemporaine* 2 (1955), 5–45.

age in the French domestic press: the *Journal de Lyon*, published on the spot, was so tightly censored that not a word about the riots appeared. There was some coverage in the other international gazettes, but the Leiden paper's five long bulletins were the most extensive and complete.

The anonymous authors of all these reports were, of course, on the side of the forces of law and order, and they all viewed the "people" who had participated in the riot from the other side of a deep social divide. Of the nine individuals identified by name in the five stories, only one was a worker, and he achieved this distinction because he was one of the three ringleaders executed afterward. But the newsletters stressed the rational economic motives behind the workers' collective behavior. The first newsletter Luzac printed explained that the trouble in Lyon had begun when the entrepreneurs of the Travaux Perrache had given their day-laborers a raise. It was this raise that led the silkworkers and hatmakers to demand pay increases for themselves—hardly an irrational action.[54] A subsequent newsletter took pains to show that the riot was not a spur-of-the-moment affair, but came after the workers had made unsuccessful attempts to gain their ends by peaceful means.[55] Admittedly the tone of this particular bulletin contrasted sharply with the "official" account furnished in the Paris newsletter carried in the same issue, which alleged that this riot, like others in Lyon earlier in the century, had "no basis, no cause, and no object." But even this harsh report made no secret of the economic causes underlying the revolt: in fact, its analysis in this regard was more thoroughgoing than that of any of the other reports the paper printed. "Some think the only cause was the natural restlessness of uneducated men, who believe themselves indispensable and independent," this story noted, but it went on to say that others "attribute [it] to the precarious way of life of the majority of the silkworkers." The periodic ups and downs of the silk industry "inevitably throw many of the inhabitants into unemployment and distress, and want naturally makes them restless and violent."[56]

The *Gazette de Leyde*'s series of reports on the Lyon uprising was not typical of its coverage of popular violence. These detailed accounts went beyond merely chronicling publicly observable events: the paper attempted to account for the cause of the unrest. But this series of articles demonstrates the paper's ability to offer a relatively objective and even sympathetic account of a popular uprising, even though it had to rely on sources who were certainly not close to the workers.[57] Compared with

54. *GL*, 25 Aug. 1786 (Lyon, 15 Aug.).
55. Ibid., 1 Sept. 1786 (Lyon, 15 Aug.).
56. Ibid. (Paris, 25 Aug.).
57. Comparison of the paper's dispatches with the correspondence from royal officials in the French archives suggests that the paper's stories were derived from the same sources as the official reports, that is, from responsible officials on the scene. Official reports in AN, F 12, 1441.

the remarks about the poor in the writings of the philosophes or even with the coverage the paper gave to many other popular uprisings of the period, its coverage of the Lyon affair attributed to the workers an unusual degree of political sophistication. Here was an instance when the *Gazette de Leyde*'s devotion to collecting as much accurate and detailed information as possible allowed the paper to break through the stereotypical categories of eighteenth-century social thought.

Selecting the News

The pages of the *Gazette de Leyde* could not contain all the news Jean Luzac was able to collect. The proceedings of the British Parliament alone would have filled the columns of a newspaper the size of the *Gazette de Leyde;* indeed, they did largely fill the pages of its London-based rival, the *Courrier de l'Europe*, for much of the 1780s. Luzac's editorial selections incorporated certain value judgments.

Luzac's selection criteria gave certain countries priority. A statistical breakdown of news reports by place of origin at five-year intervals during Luzac's editorship shows that only two European states held a more or less fixed place in Luzac's priorities: Britain and France. (See Table 1.) London and Paris datelines appeared in almost every issue of the paper in 1772, 1777, 1782, and 1787; only in 1792 did the greatly increased volume of French news lead to a virtual disappearance of English reports, which regained a modest place by 1797. The balance between these two powers depended a great deal on the specific events of each year, but the total devoted to the two countries combined amounted to more than half of the paper's total news space in five of six years sampled. Only in 1772, a year in which there was an exceptional amount of coverage of northern Europe and a sharp reduction in coverage of France, did the total of British and French news make up less than 50 percent of the *Gazette de Leyde*'s "news hole," the amount of space it could afford to devote to reporting. In 1777, the news coverage for Britain and France took up about 65 percent; in 1782, nearly 60 percent; in 1787, nearly 57 percent; in 1792, nearly 52 percent; and in 1797, about 56 percent.

The *Gazette de Leyde*'s coverage of Britain and France differed from its coverage of all other countries not only because it was more extensive, but because reports from London and Paris normally included items on several different subjects, each one of which might be a continuing story extending over several issues. The *Gazette de Leyde*'s coverage of other countries was irregular, depending on the nature of the events. This coverage also differed from the coverage given to England and France because it tended to be single-issue coverage, inspired by one particular

Table 1. Sources of news in the *Gazette de Leyde*[1]

Region	1772	1777	1782	1787	1792	1797
France	11.0%	19.6%	19.3%	42.3%	49.9%	45.9%
Britain and Ireland	20.6	45.6	40.5	14.5	2.0	10.2
Austria	2.5	0.4	3.0	2.3	1.4	6.1
Belgium	0.2	2.4	—	12.7	20.5	1.1
German states	10.6	3.1	1.2	2.7	7.6	11.6
Iberia	—	5.7	12.3	2.0	0.7	1.8
Italy	3.1	1.5	0.5	0.8	0.8	17.5
Netherlands	2.9	1.5	12.3	7.8	1.8	2.3
Poland	17.7	5.3	0.2	4.3	9.3	—
Russia	1.9	6.2	0.7	3.5	0.6	0.5
Scandinavia	19.5	2.4	0.9	0.8	5.5	0.4
Switzerland	—	0.4	4.4	—	—	1.8
Turkey	8.3	3.7	1.4	2.2	—	—
United States	—	1.3	1.4	2.7	—	0.5
Non-European	1.7	0.7	2.6	1.2	—	0.4

Totals do not equal 100% because of rounding.

1. Tables are based on a sample consisting of every fifth issue for the years 1772, 1777, 1782, 1787, 1792, and 1797, beginning with issue number 1 for each year. This sampling procedure assures that Tuesday and Friday issues of the paper are equally represented, eliminating any bias that might have been caused by the mail-coach schedules to different points. All material appearing under datelines from a given country or region has been classified as news from that region, although reports from major news centers such as London, Paris, or Hamburg often included news from other regions (for example, reports about the war in North America often appeared under London datelines); to distinguish the different news items within lengthy newsletters would have required an inordinate amount of work. Material appearing as advertisements or documentary material selected by the editor and published under a Leiden dateline has not been included in the statistical analysis.

story and ceasing when that story had reached some sort of resolution. Thus a sharp upsurge of reports from Denmark, Sweden, and Poland in 1772 faded after Struensee had been executed in Copenhagen, Gustavus III had clipped the wings of the Swedish Estates, and the partitioning powers had imposed their will on Warsaw.

Even within these zones of shifting interest, however, the *Gazette de Leyde* differentiated between countries in terms of the amount of coverage when especially newsworthy developments did take place. The paper would endeavor to obtain information from the capitals of all the major combatants during wars: thus Madrid, normally a marginal source of news, became a major source of information when Spain entered the Anglo-French conflict in 1779, and Austrian datelines became more prominent during the "phony war" with Prussia in 1778 and the campaign against Turkey in 1788.

When it came to domestic crises, however, the paper was much more selective. It made provisions for extensive special coverage only in countries where it either had significant circulation or where there were certain kinds of political institutions. It was much more attentive to the Baltic states than to the Mediterranean, for example. Poland was the most striking example, but the paper also covered major events in Sweden and Denmark with admirable thoroughness. These countries had only a rudimentary domestic press of their own, in which extraterritorial papers, both French- and German-language, played an important political role, and Luzac was aware that they constituted one of his major markets.

The *Gazette de Leyde* did also print substantial coverage of events in some European countries where its circulation was miniscule. During the simmering crisis in Ireland between 1778 and 1784, Dublin datelines became relatively common in the paper, and in 1782 it devoted considerable space to the revolutionary unrest in Geneva. Together with its ample coverage of the Polish Diet and the Swedish Estates, the paper's attention to these two regions demonstrated its sensitivity to political affairs in those countries with what the eighteenth century understood as constitutional forms of government. Sweden attracted the paper's attention when its king drastically trimmed the power of the country's quasi-parliamentary Estates, and in Poland its coverage dealt with the Diet's struggles to reform itself and protect the country from its rapacious absolutist neighbors. In all these cases, as well as in his treatment of the American War of Independence and the French troubles up to and during the Revolution, Luzac regarded events as newsworthy because he saw the issue of liberty as being at stake. Like the twentieth-century historians R. R. Palmer and Jacques Godechot, Luzac viewed the series of disturbances which we now label the "democratic" or "Atlantic" revolution as vital events.[58]

The selectivity of the *Gazette de Leyde*'s news coverage is also evident in the list of countries it normally disregarded; namely, the three great eastern monarchies. Datelines from Vienna, Berlin, and St. Petersburg were not exactly rarities in the paper, but the coverage from those capitals almost invariably consisted of short reports, limited to military and diplomatic subjects. Luzac even responded to one of the many Prussian complaints about his paper by pointing out to the Dutch authorities that he gave Prussia less coverage than any other major power.[59] The relative paucity of coverage about the eastern monarchies

58. R. R. Palmer, *The Age of the Democratic Revolution* (Princeton, N.J.: Princeton University Press, 1959–64); Jacques Godechot, *France and the Atlantic Revolution of the Eighteenth Century, 1770–1799*, trans. Herbert H. Rowen (New York: Free Press, 1965).

59. Letter (written by Jean Luzac but signed by the elder Etienne Luzac) to Grand Pensionary Van Boyen, 11 July 1776, in LGA-VH, Z(1), no. 38.

was not simply a function of difficulty in obtaining information or a lack of significant news events to cover. If Catherine II did effectively limit the amount of domestic news available about Russia, Berlin and particularly the Vienna of Joseph II were much freer. Joseph II's sweeping program of reforms was at least as significant as, say, the Irish Volunteer movement. Nor was this lack of interest in the absolutist capitals a reflection of the *Gazette de Leyde*'s inability to penetrate those markets. The paper was known in all three empires, and circulated extensively in Vienna, where it was regularly reprinted from 1786 to 1792.

Luzac may have limited coverage of the three great absolutist powers partly because they lacked the quasi-parliamentary institutions that permitted the kind of constitutionalist politics to which he was most devoted. Probably at least as important in influencing his choice of news items, however, was the fact that all three of these powers regularly sought to limit the circulation of uncensored news in their domains by methods which included using their ambassadors in The Hague to harass Dutch newspaper editors. The *Gazette de Leyde*'s archives for 1772 to 1798 preserve more complaints from the Prussian ambassador Friedrich Wilhelm von Thulemeyer alone than from the rest of the diplomatic corps combined, and Austria's Joseph II was the only ruler to adopt the brilliant but vicious stratagem of punishing the paper by authorizing a complete reprint edition of it in his capital. Clearly it made sense to minimize conflicts with such touchy states by leaving potentially controversial news from their territories out of the paper.[60] Hence the doings of Frederic II, Catherine II, and Joseph II, well publicized in their own propaganda, in the writings of the French philosophes, and in other media, were relegated to marginal status in the *Gazette de Leyde*.

Coverage of the Mediterranean world was also minimal. Although Dutch trade with Spain, Portugal, the Iberian states, and the Levant was significant and the paper could thus count on a regular network of communications, it gave little space to these areas. Italy had a significant news press of its own, which would have limited potential sales, while in Spain, where the domestic press was weak, censorship restrictions were harsher than anywhere else in western Europe. There was a fairly consistent trickle of reports datelined the Barbary Coast before the French Revolution, reflecting the persistent harassment of European shipping which was a permanent fact of life for traders in the region.

60. News coverage of the Austrian Netherlands constituted an exception to the paper's general treatment of Habsburg territories: during the unrest there in 1786–90, Belgian affairs became one of the paper's main preoccupations. But the paper's editorial bias was so strongly in favor of the Austrian authorities and against the rebellious corporate bodies in the Belgian provinces that Vienna had no reason to complain, and the London *Times* charged that Luzac's paper had been "bought up by the Emperor's Government, and is wholly at his will" (17 Mar. 1789).

The paper also provided regular correspondence from Turkey, and these stories tended to be considerably longer than those from the North African capitals. The motivation for the Turkish coverage was, of course, the fact that Constantinople was repeatedly involved in wars with various European powers.

Another customary blind spot in the *Gazette de Leyde*'s news coverage was its own immediate surroundings, the United Provinces. Regular news in the form of bulletins providing a more or less continuous narrative was almost totally lacking in the paper, even at the height of the Patriot troubles in which Jean Luzac was so intimately involved. Dutch datelines reached a peak of over 12 percent in 1782, when the stories primarily concerned the slow progress toward Dutch diplomatic recognition of the United States, and actually fell off to less than 8 percent in 1787, the year of the greatest activity and final collapse of the Patriot movement.[61] The amount of space given to Dutch affairs in 1787 was much less than that devoted to the disorders in the neighboring Austrian Netherlands. One reason was that during periods of excitement, such as the *Patriottentijd* from 1780 to 1787 and the first years of the Batavian Republic after 1795, Dutch readers had access to an extensive revolutionary press in their own language in which local events were recounted at length and freely commented upon, so they had no need of a French chronicle of their affairs. Moreover, foreign readers could not be expected to take much interest in internal Dutch politics. But Luzac also avoided domestic news because he had good reason to fear that the paper's long-term future would be jeopardized if it became an overtly partisan organ in Dutch politics. He must have been well aware that the *Gazette d'Utrecht*'s privilege was handed from editor to editor as the factional balance in the city council there shifted during the Patriot troubles, and the *Gazette d'Amsterdam*'s publisher kept his hired editor on a short leash to avoid similar problems.[62] Discretion about Dutch affairs was the wisest policy.

Although specific political reasons determined the allocation of news space in the *Gazette de Leyde*, the result was a pattern similar to that found in other major newspapers of the period. (See Table 2.) The dominance of foreign over domestic news was characteristic of the eighteenth-century press in general. Jürgen Wilke, in his study of the Hamburg

61. These figures admittedly do not take into account a considerable number of documents from various city councils, provincial estates, and extraconstitutional gatherings published in the paper's documentary section during these years. The figures for 1787 are also distorted by the fact that the Prussian intervention in September of that year put an abrupt end to reporting on Dutch domestic affairs.

62. Kluit, "Hollandsche en Fransche Utrechtse Couranten," 113–14; letters of *Gazette d'Amsterdam* editor François Bernard to Dumont-Pigalle, 8 Oct. 1786, 25 Oct. 1786, in AR, DP, carton A.

Table 2. Rank order of news sources accounting for more than 10 percent of the *Gazette de Leyde*'s news content in a given year

Year	Ranked sources
1772	Britain and Ireland
	Scandinavia
	Poland
	France
	German States
1777	Britain and Ireland
	France
1782	Britain and Ireland
	France
	Netherlands
	Iberia
1787	France
	Britain and Ireland
	Belgium
1792	France
	Belgium
1797	France
	Italy
	German states
	Britain and Ireland

papers, found that in the two eighteenth-century years he studied, 1736 and 1796, more than half the news items in the *Hamburg Correspondent* concerned foreign events with no discernible relation to the German world. The *Hamburg Correspondent*, like the *Gazette de Leyde*, gave special prominence to England and France.[63] A comparison of news coverage in English, French, German, and American papers of the period shows that a bias in favor of foreign news was characteristic of the press in all these areas down to the end of the eighteenth century.[64] The British press began to highlight domestic politics once it was given freedom to transcribe parliamentary debates after 1771, but the geographical distribution of news coverage in the *Gazette de Leyde* was characteristic of other major continental newspapers in its day.

63. Wilke, *Nachrichtenauswahl*, 149–55.
64. Jürgen Wilke, "Auslandsberichterstattung und internationaler Nachrichtenfluss im Wandel," *Publizistik* 31 (1986), 68, 77. The space given to news from various regions of Europe in 1796, the only year covered in Wilke's study that falls in the period of this analysis of the *Gazette de Leyde*, shows clear similarities to the distribution of news space in the Leiden paper for 1797: France and the two regions of major military activity, Germany and Italy, received the most coverage in the papers from England, Germany, and France that Wilke studied.

The Language of Eighteenth-Century
Journalistic Narrative

After collecting information and selecting items according to the source and the subject category, Jean Luzac worked to phrase the material in authoritative language. Journalism being a form of history, Luzac, like all historians, could not ask his readers to make a "willing suspension of disbelief." Journalists, like historians, "address themselves to distrustful readers who expect from them not only that they narrate but that they authenticate their narrative."[65] Luzac's method of accomplishing this was not the only one available to journalists in the late eighteenth century; indeed, it differed from the style the *Gazette de Leyde* itself had employed in earlier periods. But the impersonal, objective style he adopted served as a "strategic ritual" that made the paper's distinctive representation of European political reality believable to serious, well-informed readers.[66]

In the ninety-five years before Jean Luzac became its editor, the *Gazette de Leyde* had employed a variety of journalistic styles. In the late seventeenth century, its newsletters were a jumble of one- and two-sentence items, strung together with no apparent connections. A typical passage from a French report of 1688 reads, "The day before, fourteen prisoners escaped from the Abbey prison, after having soundly beaten the jailer and the guards. Yesterday a courrier arrived bringing the news that the Grand Deacon of Liège had been elected Bishop. We are assured that 5000 cavalry and 10,000 infantry are going to be raised. The King went hunting yesterday near Meudon."[67] This stream-of-consciousness style, in which no context was provided for individual items and no attempt made to give them credibility, resembles the hurried news summaries common on American commercial radio stations today; it may well have been intended for reading aloud, and presumably seventeenth-century readers were adept at inserting pauses between unrelated items as they read along. The apparent disorder of the reporting did not exclude the introduction of a definite news bias in some items. The Paris reports of 1687 show a clear sympathy with the Jansenists as opposed to the Jesuits and with the Huguenots exposed to Louis XIV's persecutions.[68] The paper was also very free in its remarks about prominent individuals, in the style of the late eighteenth-century

65. Paul Ricoeur, *Time and Narrative*, 2 vols., K. McLaughlin and D. Pellauer, trans. (Chicago: University of Chicago Press, 1984), 1:176.
66. On the notion of journalistic objectivity as a "strategic ritual," see Gaye Tuchman, "Objectivity as a Strategic Ritual: An Examination of Newsmen's Notions of Objectivity," *American Journal of Sociology* 77 (1972), 660–79.
67. *GL*, 26 Aug. 1688 (Paris, 20 Aug.).
68. Ibid., 4 Feb. 1687 (Paris, 28 Jan.).

English press. A typical item from 1687 reads, "A nun from a distinguished family has also been removed from a convent in Puy, by virtue
of a *lettre de cachet*, because, it is said, the Bishop of Puy was paying too
much attention to her."[69]

The journalistic language that Etienne Luzac employed when he first
took control of the paper in the late 1730s was the opposite of the
unstructured tone of the original *Gazette de Leyde*. The paper's political
reports now eschewed the earlier uninhibited, gossipy quality. For example, the report from Paris in the issue of 2 January 1739 devoted two-
and-a-half columns to the Imperial ambassador's state visit to the Picpus
convent, including a detailed "description of the Ambassador's car-
riages." The *Gazette de Leyde* of the 1680s and 1690s and after 1750
would never have given so much space to a purely ceremonial event. On
the other hand, the paper's material became more structured. Longer
items were broken into paragraphs, which generally corresponded to
distinct topics, so that the text lost the rambling quality characteristic of
the age of Louis XIV. The paper's reports became much more restrained and formal in character; the gap between the language of the
official press and that of the *Gazette de Leyde* had been greatly reduced.

Over the next four decades, the paper evolved away from the official
press by expanding the scope of its press coverage, but it did so without
returning to the sensational scandal-mongering tone of its early days or
of the contemporary English press. The result was a serious, high-
journalistic voice that resembled the style of the court gazettes, but the
extent of the paper's coverage clearly distinguished it from these rivals.
In his private correspondence, Jean Luzac could sling mud with the best
of his contemporaries, but he drew a strict line between language suit-
able for publication and that which was not. A story on the choice of
deputies for the French Estates-General in 1789 exemplifies the difference in tone between his paper and its more outspoken competitors. In
April 1789, both the *Gazette de Leyde* and the *Courier du Bas-Rhin* printed
a bulletin that concluded, "In the number of the representatives, there
are, no doubt, some men of great merit; but one cannot hide the fact
that, in many places, they were not the ones who were preferred to their
rivals." The *Courier du Bas-Rhin* went on to add a phrase that would
never have sullied the columns of the Leiden paper, however: "No
doubt the people have their reasons for choosing them, and perhaps
they thought that the Estates-General would be a bath that would rein-
vigorate all the impotent ones and cleanse all the lepers."[70] Both the
papers thus commented critically on the deputies and on the electorate
that had chosen them, but the *Gazette de Leyde*'s criticism was restrained

69. Ibid., 19 Aug. 1687 (Paris, 12 Aug.).
70. Ibid., 24 Apr. 1789; *Courier du Bas-Rhin*, 25 Apr. 1789.

and impersonal; the *Courier du Bas-Rhin*, by contrast, chose to be vivid, concrete, and, no doubt, more entertaining, but at the price of making even the dullest reader alert to the fact that this news source had a distinct bias.

Serious, dignified, and somewhat dull language contributed to the *Gazette de Leyde*'s image as a dependable news source, but so did the manner in which it unfolded its stories. Luzac always reminded readers of how uncertain the details of his news were. He was acutely aware that "the first reports of a striking event are always full of errors, and that the clouds that hide the truth are greater, the farther away one is from it."[71] Despite his best efforts, there were bound to be mistaken reports in his paper, and the only way he could maintain a reputation for truthfulness was to structure narratives in such a way that readers were drawn into what another journalist of the time called "this not unphilosophical occupation in which one follows the growth or diminution of the truth, and sees it emerge bit by bit from the coverings with which error has distorted it, or, after having dazzled for a moment with misleading rays, dissolve like a mirage and rejoin the pack of lies from which it came."[72]

An essential feature of the *Gazette de Leyde*'s journalistic strategy was the frequent publication of significant official documents: royal edicts, texts of parliamentary speeches and contestatory groups' manifestoes, international treaties, and the like. Like modern "newspapers of record," the paper lent veracity to its own news accounts by inviting readers to examine for themselves the evidence it cited. Even if they did not labor through the columns of tiny type in which the documents were printed, readers would be persuaded by their presence. Luzac added to the impact of these published documents by the caution with which he presented them: in a world in which rulers were under no obligation to inform their subjects of their actions, readers had good reason to wonder how authentic the materials a newspaper published were. The *Gazette de Leyde* sought to reassure them by indicating the source of its texts or by stating that they came from reliable informants.

But the *Gazette de Leyde* was much more than simply a collection of unrelated documents. Its main feature was its news reports, and Luzac established their veracity by repeatedly but unobtrusively demonstrating to readers the caution with which he proceeded before publishing any item. In his paper, news stories rarely recounted events in the form of a closed narrative of a completed action. Even an event as sharply limited in time and space as the storming of the Bastille on 14 July 1789 came to be reported in the *Gazette de Leyde* as a suspense story spread

71. Jean Luzac to the Grand Master of the Order of Malta, 12 Dec. 1775, in LGA-VH, Z(1), no. 37.
72. [Pidansat de Mairobert, attrib.], *Mémoires secrets*, 25:8–9.

over several issues. The issue of 21 July 1789, which printed a newsletter from Paris written on 13 July, concluded with an editor's note dated 20 July, bringing readers the first intimation that something extraordinary had happened in the French capital. But because the paper wanted to be as truthful as possible, Luzac explained that he was not publishing the latest, unverified reports from Paris: "There are some that speak of blood spilled by troops in the middle of the capital, and of all the horrors that announce a civil war." This alarming anticipation must have sent readers scurrying for their papers three days later, where they found a letter from Paris, dated 17 July, which brought them up to date on what Luzac, in an editorial note dated 22 July, called a series of events "more striking, more sudden, more astounding in all their details" than any others in modern history. But this rapid summary of the storming of the Bastille was not the end of the matter. The supplement to the same issue, printed a day later, went over the same ground, but in much greater detail, and subsequent issues continued to fill in the background of the event, whose significance thus only became clear over a period of several weeks. This cautious, cumulative depiction of the storming of the Bastille was not merely a result of the Leiden paper's distance from Paris: it was a journalistic strategy quite different from that of the excited pamphlet-journalists in Paris, who, despite protestations that "it is impossible to provide immediately a detailed and exact report," in fact claimed to have produced an instant chronicle that could serve as "an immortal monument" to an event whose significance they were ready to define on the spot.[73] Unlike the French journalists, who immediately made the 14 July event a mythic occurrence,[74] Luzac's journalistic strategy was deliberately designed to demystify it, to keep readers from jumping to conclusions about it, and to embed even such an unusual occurrence in the continuously flowing stream of events.

This cautious, piecemeal method of reporting, applied even to such sharply defined events as the storming of the Bastille, was even more evident in the *Gazette de Leyde*'s coverage of more routine news. Typically, whether the paper's focus was on a war, a diplomatic negotiation,

73. Citations from *Paris sauvé, ou Récit détaillé des evènemens qui ont eu lieu à Paris, depuis le dimanche 12 Juillet 1789, une heure après-midi jusqu'au vendredi suivant au soir* (Paris: n.p., 1789), 3; and [Jacques Beffroy de Reigny], *Précis exact de la prise de la Bastille, rédigé sous les yeux des principaux acteurs qui ont joué un rôle dans cette expédition, & lu le même jour à l'Hotel-de-Ville* (Paris: Baudouin, 1789), 1. On the earliest printed narratives of the storming of the Bastille, see Hans-Jürgen Lüsebrink and Rolf Reichardt, "La prise de la Bastille comme 'événement total.' Jalons pour une théorie historique de l'événement à l'époque moderne," in Centre Meridional d'Histoire Sociale, *L'Evénement* (colloque d'Aix-en-Provence, 1983) (Marseille: Laffitte, 1986), 77–102.

74. See Claude Labrosse and Pierre Rétat, "La légende immédiate de la Révolution dans la presse de 1789," in *La légende de la Révolution* (Clermont-Ferrand: Faculté des Lettres et Sciences Humaines de l'Université Blaise-Pascal, 1988), 127–36.

or a domestic constitutional crisis, news coverage was spread out over many weeks, if not months or even years. The events that the *Gazette de Leyde* considered worth reporting in any detail usually cast a long shadow ahead of them. In covering the outbreak of a typical eighteenth-century war, the paper was likely to pick up warning tremors months or even years before anything specific occurred. An article on 9 January 1784 complained that war between Russia and Turkey had been imminent for a whole year and yet nothing definite had happened; as it turned out, this brewing conflict did not explode until 1787. This war was an extreme case, made more difficult for the paper because of poor access to information in Constantinople and St. Petersburg, but even in capitals where correspondents were well informed, decisions to make war were usually bruited about long before real consequences ensued. Thus Luzac had reported as early as 18 April 1777 that there was discussion in Paris about a war with England in support of the Americans, but at that date, the paper considered the prospect unlikely. By 27 June 1777, the gazette had reports of American privateers operating out of French ports; on 1 August 1777 it told readers that a French declaration of war was imminent. In fact the treaty between France and the United States committing the Bourbon monarchy to the war was not signed until December 1777, and France did not officially break off relations with the British until March 1778; fighting only began with the British naval attack on the *Belle Poule* in June. The way the French involvement in the war progressed from a speculative possibility to a probability and then, slowly, took on the lineaments of reality was typical of the way many of the *Gazette de Leyde*'s news stories developed. It reflected a sense that important events did not happen suddenly but evolved over time. The paper depicted the actions of states, and of major groups within them, as calculable and hence predictable: indeed, events followed stereotypical patterns, so that although the journalist's function was to tell what was new, in fact, "contrary to what the journalist would like to make us believe," there is no "real innovation in history . . . but merely the coming about of already known possibilities."[75]

Because the limits of historical possibility were assumed to be known in advance, the *Gazette de Leyde* had merely to sketch in the exact details of the processes it recorded. The drama and tension in its reports came from the episodic manner in which it necessarily had to chronicle the world around it. Thanks to the regular interruption of the story imposed by periodic publication, readers were kept in suspense, waiting for the always-promised "continuation in the next number": as Pierre Rétat comments, "the report comes as a reappearance that fulfills an expecta-

75. Pierre Rétat, "Les gazettes: De l'événement à l'histoire," in Henri Duranton et al., *Etudes sur la presse* 3 (1978), 27.

tion."[76] Through this narrative style, journalist and reader became part-
ners in the difficult discovery of the truth about contemporary history.
And by his constant reiteration of the tentativeness of all his reports and
the unofficial nature of the documentary texts in his paper, Luzac
safeguarded himself against interference from governments, as he
could always excuse what he had printed on the grounds that he had
made an honest error. Luzac did not preach or thunder at his readers to
convince them of the truth of his accounts, nor did he resort to sensa-
tionalism. Instead, by constantly striking the pose of a mere mortal,
limited in his ability to discover the truth, he won readers' trust for the
version of historical reality that he had painstakingly assembled.

From the diversity of materials that he assembled twice each week at
his desk in Leiden Jean Luzac created a journalistic text whose words
were often taken verbatim from the letters and documents his correspondents provided, but whose spirit arose from the frame within which
they were set: the continuously appearing *Gazette de Leyde*. Luzac accomplished his task of "making news" in such a way that the significance of a
report or a document in his paper was different from the significance of
the same item as it appeared in any other source of the period. Before
his readers could receive the fruits of his labors, however, Luzac had to
see the *Gazette de Leyde* through the press, and eighteenth-century technology severely restricted the amount of information he could furnish
readers.

76. Ibid., 31.

[5]

Producing a
Newspaper in the
Eighteenth Century

Once he had selected the news and documents destined for each issue of the paper, Jean Luzac's personal role in the production of the *Gazette de Leyde* was at an end. Unlike Benjamin Franklin in Philadelphia in the 1730s, most of the European newspaper editors of the eighteenth century were incapable of setting type or operating a printing press. Nor did they usually have much to do with the distribution of the printed copies or the management of their enterprise's business affairs. Yet all these aspects of newspaper production vitally affected the content of newspapers and their impact. Jean Luzac may have left the hard work of printing and distributing the *Gazette de Leyde* to others, but he was acutely aware of the many ways in which printing technology and the necessities of marketing impinged on his freedom to disseminate the news.

Printing the *Gazette de Leyde*

Of all the constraints that helped shape the *Gazette de Leyde*, none would have seemed more immutable to Jean Luzac than the technology of the wooden handpress on which his newspaper, like every other printed work before 1800, was produced. Ironically, no other aspect of journalism would be so rapidly transformed in the nineteenth century. Dependence on the wooden, hand-powered printing press had profound consequences for the nature of every journalistic text of Luzac's day. Technology restricted the amount of information Jean Luzac could fit into the two weekly editions of his paper. It limited the number of copies he could sell and therefore the size of the audience and the revenue he could obtain, and those limits in turn set bounds to the amount and quality of information he could publish and the impact his paper could have. A close analysis of the methods used to transmute the news reports Luzac obtained into black marks on white paper is no mere antiquarian exercise: it is central to an understanding of the nature of the *Gazette de Leyde*'s historical role.

In recent years, historians have taken a keen interest in the details of printing processes before 1800, a subject formerly reserved for specialists in material bibliography and the narrow field of printing history. In the English-speaking world, Robert Darnton has done more than anyone else to describe the ways in which words were turned into print in the age of the Enlightenment. Using the very rich records of the Société Typographique de Neuchâtel (STN), he and the Swiss scholar Jacques Rychner have been able to reconstruct the process by which books such as the STN edition of Diderot's *Encyclopédie* were published. Darnton has even accomplished the tour de force of identifying the pressman whose thumbprint appears in the margin of a surviving copy of that work. But the text of the third edition of the *Encyclopédie*, the subject of Darnton's *Business of Enlightenment*, was little affected by the mechanical process that made its reproduction possible.[1] Authors of books in the eighteenth century could afford to remain relatively ignorant of the mechanics of printing. Prevailing technology set some limits on the nature of the texts they could create if they wished to see them in print: they could not demand the complete integration of text and illustrations that modern methods allow, or insist on exotic typefaces. But those constraints probably did not bother most authors: these were constants that had prevailed since Gutenberg's day.

On the other hand, journalists were continually reminded of the constraints technology imposed. To function at all within the restrictions imposed by their printing equipment, they had to organize the work of producing their gazettes according to principles entirely different from those followed in book publication, and they had to push the balky wooden press to the limits of its possibilities. It is not surprising that the greatest European newspaper of the first half of the nineteenth century, the London *Times*, was also the first printing enterprise to adopt the steam-powered rotary press, which allowed a quantum jump in its press run, a massive increase in its total audience, and consequently an unmistakable growth in the newspaper's political and cultural influence.[2] In view of the special importance of printing technology to the production of newspapers, it is surprising that so little recent scholar-

1. Robert Darnton, *The Business of Enlightenment* (Cambridge, Mass.: Harvard University Press, 1979).

2. [Morison et al.], *History of the "Times,"* 1:110–15. The first Koenig press, installed for the *Times* in 1814, could print four times as many sheets per hour as the handpress.

ship on hand-printing methods pays attention to the peculiarities of newspaper printing.

Although records of the *Gazette de Leyde*'s printing operations do not seem to have survived, a Dutch scholar has recently published an early-nineteenth-century Dutch manuscript on printing techniques written by a certain David Wardenaar—and Wardenaar had almost certainly practiced his trade in the *Gazette de Leyde*'s printing shop.[3] His manuscript is the only manual for the printing trade from the handpress era known to have been written by a man experienced in newspaper publication.

As the references to newspaper printing scattered through Wardenaar's work indicate, the basic difference between newspaper printing and other forms of printing work was that the printers of newspapers constantly faced the pressure of deadlines. Workers in a newspaper shop "must frequently work as if on a forced march," Waardenaar remarked, "often hastily, as fast as a bird's flight."[4] Unlike most books, the newspaper had to be ready by a specified time or it lost all value. Consequently, newspaper printing required a work rhythm very different from that prevailing in most other printing shops in the eighteenth century. Darnton and Rychner have shown how irregular the working patterns in the STN shop were: the amount of type set and the number of sheets printed varied widely from day to day, and even the same worker might work twice as fast one day as he did the next. Printers working on a book might have to do some of their tasks in haste, to finish the job, but they could look forward to some slack time afterward.[5] This pattern was not accidental, but represented a functional adaptation to the unpredictable fluctuations of book and job printing. Paul Gaskell notes that "the printing trade has always had to accommodate great variation of demand, and its operations have had to be correspondingly flexible."[6] But a newspaper shop did not operate under these conditions. For newspaper publishers, there was a steady flow of work on a predictable schedule. Consequently, newspaper printing required a sense of time and a degree of organization quite foreign to the habits that prevailed in a book publishing firm such as the STN.

The records of the Dutch-language *Amsterdamsche Courant* from the

3. Wardenaar, whose manuscript dates from 1801, had worked in a newspaper printing shop in Leiden from 1767 to 1773. There were two newspapers in the city at that time, Luzac's enterprise and the Dutch-language *Leydse Courant*. Given that Wardenaar moved on to work in the French-language printing shop of Reinier Arrenberg in Rotterdam after 1773, it seems plausible that his earlier experience had been in the *Gazette de Leyde* shop. Frans A. Janssen, ed., *Zetten en Drukken in de achttiende Eeuw: David Wardenaar's Beschrijving der Boekdrukkunst (1801)* (Haarlem: Enschedé, 1982), 53–55.

4. Janssen, ed., *Drukken*, 427, 429.

5. Darnton, *Business*, 219–227; Jacques Rychner, "A l'ombre des Lumières: Coup d'oeil sur la main-d'oeuvre de quelques imprimeries du XVIIIe siècle," *Studies on Voltaire and the Eighteenth Century* 155 (1976), 1938.

6. Paul Gaskell, *A New Introduction to Bibliography* (Oxford: Clarendon, 1972), 160.

mid-eighteenth century clarify the difference between book printing and newspaper work. The eight printing-shop workers who put out the triweekly paper kept a rigid schedule. On the three printing days, they put in twenty hours on the job, from 8 A.M. to 4 or 5 A.M. the next day. They could sleep late the following morning, but still had to work at least a four-hour shift cleaning and redistributing type to be ready for the next day's marathon. Not only were the working hours more regular than in the STN shop, but the workers' productivity had to be relatively constant, too: each issue of the paper contained roughly the same amount of type and had to be printed in the same number of copies. The erratic performances typical of the STN labor force could never have been tolerated. In return for their greater discipline, of course, the workers were assured of a more regular income. They were not likely to be laid off during slack periods, and in fact the *Amsterdamsche Courant*'s printers were generally long-termers: in 1767, they had been with the paper from four to forty years, and turnover in the printing shop was almost nonexistent.[7] This was evidently the case for the *Gazette de Leyde* as well. When he finally sold the paper to Napoleon's brother Louis in 1807, Etienne Luzac made a special point of asking for pensions for his printing-shop workers, "who have served me in this undertaking, some for thirty or forty years."[8] To assure this loyalty, newspaper publishers paid their printers well, in contrast to publishers of books and other materials, and even gave them such benefits as retirement pay.[9] The Luzacs' paper required the same dependable publishing operation that its Amsterdam neighbor did, and must have adopted similar procedures to obtain it.

Twice a week, the printing-shop workers on whom the production of the *Gazette de Leyde* depended began the well-worn routine that resulted in an eight-page newspaper. Jean Luzac himself probably did not supervise the work they did, but he must have known from long experience just how much text the compositors could set in the time available for each issue, and his editorial decisions had to be made accordingly.[10] The

7. Eeghen, "Amsterdamsche Courant," 36.

8. LGA-VH, Z(2), no. 119 (1807).

9. Janssen, ed., *Drukken*, 443. In 1767, the four compositors who worked for the *Amsterdamsche Courant* earned 8.5 gulden a week, and the two pressmen 6.5 gulden, higher wages than their contemporaries in Paris would have received, but less than half of the 27 shillings a week that London newspaper printing workers earned in 1785. Eeghen, "Amsterdamsche Courant," 36; Anon., *Printing the 'Times' since 1785* (London: Printing House Square, 1953), 15–16.

10. The archives of the *Gazette de Leyde* do not indicate when the younger Etienne Luzac took over the direction of the paper's printing operations from his father. Article 11 of the contract between the senior Etienne Luzac and his two nephews, signed at the time of their father's death in 1783, specified that one or the other would have the presses in his house, and receive a fixed sum of 500 gulden annually for the incidental expenses of the printing operation. To guarantee Etienne Luzac's devotion to this end of the newspaper's operation, the contract bound him to refrain from any other business activity. LGA-VH, Z(2), no. 51.

actual printing shop could not have been very large. Throughout the period with which we are concerned, the paper's presses were housed in the building where Etienne Luzac and his family lived. At some point after Jean Luzac had ceased to be the editor, Etienne invested in a new shop, located in a building of its own. When he sold the paper to the Dutch government in 1807, Etienne Luzac put the value of this shop and its equipment at 5,000 gulden, the equivalent of 10,000 French livres.[11] This was a modest price: a French author of a handbook for printers, published in 1791, had estimated that the cost of type and two presses for a small printing shop, exclusive of the building it was housed in, would cost 8,255 livres, and a French newspaper publisher whose printing shop had been destroyed in 1797 estimated his losses at 40,000 livres.[12] The shop that the *Gazette de Leyde* had used before Etienne Luzac decided to house it separately was probably smaller and less valuable than the premises it occupied in 1807.

Internal evidence from surviving copies of the paper helps us reconstruct the tasks in the *Gazette de Leyde*'s printing shop. Each issue actually consisted of two separate four-page newspapers: the *ordinaire*, the first four pages of the issue, was set in type and handed over to the pressmen a day ahead of the four-page *supplement*, even though both bore the same date.[13] The printed area of the pages measured 19 cm by 13 cm, slightly larger than the format the paper had employed a hundred years earlier, but much smaller than the English or Dutch newspapers of the period. The pages of the *ordinaire* were divided into two columns; the *supplement* was set in long lines running across the page. Perhaps this procedure made it easier to sort the printed sheets and put together complete copies. Both sections of the paper were set in the same miniscule body type, a size that French printers called *petit romain*. One good compositor could set about two-thirds of a printing form—the wooden frame that contained the type used to print one sheet—in this size per day; each eight-page issue of the *Gazette de Leyde* required two such forms and thus represented at least three man-days of setting work.[14] In fact, it probably came to even more, because a good part of the paper was usually in even smaller *petit texte* type, which the Luzacs employed for the numerous documents they published.

11. Etienne Luzac, letter of 31 May 1807, ibid., no. 118.

12. M. S. Boulard, *Le manuel de l'imprimeur* (Paris: Boulard, 1791), 81–84; Poncelin, bankruptcy dossier, 10 Feb. 1804, in Archives départementales de la Seine (Paris), D 11 U(3) 24, d. 1638.

13. The editor's note that normally appeared on page 4 of the *ordinaire* customarily bore a date one day earlier than the date of publication, whereas the editorial note at the top of page 5, the first page of the *supplement*, bore the date of publication, and last-minute material always appeared on page 8 of that section, indicating that it was the last to go to press. The *Gazette de Cologne*, whose format was identical to the *Gazette de Leyde*'s, acknowledged the one-day delay between its two four-page sections by giving them different dates.

14. Feyel, *Gazette*, 101.

Theoretically, two skilled compositors could have set the type each issue required in two days, but it is more likely that the paper employed at least four typesetters, like the *Amsterdamsche Courant* whose three four-page issues (in a slightly larger format) contained somewhat less type.[15] A composing-room staff working at top speed could hardly have produced work of the quality found in the paper, or coped with the accidents bound to accompany newspaper production. As it is, the compositors of the *Gazette de Leyde* were certainly among the most careful and accurate to be found anywhere in the eighteenth century. Typographical errors of any sort are exceedingly rare in the paper, and the grosser mistakes common in most newspapers of that age and our own—misplacement of whole lines or paragraphs, for example—are simply not found. The Luzacs must have understood intuitively that inaccuracies in detail would cast doubt on the paper's reputation for accuracy on more important matters: the exterior appearance of the text had to match its content. Such a result could only be obtained with a workforce large enough to allow for a reasonable pace of work and proper attention to tasks such as redistributing the tiny *petit romain* and *petit texte* characters properly after use.

Not only did the *Gazette de Leyde*'s diligent compositors carefully avoid errors, they also followed some complicated typographical conventions designed to make the paper easier to read, although to modern eyes, it seems to lack the devices that today's newspapers use to make their copy easily legible. It is true that the Luzacs resolutely ignored the experiments in typographical design in England and in the Netherlands during this period which foreshadowed modern newspaper design, such as individual titles for specific stories and various forms of typographical ornaments or rules to separate stories. Because the *Gazette de Leyde* carried little advertising, and what it did carry was always confined to a single block at the bottom of the last page of the *ordinaire*, its pages did not have the distinctive mosaic appearance of the London papers, whose front page was often partially or totally covered with ads, each beginning with an oversized initial. Nor did the *Gazette de Leyde* ever emulate the common practice of the Dutch-language papers in running advertisements sideways in the spaces between news columns.

These English and Dutch expedients were steps on the road to separating newspaper typography from book layout. They showed some recognition of what English printing historian Stanley Morison called "the fundamental problem of newspaper display: to order the material for rapid reading." By the mid-1780s, English newspaper publishers, such as John Walter I, founder of the *Times*, were coming to realize that "the book is composed on the understanding that it will be read atten-

15. Eeghen, "Amsterdamsche Courant," 35.

N U M E R·O XXVI.

NOUVELLES EXTRAORDINAIRES

D E

DIVERS ENDROITS

du MARDI 1. Avril, 1777.

De PARIS, *le* 24. *Mars.*

LE Parlement vient de rendre & faire publier un Arrêt, lequel, fur l'appel à *minimâ* de la Sentence du Bailliage d'*Orléans* du 22. Mai 1776. condamne au carcan & au banniffement plufieurs Particuliers de la dite Ville, convaincus d'ufure, quelques-uns pour avoir escompté ou prêté fur gages à 20. Sous par Louis par mois. Parmi ces Uforiers font un Commiffaire de Police, un Chirurgien, un Apothicaire, un Huiffier. Le même Arrêt décharge d'accufation le Prieur de *Saint-Laurent*, Chanoine de la Cathédfale d'*Orléans*, & le Curé de la Paroiffe de *St. Donatien* de la même Ville. Il ordonne "que les Loix, citées dans l'Ar-„ rêt, depuis le Capitulaire de *Charlemagne* „ de l'année 789. jufqu'à l'Arrêt de la Cour „ du 27. Août 1764. feront exécutées felon „ leur forme & teneur. En conféquence, „ fait défenfes à toutes Perfonnes d'exercer „ aucunes efpèces d'ufures prohibées par les „ Saints Canons reçus dans le Royaume, Or-„ donnances, Arrêts, & Règlemens de la „ Cour, en quelque manière que ce foit ou „ puiffe être, & même fous apparences fein-„ tes & controuvées de faits de Commerce, „ &c. " Cet Arrêt eft d'autant plus remarquable, qu'on fe rappelle que, malgré les repréfentations du Parlement, les pourfuites dans une pareille affaire contre des Particu-

liers d'*Angoulême* ont été annullées par des Arrêts du Confeil au rapport de Mr. *Turgot*, alors Contrôleur-Général, dont le fyftème étoit, qu'il falloit, pour l'avantage du Commerce, regarder l'Argent comme Marchandife, fujet conféquemment à une variation de prix telle qu'elle a lieu pour les Denrées ou pour le cours des Effets à la Bourfe, &c.

On dit, que le Sr. *Tort* veut fe pourvoir au Conf·il en caffation de l'Arrêt du Parlement, du 19. Mars, dont nous avons déjà rendu compte (*l'Ordinaire dernier :*) Cependant, comme nous venons d'en recevoir un Précis plus ample, nous croyons devoir le donner à nos Lecteurs. Le voici.

Le Procès de M. le Duc de Guines a été jugé le 19. de ce mois par quarante-cinq Juges. Il l'a gagné tout d'une voix. La plainte de Tort, *en ce qu'il impute à M. le Duc de Guines de l'avoir fait jouer dans les Fonds d'Angleterre, & de l'avoir fait fuir, déclarée injurieufe & calomnieufe. M. le Duc de Guines & M. de Monval déchargés de l'accufation.* Tort *blâmé, (ce qui s'exécute en faifant mettre le condamné à genoux & lui difant : La Cour te b'âme & te déclare infame :* Va-t-en.) *Condamné en outre en des dommages-intérêts envers M. le Duc de Guines, M. de Monval, & M. de Saudray, par forme de réparation civile, applicables de leur confentement aux pauvres Prifonniers, & à tous les dépens du Procès, (qui emportent prifon.) Enjoint à* Roger *&* Delpech *d'être plus circonfpects à l'avenir, leur fcrou ou acte d'emprifonnement fubfiftant ; & les dits* Roger *&*

tively," whereas "the newspaper must be set-up on the understanding that it will be read inattentively. Moreover, the book is composed for consecutive, the newspaper for inconsecutive reading; the nature of the book-page is homogeneous, of the newspaper, heterogeneous."[16] The Luzacs, and the French-language press both inside and outside the kingdom in general, remained more conservative and adhered to traditions of typographical form overtly derived from book composition. Even the French Revolution led to only modest experiments in newspaper layout: it was during the Napoleonic period that the basic principle of laying out the paper as though it were to be read consecutively from the top of the left-hand column of the front page to the bottom of the right-hand column on the last page was finally abandoned in the French-language press.[17]

Within the limits of this conservative tradition, however, the *Gazette de Leyde* had gradually adopted some innovations that made the newspaper of Jean Luzac's day much more readable than its late-seventeenth-century predecessors. These conventions were so modest, compared to the large-type headlines, the illustrations, and the jigsaw puzzle format that newspapers adopted during the nineteenth century, that they can easily pass unnoticed by today's reader, but when one immerses oneself in the text, one gradually becomes aware of how much the typography in the *Gazette de Leyde* actually does facilitate the rapid digestion of the content; it is a shock to move from the Luzacs' paper to an eighteenth-century text that lacks such aids to reading. The seventeenth-century *Gazette de Leyde* had been set entirely in a single typeface, and news bulletins from a given source were set without paragraph indentations, regardless of length. Etienne Luzac had taken to printing the lengthy documents that were the paper's specialty in a typeface smaller than the paper's standard body type: this saved space and also distinguished the documents from the ordinary news items, even if it did make the documents harder to read. The block of advertising copy in the *ordinaire* came to be distinguished from the news because it was set in long lines, unlike the rest of that section, and in italic type.

Although the paper still used no headlines or titles, the headings on stories had become somewhat larger and more varied. By Jean Luzac's day, the *Gazette de Leyde* distinguished between "lettres," which were usually the longer newsletters from his correspondents, and "nouvelles," shorter reports whose source may have been other newspapers. The headings on longer items were set in a mixture of types: thus a

16. Stanley Morison, *The English Newspaper* (Cambridge: Cambridge University Press, 1932), 184–85.
17. On French newspaper design during the Revolution, see Jeremy D. Popkin, "Une réprise en main et un nouveau départ: La présentation de texte dans les journaux entre 1794 et 1807," in Pierre Rétat, ed., *Textologie du journal* (Paris: Minard, 1989).

heading in a typical issue from 1772 reads "*SUITE des Nouvelles de* STOK-HOLM *du 4 Septembre.*" Such headings stand out even though the type was no larger than that employed for the story itself. Longer items were broken into paragraphs, which generally corresponded to distinct topics, and within these paragraphs, proper names and direct quotations were set in italics. The *Gazette de Leyde* was also generous with capital letters at the beginning of nouns, coming closer to German practice than to modern French habits in this regard. A typical line from a news dispatch printed in 1772 reads: "Hier, il se tint à *Whitehall* une grande Conférence entre les Ministres d'Etat: La Colonie projettée sur l'*Ohio* en a fait l'objet."[18] All these typographical conventions, minor though they seem in retrospect, made definite contributions to the legibility of the paper.

Ensuring that the compositors could set enough of this intricately patterned type for the paper required careful scheduling. The Luzacs had the first half of each issue printed a day in advance of the second because this spread the work of composing and printing the paper more evenly through the week and made the most efficient use of both manpower and machinery. Had the entire paper been printed on the day before it was released, as a daily newspaper is, they would have needed twice as many compositors, pressmen, and presses and the workers and the presses would have been idle five days out of seven. With the procedure they actually adopted, a smaller workforce could be kept going at optimal speed for at least four days out of seven, and the two "off" days would have been needed for such jobs as cleaning and redistributing type, as they were in the *Amsterdamsche Courant*'s shop. But such a schedule complicated the task of making the paper as timely as possible by lengthening the production process. Jean Luzac had to plan carefully to minimize the disadvantages of this procedure.

Careful examination of typical issues of the *Gazette de Leyde* shows that each issue was an intricate mosaic of items, some set in type well in advance of the printing deadline, and others composed as close to press time as possible. A few items in each issue were either permanently on hand or could be prepared a week or more in advance: the half-page logo with the paper's title and the provincial coat of arms, of course, and the block of advertising copy that normally occupied the lower half of page 4.[19] The front page of the *supplement* (page 5) also contained material that could be set in advance. It typically began with a paragraph of editorial comment, datelined Leiden, followed by the reproduction of one or more substantial documents bearing on some major ongoing

18. *GL*, 22 Sept. 1772.
19. Copies from a year of peak circulation, 1789, show that the *Gazette de Leyde* had at least three different logo blocks, which can be differentiated from each other on the basis of the size of the type in the title.

news story—proclamations of the Continental Congress during the American Revolution, for instance. Many of the smaller news items had probably also been set in type some time in advance of printing. The first news story in the left-hand column on page 1 was almost always of this sort. Rarely a major item, such as the beginning of the newsletter from Paris or London, this was usually a report from some distant part of the world, such as Constantinople or Algiers, which took so long to reach Leiden that there was no need to rush it into print. Very likely Luzac also favored putting such news in this prominent location because the beginning item could be shortened if necessary to make way for more significant news.

The heart of each issue of the *Gazette de Leyde* was made up not of such relatively short news items from exotic places, but of lengthy newsletters from major European capitals, most often Paris and London. These newsletters were often accompanied by substantial documents—parliamentary speeches from England, or parlementary remonstrances from France. These documents were often so long that they had to be printed in installments over several issues, and because of the very small type used, they involved a great deal of slow, painstaking composition. The newsletters were the items to be printed as quickly as possible, and, as a result, they were undoubtedly the last material to be set in type. The newsletters were usually concentrated on the interior pages of the *ordinaire* and the *supplement*—that is, pages 2–3 and 6–7 of the paper— suggesting that the printer laid out those pages first, observing how much additional room would be needed on the exterior pages for the rest of the vital last-minute newsletters and choosing shorter stories already set in type to fill the remaining space on those pages.

The foreman in the Luzacs' shop worked on the four pages of each issue's *ordinaire* first, often using material from a Paris or London newsletter that had already been partially printed in the previous issue. In a typical issue, the copy of 2 June 1786, the main feature of the *ordinaire* was an "extract of a letter from Paris" dated 22 May 1786, which began halfway down the right-hand column of page 2 and ended halfway down the left-hand column of page 3 (see Figure 1). This was followed by three full columns of a document, a section of the lawyer Target's *mémoire* on behalf of Cardinal de Rohan in the Diamond Necklace case, which gave the appearance of being directly related to the Paris newsletter. In fact, it was an installment of a document that had arrived in Leiden more than a week earlier, and which the paper's compositors could have been working on well in advance of the deadline for the June 2 issue. Page 1 and the left-hand column of page 2 were taken up by a set of items from the Iberian peninsula, datelined Algiers, 15 April; Lisbon, 2 May; Cadiz, 28 April; and Madrid, 9 May. All had presumably reached

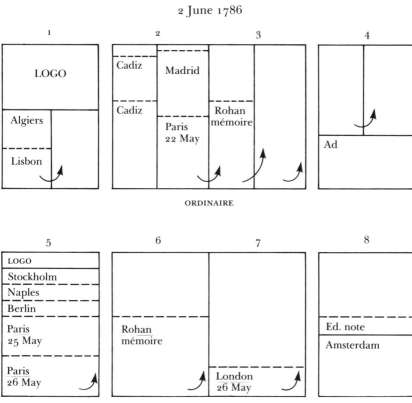

Figure 1. LAYOUT OF GAZETTE DE LEYDE

2 June 1786

ORDINAIRE

SUPPLEMENT

the paper in a single packet, sent via Madrid, and since the most recent was already more than three weeks old, they were typical of material the editor could hold over for one or more issues without making it appear stale. Consequently, there was nothing in the *ordinaire* for this particular issue that was likely to have arrived in the office less than a week before the paper's date of publication. In other words, the *ordinaire* for this issue had undoubtedly been locked up and sent to press well before the final deadline for the paper, a situation most satisfying for all concerned. When there was too much pressing news to be contained solely in the *supplement*, however, the most recent newsletter from Paris or London might be started in the *ordinaire*. If this newsletter was fleshed out sufficiently with documents that had been received earlier, the *ordinaire* could appear to give late-breaking news while in fact containing only a column or so of material composed on a rush basis.

With the *ordinaire* out of the way, the paper's printers, fortified no doubt by ample portions of the beer, coffee, and tea that Etienne Luzac was obliged to furnish them, turned their attention to the *supplement*, which would be printed twenty-four hours later. Its interior pages usually contained the latest-breaking news that the paper was going to carry. In the case of the issue of 2 June 1786, this consisted of Paris and London newsletters dated 26 May—that is, four days later than any material contained in the *ordinaire* of the same issue. Because the paper arranged for twice-weekly newsletters from both major capitals, this was one mail delivery later than that which had brought the Paris newsletter excerpted in the *ordinaire*. Mail from both London and Paris took about three days to reach Leiden, so Luzac would have received his 26 May newsletters on the twenty-ninth, leaving three days to get them set up in type and printed. For the 2 June 1786 issue, he had the lower half of page 5 and the upper half of page 6 filled with late-breaking Paris news, and then helped himself to another generous slice of the lengthy *mémoire* concerning Cardinal de Rohan, finishing out page 7 with the first few lines of his latest dispatch from London. He had already taken care of the top of page 5 with some short items from Stockholm, Naples, and Berlin, of which only the Berlin letter seems likely to have arrived in the interval since the previous paper. The bottom of page 8 carried an installment of the official program of the Amsterdam society for the improvement of agriculture. A few lines of editorial comment that Jean Luzac had dashed off, datelined 1 June, were inserted into the middle of page 8. They constituted the only item of truly last-minute copy in the paper, and served to assure readers that their paper had been put to bed as late as possible. With that, the *supplement* was ready to go to press. Yet even as he handed over the copy for each issue, Luzac was already in possession of more up-to-date material. Some issues of the paper carried small stop-press items at the bottom of page 4 or page 8 which prove that another mail delivery from Paris or London had already arrived in Leiden. But only a tremendously important news story justified the delaying of the printing process to incorporate urgent last-minute information into the paper.

The actual printing of the paper, like the typesetting, required skilled and dedicated workers. In eighteenth-century book production, the normal ratio of composers to pressmen was about one to one, but the Dutch newspaper enterprises of the eighteenth century employed many more compositors per press.[20] However many pressmen the *Gazette de Leyde* may have employed, the paper probably tried to get by with only

---

20. The *Amsterdamsche Courant* needed only two pressmen to put out its three weekly issues in 6,000 copies apiece, and the *Oprechte Haarlemse Courant* typically paid out four times as much in wages to compositors as it did to pressmen. Eeghen, "Amsterdamsche Courant," 36; Couvée, "The Administration of the 'Oprechte Haarlemse Courant,'" 107.

one set of forms for the *ordinaire* and one for the *supplement:* two sets of forms meant a doubling of the number of compositors and a steep increase in printing costs. In 1789, the year when the paper's profits and, presumably, its circulation hit an all-time high, the Luzacs were forced to set the copy for the paper twice in order to meet demand, but this does not seem to have been the case in more normal years.[21] Even when all the copies were printed from a single set of forms, the time needed to produce the paper could not be compressed. Indeed, the more successful the paper became and the larger the press run, the harder it was to fit late-breaking news into the forms. In the mid-1780s, when the paper was selling more than 4,000 copies of each issue, requiring more than 8,000 pulls of the press,[22] it would have taken a team of pressmen considerable time to work their way through the printing of the paper. True, newspaper pressmen worked fast: Leiden printer David Wardenaar boasted that when he had to, he had "done 250 sheets on one side in a half an hour . . . many times," so that his partner "barely had enough time to smear the letters [with ink]." The duc de Croÿ claimed to have witnessed the printers of the *Courrier de l'Europe* putting out 7,000 copies of the paper in six hours.[23] But normal printing work proceeded less quickly. The STN press teams of two men averaged between 10,000 and 16,000 printed sides, or 5,000 to 8,000 completed sheets, in a six-day work week.[24] At a press run of 4,000, the *Gazette de Leyde* would have required 16,000 printed sides for its two issues a week, just about the maximum that single press team could produce under ideal conditions. But as Wardenaar emphasized, conditions for newspaper printing were rarely ideal. Papers often had to be printed at night, when the lower temperatures made the ink harder to work with.[25] Skill

21. A comparison of the copies of the paper in the Library of Congress, Washington, D.C., and the Leiden University Library for the dates of 6 and 13 Feb. 1789 shows that they were printed from different forms, although their text is identical. The Library of Congress collection for 1789 also has copies using two different fonts of body type, one considerably more worn than the other, suggesting that the increased demand for the paper had forced the Luzacs to double their type supply.

22. The *Gazette de Leyde* was printed in quarto format, so that after being run through the press twice (to print each side), each printed sheet of paper yielded two complete copies of either the *ordinaire* or the *supplement*. Thus 4,000 copies of the *ordinaire* were produced by running 2,000 sheets of paper through the press, turning the sheets over and rotating them 180 degrees, and running them through the press again, and then cutting the sheets in half to produce 4,000 *ordinaires*, each one consisting of a half-sheet of paper printed on both sides. Because each subscriber's copy of the paper included two sections, this whole process had to be carried out twice for each issue; hence the figure of 8,000 pulls of the press to produce a press run of 4,000 complete copies.

23. Janssen, ed., *Drukken*, 427; "Journal du Duc de Croÿ," in Bibliothèque de l'Institut (Paris), Ms. 1675, entry of 26 Aug. 1779. The duc de Croÿ had visited the *Courrier de l'Europe*'s shop in Boulogne. Unfortunately, he does not indicate how many presses and pressmen were needed to work off that paper's press run.

24. Rychner, "Ombre," 1942.

25. Janssen, ed., *Drukken*, 315.

was needed to obtain a clean impression from forms filled with small-sized type. It seems unlikely that a single pair of men could have handled the paper's work load; unlike the single team that managed to manhandle a press into producing the three-day-a-week *Amsterdamsche Courant*, these men would have had to work more than twelve hours on two consecutive days twice every week. We can safely conclude that the *Gazette de Leyde* needed two teams of pressmen, essentially one for the *ordinaire* and one for the *supplement* of each issue. Each team would have been responsible for putting out slightly more than 8,000 sheets of printed paper a week, a load well within the known capacities of the printing equipment available to them, although they must have been working up a healthy sweat on the nights before publication.

The printing of the paper was carried out according to standard procedures. Each copy of the *ordinaire* or the *supplement* occupied only a half-sheet. The printers working on either of the paper's two sections had a form on the marble of their press containing blocks of type representing all four pages of that section. The type for pages 1 and 4 would have been on one half of the form, the type for pages 2 and 3 on the other, with the heads of all four pages toward the middle of the form. The printers would take full sheets of paper and print half the number necessary to make up the paper's required press run. They would then turn the sheets over, rotate them 180 degrees, and run them through the press again. In this way, the half of each sheet that had already received the impressions for pages 1 and 4 would receive the impressions of pages 2 and 3 on the backs of those pages during its second run. The other half of the sheet, already printed with pages 2 and 3, would end up with pages 1 and 4 on its second pass through the press.[26] The full sheets, each containing, like any printed sheet in quarto format, eight pages of impression (four on the front and four on the back), would then be cut in half, each one yielding two copies of the section of the *Gazette de Leyde* it represented. Surviving copies of the paper bear the telltale sign of this printing method: they have been cut just above the top of the printed area, whereas their left, right, and bottom margins are somewhat more generous. Assuming that the *Gazette de Leyde*, like some other eighteenth-century papers, used a press modified so that all four pages of a quarto form could be printed with a single pull of the bar, this method was the most rapid and efficient available for producing the number of copies the paper needed.

This twice-a-week rush to print conditioned every aspect of Jean Luzac's newspaper. Out of the seven or eight days that normally elapsed

26. The German newspaper historian Martin Welke has verified the use of this technique by finding an uncut proof sheet for an eighteenth-century German paper, the *Wolfenbütteler Zeitung*, in the city archives at Wolfenbüttel (personal communication).

between the occurrence of a major event in Paris or London and the publication of a report in Leiden, at least three represented the time necessary for printing after the news reached Luzac's desk. Furthermore, the limit on the amount of type that could actually be set on a rush basis just before the paper went to press meant that only a small portion of each issue's contents could be even that fresh. The *Gazette de Leyde* rarely had more than two genuine newsletters from correspondents in any one issue, and these rarely furnished more than 25 to 30 percent of the paper's total contents. Even if Luzac could have collected more fast-breaking news from around the world, he still could not have used it without hiring several additional compositors who would then be unemployed most of the week. The nature of the printing process thus forced Luzac, and all other newspaper editors of the period, to be extremely selective and to limit the quantity of the "freshest advices" they actually placed in their paper; the constraints of technology made the recruitment of a really extensive network of correspondents a useless luxury.

There were ways in which newspapers relying on the same printing equipment as the *Gazette de Leyde* could expand the number of copies that could be printed and the amount of late news they could contain. But these alternatives required sufficient income to employ more typesetters and printers. Simply raising the paper's subscription price would have been difficult: competition would mean lost sales to cheaper rivals. Income could be obtained by allowing the paper to become dependent on political subsidies, as the London dailies and the *Courrier de l'Europe* were, or by greatly increasing the amount of advertising. The latter strategy was adopted by the most widely circulated European newspaper in Luzac's day, the German-language *Hamburg Correspondent*, which achieved its press run of over 20,000 around the time of the French Revolution by employing up to six printing presses. But it managed to pay for this extravagance by filling half its pages with advertising, and its weekly "news hole" was actually smaller than that of the *Gazette de Leyde*. The daily papers of the French Revolution also used multiple printing presses: in 1792, the *Gazette universelle* of Luzac's former Paris correspondent Pascal Boyer and his one-time editor Cerisier had eight to ten presses to handle its print run of 11,000 copies.[27] It probably needed four sets of forms each day, and would have required a workforce at least four times the size of the *Gazette de Leyde*'s. The *Moniteur*, the largest of the French revolutionary papers (each four-page folio-sized issue occupied a full printing sheet, not simply a half-sheet), needed an even larger printing establishment. Even so, it could not set type fast enough to keep up with the latest news and settled for publishing its accounts of

27. Dumont-Pigalle to Johan Valckenaer, 21 Aug. 1792, in LUL, Ms. BPL 1031(I), ff. 3–6.

the revolutionary assemblies' debates one or more days late. In 1794, the printing shop responsible for putting out the *Moniteur* had twenty-seven presses, thirty-seven compositors, and fifty-four pressmen.[28] Only the development of power-driven printing machinery in the nineteenth century allowed journalists to expand substantially the amount of late-breaking information they could accommodate in their papers, while simultaneously increasing their press runs (thereby raising income) and enlarging their papers.

Modest as its regular portion of up-to-the-minute news was, the *Gazette de Leyde* represented an outstanding achievement for a news enterprise forced to rely on the wooden printing press and unable to afford the expanded workforce employed by the large London and Paris dailies. To be sure, the Luzacs did not try to achieve the fastest results possible with their equipment: they could not afford to demand herculean efforts from their staff every week. Furthermore, they demanded exceedingly high standards in their finished product. One has only to compare the neat, errorless columns of a typical number of the *Gazette de Leyde* with the pages of any Parisian daily during the French Revolution to see how many typographical errors, jumbled lines and paragraphs, and other mistakes were bound to creep into papers that had to meet the more demanding requirements of daily publication. But compared to other sorts of printing jobs in the eighteenth century, the production of the *Gazette de Leyde* was already a hurried procedure. The masses of miniscule gray type wedged into its columns twice a week represent one of the outstanding technical achievements of eighteenth-century typography, fit to take their place alongside the fine editions of a Baskerville or a Didot.

Distribution and Marketing

Once the *Gazette de Leyde*'s pressmen had completed their work, the paper was sent throughout Europe. To do this, the paper relied on the postal systems of the states in which it circulated. Most copies were destined for export, but the Dutch post carried them as far as the frontier. Each Dutch newspaper publisher had to negotiate an annual contract with the directors of the post, bargaining for the best rate he could get. In 1772, the Luzacs had signed an agreement with the Dutch postal carriers specifying an annual charge of 600 gulden for the transport of their shipments to the three frontier points leading to France and southern and northern Germany. With increases to allow for the

28. Robert Darnton, "L'imprimerie de Panckoucke en l'an II," *Revue française d'histoire du livre* 9 (1979), 365.

growing weight of the paper's bundles, this contract remained in effect until the abolition of all special postal concessions after the Batavian Revolution.[29] Beyond the frontiers, the paper's bundles became the responsibility of the distribution agents in the receiving countries, either the postmasters or, in the French case, a privileged vendor. These distributors received a healthy commission for their services. Indeed, the cost of postage was the major part of an international journal's subscription price. In 1770, Pierre Gosse, one of the Luzacs' Dutch competitors, offered his Swiss distributor copies of his *Gazette de La Haye* for the wholesale price of 11 livres, 14 sous per copy; the subscription price was 36 livres, and the difference was meant to cover the distributor's profit and the cost of transportation.[30] The distributors in turn remitted payments to the publisher, usually once a year. The system posed great risks for the newspaper publishers. When he took over the paper in 1738, the elder Etienne Luzac inherited an unpaid balance owed by the Prussian postmaster in Emmerich that amounted to nearly four times the paper's annual profits; for a time, this loss alone threatened to bankrupt the paper.[31] The records show that in 1745–49, payments from just two of the more than ninety distributors accounted for more than half of total sales. Defaults by distributors averaged more than 700 gulden a year, about a twelfth of gross revenues.[32]

From 1759, foreign newspaper sales in France were handled by a special arrangement. A privileged bookseller, David, had been given a monopoly for the distribution of all foreign gazettes. His Bureau général des gazettes étrangères sold the papers in Paris both by subscription and through street vendors, and transshipped copies bound for the French provinces.[33] To accommodate subscribers in provincial towns closer to Leiden, David apparently granted booksellers or postmasters a franchise to receive the paper directly.[34] This arrangement normally ran smoothly, but there were occasional problems. In 1779–80, the

29. The 1772 contract is in AR, Derde Afdeling, Familiearchief Le Jeune (1747–1810), inv. no. 271; Overvoorde, *Postwezen*, 127–128.

30. Pierre Gosse, Jr., to STN, 31 Aug. 1770, in Bibliothèque publique et universitaire, Neuchâtel, STN Archive, Ms. 1159, ff. 132–33.

31. Etienne Luzac to Frederic II of Prussia, 6 Mar. 1744, in LGA-VH, Z(1), no. 22. Profit figure from petition to Stadholder, n.d., in ibid., no. 25.

32. Profit statements for 1745–49, in ibid., no. 29. Unfortunately, the distributors are not identified by location. It is also unfortunate that no comparable documents record the distribution of the paper in Jean Luzac's day. One would suppose that the two largest shipments went to Paris and to the Prussian postmaster at Emmerich who handled distribution in northern Germany, Poland, and the rest of the Baltic.

33. An "Avis aux Colporteurs," dated 15 Sept. 1759, announced the creation of the new monopoly and informed the street vendors that they would pay a wholesale price of 12 sous per copy of the foreign papers. BN, Anisson-Duperron, Ms. fr. 22084, f. 111.

34. See the lists of subscription points in *GL*, 24 May 1768 (seventeen cities) and 24 Dec. 1784 (nineteen French cities plus Geneva).

Luzacs quarreled with the Bureau général about who was responsible for paying the increased cost of postal transport in Belgium.[35] In 1783, they complained that French sales were falling off and suspected the French government of tolerating a counterfeit edition; the Bureau général's agent assured them that all the international papers had lost sales with the ending of the American war.[36]

By Jean Luzac's day, the *Gazette de Leyde* was a well-known title with a century of continuous publication behind it; to a large extent, the paper sold itself. There is no indication that the Luzacs felt any need to circulate prospectuses or advertise in other publications, the way the backers of newly created periodicals did. Local distributors, on the other hand, frequently did advertise the full list of periodicals for which they took subscriptions. The French Bureau général issued regular prospectuses listing all the newspapers it handled, their prices, and the days on which they arrived.[37] The publishers of the *Annonces, Affiches et Avis Divers pour la Ville de Marseille*, who doubled as subscription agents for out-of-town periodicals, issued an annual notice to clients when it was time to renew their subscriptions, noting that otherwise "we are sometimes exposed to unmerited reproaches from forgetful subscribers."[38] In this way, the *Gazette de Leyde* profited from the growth of local periodicals throughout Europe: rather than competing with the international gazettes, these provincial advertisers, ever more numerous in the 1770s and 1780s, offered a useful channel of publicity for them.

The *Gazette de Leyde* as a Business Enterprise

Not having to organize their own distribution system simplified the administrative affairs of the *Gazette de Leyde* considerably for the Luzacs. Nevertheless, bookkeeping was a necessary part of the paper's business. The contract of 1783 assigned the task of corresponding with distributors and keeping the books to the paper's printer, Jean Luzac's brother Etienne. As co-owner of the newspaper, Jean Luzac was guaranteed a right to inspect the books. Until the two brothers had a falling-out over politics after 1795, the division of the profits apparently went smoothly.[39] Except for drafting letters to government officials when the paper's

35. Letter of De Lopes, postmaster at Brussels, to *GL*, 10 June 1779, reply, and letter of De Lormes (Paris agent) to *GL*, 4 Sept. 1780, in LGA-VH, Z(1), nos. 43–45. It is not clear how this dispute was resolved.
36. De Lormes to *GL*, 14 July 1783, in LGA-VH, Z(1), no. 55.
37. Prospectus, 1763, in BN, Anisson-Duperron, Ms. fr. 22084, f. 113.
38. 12 Dec. 1776. In 1773, the Marseille bureau had advertised twenty-one different periodicals, including the *Gazette de Leyde* and all its rivals. In 1774, it offered seventeen.
39. Contract, 18 Feb. 1783, in LGA-VH, Z(2), no. 51.

circulation was interrupted for political reasons, Jean Luzac had little concern with the business side of the paper.

The business affairs of the *Gazette de Leyde* were uncomplicated, particularly in comparison with the British papers of the period, which were usually structured as joint partnerships with as many as a dozen shares.[40] The paper's income came almost entirely from subscription sales, forwarded by the various postmasters and booksellers. Payments for advertisements, the paper's only other source of income, amounted to less than 3 percent of the gross income.[41] Expenses generally fell into simple categories: acquisition of paper, maintenance of printing equipment, wages for the printers, and payments to the city government. The *Gazette de Leyde*'s registers do not seem to have been preserved, but if one estimates the costs for paper and labor as about the same as the *Amsterdamsche Courant*, for which such records do exist, we can construct a hypothetical balance sheet that yields annual profit figures in the neighborhood of those given in the remaining documents in the paper's archives (see Figure 2).

These hypothetical calculations leave a balance of 68,850 gulden. Jean Luzac's actual figures for the paper's net profit in 1783–86 range from approximately 14,000 to 19,000 gulden. The difference, a figure representing about half the paper's gross income, probably went to the postal services and agents who distributed the paper.[42] Since the record books of the *Gazette de Leyde* do not seem to have been preserved, there is necessarily a large margin of uncertainty in these calculations, but they do demonstrate that the figures given in the Luzacs' papers for the enterprise's net profits are consistent with what we know about the actual costs of producing a newspaper in the eighteenth-century Netherlands.

As a business enterprise, the *Gazette de Leyde* was highly profitable. The 1783 contract between Etienne Luzac and his nephews specified that when the elder Luzac died, they were to buy out their uncle's stake in the business by putting up 8,000 gulden each to provide the paper with working capital.[43] This was a large sum, more than five times what Jean Luzac paid for a house for himself and his family in 1790.[44] But the investment was well worth it: during the four years in which they had to

40. Michael Harris, "The Management of the London Newspaper Press during the Eighteenth Century," *Publishing History* 4 (1978), 95–112.

41. Figures for 1783–86, from "Portie van Oom in de affaire," in LUL, Luzac, carton 30.

42. The letters of Pierre Gosse, Jr., publisher of the *Gazette de la Haye*, to STN show him offering them bulk orders of his paper for a third of the retail price. But the more successful *Gazette de Leyde* may have been able to negotiate a more favorable contract with its postal services. Gosse, letter of 31 Aug. 1770, in Bibliothèque publique et universitaire de Neuchâtel, STN Archive, Ms. 1159.

43. Article 2 of contract in LGA-VH, Z(2), no. 51.

44. Knappert, "Gedenksteen," 113.

Figure 2. Hypothetical annual balance sheet for the *Gazette de Leyde*

Income (gulden)		*Expenditures* (gulden)	
Subscriptions (5,000)	90,000	Wages[1]	c. 4,000
Advertisements	750	Paper[2]	c. 2,100
Total	90,750	Misc.[3]	500
		Correspondents[4]	9,000
		Payment to city	3,000
		Editor[5]	2,000
		Misc. losses[6]	500
		To. M. J. Luzac[7]	800
		Total	21,900

1. Based on wage rates for *Amsterdamsche Courant* in 1767, on the assumption that the paper employed one foreman at 10 gulden per week, four compositors at 8.5 gulden per week each, four pressmen at 6.5 gulden per week each, and one apprentice at 6 gulden per week. Figures in this and the following note from Eeghen, "Amsterdamsche Courant," 35–36.

2. In 1770, the *Amsterdamsche Courant* paid 36 stuivers (1.8 gulden) per ream for ordinary newsprint: 5,000 copies of the *Gazette de Leyde* came to 10 reams per issue, and there were 105 issues per year, making a total of 1,050 reams. I have assumed a price of 2 gulden per ream to simplify calculations.

3. Specified in the 1783 contract, LGA-VH, Z(2), no. 51.

4. In the 1780s, the Paris correspondent, Boyer, earned 1,500 gulden (3,000 livres) a year, and the equally active London correspondent presumably earned a comparable salary. If the paper maintained eight less-active correspondents paid 750 gulden a year (a figure extrapolated from the known payments to Baudus, the Hamburg correspondent, for 1794), the total in this category would have come to about 9,000 gulden a year. This may be the expenditure represented in Jean Luzac's notes on the paper's expenses for the years 1783–87 ("Portie van Oom in de affaire," LUL, Luzac, carton 30), which include an annual item, "Fraix et dépenses," which ranges from 7,500 to 10,000 gulden per year.

5. Figure guaranteed to Jean Luzac, beyond his share of the profits, under the 1783 contract.

6. Defaults from subscription agencies and advertisers. Figures based on figures shown in Luzac's notes on "Portie van Oom in de affaire."

7. The 1783 contract specified an annual payment to one Martha Jacob Luzac of 500 gulden plus the profit on one hundred subscriptions and one-third of the profit from advertising.

split the profits with their uncle, the two nephews earned close to half their original investment every year, and once they became the sole owners in 1787, they recouped more than 100 percent of their stake annually until the unforeseen events of the French Revolution drove profits down (see Table 3).

In addition to demonstrating that the Luzac brothers did very well running their newspaper, the figures in Table 3 show that the *Gazette de Leyde* was one of the most successful newspapers in the Western world. A major London daily, the *Morning Chronicle*, had a profit equivalent to 18,000 gulden in 1785, just about the same figure as the Leiden paper,

Table 3. Annual profit of *Gazette de Leyde*, 1783–1805[1] (gulden)

1783	13,999	1791	17,700	1799	9,300
1784	15,477	1792	17,600	1800	6,000
1785	17,010	1793	26,600	1801	6,900
1786	19,500	1794	22,700	1802	6,600
1787	22,900	1795	13,200	1803	7,600
1788	27,500	1796	15,300	1804	9,500
1789	29,400	1797	13,400	1805	6,500
1790	22,900	1798	10,100		

1. Figures from sheet headed "Portie van Oom in de affaire," apparently Jean Luzac's calculations of his uncle's share of the paper's profits in the four years from the time the nephews took over the running of the paper in 1783 to the death of the elder Etienne Luzac in January 1787 (in LUL, Luzac, carton 30) and from the figures the younger Etienne Luzac submitted to the Dutch government during negotiations for sale of the paper in 1807 (in LGA-VH, Z[2], no. 119). There is a small discrepancy in the figures for 1786, the only year for which the two sources overlap: Jean Luzac's detailed calculations give a profit figure of 18,947 gulden, whereas his brother's figures, which have clearly been rounded off, list 19,500 gulden, which approximates the figure that would result from adding Jean Luzac's total for unpaid bills from 1786 to his figure for net profits.

and in 1780 the *Gazette de France*, with 12,000 subscriptions, returned a profit equal to only 5,905 gulden. The *Courrier d'Avignon*'s annual profits never topped the equivalent of 10,000 gulden per year and they probably averaged considerably less.[45] The *Gazette de Leyde* was a very substantial enterprise, equal to the other major papers of the European world. Certainly it prospered so handsomely in the last years of the Old Regime that Jean and Etienne Luzac had very little reason to tinker with the journalistic formula that was bringing them such success. They accepted the technological restrictions that limited the paper's press run and the amount of news it could carry because they were thus able to make large profits on a modest investment and with very little risk.

45. Figures for *Morning Chronicle* from Ian R. Christie, *Myth and Reality in Late Eighteenth-Century British Politics* (Berkeley: University of California Press, 1970), 320; for *Gazette de France* see Denise Aimé Azam, "Le Ministère des Affaires étrangères et la presse à la fin de l'ancien régime," *Cahiers de la presse* 1 (1938), 430; for *Courrier d'Avignon* see Moulinas, *L'imprimerie*, 354–59. Both the *Gazette de France* and the *Courrier d'Avignon* had to pay large sums to the governments that licensed them; the *Morning Chronicle* and other British papers also paid heavily for the right to publish through the stamp tax and a steep tax on advertisements. But the *Gazette de Leyde* also paid the Leiden government handsomely for its privilege.

[6]

The *Gazette de Leyde*'s Readership

Copies of the *Gazette de Leyde* left Leiden to circle the world: from the Netherlands to Philadelphia, and via Vienna and Aleppo, Syria, to India. Subscribers were of course thinly and unevenly spread across the globe, and they made up a minority of the reading public even in those countries where the paper was most popular, but the steady flow of subscription orders, reflected in the paper's substantial profits, assured Luzac that there were eager recipients for his product.

Numbers and Distribution

The *Gazette de Leyde*'s total press run varied from year to year, depending on the public's interest in the paper's news and the nature of the competition. When Jean Luzac briefly experimented with leaving the paper to a hired editor, in the mid-1780s, the press run appears to have been around 4,200.[1] This put the paper in the same league as the most

1. When Antoine Cerisier was hired to edit the paper in 1785, his salary was set at 1,400 gulden a year, with a bonus of 50 gulden for each additional 100 subscriptions sold. If the base rate for his salary was calculated on the same basis of 50 gulden for each 100 subscriptions, the press run in 1785, when he received a 600 gulden bonus, would have been 4,000 copies per issue. If the 1,400 gulden payment to Cerisier listed for 1786 represented a bonus, the press run that year would have been 5,600. Figures from LUL, Luzac, carton 30, "Portie van Oom in de affaire," a set of figures for the paper's profits from 1783 to 1786. These figures are in the same range as those derived from records of the paper's payments to the Dutch post office for the mailing of copies. Dutch postal historian Overvoorde, using a figure of 10 grams per copy, calculates that for 1788, the paper's payment of 1,464 gulden represented postage for 7,330 copies per issue, although he notes that Luzac may have paid extra postage on copies sent to distant destinations.

successful Dutch-language papers, such as the *Oprechte Haarlemsche Courant*, whose press run was about 6,000, and the most successful London newspapers, whose sales were about 4,500 in this period. The *Gazette de Leyde*'s press run was considerably below that of the *Hamburg Correspondent*, whose 20,000 copies per issue probably made it the most widely read newspaper in the world up to 1789.[2]

The figure for the late 1780s represented a considerable increase over the sales in the early 1770s, when Jean Luzac took over the paper. Sales certainly rose during the years of the American war. The number of subscriptions in France alone had been only 287 copies in 1767, and 300 in 1773, but it climbed to 2,560 in 1778, slumping to 1490 when peace broke out in 1783.[3] The prerevolutionary crisis in France also stimulated sales. The paper's net profits rose nearly 50 percent from 1786, when they stood at 19,500 gulden, to 1789, when they reached 29,400 gulden, the paper's all-time high (see Table 3). Profits then dropped sharply in the first few years of the French Revolution, due to the loss of the French market, but the outbreak of war in 1792 brought profits of 26,600 gulden in 1793. The figure fell to 13,200 in 1795, however, and never rose above 15,300 again. Whether this reduction reflected falling sales, rising expenses, or both cannot be determined. During the Napoleonic period, the paper continued its decline. By 1810, when it had become an official publication of Louis Bonaparte's government, the press run had fallen to a mere 400.[4]

The total audience of the *Gazette de Leyde* was not tied to the number of copies printed in Leiden, however. In the first place, these were not the only copies in circulation. Throughout the paper's life, pirate reprints diminished the sales of the original; yet by offering distant subscribers a cheaper version, they probably increased its total readership. In 1791, Luzac complained that there were five or six such pirate editions.[5] The Vienna reprint, which appeared from 1786 to 1792, had an official privilege granted by Joseph II. In 1788, it had 219 subscribers outside of

(Overvoorde, *Postwezen*, 128). Calculations on the same basis give a figure of 5,382 copies per issue for 1787, not far from the estimate derived from the figures for Cerisier's salary if the 1786 payment of 1,400 gulden is interpreted as his bonus. A total circulation of between 5,000 and 7,000 copies per issue during the late 1780s thus seems a reasonable assumption.

2. The German pastor Wendeborn, the Hamburg paper's London correspondent during the 1780s, was told that the Hamburg paper reached a circulation of 21,000 during the American War of Independence. Gebhard F. A. Wendeborn, *D. Gebh. Fr. Aug. Wendeborn's Erinnerungen aus seinem Leben* (Hamburg: Bohn, 1813), 291. During the Napoleonic period, French sources put this paper's press run as high as 56,000. (AN, F 7 3461, anonymous note; a more detailed report after the French occupation of Hamburg in 1811 gives a figure of 20,000. AN, F 18 12, plaq. 4, report of 26 Aug. 1811.)

3. De Lormes to Luzac, letter of 14 July 1783, in LGA-VH, Z(2), no. 55.
4. AN, F 7 3459, police report, n.d. but 1810 or 1811.
5. Jean Luzac to Mercy d'Argenteau, 8 Feb. 1791, in LGA-VH, Z(2), no. 79.

Vienna, and sales within the capital were presumably at least as large.[6] Another counterfeit edition appeared in Naples.[7] Five counterfeit editions with an average press run of 400 copies would have boosted the total circulation of the paper to 7,000 to 9,000 during its peak years.

Moreover, parts of the paper's contents were disseminated through the reprinting of selected articles in other periodicals. Luzac and other editors had to contend with enterprises such as the Brussels-based *Esprit des Gazettes*, established in 1786 with the avowed purpose of "making available to everyone, at a bargain price, all the political news" by systematically pillaging the *Gazette de Leyde* and its competitors; the *Esprit des Gazettes* differed from other newspapers that lived by reprinting news from their rivals only in that it diligently listed the sources of all its articles.[8] Even those who could not read French sometimes found the *Gazette de Leyde*'s stories in their papers. During his term as secretary of state in the first Washington administration, Thomas Jefferson translated some of the *Gazette de Leyde*'s European reports for the Philadelphia *Gazette of the United States* and for several other papers, to offset what he believed were excessively anti-French articles reprinted from the London journals.[9] Through counterfeit editions and reprints of selected news items in other newspapers, Jean Luzac's news-gathering activities had an impact well beyond the circle of readers of the original edition.

Several readers undoubtedly saw each copy of the *Gazette de Leyde*, but it is difficult to calculate the exact extent of this multiplier effect. A copy sent to a large reading room, such as the Grand Société in The Hague with its 200 members, might have been scanned by as many as several dozen people, whereas a copy sent to a nobleman in the French countryside might serve no more than a handful. If one accepts a common estimate of 10 to 12 readers per copy for a typical eighteenth-century periodical, and if one takes the counterfeit editions of the paper into account, the total number of people who held a copy of each issue in their hands during the paper's peak years would have been about 50,000 to 100,000. Modest as this figure appears in comparison with the total readership of nineteenth-century or twentieth-century elite newspapers, it was enough to allow the *Gazette de Leyde* to serve as the medium for a common political culture spanning much of the European world.

The sales and readership of the *Gazette de Leyde* varied greatly from country to country. Before 1789, the paper appears to have circulated without censorship restrictions in almost all parts of Europe but it was most in demand in French-speaking countries and in countries with no

6. Strasser, *Die Wiener Presse in der josephinischen Zeit*, 39–40.
7. Castronovo, Ricuperati, and Capra, *La stampa italiana dal cinquecento all'ottocento*, 351.
8. Prospectus, *Esprit des Gazettes*, tipped in at front of v. 1, 1786, in University of Chicago copy.
9. Boyd, ed., *Jefferson*, 16:237n–47n.

significant political press of their own. It is no surprise that France was Luzac's largest single market. The extensive and systematic coverage given to the country's affairs and the lack of comparable newspapers published inside the country made the *Gazette de Leyde* the kingdom's "newspaper of record." Etienne Luzac's contract with the Dutch post office in 1772 indicated that more than two-thirds of the copies sent abroad at that date were headed for France and Brabant.[10] The French sales agent assured Luzac that its circulation there in the early 1780s was considerably higher than that of the other international gazettes, with the exception of the government-subsidized *Courrier de l'Europe*.[11] The figures for sales in France, cited earlier, indicate that peak circulation there during the American war was almost 2,500 copies, and the sharp drop in the paper's income from 1790 to 1792, reflecting the impact of the loss of the French market to the new domestic papers, is a measure of the paper's earlier dependence on its French readership.

The *Gazette de Leyde* also had readers in other regions of Europe where French was the common language. There was a regular subscription agent in Geneva, where the paper benefited from the absence of a local gazette and from the fact that local authorities had restricted the development of the Swiss press in general.[12] The paper printed occasional notices to subscribers in the Austrian Netherlands, which had a significant French-language press of its own but one that was prevented from covering local events as fully as many readers would have liked. But the paper also found readers in countries where only the educated elites could read it. In his survey of the European newspaper world, the German diplomat Joachim von Schwarzkopf made special note of the paper's presence in Spain and Portugal.[13] In Italy, the American representative William Short reported to Jefferson in 1788 that "the Leyden gazette is not so generally found in the coffee houses as I had imagined," but he did manage to procure copies that were less than two weeks old everywhere he stopped north of Rome.[14] Horace Walpole's correspondent Horace Mann read it regularly in Florence. Copies also went to the European merchant colonies in Turkey.[15]

The paper had a following in the German-speaking world, too, de-

10. Contract, 7 Mar. 1772, in AR, Derde Afdeling, Familiearchief Le Jeune (1747–1810), inv. no. 271. The contract was based on bundles of 30 Dutch pounds for France and Brabant, 8 pounds for the postal route via Maseyk (which served southern Germany, Austria, and Italy), and 6 pounds for the route via Emmerich (serving northern Germany and Scandinavia).

11. De Lormes to Jean Luzac, 14 July 1783, in LGA-VH, Z(2), no. 55.

12. Schwarzkopf, in *Allgemeiner Literarische Anzeiger* (1800), 1481–83.

13. Ibid., 1461, and (1801), 334–36.

14. William Short to Jefferson, 18 Oct. 1788, and 14 Jan. 1789, in Boyd, ed., *Jefferson*, 14:28.

15. Mann to Walpole, 23 July 1768 (23:77), 19 Oct. 1776 (24:250), 27 May 1783 (25:405) in W. S. Lewis, ed., *Horace Walpole's Correspondence* (New Haven: Yale University Press, 1960–). Schwarzkopf, in *Allgemeiner Literarische Anzeiger* (1800), 66.

spite the competition of French-language gazettes published along the Rhine and of the *Hamburg Correspondent*, the closest equivalent to the French-language international gazettes. The 1772 postal contract indicated that slightly more copies went to southern Germany and Austria than to Prussia and Scandinavia. A German satirical print of a newspaper reading room of 1788 clearly shows Luzac's journal along with the gazettes of Cologne and Cleves and a variety of German-language papers, and this reflected the actual practice of well-stocked reading rooms such as the Harmonie establishment in Hamburg.[16] German journalists routinely cited the paper as a publication that their readers would know at least by name. According to a magazine article of 1792, "a fashionable lady must have at least glanced at the latest numbers of the *Moniteur*, the *Journal de Paris*, or the *Gazette de Leyde*, before she goes to her tea-party."[17] The paper had some sales in Luzac's home country as well, but here, too, it had to contend with competition from well-informed papers in the language of the country.

The foreign markets that concerned Luzac most after France, however, were those in the Baltic states, even though sales there were much lower than in France. Poland, Sweden, and Denmark had only rudimentary domestic presses and the aristocracy read French. The paper's close relationship with reform-minded circles in Poland is well documented, and the paper became a subject of debate in the Diet in 1774.[18] Denmark, which lacked even an officially sponsored court gazette, and Sweden depended heavily on the German-language press for their news, but some French newspapers sold there as well.[19] A few copies of the *Gazette de Leyde* reached Russia, but the small potential audience and heavy censorship apparently kept the paper from finding much of a market there.

Of the major language areas of the Western world, the *Gazette de Leyde* seems to have been least successful in the English-speaking countries, despite Luzac's boast in one letter that the accuracy of his predictions of American success in the revolutionary war was bringing rising sales across the Channel.[20] The London papers were not Luzac's equals in obtaining thorough and accurate continental news, but they satisfied the demands of most of their audience. The *Gazette de Leyde*'s primary English audience was probably the diplomatic community and the editors of English newspapers. During and after the War of Independence,

16. Irene Jentsch, *Zur Geschichte des Zeitungslesens in Deutschland am Ende des 18. Jahrhunderts* (Ph.D. diss., Leipzig, 1937), 53.

17. *Journal des Luxus und des Moden*, 1792, cited in Elgar Blühm and Rolf Engelsing, eds., *Die Zeitung* (Bremen: Schünemann, 1967), 141–42.

18. Lojek, "International French Newspapers and Their Role in Polish Affairs during the Second Half of the Eighteenth Century," 54–64.

19. Schwarzkopf, in *Allgemeiner Literarische Anzeiger* (1800), 41–43, 49–51.

20. Notes in margin to letter of the English ambassador Joseph Yorke to the Dutch States-General, 25 May 1779, in LGA-VH, Z(2), no. 42.

American representatives on the continent arranged for the regular dispatch of a handful of copies to the Continental Congress's members back home, and Luzac sent copies to a few other individuals in the American states, but it is doubtful that the paper had any general readership in the New World, either.[21] Occasional subscriptions went to individuals in European colonies around the world, such as a certain Edmund Morris in Calcutta, whose brother William wrote to Luzac in 1787 saying that his brother, "being very desirous to have the earliest news from Europe, and being very partial to your Gazette," asked to have his copies sent via the English consul in Aleppo.[22] One of Luzac's friends later recalled "meeting at his house travelers arriving from America, from India, from China, who came to tell him how pleased they had been to find his paper in those distant countries, where it was their only way to find out about the political state of Europe."[23]

The French Revolution brought a sharp change in the paper's readership: it virtually lost its most important market. Major Paris reading rooms continued to subscribe to the *Gazette de Leyde*, and even some of the early Jacobin clubs received it, but the paper could hardly hope to compete in the general French market.[24] The paper survived this blow, and even prospered during the first years of the Revolution, because rising interest in the news elsewhere in Europe offset this loss. And before long the French Revolution created a new audience for the *Gazette de Leyde:* the French emigrés who formed colonies in towns all over Europe. These displaced aristocrats and well-to-do bourgeois were drawn from precisely the social groups that had always been most interested in the paper, and their precarious situation made them even more avid for news than they would normally have been. An advertisement for a German grammar in the paper in 1794 which began, "Since there are now many French who are obliged by existing circumstances to learn German," was obviously addressed to this group.[25] Even after the French invasion of the Netherlands and the proclamation of the Bata-

21. Dumas to Congress, 17 Apr. 1777, in AR, Dumas, carton I; Jefferson to John Jay, 17 June 1785, in Boyd, ed., *Jefferson*, 8:226; Benjamin Gerrish to Luzac, Boston, 23 Nov. 1782, in Huntington Library, Rufus King collection, RK 485.

22. William Morris to Luzac, 18 Oct. 1787, in Huntington Library, Rufus King collection, RK 487.

23. [Baudus], "Notice sur M. Luzac."

24. The *Gazette de Leyde* appears on the lists of titles available at two important Parisian reading rooms in 1791, the Chambre patriotique et littéraire and the Cabinet littéraire national. It was one of only two foreign papers available at the former institution, and one of six offered by the latter. Prospectuses in Newberry Library, French Revolution Collection. A study of Jacobin clubs' newspaper subscriptions in 1789–91 shows that four of them took the paper, compared with thirty-five that subscribed to the popular revolutionary *Annales patriotiques* and twenty-seven that took the Revolution's own "journal of record," the *Moniteur*. Michael L. Kennedy, *The Jacobin Clubs in the French Revolution: The First Years* (Princeton, N.J.: Princeton University Press, 1982), Appendix E.

25. *GL*, 16 Dec. 1794.

vian Republic, the paper continued to hold its own against the Paris press, particularly in the newly annexed Belgian departments of France where counterrevolutionary sentiment was strong. French authorities included it in a list of papers whose circulation on French soil was banned on 24 nivose, An VII, but a police report from Bruges six months later indicates that it was still reaching Belgian readers.[26] The Revolution thus altered the distribution of the *Gazette de Leyde*'s readership but did not reduce it so drastically that the paper's survival was threatened. Indeed, as late as 1807, Etienne Luzac was still confident that the paper could regain its prerevolutionary level of readership on the basis of markets in Belgium and the Rhineland if French political interference could be prevented.[27]

Readers' Interests

The people who sought out the *Gazette de Leyde*, like all eighteenth-century newspaper readers, had several motives. As the publisher of another French-language gazette of the period put it, people read newspapers because "a certain natural curiosity, on the one hand, and our interests, on the other . . . drive us to find out about events in which we have taken and are continuing to take part."[28] But the readers of the *Gazette de Leyde* were either more curious or took a stronger interest in public affairs than most of their contemporaries. They were among those whose interest in public events was so great that they "must have the latest news at all costs, and read the papers daily," rather than the broader public of "the curious who, either because of the number of other things they have to do or because of the location where they live, are not in a position to read all the papers."[29] These readers were of necessity fairly wealthy. An annual subscription to the *Gazette de Leyde* cost 36 livres a year in France, twice as much as the *Gazette de France* or the *Courrier d'Avignon*, four times as much as most of the small provincial *Affiches*, and many times the cost of an ordinary book. The paper's readers were also well educated and could read French. The paper presumed that its audience knew who the sovereigns and leading ministers of major European states were, and it assumed a familiarity with European geography. The dense columns of small type presupposed a readership thoroughly at home with the printed word.

Before 1789, these serious, educated readers shared a clear notion of

26. Documents in AN, F 7 3451.

27. Etienne Luzac, letter of 31 May 1807, in LGA-VH, Z(2), no. 118.

28. Prospectus, *Courier François en Italie* (Florence), 1779, cited in Morelli Timpanaro, "Persone e Momenti," 463.

29. Prospectus, *Esprit des Gazettes* (1786).

what a good newspaper should be. For these participants in the era's high culture, the ephemeral newspaper was by definition a lesser form of reading matter: as we have seen, even Jean Luzac himself had itemized "the shortcomings of this genre of publication." The standard wisdom held that newspapers were supposed to contain "materials for history"; they were supposed to serve as modest helps for the production of a more important genre of texts. Luzac expressed his distress at the way "the public's demand to have something new" prevented him from fulfilling this documentary function.[30] Even in their appearance, the newspapers of the continent, unlike their British contemporaries, continued to model themselves after books. The small, two-column format, and preprinted title pages allowed readers to have collections bound in volumes.

Although their enterprise was essentially secondary to the production of more prestigious books, journalists still aspired to certain ideals. Writing in the *Encyclopédie*, Voltaire maintained that "a good gazetteer should be promptly informed, truthful, impartial, simple, and correct in his style; this means," Voltaire added, "that good gazetteers are very rare."[31] Baron Bielfeld, author of a standard handbook for diplomats, echoed Voltaire in demanding that journalists limit themselves to "a clear, truthful and succinct narration of public events" and that they eschew all commentary on their news. "A gazetteer who comments is a vulgar person. His reflections are usually either biased, or dictated by corruption, or banal, or wrong." The eighteenth-century public did not trust journalists to shape its opinions: Bielfeld echoed the consensus in insisting that the journalist "should leave to his readers the business of making reflections."[32] Although much of the European press did contain satirical and anecdotal items about important people, it was generally held that these had no place in a proper newspaper: Voltaire added that "it is unnecessary to say that offensive language should never be employed, under any pretext."[33] To be sure, these austere prescriptions were often honored only sporadically. But the *Gazette de Leyde* prospered precisely because there were some readers who wanted a newspaper that seemed to conform to them.

Those who did want a serious newspaper included a number of sov-

30. Luzac to unidentified correspondent, n.d. but 1785–87, in LUL, Luzac, carton 28, no. 69.

31. Article "Gazetier," in Denis Diderot and Jean d'Alembert, eds., *Encyclopédie, ou Dictionnaire raisonné des sciences et des arts et des métiers*, 17 vols. (Paris: Lebreton, 1757–65), 7:535.

32. Jacob Friedrich von Bielfeld, *Institutions politiques*, 2d ed. (Leiden: Luchtmans, 1767–72), 2:369–70. On the period's general rejection of journalists' claims to guide public opinion, see Jack R. Censer, "The Self-Image of the Press: The Prospectus and the Revolutionary Reader," in Pierre Rétat, and Jean Sgard, eds., *La presse devant la Révolution, 1788–1793* (Lyon: Presses universitaires de Lyon, 1989).

33. Article "Gazette," in Diderot and d'Alembert, eds., *Encyclopédie*, 7:534.

ereigns and their familiars: Louis XVI was said to prefer the paper to all others; his aunt, Madame Victoire, had the French ambassador arrange for a personal subscription for her. In 1784 the French consul in Amsterdam undertook to obtain a bulk shipment of the paper to be given out to the courtiers at Versailles.[34] Walpole's correspondent Horace Mann reported that Leopold of Tuscany read it.[35] Intellectuals with an interest in politics kept up with it. The French philosophe Condorcet used it to keep abreast of the news during his trips away from Paris. From her exile in Switzerland, the Dutch-born Isabelle de Charrière followed events in her native country through its pages.[36]

Although little can be said about the mass of individual subscribers, since no subscription registers for the paper have survived, certain identifiable social and professional groups depended on its services. The *Gazette de Leyde* was required reading for all those involved in diplomacy and international affairs. Walpole's correspondent Horace Mann, the British representative at the court of Tuscany, Thomas Jefferson, the American ambassador in Paris, and all the other ambassadors, envoys, secretaries of legations, and hangers-on who clustered around Europe's dozens of large and small capitals relied on the press in general and on the *Gazette de Leyde* in particular for their overall news. "It had become . . . almost an official part of diplomacy. There was not a minister, not a statesman who did not prefer it to all others," a former correspondent for the paper recalled after Jean Luzac's death.[37] Wherever a diplomat might be posted, he needed to stay informed about events all over Europe, since, as the *Encyclopédie methodique*'s article on negotiations put it, "the different European states have so many exchanges and connections among themselves, that a change in any one of these states is almost always capable of affecting the security of others."[38]

Baron Bielfeld, as tutor to those entering a diplomatic career, told his pupils that "a negotiator must not neglect to read the public newspapers . . . , but since they are certainly not all equally good, one must make a choice." He recommended the Dutch papers, specifically including the *Gazette de Leyde*, as they were "less likely than all the others to

34. [Pidansat de Mairobert, attrib.], *Mémoires secrets*, 28:166 (8 Mar. 1785); instructions to ambassador, 1 Aug. 1772, in MAE, Corr. Pol.—Hollande, 524; Chevalier de Lironcourt to Ministry of Foreign Affairs, n.d., in Annie Versprille, "Oordeel over de Gazette de Leyde," *Jaarboekje voor Geschiedenis en Oudheidkunde van Leiden en Omstreken* 52 (1960), 160–61.

35. Mann to Walpole, 27 May 1783, in Lewis, ed., *Walpole Correspondence*, 25:405.

36. Condorcet to Mme Suard, n.d. but 1774, in BN, Ms. N.a.f. 23639, f. 192; Isabelle de Charrière, letters of 20 June 1784, February 1795, 2 Sept. 1799, in *Oeuvres complètes*, 10 vols. (Amsterdam: Van Oorschot, 1979–81), 2:626, 5:23, 621.

37. [Baudus], "Notice sur M. Luzac."

38. Jean-Nicolas Démeunier, in *Encyclopédie methodique. Economie politique et diplomatique* (Paris: Panckoucke, 1788), 3:406.

keep things quiet, or to disguise facts that may be disagreeable to certain governments."[39] Even though the diplomatic services of major governments were far more extensive than the network of correspondents that a newspaper could afford to maintain, newspapers such as the *Gazette de Leyde* filled major needs. They were frequently first with the news: Luzac's paper appeared twice a week, whereas French ambassadors normally wrote to Versailles only once a week. And a paper such as Luzac's solved the problem of communication among embassies in different countries.[40] According to one source, the Turkish government, which did not maintain regular embassies in the European capitals, had the *Gazette de Leyde* translated in order to keep up with foreign affairs.[41]

Military officers were another professional group with a strong interest in the *Gazette de Leyde*. Often stationed far from major capitals where decisions to make war were taken, they needed to know about any quarrels that might lead to war and were professionally interested in the events of any conflict. To advertise the value of the index they proposed to include with their paper, the creators of the *Esprit des Gazettes* cited the example of a reader who might want to know "what a commander in a particular campaign had done."[42] Eighteenth-century governments normally provided regular reports about the progress of their armies in the field, but these official sources were always suspected of following one writer's advice to not only "publicize a victory" but "to exaggerate it."[43] By bringing together the official bulletins of all combatants in one convenient place, the *Gazette de Leyde* offered readers who were or had been officers the opportunity to compare conflicting accounts and determine for themselves where the truth lay. The *Gazette de Leyde*'s military news was often provided by serving officers and was written for an audience familiar with the technical vocabulary; it presumed that readers would know the organizational structures of major European armies and be able to evaluate the competence of commanders on the basis of their maneuvers. Only in the course of the French revolutionary wars did the paper's military coverage take on a less technical tone and give some indication of the emotional intensity of the battles and of their broader political impact.

The *Gazette de Leyde*'s appeal to diplomats and military officers gave it a significant base of readers, but these groups were by no means the only ones interested in the high-quality information the paper purveyed.

39. Bielfeld, *Institutions politiques*, 2:369.
40. On the French diplomatic service's internal communications, see *Les affaires étrangères et le corps diplomatique français*, 1:210–13.
41. [Baudus], "Notice sur M. Luzac."
42. Prospectus, *Esprit des Gazettes* (1786).
43. Article "Bataille," in Louis de Keralio, ed., *Encyclopédie methodique. Art militaire* (Paris: Panckoucke, 1784), 1:231.

Certainly it held a strong interest for officials in the steadily swelling ranks of Europe's numerous bureaucracies. Even those in states with strong censorship laws had other means of keeping up with events taking place in their own country, but they had an interest in knowing what was happening in other countries, and also in keeping up with what was being reported publicly about their own government.

The paper was probably equally important to rentiers, those who invested in governments rather than working for them. This was a particularly important social group in the Netherlands, whose capital market remained the most important in Europe down to the time of the revolutionary wars. Dutch investors had access to a sophisticated economic press, mostly in their own language, which provided them with up-to-date information on market conditions, including the latest changes in commodity and stock prices in London, Hamburg, and other major financial centers.[44] But then as now, investors needed the best possible political and diplomatic intelligence, to enable them to forecast events that might affect the market. As historian James Riley remarks, "Such news, and in particular informed speculation about the prospects of war and peace, was important for investment planning."[45] It was this need for accurate foreign news that provided the French-language *Gazette de Leyde* with a steady market in the Netherlands itself, but the rentier class was an international phenomenon, and there is no doubt that part of the paper's appeal in France, as well as in other wealthy communities such as Geneva, was its success in giving investors the confidence that they could make informed choices.

Another specialized readership was made up of professionals in the collection and distribution of news. Like most other eighteenth-century editors, Luzac undoubtedly exchanged copies of his paper for other publications as part of his own news-gathering operation. But he certainly did not provide free copies to the owners of coffeehouses, reading rooms, and other places where readers who did not purchase individual copies came to find newspapers. In Europe as a whole, the number of reading rooms at the time of the French Revolution was probably more than 1,000, and the *Gazette de Leyde* and other international papers were stocked in the larger and more sophisticated ones. Paris alone had more than 600 cafés, and Louis-Sébastien Mercier complained that while literature was discussed in a few of them, "in most, the gossip is even more boring: it is always about the gazette."[46] A number of literary

44. Larry Neal, "The Flow of Financial Information in the Eighteenth Century: London and Amsterdam," paper presented to the Social Science History Association, Chicago, November 1985.
45. James C. Riley, *International Government Finance and the Amsterdam Capital Market, 1740–1815* (New York: Cambridge University Press, 1980), 38.
46. Mercier, *Tableau*, 1:227.

sources from the period depict the *Gazette de Leyde* being read in such establishments. In 1788, Isabelle de Charrière began a play set in a Parisian *cabinet de lecture* by having one character ask another, "Would you be interested in reading the most recent *Gazette de Leyde*?" The author of the fictionalized memoirs of Countess de la Motte, one of the main figures in the Diamond Necklace scandal, had the countess's husband make a special trip from Edinburgh to Glasgow where he had "remarked that a certain café received the *Gazette de Leyde*" in order to consult its coverage of his wife's trial.[47] Such fictional depictions had a strong base in reality: the *Gazette de Leyde* appears in the list of journals featured in a number of prerevolutionary reading rooms, such as the Cabinet politique et littéraire of Angers.[48]

Diplomats, military officers, rentiers, and reading room and coffee-house owners provided the *Gazette de Leyde* with a core of regular subscribers. A less stable market of general readers read the papers more out of curiosity than necessity; their interest in the press rose and fell depending on the nature of the news. The number of such readers was certainly significant for the paper's circulation. An exasperated Dutch Patriot critic accused Luzac of neglecting the serious issues of Dutch politics in the 1780s in order to "pique the curiosity of the public with silly stories like that of the Diamond Necklace . . . [Luzac] seized this opportunity to fill his paper up with such stuff, and that gained him 500 extra subscriptions."[49]

Whether attracted by professional interest or curiosity, the readers of the *Gazette de Leyde* came from the wealthiest strata of the European aristocracy and bourgeoisie. The *Gazette de Leyde*'s advertising was unquestionably aimed at this "up-scale" market. A statistical analysis of the paid advertisements printed in the last trimester of 1787 shows that the largest category of commercial advertising in the paper had to do with investment opportunities and announcements directed at holders of various governments' bond issues. A third of the advertisements in the paper fell into this category. Just over a quarter were placed by booksellers, but what the *Gazette de Leyde* promoted was not the common run of new titles. It did advertise specifically political books, but it was equally likely to announce auctions of rare book collections, of interest primarily to wealthy amateurs rather than to ordinary readers. The patent-medicine ads ubiquitous in the eighteenth-century European

47. Isabelle de Charrière, "Attendez revenez ou les delais cruels," (1788), in *Oeuvres complètes*, 7:115; *Mémoires justificatifs de la Comtesse de Valois de la Motte, écrit par elle-même* (London: n.p., 1789), 111.
48. François Lebrun, "Une source d'histoire sociale: La presse provinciale à la fin de l'ancien régime. Les 'Affiches d'Angers' (1773–1789)," *Mouvement social*, no. 40 (1962), 62, advertisement for 1779.
49. Dumont-Pigalle, "Contre Luzac," in AR, DP, carton 59.

press were also common in the *Gazette de Leyde*—these preparations were among the few products that interested members of all social classes—but the enticements to bid on jewels from the estate of a titled French aristocrat, the ads for costly French perfumes, and the come-ons for fancy Dutch tulip bulbs clearly were meant for those with substantial discretionary income. The occasional real estate advertisements in the paper almost always promoted seigneurial estates or substantial town-houses. As an advertising medium, the *Gazette de Leyde* evidently ap-pealed above all to entrepreneurs, primarily Dutchmen and Parisians, who were interested in improving the life-styles of the rich and famous, rather than to those seeking to extend the benefits of commercialization to more humble folk. Until the outbreak of the French Revolution, then, the *Gazette de Leyde*'s audience consisted of Europe's cosmopolitan elite, aristocrats and bourgeoisie with a strong interest in political, diplomatic, and military events.

The Art of Reading a Gazette

Like a book, a newspaper "can be read in many ways."[50] Unfortu-nately, we have all too few testimonies to the ways in which the *Gazette de Leyde*'s readers engaged themselves with their newspaper. Unquestion-ably newspapers were read very differently from books. They were by their nature ephemeral works, appreciated only if they were fresh. As Mercier noted, "These details . . . that are so much in demand today, will be completely without interest in two weeks."[51] Some readers obviously did value their copies of Luzac's paper as a permanent record, else the bound collections preserved in libraries today would not exist, but such serious readers were a minority, and only a reader with a strong profes-sional incentive, such as the American ambassador to the Netherlands William Vans Murray, would go to the extent of making a personal index to his collection.[52]

Readers who wanted the latest news were likely to set aside scheduled times to read newspapers, times regulated by the predictable schedules of publication and mail delivery. Unlike the book, which accommodated itself to the reader's schedule, the newspaper forced the reader to com-ply with its schedule. In some cases, a reading group banded together to share the cost of a newspaper subscription and members each had a set time during the day to read the shared copy, before handing it on to the

50. Roger Chartier, *Lectures et lecteurs dans la France d'ancien régime* (Paris: Seuil, 1987), 165.
51. Mercier, *Tableau*, 5:303.
52. "Diary," vol. for 1798, in William Vans Murray papers, LC.

next subscriber.[53] Advertisements for newspaper subscriptions in the prerevolutionary era, before daily papers became common in the French-speaking world, regularly listed the days of the week on which issues would be distributed, and coffeehouse and reading room subscribers undoubtedly knew when they would find new issues in their favorite haunts. Newspaper readers were thus time-conscious readers; newspaper reading served to integrate them into the broader flow of public time, rather than serving, like book reading, as an escape into a private realm divorced from external constraints.

The newspaper integrated its reader into the public realm, but readers understood that any one periodical could give them only an incomplete picture of that public world. Whether they read their newspapers in public, at a café or reading room, or privately at home, dedicated readers rarely limited themselves to a single periodical. The philosophe Condorcet, away from Paris during a vacation, wrote to a friend that "with the daily sheet . . . , the *Petites Affiches* . . . and the *Gazette de Leyde* . . . , I occupied myself for the whole morning."[54] Condorcet's three periodicals offered three different and complementary kinds of content, but readers often perused several titles offering the same type of content for the purpose of making a critical comparison. The Paris bookseller Siméon-Prosper Hardy recorded one instance of such comparative reading involving the *Gazette de Leyde* in his journal. He had been "singularly struck" by the conflicting accounts of an insurrection on the island of Malta that appeared in the *Gazette de Leyde* and the *Gazette de France*. "How can one reconcile two reports of the same event that are so much opposed to each other, and avoid the natural idea that a partisan bias must have influenced one writer or another? . . . most of the intelligent readers will not make up their minds until more information is available."[55] Serious readers regarded any one newspaper, including the *Gazette de Leyde*, as potentially incomplete; they exercised their critical faculties to determine what was true and what was false.

Having perused the texts of various journals, the readers of the eighteenth century were eager to discuss what they had read. Most depictions of newspaper reading from the period show readers in company. Either one member of the group reads a paper aloud to the others, or members of the group combine reading and talk. Being up on the latest

53. Jentsch, *Zur Geschichte des Zeitungslesens*, 37.

54. Condorcet to Mme Suard, n.d. but 1774, in BN, Ms. N.a.f. 23639, f. 192. The *feuille du jour* that Condorcet refers to may have been a manuscript newsletter; there was no daily printed newspaper in France before the establishment of the *Journal de Paris* in 1777.

55. Hardy, "Mes Loisirs," entry for 23 Oct. 1775, in BN, Ms. fr. 6682. In this case, Hardy preferred the version printed in the *Gazette de France*, more anticlerical than the Leiden paper's version. As it happens, Jean Luzac himself later decided that his report of this incident had been misleading. Letter to Grand Master of the Order of Malta, 12 Dec. 1775, in LGA-VH, Z(1), no. 37.

"The Newspaper Feast" ("Die Zeitungs-Schmaus"). German satirical engraving, 1788. Note the donkey at right representing a newspaper editor, ingesting newsletters and excreting "bulletins" ready for publication. The *Gazette de Divers Endroits* on the wall at lower left is probably meant to represent the *Gazette de Leyde*. Courtesy of Dr. Martin Welke, Deutsche Zeitungsmuseum.

events was an essential part of eighteenth-century sociability. As the marquis de Caraccioli wrote in 1777, "Whoever does not read gazettes and magazines, might as well consider himself left out of the political and literary world."[56] Mercier ridiculed the Parisian consumers of *nouvelles* who studied the newspapers "like a lesson they need to memorize" and could then be overheard "talking about cities, fortresses, strongpoints . . . without knowing where they are or what country they belong to," but he admitted that this political news was the main substance of Parisian public conversation.[57] Travel writers made the same point about other parts of Europe, such as the Netherlands.[58]

The natural extension of this process was for the readers to communi-

56. Louis-Antoine de Caraccioli, *Paris, le modèle des nations étrangères, ou l'Europe française* (Venice and Paris: Duchesne, 1777), 227–28.

57. Louis-Sébastien Mercier, *Les entretiens du Palais-Royal* (Paris: Buisson, 1786), 186.

58. Grabner, *Briefe über der vereinigten Niederlände*, 285.

cate to the editors of their preferred periodicals the result of their reflections on its content. This dialogue between readers and journalists was a common feature of many eighteenth-century periodicals, but it was not characteristic of the *Gazette de Leyde*. Jean Luzac did not publish readers' letters on a regular basis, and the tiny sample of readers whose letters were referred to—only twenty-five from January 1787 to July 1789—tended to be individuals who had been mentioned in the paper, rather than ordinary subscribers. Luzac's extensive correspondence bears no trace of contact with ordinary readers who were not also sources of political information. Prominent intellectual figures, such as Madame de Charrière, occasionally wrote letters to the editor, but these were not published.[59] Since subscriptions to the paper were handled by agents in their respective countries, the Luzacs did not even receive routine letters of renewal from individual subscribers. Their foreign subscription agents might forward a general impression of audience reaction to the paper, as the French agent De Lormes did in 1783, when he told Jean Luzac that "I have always heard your work praised in general, although I meet many people who complain that the type size is very small."[60] The Luzacs had a general conception of what readers wanted to find in a newspaper: in 1772, they justified their resistance to French government pressures in terms of their obligation to meet their readers' demands, and, as we have seen, Jean Luzac expressed frustration at the way readers' expectations forced him to be a journalist rather than a historian.[61] But what the Luzacs were responding to was an abstract notion of their readers' interests, communicated indirectly through sales figures. They had little direct contact with their widely scattered audience.

The Luzacs were more responsive, of course, when the "reader" of their paper was a sovereign. The occasional editor's notes repudiating reports published a few issues previously were the public signs of this unequal dialogue between the *Gazette de Leyde* and its most powerful readers. Rulers and ministers might demand such retractions for their own reasons, or to ward off complaints from influential individuals and groups in their own country. Luzac and other journalists, dependent on governments for information and for the opportunity to sell their papers, rarely resisted these pressures; their general readers probably knew what to make of these forced retractions.[62] This distinction between the paper's responsiveness to public authorities and its indif-

---

59. Isabelle de Charrière to *Gazette de Leyde*, 20 June 1784, in Charrière, *Oeuvres*, 2:626.
60. De Lormes to Luzac, 14 July 1783, in LGA-VH, Z(2), no. 55.
61. Etienne Luzac to Desnoyers, 28 May 1772, in ibid., Z(1), no. 34; Luzac to unidentified correspondent, in LUL, Luzac, carton 28, no. 69.
62. Jeroom Vercruysse, "La réception politique des journaux de Hollande, une lecture diplomatique," in Hans Bots, ed., *La diffusion et la lecture des journaux de langue française sous l'ancien régime* 39–47.

ference to the private members of civil society who made up its ordinary
readership reflected the difference between the eighteenth-century political gazette and the literary journal. The gazette was part of public life,
in an era when rulers were the only acknowledged participants in political dialogue; the literary journal dealt with matters that were recognized
as open for discussion by private individuals. The very existence of such
newspapers as the *Gazette de Leyde* indicated that this distinction was not
absolute: by making political news available to anyone with the price of a
subscription, Luzac's paper and its rivals gave private members of civil
society the raw material for critical judgments of their rulers. But the
paper's refusal to publicize the "public opinion" that emerged from
these private discussions symbolized its continued adherence to a political order in which authority was not formally derived from popular
consent. In reading the *Gazette de Leyde*, ordinary subscribers were simultaneously admitted to the realm of public affairs and yet reminded of
their powerlessness to affect it. This was a situation that became increasingly difficult to accept as the paper itself, through its content,
emphasized the importance of the events shaking the European world
in the 1770s and 1780s.

[7]

The *Gazette de Leyde* and the Crises of the 1770s

The year 1772, in which the elder Etienne Luzac summoned his nephew Jean to take over the editorship of the *Gazette de Leyde*, was a year during which the paper had many crises to report to its widely dispersed readers. In four states—France, Sweden, Denmark, and Poland—fundamental principles of Europe's long-standing order seemed threatened by governments grasping for unrestrained power. According to historian Franco Venturi, the "republican forms of government and those that protected freedom seemed increasingly unable to resist the thrust of absolutism, of standing armies, of bureaucracy, of the diplomacy of countries where power was the most centralized."[1]

Contemporary observers recognized these disparate events as part of a larger whole. A critic of the measures undertaken in France to strengthen royal authority in 1771 made a direct connection between affairs in his own country and Gustav III's coup in Sweden the following year, accusing the French government of revealing its own secret intentions "by its care in propagating the *doctrine of despotism*, by thus publicizing the acts of other rulers." Linguet claimed that the partition of Poland had marked the moment at which "the terrible principle that force is the strongest argument of kings, so often practiced but always so carefully disguised, was for the first time exposed and put into practice openly and without concealment."[2]

---

1. Franco Venturi, *Settecento riformatore* (Turin: Einaudi, 1976–84), 3:xiii.

2. *Journal historique*, 3:254 (8 Sept. 1772); *Annales politiques*, 1:78 (Apr. or May 1777). In fact, there was a very real connection between the French and Swedish events: the French government had supported Gustav III's plan and provided funds for him. Orville Murphy, *Charles Gravier, Comte de Vergennes* (Albany: State University of New York Press,

Etienne Luzac, who had lent the columns of his newspaper to the defenders of the French parlements for more than twenty years, and whose concern with constitutional liberties in other states had been equally evident, was certainly not indifferent to these crises; his nephew was to engage himself even more deeply in them. The events of 1772 launched the younger Luzac into an intimate relationship with the revolutions that shook European civilization for the next twenty-five years. As he set about chronicling the complex events of the age of revolutions, Jean Luzac found himself straining the limits within which the European press had learned to operate in its first century and a half of existence. As scrupulous as he might be in assembling the information he published, he was simultaneously involving himself in the events his reports described: he had increasing difficulty maintaining the appearance of impartiality that justified his paper's existence in the face of established governments' claims of a right to control the news. Luzac's correspondence allows us to follow the drama of his efforts to maintain the existence and the reputation of his newspaper and to promote causes he deeply believed in during those decades in which both the European world and the world of journalism were profoundly transformed.

The First Crisis of Liberty, 1772–1774

The crisis of constitutional freedom in European politics in the early 1770s was not just a news story for the *Gazette de Leyde:* it was also a direct threat to what Etienne Luzac had made of the newspaper since he had become its owner in 1751. For twenty years, the elder Luzac had labored to make his publication the best source of political news on the continent, and for twenty years, he had quietly but firmly placed it on the side of those he considered the true defenders of ordered liberty in each major European country. The most long-lasting of these commitments had been his identification with the French parlements in their seemingly unending series of confrontations with the French crown after 1751. Throughout this period, the *Gazette de Leyde* had faithfully reprinted the parlementary remonstrances that constituted the refractory judges' main form of propaganda, and its news stories had consistently reflected a conviction that these judicial institutions were an essential safeguard of French liberty. The paper had documented and applauded

---

1982), 184–201. Linguet's comments on Poland were paradoxical, in that he had actually put forward his own plan for a partition of the country under French direction in 1771 and in that he was normally a proponent of absolutism, but he nevertheless recognized the significance of what had taken place in 1772–74.

the parlements' successful campaign for the abolition of the Jesuit Order; it had given sympathetic coverage to the parlements' resistance to
new taxes in the wake of the Seven Years' War, remarking that the
judges "have redoubled their efforts to maintain the splendor of the
crown, without crushing the subjects under new burdens."[3]

In 1765, when the French government became locked in a struggle
with the parlement of Brittany, the paper took up the Breton cause,
publishing inflammatory texts in which the judges of the various parlements identified themselves as the only true defenders of the nation's
freedoms.[4] As this *affaire de Bretagne* dragged on and became more
embittered, the paper publicized the increasingly shrill remonstrances
in which the parlementary magistrates denounced the French government, culminating in the Paris Parlement's vehement protest of 6 September 1770 against "the multiplicity of acts committed by an unrestrained power against the spirit and the letter of the fundamental laws
of the French monarchy" which demonstrated "a premeditated project
to change the form of government and substitute for the equitable force
of the law the unregulated movements of an arbitrary power."[5] From
this point, events in France moved rapidly to a crisis: on 7 December
1770, Louis XV's chancellor, Maupeou, forced the Paris Parlement to
register an edict disavowing all the court's attempts to restrict the king's
powers, and when the judges protested by declaring a judicial strike,
they were arrested and exiled on 20 January 1771.[6]

The Maupeou "coup" did not immediately change the tone of the
Gazette de Leyde's French news coverage. The paper sided emphatically
with the exiled judges. It announced that no one in Paris believed that
the government could force through its "morally impossible plan for a
new court of justice," and it condemned the harsh treatment of the
parlementaires, "stuck away in villages where they can hardly find anything to eat."[7] But Chancellor Maupeou and his ministerial colleagues,
the abbé Terray and the duc d'Aiguillon, intended to go beyond the
measures their predecessors had taken in dealing with the parlements

3. *GL*, 2 Sept. 1763 (Paris, 26 Aug.).
4. Typical was the remonstrance of the Metz parlement in 1765, which asserted that the
cause of the parlement of Rennes was that of all the courts, and expostulated that "if a
spirit of indifference [to public affairs] is substituted for the spirit of patriotism, France will
continue to have inhabitants, but it will cease to have citizens." Printed in *GL*, 20 Aug. 1765
(Paris, 12 Aug.).
5. Ibid., 18 Sept. 1770 (Paris, 10 Sept.).
6. There has been a considerable outpouring of recent literature on this "Maupeou
coup." For a brief summary of events, see Durand Echeverria, *The Maupeou Revolution*
(Baton Rouge: Louisiana State University Press, 1985), 1–34. A brilliant but regrettably
unpublished look at the political causes behind the "coup" is Martin Mansergh, "The
Revolution of 1771, or the Exile of the Parlement of Paris" (Ph.D. diss., Oxford University,
1973).
7. *GL*, 22 Feb. 1771 (Paris, 15 Feb.).

and their extraterritorial journalistic allies. The duc d'Aiguillon told the French ambassador in The Hague, "It would be very desirable if the Dutch gazettes were more circumspect than they are concerning the details about our internal affairs with which they fill their papers. If they are not more careful and more measured in their reports, they will force us to prohibit the introduction of their papers into the kingdom."[8] Several foreign gazettes were banned altogether, and the *Gazette de Leyde*'s issue of 30 July 1771 bore mute witness to the effectiveness of the French government's pressures. The paper, which until then had been full of reprinted remonstrances denouncing the court reform plan, suddenly fell silent on French affairs. For the next two and a half years, the *Gazette de Leyde* could do little more than print the official edicts put out by the ministers and the remodeled "Maupeou parlements."

Behind the scene, Etienne Luzac exchanged angry letters with the French ambassador in The Hague, complaining about the way in which the Maupeou government was changing the traditional rules of the journalistic game. "For more than a century, . . . the authors of periodicals have been able to publish edicts, remonstrances, and other pieces relative to political matters," he protested. "I have done so myself for fifty years and no minister has ever taken offense." He pleaded for the French government to consider "the delicacy of my situation. How can I satisfy the readers, on the one hand, who want to be accurately informed about political affairs, and on the other hand, those who are involved in these affairs? If a public newspaper leaves out everything the people in high office in all European countries would like kept secret, would this paper deserve the public's confidence and esteem? Would it keep any of its readers?"[9] But the French government remained implacable. The French ambassador warned Etienne Luzac, "If you do not change your correspondents, you will lose your readers permanently,"[10] and the *Gazette de Leyde* had to recognize that if the restructuring of the French government undertaken by Maupeou and his colleagues succeeded, the scope of the journalistic freedom permitted to the extraterritorial press would be reduced for good.

Meanwhile, other pressures on the *Gazette de Leyde* intensified. The Danish government complained vociferously about the paper's refusal to endorse the charges brought against the arrested minister Struensee, whose reforming efforts fell victim to a palace coup in February 1772.[11]

8. Aiguillon to Noailles, 28 Apr. 1771, in MAE, Corr. Pol.—Hollande, 523.
9. Etienne Luzac to Desnoyers, secretary of the French embassy in The Hague, 5 July 1772, 27 May 1772, in LGA-VH, Z(1), no. 34.
10. Desnoyers to Etienne Luzac, 27 May 1772, in MAE, Corr. pol.—Hollande, 524.
11. The French ambassador in The Hague reported that the Danes had singled out the *Gazette de Leyde* for special attention in this regard. Desnoyers to Aiguillon, 17 July 1772, in MAE, Corr. Pol.—Hollande, 524.

The paper's judgment on the fallen minister had been nuanced, concluding that his reforms had been motivated by good intentions "but the changes were too sudden and carried out too brusqucly."[12] But this did not satisfy the victors in Copenhagen. In response, Etienne Luzac warned the Danes that he had already rejected similar complaints from France. "You would not want an honest man to act like the most vile populace or the most insipid flatterers, by judging a minister simply because he is a prisoner," Etienne Luzac wrote to the Danish minister in The Hague, ending with the emphatic declaration, "I will never depart from the truth, either out of enmity or from a desire to please men in high places."[13]

The paper made no effort to conceal its condemnation of the hasty execution of Struensee, saying that his conduct on the scaffold disproved the charges that he was an atheist and a libertine, and labeling the whole sequence of events in the Scandinavian kingdom "this tragic affair."[14] The Danish authorities continued to complain, finally driving Etienne Luzac to tell the Danish ambassador that if he acceded to Copenhagen's demands, "it would be a major point gained, especially for those who fear that their conduct cannot stand the light of day, and I would invite all the Oriental princes to come learn from our reports political lessons and principles of which they have certainly been ignorant up to now."[15] Denmark was small and relatively powerless, so the *Gazette de Leyde* could afford this haughty tone, but two years of such exchanges could only contribute to the editor's sense that not only liberty but his own publication were under siege. Gustav III's coup against the aristocratic faction in the Swedish Diet in 1772 brought the paper into conflict with one more northern court. As in the case of Denmark, the paper did not openly condemn the changes, but it explicitly warned readers not to accept everything the victors said against the defeated party. "As in all revolutions, the people of Sweden gives the appearance of accepting the change that has just occurred with joy," one of the *Gazette de Leyde*'s early reports from Hamburg began, "but it has been learned that the new form of government has been rejected in several places, among others in Gothenburg."[16]

Even more than Denmark and Sweden, however, it was Poland that preoccupied the paper after it was forced to mute its coverage of French events. The paper's interest in Polish politics was not new. Even if Dutch republicans could be forgiven for not wanting to acknowledge the sim-

12. *GL*, 4 Feb. 1772 (Leiden, 3 Feb.).

13. Etienne Luzac to De la Pottrie, letters of ? Mar. 1772 and 13 Mar. 1772, in LGA-VH, Z(1), nos. 33, 34.

14. *GL*, 15 May 1772 (Hamburg, 8 May).

15. Etienne Luzac to Danish ambassador, 14 Apr. 1774, in LGA-VH, Z(1), no. 34.

16. *GL*, 22 Sept. 1772 (Hamburg, 15 Sept.).

ilarities between the two countries' weak central institutions, the Netherlands was vitally interested in Polish trade and the fate of the Polish
kingdom was always a matter of immediate concern to the Dutch. When
Stanislas-August Poniatowski—who had been impressed by visits to the
Netherlands as a young man—came to the Polish throne in 1764 and
began to try to reform the country's archaic institutions, the *Gazette de
Leyde* printed coverage supportive of his efforts.[17] At the beginning of
1768, it began its reporting of a new session of the Polish Diet with the
remark, "What is now happening in this Kingdom marks a new epoch
for us in this century of reform."[18] By 1772, the paper recognized that
Polish reform was going to have to be purchased at the price of cessions
of territory to the kingdom's three powerful absolutist neighbors, Prussia, Russia, and Austria. The *Gazette de Leyde* made itself a conduit for
King Stanislas-August's hopes to achieve significant internal reforms
that would revitalize the country and, to some extent, offset the disaster
of the First Partition. With the king himself arranging to supply the
paper with articles, it is not surprising that the paper expressed the hope
that his program would succeed and "make the basis of this government
more conformable to reason and order. . . . Polish freedom, that is, the
despotism of the magnates, may suffer as a result of the project attributed to the Allied Powers, but true freedom and justice will rejoice in
advance at the destruction of these pretended rights, which outrage
humanity."[19]

While the paper was careful to avoid outspoken criticism of the partitioning powers, it was unmistakably sympathetic with the cause of Polish
independence and sought to remind the states of western Europe that
they had at least an economic stake in Polish freedom: "The trading
nations cannot help being alarmed at the possible disappearance of one
of the principal branches of their commerce, and at the disruption or
total cut-off of exchanges by arrangements contrary to liberty, without
which trade cannot survive."[20] The paper's coverage served to counter
the propaganda in favor of Prussia and Russia emanating from many of
the leading French philosophes.[21] This position matched the policy of
the French government as well, which viewed the First Partition with
alarm but was unable to prevent it; at a time when the paper was in
potential conflict with Versailles over its attitude toward French affairs,

17. Jean Fabre, *Stanislas-Auguste Poniatowski et l'Europe des lumières* (Paris: Les Belles
Lettres, 1952), 181, 184.
18. *GL*, 5 Jan. 1768 (Warsaw, 15 Dec. 1767).
19. Ibid., 9 June 1772 (from the Vistula, 28 May). On the paper's connection with
Stanislas-August in this period, see Fabre, *Stanislas-Auguste*, 475.
20. *GL*, 30 Nov. 1773 (Poland, 15 Nov.).
21. On the extent and effects of the philosophes' support for their heroes Frederic II
and Catherine II, see Fabre, *Stanislas-Auguste*, 359.

the coincidence of its views with those of the French over the Polish issue may have helped smooth over the difficulties between France and the Luzacs.

Unable to mount a frontal assault on Poland's foreign enemies—although its coverage inspired a vehement Prussian protest—the *Gazette de Leyde* distinguished itself by its ferocity toward their agents within the Polish Diet.[22] Its main target was Adam Poninski, whom it accurately identified as the principal Russian agent in that body. Although the Diet sessions in 1773 were supposed to be secret, the paper managed through its connection with Stanislas-August to obtain summaries of the debates and texts of some major speeches, including Poninski's.[23] The king's opponents had destroyed all hostile newspapers in the country, leaving only one pliable journal there.[24] This meant that the *Gazette de Leyde* and the *Courier du Bas-Rhin*, with which Stanislas-August had entered into arrangements in late 1772, had to serve as the king's main organs, not only for appealing to foreign public opinion but for addressing Poles who were able to read French.[25] The *Gazette de Leyde* was sufficiently successful in this role for Poninski to denounce it openly in the Diet, which duly voted to ban the paper's circulation in Poland. Writing in his own name, the paper's editor responded to the news of this ban with an even more explicit denunciation of Poninski for lining his own pockets at his country's expense: "One needs considerable resources to rise so quickly from a mediocre situation to the most magnificent opulence." And, referring to the dismissal of the unpopular French ministers d'Aiguillon, Maupeou, and Terray after Louis XV's death in 1774, the paper warned Poninski that "there is an end to all things, and . . . disgraces are all the more striking, when the motives that inspire them need no justification."[26]

From Warsaw, the outraged Poninski appealed to the Estates of Holland to take action against the editor of the *Gazette de Leyde*, who "instead of showing the natural comprehension of one republican for another, has continually put the most innocent actions in the most odious light."[27] The Luzacs, who had just witnessed the disgrace of their enemies in France, seized the opportunity to respond aggressively: they answered Poninski's one-page letter of complaint with a twenty-four-

22. Thulemeyer (Prussian ambassador to The Hague) to States-General, 29 Dec. 1774, in LGA-VH, Z(1), no. 36.

23. *GL*, 21 May 1773 (Warsaw, 5 May); and 8 June 1773 (Poland, 21 May).

24. Julien Grossbart, "La presse polonaise et la Révolution française," *Annales historiques de la Révolution française* 14 (1937), 143.

25. Łojek, "International French Newspapers and Their Role in Polish Affairs during the Second Half of the Eighteenth Century," 60.

26. *GL*, 6 Sept. 1774 (Leiden, 5 Sept.).

27. Poninski, letter of 19 Sept. 1774, in LGA-VH, Z(1), no. 35.

page statement of principles and an additional eight pages of hand-copied citations from other European newspapers. The Polish count was not "a sacred person," and the Luzacs demanded to know "where the law of nature states that no one can speak critically of him."28

Located far from the scene, the *Gazette de Leyde* could not really hope to affect the outcome of the Polish crisis; its pro-Polish publicity was no match for the armed might of the partitioning powers. But its narration of the Polish crisis embarrassed and irritated the Polish agents of the partitioning powers, and served to make the opponents of partition appear as models for emulation elsewhere because of their willingness to put the defense of their country's independence above selfish private interests. Casting the Polish Patriots as heroes, the paper helped offset the admiration expressed by many of the philosophes for the enlightened absolutist rulers who were undermining the country, and it helped prepare readers to react appropriately to other struggles for liberty about to break out in countries where the press could have more impact.

Turning Tides

By the fall of 1774, the *Gazette de Leyde* could afford to respond more energetically to such outrages as the Polish Diet's vote to ban it, because the menace to European liberty that had clouded the horizon in 1772 began to recede. What the paper had seen as the threat of despotism in France dissolved, and in North America new champions entered the lists on behalf of liberty. Etienne Luzac could at last withdraw altogether from the paper's operations in 1775, knowing that an environment favorable to the *Gazette de Leyde* had been restored.

Already in 1773 the crisis menacing Europe's traditional liberties had begun to ease. The final abolition of the Jesuit Order, the culmination of a fifteen-year campaign in Spain, Portugal, and France, proved to the paper that the forces of evil were not invincible. "The suppression of the Jesuit Order goes forward everywhere without any difficulty, and this colossus, whose fall was expected to crush those who toppled it, has collapsed without the slightest shock," the paper commented.29 From Britain's North American colonies, where the paper had covered opposition to the innovations of the British government sympathetically since the Stamp Act crisis of 1765, came encouraging reports that "the spirit of liberty is unanimous, and declares itself openly against the despotism that the Ministry is suspected of trying to establish."30 Even

28. Etienne Luzac to Estates of Holland, 25 Oct. 1774, ibid.
29. *GL*, 20 Sept. 1773 (Leiden, 20 Sept.).
30. Ibid., 17 Aug. 1773 (London, 10 Aug.).

the French news occasionally indicated that the Maupeou reforms were less effective than the government there claimed. The paper published a few letters and documents from opponents of the new parlements, such as the former Parlement de Paris member Le Camus de Neville, who had gone into hiding to avoid arrest, and it sniped at Maupeou's most prominent supporters, such as Voltaire, of whom it remarked that "the public has long since been on its guard against both the attacks and the eulogies that flow from his pen, which is rarely safe from bias."[31]

It was the unanticipated death of Louis XV in May 1774 that definitively removed the threat to liberty in France and allowed the *Gazette de Leyde* to resume its normal role of spokesman for the forces of parlementary constitutionalism there. The paper's treatment of the deceased monarch was eminently respectful; indeed, its main story on the event was simply the report the French government had prepared for the official *Gazette de France*, although the text was apparently communicated to the Leiden paper even before it appeared in print in Paris.[32] There was no hint in the *Gazette de Leyde* of the animosity toward the king that led the court to have his body taken to Saint-Denis by a roundabout route to avoid hostile demonstrations in Paris. But within a few days of Louis XVI's accession to the throne, the Leiden paper became a privileged conduit for leaks from Versailles indicating the new ruler's desire to separate himself from his unpopular predecessor, such as details about the exile of Madame Du Barry and the recall of exiled supporters of the former minister Choiseul, whose disgrace had coincided with the Maupeou "coup" in 1770.[33]

The burning question throughout the summer of 1774 was whether the new monarch would dismiss Maupeou and restore the old parlements. After months of speculation, the *Gazette de Leyde* of 2 September 1774 was finally able to trumpet the news of "a great revolution in the ministry," as Maupeou was toppled and his "Patriot" victims, such as the Breton magistrate Caradeuc de La Chalotais, allowed to return to their homes. The restoration of the parlements took two months longer, because of squabbles about the fate of the judges Maupeou had appointed, but the appointment of a former parlementary leader, Hue de Miromesnil, as *garde des sceaux* (minister of justice) and of the reform-minded Jacques Turgot to the ministry convinced the paper that France was finally out of danger. Indeed, in comparing Turgot's rumored plan to give the French provinces the right to tax themselves with Britain's increasingly harsh measures in North America, the *Gazette de Leyde*

31. Ibid., 5 Feb. 1773 (Paris, 29 Jan.); and 1 Oct. 1773 (Paris, 24 Sept.).
32. Ibid., 20 May 1774 (Versailles, 12 May). The same story appeared in the *Gazette de France* of 13 May 1774.
33. *GL*, 24 May 1774 (Brussels, 19 May). A series of similar reports appeared under Brussels datelines in the next few issues.

commented that "it would be one of the more remarkable singularities of our century, if France restored to the nation the right to tax itself, a right so sacred [that] it would seem to be imprescriptible for every people that is not enslaved, at the same moment that England works to strip that right from its American subjects."[34] Optimism was obviously running high in Leiden.

Much of this optimism focused on affairs in North America. Jean Luzac inherited from his uncle an editorial policy on American affairs that anticipated the position the paper took in the 1770s. From the end of the Seven Years' War, the Leiden paper had begun to publicize colonial protests against British rule. As early as 1764, before Benjamin Franklin's 1766 visit to the Netherlands that laid the basis for later pro-American agitation there, the paper printed an article from Virginia suggesting that the colonies would be better off if they made themselves economically independent of Britain.[35] The paper gave ample coverage to American reaction against the Stamp Act in 1765. One of its dispatches announced, "There is a violent and universal alarm in the Colonies about the latest arrangements made with regard to them," and ended with the ominous remark, "There is no one who can foresee what may result from a general discontent among the people of this vast continent. But you and I, Sir, agree at least on this, that religion does not require any people to submit to slavery, if it is in a position to free itself, and to maintain that freedom."[36] To be sure, the paper hesitated to endorse the violence of the colonists' protests; following its normal tendency, it seemed to agree with articles that preached moderation and compromise, such as a 1766 dispatch datelined Philadelphia which concluded, "One may hope that a little good sense will forestall, before it is too late, ideas and enterprises whose beginnings can be foreseen more easily than their consequences, and that the commercial circles of Great Britain will come to see that their fortune depends more on making changes in public arrangements, and the introduction of a reasonable policy, than on anything else."[37]

In the years that followed, the paper continued to give sporadic attention to colonial events, and to express its hopes that violence would be avoided and that moderation would prevail. From time to time, it provided readers with significant documents from British North America, such as the text of Governor Charles Greville Montagu's proclamation dissolving the refractory South Carolina General Assembly or the text of a speech by the pro-British Governor Thomas Hutchinson to the

34. Ibid., 16 Sept. 1774 (Amsterdam, 14 Sept.).
35. Ibid., 6 Nov. 1764 (Virginia, 4 Sept.).
36. Ibid., 4 Oct. 1765 (North America, 25 July).
37. Ibid., 17 Jan. 1766 (Philadelphia, 9 Nov. 1765).

Massachusetts General Assembly.[38] The *Gazette de Leyde*'s audience was thus regularly reminded of the extent of colonial dissatisfaction with British rule. In 1773, when it published the text of the Massachusetts Assembly's response to Governor Hutchinson's assertion that the king had the right to tax the colonists without their consent, the paper took pains to frame the issue clearly for its readers, so that they could not mistake its significance: "Since one finds in it a clear and precise statement of the arguments on which the colonies base their claim to tax themselves, and since this quarrel seems to be becoming increasingly serious, we believe we will please our readers, by presenting them with a document so essential for the understanding of the public law of the American colonies."[39]

What was surprising about the *Gazette de Leyde*'s coverage of the American crisis in 1774 was that the paper committed itself so firmly to the colonists' cause and reacted so mildly to the rising tide of violence that was leading toward an armed conflict, a development that normally led the paper to condemn protest movements. The decision to back the Americans was a fully conscious one on Jean Luzac's part, taken at a time when he had no direct personal contact with any of the American leaders and long before any European power had decided to support them. As Luzac proudly reminded John Adams in 1781, "I dare to say, we, in those early times (already in 1774) contributed a great deal to awake the French Court on that subject," and he was also happy to recall that he had predicted the creation of an independent American republic as early as 1775.[40] Prepared by its detailed coverage of earlier stages of the American conflict, the *Gazette de Leyde* could not help seeing the colonists' revolt as one more instance of the struggle between liberty and despotism that it chronicled in so many European contexts. In the distant events in North America, Jean Luzac found the great cause of his life: from 1774 to 1783, he promoted American independence both through his newspaper and by his personal efforts.

The *Gazette de Leyde* was well informed about American events, even before Luzac established a regular connection with Charles Dumas, the American representative in The Hague, in 1777. He did not shrink from reporting incidents of violence, such as the Boston Tea Party, which was detailed in two letters in a single issue warning that "all America is in flames over tea."[41] But until 1774, the paper emphasized that the Americans had taken no steps toward actual insurrection and stressed the firmness and unanimity with which the entire population was resisting

38. Ibid., 19 Jan. 1773 (Charlestown, 12 Nov. 1772); 12 March 1773 (Boston, 7 Jan.).
39. Ibid., 14 Sept. 1773 (Boston, 27 July).
40. Luzac to John Adams, 10 Dec. 1781, in Adams Papers microfilms, r. 355; draft of response to English ambassador Joseph Yorke, 1779, in LGA-VH, Z(2), no. 42.
41. *GL*, 11 Feb. 1774 (New York, 1 Nov. 1773).

the threat of British reprisals.[42] Luzac was quick to print the colonists' version of the events surrounding the Battle of Lexington in 1775, making no comment on their assertion that "the fate of British America is settled . . . it seems to have no alternatives other than to perish or to make itself entirely independent of the Mother-Country," a bold claim at a time when sentiment among the colonists was by no means unanimous in favor of separation from England.[43] One reason for the paper's attitude was that even after Lexington, it managed to believe that the level of violence in the colonies was relatively insignificant: in December 1775, a rare article with no dateline claimed that the takeover of power in most of the American colonies had been relatively bloodless and that the recent attack on the royal governor of North Carolina was a new and unusual phenomenon.[44] Luzac was also shocked by the reports of British atrocities that he received: letters describing the burning of the port city of Falmouth inspired him to comment, "Time will tell us whether these harsh methods will serve to recover the colonies. To judge by present appearances, their effect will probably be to stiffen their resistance, since the British character which animates them hardly ever allows itself to be intimidated by violence."[45]

But the most important reason for Luzac's willingness to overlook possible flaws in the Americans' conduct at the outset of the Revolution was his admiration for the goals adopted by the rebels. Like his friend Pieter Paulus, the leading political thinker among the Dutch Patriots, who praised the Articles of Confederation as a worthy imitation of the Union of Utrecht by which the United Provinces had consolidated their independence from Spain, Luzac was highly impressed by the Americans' political wisdom.[46] After he had published the full text of the Continental Congress's Plan for a Confederation of the United Colonies in early 1776, Luzac added that

> one has few doubts that the inhabitants of North America will accept these articles, because they seem to have included everything that could establish and maintain a sincere union, disinterested and serving the good of all . . . the people has the deepest respect for the Congress and for every one of the members who compose it. . . . This veneration, which verges on enthusiasm, is kept up and augmented by the humanity that one observes in all the resolutions, the ordinances, and the actions of those who direct policy, and who direct and carry out the Confederation's military operations.[47]

42. Ibid., 5 July 1774 (London, 28 June); 9 Sept. 1774 (Boston, 18 July).
43. Ibid., 13 June 1775 (Boston, 30 Apr.).
44. Ibid., 15 Dec. 1775.
45. Ibid., 2 Jan. 1776 (Leiden, 2 Jan.).
46. Jan Willem Schulte Nordholt, *The Dutch Republic and American Independence*, Herbert Rowen, trans. (Chapel Hill: University of North Carolina Press, 1982), 12.
47. *GL*, 6 Feb. 1776.

For the young man who had just assumed control of the *Gazette de Leyde*, there could be no doubt that a movement committed to attaining such worthy goals by such worthy means deserved support.

The years in which Jean Luzac was indulging in this unbridled enthusiasm for the American Revolution were also years of high hopes in the paper's main marketplace, France. With the appointment of Turgot and the restoration of the parlements, the paper hoped for the coming of a great age of reform. Whereas the Americans' prospects seemed to depend on their valor in opposing an armed foe, however, it soon became clear that French affairs were more complicated. Who to support in France was not as clear to Luzac as it was in America. Although the paper regularly praised Turgot, it was less firm in supporting his reform measures. On the eve of the grain riots of May 1775, it expressed doubts about Turgot's decision to remove all restrictions on the sale of grain inside France: "A middle course would probably be, in this as in all things, the most sure."[48] As Turgot found himself embroiled in conflict with the restored parlements in the spring of 1776, the paper, which gave an accurate enough summary of the growing dispute, gave the minister no overt support until after his disgrace, when it commented, "Even though his ministry was not of long duration, he has at least the satisfaction of leaving it with a reputation that is not always given to statesmen, that of a true patriotism and the most complete probity."[49] Once Turgot was gone, the paper fought a rearguard action, assuring readers that the king still meant to see his former minister's policies implemented. But it was realistic about the extent of opposition his program had encountered, noting that "the major commercial cities seemed to oppose the principle of general free trade."[50] And it expressed no resentment toward the parlements for their role in Turgot's downfall.

With the ouster of Turgot, however, the clash of fundamental political principles that had given life to the *Gazette de Leyde*'s coverage of French affairs up to 1771 and from 1774 to 1776 came to an end. The French authorities undertook a vigorous campaign against the outspoken journalists who had surfaced in Paris after Maupeou's dismissal,[51] and in any event, the *Gazette de Leyde*, which had feared that Turgot was trying to accomplish too much too quickly, accommodated itself easily to his successor, Necker, who limited himself to more modest reforms. The publicity-conscious Necker must have been pleased with the *Gazette de Leyde*'s favorable comments about his measures, even

48. Ibid., 9 May 1775 (Paris, 1 May).
49. Ibid., 24 May 1776 (Paris, 16 May).
50. Ibid., 28 May 1776 (Brussels, 23 May); and 31 May 1776 (Paris, 24 May).
51. Nina R. Gelbart, *Feminine and Opposition Journalism in Old Regime France* (Berkeley: University of California Press, 1987), 143–47.

though its articles were generally very brief. But when Necker came under fire from powerful domestic opponents in 1781, it became clear that the *Gazette de Leyde* was not in a position to provide the kind of detailed coverage of a ministerial crisis that it had under Turgot. The paper praised the publication of Necker's *Compte rendu au Roi*, but rather than explaining realistically where the opposition to him came from, it referred vaguely to "people who found their private advantage in general disorder." When he was finally dismissed, the *Gazette de Leyde*'s report was scarcely more informative than that of the *Gazette de France:* it consisted of a one-sentence announcement, supplemented elsewhere by two sentences of superficial explanation.[52]

This muzzling of the paper's coverage was part of a broader crackdown on the Paris *bulletinistes* and pamphleteers. "The Bastille is full of people who wrote too freely about what is going on. . . . The papers arriving from abroad have been rigorously screened," one manuscript newsletter reported three months before Necker's dismissal.[53] The offensive continued after Necker's fall, and extended even beyond France's borders, as French agents followed Foreign Minister Vergennes's orders to pursue *libellistes* into their lairs abroad.[54] The result was noticeable not only in the *Gazette de Leyde* but in all its competitors: until the middle 1780s, news reports about domestic affairs in France were singularly dry and dull. This period of calm also reflected the absence of sharp controversies in France: Necker's successor Jean François Joly de Fleury successfully avoided all confrontations with the parlements, and the French government basked in the glory of its successful intervention on behalf of the Americans. Only when Joly de Fleury's replacement, Calonne, had to face the bills from the American war did French politics become heated again.[55] Until that happened, however, the *Gazette de Leyde* and its competitors had to look elsewhere for news.

The *Gazette de Leyde* and the American War of Independence

Fortunately for the European news industry, at the same time that court intrigues and opposition from the parlements were undermining

52. *GL*, 13 Mar. 1781 (Paris, 6 Mar.), and 29 May (Paris, 21 May).

53. Lescure, ed., *Correspondance secrète*, 1:363 (entry for 1 Feb. 1781).

54. Vergennes to La Grèze, 5 Nov. 1781, in Eugène Hubert, ed., *Correspondance des ministres de France accrédités à Bruxelles de 1780 à 1790* (Brussels: Kiesling, 1920–24), 1:34. The campaign caused a dip in the production of all forms of controversial pamphlet literature. Robert Darnton, *The Literary Underground of the Old Regime* (Cambridge: Harvard University Press, 1982), 191–95.

55. Bailey Stone, *The Parlement of Paris, 1774–1789* (Chapel Hill: University of North Carolina Press, 1981), 83–86.

Turgot's government, the Americans were moving toward a definitive break with Britain. As late as 25 June 1776, the *Gazette de Leyde* still expressed the hope that the differences between the colonists and the mother country could be worked out, although the paper commented that the program of independence set out in Tom Paine's *Common Sense* had increasing support in America. Readers thus were not taken by surprise when the paper published the first state resolutions calling for American independence.[56] Luzac followed up by giving his readers the first version of the Declaration of Independence published on the continent.[57] Surprisingly, the paper made no editorial comment on this document. The *Gazette de Leyde* continued to cover the American war closely, but the conflict had ceased to be a matter of ideology and was now presented as a conventional military and diplomatic story.

The outbreak of fighting between the British and the Americans complicated the task of obtaining news from North America, as the British tried to cut off American contact with the rest of Europe. The vast majority of the *Gazette de Leyde*'s news about the war arrived via London, and it tended to put the American situation in an unfavorable light. Because Luzac was sure that his readers "desire above all to be kept informed with impartiality of all the events in the war . . . since it is the most interesting subject at the present time,"[58] he had no choice but to use much of this English material, which swelled the percentage of the paper filled with material datelined London to more than 40 percent from 1777 to 1782. In addition, his correspondent in the British army, an officer stationed in New York, was labeled "a true Satan" by Charles Dumas, the American agent in The Hague.[59] To be sure, not all the items from London were unfavorable to the American cause. The British parliamentary opposition continued to clamor for peace negotiations with the rebels and to condemn Lord North's conduct of the war, thus generating a steady stream of pro-American speeches and pamphlets that Luzac could reproduce.[60] But he was consistently on the

56. The Virginia Assembly's independence resolution appeared on 9 Aug. 1776, that of Rhode Island on 13 Aug.

57. Luzac obtained his copy of the Declaration of Independence from English sources; the document had been published in London before it appeared in his paper on 30 Aug. 1776. On the first publications of the Declaration, see Durand Echeverria, "French Publications of the Declaration of Independence and the American Constitutions, 1776–1783," *Papers of the Bibliographical Society of America* 47 (1953), 313–38.

58. *GL*, 3 Jan. 1777 (Leiden, n.d.).

59. Dumas, letter to William Carmichael, 22 Apr. 1777, in AR, Dumas, carton I.

60. Thus the paper's London dispatch for 7 Feb. 1777 said that the Opposition would soon attack the Ministry over the unexpected size of the expenses engendered by the war, although the correspondent added that the English people would be willing to pay them. (London, 31 Jan.) Later that winter, the paper printed translated excerpts from one of Richard Price's pro-American pamphlets (14 Mar. 1777 [London, 7 Mar.]). On British press coverage of the war, see Solomon Lutnick, *The American Revolution and the British Press, 1775–1783* (Columbia: University of Missouri Press, 1967).

lookout for information that would counter the impression of grave difficulties for the American side, which much of this reportage created.

Exactly when Luzac established direct links with American sources is not clear. By March 1777, Charles Dumas (the Dutch zealot for the American cause recruited by Franklin as an agent in November 1775) was writing to Franklin and Deane in Paris that "I have been in close contact with the French gazetteer in Leiden for some time." And Dumas assured them that Luzac would publish whatever material the Americans furnished.[61] When John Adams arrived in the Netherlands in 1780, he personally contacted Luzac, who also continued to receive American news and propaganda via Dumas. The paper's pro-American coverage was thus coordinated with the official American representatives in Europe, and the paper had the benefit of whatever information about events in North America they were able to pass along. The *Gazette de Leyde* was never the Americans' sole journalistic supporter in Europe: other newspapers throughout the continent gave considerable attention to the conflict. The official *Gazette de France* and the French-government-controlled *Courrier d'Avignon* and *Courrier de l'Europe* (the latter having relocated from London to French soil as a result of the war) were visibly pro-American, but the first two had much less space to devote to the revolutionary war than Luzac's journal, and all three lacked its credibility.

By 1777, a journal exclusively devoted to the American cause, the *Affaires de l'Angleterre et l'Amérique*, was published in neutral Antwerp but supported by the French government. When it was discontinued in 1779, its place was soon taken by the Dutch-based *Politique hollandois*, edited by Antoine-Marie Cerisier, later the editor of the *Gazette de Leyde* itself.[62] But these magazine-style publications could not really replace the *Gazette de Leyde* as a source of pro-American news. They appeared much less frequently than the biweekly Leiden paper, and they could hardly aspire to the reputation for impartiality and veracity that the *Gazette de Leyde* enjoyed. Not only were they openly partisan, but the *Affaires de l'Angleterre* was secretly censored and shaped by the French

61. Letter of 11 Mar. 1777, in AR, Dumas, carton I. On Dumas, an enthusiast for America who had been in correspondence with Franklin since the latter's visit to the Netherlands in 1766, see Schulte Nordholt, *The Dutch Republic and American Independence*, 47–52.

62. On the *Affaires de l'Angleterre*, see Bernard Faÿ, *L'esprit révolutionnaire en France et aux Etats-Unis à la fin du XVIIIe siècle* (Paris: Champion, 1925), 61–63; and Peter M. Ascoli, "American Propaganda in the French Language Press during the American Revolution," in *La Révolution américaine et l'Europe* (Colloque de Toulouse, 1979) (Paris: Centre national de la recherche scientifique, 1979), 294–8. John Adams strongly endorsed Cerisier's *Politique hollandois* and provided a number of articles for it. Adams to Cerisier, 22 Jan. 1782, in Adams Papers microfilms, r. 101; see also his note about the paper in r. 601.

Ministry of Foreign Affairs, which, for example, mutilated the text of Thomas Paine's pamphlet *The Crisis* to give it a pro-monarchist twist.[63]

The Americans in Europe were not always satisfied with the *Gazette de Leyde*'s treatment of their affairs. At a low point in the colonists' fortunes at the end of 1780, Luzac published several news reports that the touchy American representative in the Netherlands, John Adams, regarded as defeatist. Adams, who had had to confess to other correspondents that things did indeed look gloomy for the American cause,[64] exploded, provoking Luzac to reply that in his view the rebels might well have to settle for less than the complete independence of all thirteen colonies. Comparing the American Revolution to the Dutch revolt of the 1570s, he reminded Adams that "out of the number of seventeen Provinces, which revolted against the Spanish Yoke, no more than eight obtained the aim of their endeavours," and he suggested that history proved "that the end of all wars is a sort of middle way between the different aims of the two contending Partys."[65] Luzac was unrepentant, and Adams, unwilling to break with one of his most important journalistic supporters, finally had to content himself with the assurance that "those ideas were not held up to the public by any one who meant to do mischief or to carry any point."[66] This episode cooled the relations between Adams and Luzac, but the American agent Dumas continued to regard the paper as the most dependable friend the Americans had and to forward vital information to the editor, including the text of the secret treaty between the United States and France.[67]

In general, however, the Americans had little to complain about concerning the *Gazette de Leyde*'s coverage of the war. To put the best face on the Americans' situation, the *Gazette de Leyde* worked consistently to deny unfavorable reports from other sources, usually in the British press. The paper repeatedly warned continental readers against the London papers, accusing them of obtaining their articles from "a certain class of manufacturers of reports, exiled Americans and others." It remarked that the well-informed "know how readily they print every kind of article and document, however evident its falsity."[68] When the

63. Faÿ, *Esprit*, 61–63.

64. Adams to Arthur Lee, 6 Dec. 1780, in Adams Papers microfilms, r. 102.

65. Luzac to Adams, 19 Jan. 1781, ibid., r. 354. I have been unable to identify the specific article that roused Adams's ire, but the paper had published several articles in late December 1780 and early January 1781 suggesting that Vermont might become a separate republic. Adams also accused Luzac of implying that the Americans might have to make peace at the cost of leaving Georgia to the British.

66. Adams to Luzac, 22 Jan. 1781, ibid., r. 102.

67. Dumas to Luzac, 19 May 1782, in AR, Dumas, carton I. Luzac does not seem to have published this document until after it appeared in the American press at the end of 1778.

68. *GL*, 22 Dec. 1780 (Leiden, 22 Dec.); and 8 Dec. 1780 (Leiden, 8 Dec.).

London papers claimed that Congress was divided over war policy, and that conditions in the rebel-held area were so bad that the Americans would have to sue for peace, the Leiden paper replied that the stories were exaggerated.[69] When some of the French officers who had fought with the Americans returned to Europe, the paper denied that they were, as the British press claimed, fed up with their American allies.[70] Luzac was always ready to soften the impact of any military defeat, as he did when he rebutted English claims that the defenders of Charlestown, South Carolina, had been so demoralized that they had surrendered long before they were forced to.[71]

The *Gazette de Leyde* stressed American advantages and successes whenever they occurred. Early in the war, the *Gazette de Leyde's* greatest concern was to demonstrate French sympathy with the American cause. Even before the French court had taken a definite decision to back the rebels, the paper was highlighting the involvement of individuals in France and elsewhere.[72] An article in February 1777 reported that French merchants had agreed with agents of the Continental Congress to buy American tobacco exports.[73] In June 1777, the paper reported on American privateers operating from French ports, suggesting for the first time that this might lead to a Franco-British war.[74] An editorial comment at the beginning of August 1777, following the news of the American victory at New Brunswick, claimed that French entry into the war was imminent.[75] The news was premature: Vergennes had indeed urged such action, but the king had not yet consented. Nevertheless, the steady flow of reports justifying British accusations that France was aiding the rebels, printed without provoking any protest from the French Ministry of Foreign Affairs, suggests that the pro-American faction in the French government was actively using the *Gazette de Leyde* to increase tensions with England.

As is well known, the French government did not finally commit itself to an alliance with the Americans until after it received news of Burgoyne's surrender at Saratoga. The *Gazette de Leyde* was one of the first continental papers to print news of the momentous American victory,

69. Ibid., 9 Mar. 1779 (Leiden, n.d.); and 24 Apr. 1781.
70. Ibid., 13 Apr. 1779 (n.d.).
71. Ibid., 27 June 1780.
72. Ibid., 25 June 1776. Secret French governmental aid to the rebels had begun in May 1776. Jonathan R. Dull, *A Diplomatic History of the American Revolution* (New Haven, Conn.: Yale University Press, 1985), 60.
73. *GL*, 25 Feb. 1777 (Rotterdam, 22 Feb.).
74. Ibid., 27 June 1777 (Leiden, 25 June).
75. Ibid., 1 Aug. 1777 (Leiden, 30 July). This article probably reflected a tip about Vergennes's memorandum to Louis XVI recommending intervention, prepared during July 1777 and forwarded to France's Spanish ally on 26 July. Murphy, *Vergennes*, 245. On French policy at this point, see also Jonathan R. Dull, *The French Navy and American Independence* (Princeton, N.J.: Princeton University Press, 1975), 75–90.

and it provided the most complete and best-documented coverage to be found in the European press.[76] The French government needed to justify intervention when it finally made its decision public; it was obviously an asset to have the continent's most reputable newspaper reporting favorably on American chances.

Although the Franco-American treaty was signed on 6 February 1778, it was not made public until the French government officially informed the British in late March. It is hard to believe that the French government had not encouraged Luzac to write the editorial note he published a few days after the secret signing, however: it was a list of all the evidence that seemed to indicate that France must have taken the plunge. The paper cited the rumors swirling around Versailles and Paris and the unusual number of ministerial conferences being held, the outspoken eagerness of the army and navy to teach the British a lesson, the fears expressed by merchants in Bordeaux and Paris, the naval preparations being made in Brittany, and several other signs.[77] The *Gazette de Leyde*'s articles could well have been part of Vergennes's elaborate efforts to provoke the British into taking the initiative in starting hostilities. If so, the maneuver was not successful: even after the French announcement of their pact with the Americans, military operations did not begin for three months. But the Leiden paper had kept its readers at least as well informed about the prospects for war as His Majesty George III, who, despite British diplomatic and naval intelligence, had still hoped as late as the beginning of March 1778 that the French might stay out.[78] And it had certainly been more accurate than its London rival, the *Courrier de l'Europe*, which maintained as late as 10 March 1778 that the French government's attitude was still undecided.

The best evidence on behalf of the Americans was, of course, good news from the battlefront—something that was often in short supply during the long middle period of the war, from 1778 to 1780. The paper's successful exploitation of the triumph at Saratoga has been mentioned; it was naturally even more pleased to be able to report the decisive American victory at Yorktown four years later. Even before hard news of the American success arrived, the paper had gone out on a limb and forecast a great event when it noticed that the British government had stopped printing bulletins about Cornwallis's army in the late summer of 1781.[79] The first definite news of the battle actually came via Versailles and the *Gazette de France*, but the Leiden paper was quick to

76. Peter M. Ascoli, "The French Press and the American Revolution: The Battle of Saratoga," *Proceedings of the Western Society for French History* 5 (1977), 46–55.

77. *GL*, 17 Feb. 1778 (Leiden, 14 Feb.).

78. George III to Lord North, 6 Mar. 1778, in John Fortescue, ed., *The Correspondence of King George the Third* (London: Macmillan, 1928), 4:46.

79. *GL*, 18 Sept. 1781.

add more information and its own commentary to underline the significance of the event.[80] The *Gazette de Leyde*'s Paris correspondent wrote that the battle might not mark the end of the war, but "it cannot help but be decisive," and an editorial note crowed, "If ever a plan of military operations was skillfully arranged, prudently carried out, and happily concluded, it was this one."[81]

The American War of Independence had provided the *Gazette de Leyde* with a splendid opportunity for doing well by doing good. Public interest in the conflict caused sales of all newspapers to soar: the *Gazette de Leyde*'s sales in France alone were 2,560 in 1778, and sales of the *Gazette de France* reached an all-time high of over 12,000 in 1780.[82] At the same time, Jean Luzac was able to take pride in having assisted a cause to which he was personally devoted. Not only did he help the Americans by publishing articles favorable to their cause, he also worked personally to assist them. He furnished the American representatives in Europe with secret reports on Dutch politics; at John Adams's request, he translated pamphlets and documents into French and sometimes arranged for their publication.[83] In 1781, Luzac was one of the handful of Dutch citizens who offered to subscribe to the first loan the American rebels attempted to float in Amsterdam.[84]

In the spring of 1782, when the Dutch cities represented in the States-General were polled on the question of extending official recognition to the Americans, Luzac drafted a petition in the name of Leiden's merchants that led to the city council's instructing its delegates to support the move. Replying to a letter of thanks from representatives of the merchants, Luzac said that his contribution to winning his native city's support for the American cause had been "one of the most agreeable and honorable . . . moments in my life."[85] Once ultimate American success was assured, John Adams put aside minor disagreements with his friend and gratefully acknowledged "your constant attachment to the principles of the American Revolution, and the respect which has been long paid, and the services rendered to the American cause in Europe, by the Leyden Gazette."[86] The triumph of the American cause seemed to mark both a great step forward for the cause of liberty and a

80. Ibid., 27 Nov. 1781 (Versailles, 19 Nov.).

81. Ibid., 30 Nov. 1781 (Paris, 23 Nov., and Leiden, 30 Nov.).

82. De Lormes to Jean Luzac, 14 July 1783, in LGA-VH, Z(2), no. 55; Tucoo-Chala, *Charles-Joseph Panckoucke*, 228.

83. Dumas to Benjamin Franklin, 11 June 1779, in AR, Dumas, carton I; Jean Luzac to John Adams, 19 Oct. 1780, 14 Nov. 1780, 16 Nov. 1780, in Adams Papers microfilms, r. 353.

84. Schulte Nordholt, *The Dutch Republic and American Independence*, 146. This attempt at borrowing ended in complete failure.

85. Luzac to Jan de Kruyff and Jan van Heukelom, 4 Oct. 1782, in LGA-VH, P(VII).

86. Adams to Jean Luzac, 13 Dec. 1781, in Adams Papers microfilms, r. 102.

major achievement for Jean Luzac himself, in his double role as news-paper editor and as activist. The dark days of 1772 when both liberty and the *Gazette de Leyde* had been under siege had given way to a climate of hope, and Luzac already looked forward to bringing his own country-men the benefits of the new principles exemplified by the American Revolution.

[8]

Engagement and Disillusionment: Jean Luzac and the *Gazette de Leyde* from 1782 to 1787

Even as Jean Luzac was accepting the praise of his fellow towns-men for his role in promoting the cause of American independence, affairs in Europe were moving in directions that posed new problems for him and for the *Gazette de Leyde*. During the 1770s and early 1780s, movements for constitutional liberty in Europe and the New World had been gaining strength, and the paper had not hesitated to support the reaction against Maupeou's reforms in France and the American Revolution. By 1782, however, the *Gazette de Leyde* found itself questioning movements in Europe that seemed superficially similar to the American Revolution. In the years that followed, the happy conjunction between world politics and the paper's editorial policies disintegrated, and Jean Luzac found himself under attack as an enemy of liberty in his native city. In reaction, he attempted to distance himself from the running of the *Gazette de Leyde*, but he was unable to disengage himself from the paper or to ensure the success of his views in the heated controversies of the Dutch Patriot period. The man and the newspaper which had radiated optimism about the future in 1781 and 1782 had become profoundly pessimistic about the future of liberty by 1787, just as the crisis that was to lead to the French Revolution began to unfold.

European Crises, 1782–1784

From late 1781 to 1784, the *Gazette de Leyde* gave particularly extensive coverage to three "democratic revolutions" in Europe: the troubles in the Swiss city-republic of Geneva, the Irish Volunteer movement and the parliamentary turmoil in Britain after the fall of Lord North in April of 1782. The outcome of all three struggles gave pause to those who thought that the American experience could be duplicated in the Old World. The Genevan crisis of 1781–82 was a sequel to the violent political disputes that had rocked that city in the 1760s and made it a crucible for the articulation of new ideas about political participation and democracy. When these disputes about which groups in the city deserved political representation had led to outright violence in 1768, the *Gazette de Leyde*'s news coverage had been distinctly hostile to the party demanding broader political participation, the Représentants, claiming that their program would "replace honor and virtue, which have heretofore guided the magistrates, with fear and self-interest, and thus completely degrade them, by making them victims of their resistance to a blind multitude."[1] This attitude placed the paper in agreement with the French government, which exercised a considerable influence in Genevan affairs, but the paper's views also reflected the fact that Etienne Luzac saw in Geneva's oligarchical republican constitution, so similar to that of the cities of the Netherlands, a form of government that met his criteria for constitutional freedom. Jean Luzac's enthusiasm for the Americans concealed the similarity between his attitudes and his uncle's; the revival of controversy in Geneva in 1781–82 brought that underlying distrust of popular sovereignty to the fore again. Jean Luzac's treatment of the Genevan crisis foreshadowed both the *Gazette de Leyde*'s editorial position on subsequent European constitutional crises and his own involvement in the Dutch Patriot movement of the 1780s.

The Genevan crisis of 1768 had ended with a compromise offering some concessions to the Représentants, and mention of the city had disappeared from the pages of the *Gazette de Leyde* for many years afterward. In 1781, however, the old dispute revived. The paper promptly began to publish reports, datelined Berne and Paris, denouncing the Représentants for trying to "change the form of government, now a mixture of democracy and aristocracy, into a pure democracy," and for threatening to resort to violence.[2] These articles obviously reflected the views of the French government and the leaders of the Swiss Confederation, both of them hostile to the Genevan reformers, but they were also consistent with the views about Geneva the paper had held in the 1760s. As Genevan politics became increasingly uproarious in 1782, the paper continued to draw its information largely from sources favorable to the city's oligarchy, the Négatifs. Luzac conceded in one of his

1. *GL*, 19 Apr. 1768 (Geneva, 15 Mar.). This article took up five columns of news space, indicating the importance Etienne Luzac attached to the Genevan affair. For a short summary of the Genevan crisis of the 1760s, see Palmer, *Democratic Revolution*, 1:111–42.
2. *GL*, 27 Feb. 1781 (Paris, 19 Feb.); and 23 Feb. 1781 (Berne, 6 and 11 Feb.).

editorial notes that the reports he had received via Paris, denouncing the Représentants and their supporters from the lower classes, the Natifs, conflicted with the mail he was receiving directly from Geneva, where an insurrection had installed a more democratic government in power in April 1782. He even printed one reader's letter complaining about the paper's bias.[3] Given a choice between competing printed accounts of the April revolt, however, the paper made only passing reference to François d'Yvernois's *Précis historique de la dernière Révolution de Genève*, favorable to the Représentants, while it excerpted generously from an anonymous *Relation de la conjuration contre le gouvernement et le magistrat de Genève*, which was hostile to them.[4]

Bombarded with complaints about his paper's Genevan coverage, Luzac came forth with an unusually explicit statement of editorial policy. He asserted that he meant to be impartial, and that he would publish statements from both sides in the dispute, and indeed he made critical comments about the intolerability of "aristocratic hauteur" in a "republic where the equality of all citizens is the basis of the constitution." But he found the opponents of the oligarchic Négatifs more blameworthy, because it was they who had resorted to arms and "plunged the country into an abyss of misfortunes" in pursuit of goals that were "more attractive in the abstract than truly essential to [the city's] welfare."[5] The paper thus had no difficulty in endorsing the French military intervention that overturned the insurrectionary government. The *Gazette de Leyde*'s attitude toward the Genevan revolution of 1782 certainly reflected the views of the French and Swiss authorities, on whom the paper was dependent for permission to circulate in those two countries, but it was also fully consistent with Jean Luzac's personal attitude toward movements that appealed to the doctrine of popular sovereignty and used force to achieve their goals.

Crises in Ireland and England

During its coverage of the American war and the Genevan revolution of 1781–82, the *Gazette de Leyde* found itself devoting considerable space

3. Ibid., 26 Apr. 1782 (Paris, 19 Apr. and Leiden, 24 Apr.); reader's letter, *GL*, 5 July 1782 (Leiden, 4 July).
4. Ibid., 18 June 1782 (Lausanne, 3 June). Both these works had appeared as printed pamphlets, and Luzac undoubtedly had access to both texts. The *Rélation de la conjuration* had been prepared for the ministers of the "protecting powers" that had guaranteed the compromise settlement of 1768 and stated that it was published explicitly as a response to pro-Représentant propaganda; Luzac thus knew precisely what the significance of the text he chose to republish was. *Rélation de la conjuration contre le gouvernement et le magistrat de Genève qui a éclaté le 8 Avril 1782* (N.p., n.d.), "Avis."
5. *GL*, 25 June 1782 (Leiden, 24 June).

to events in the British Isles. The Irish Volunteer movement of 1779–84 and the agitation for reform in England, together with the parliamentary crises following from the downfall of Lord North in March 1782, raised fundamental questions about the nature of the British constitutional system. Unlike his situation in dealing with French or Genevan affairs, Jean Luzac was under few constraints in dealing with British politics. His paper had almost no circulation there: thanks to the extensive English-language press, English citizens did not need a foreign gazette to learn what was going on in their own country. The French government, for its part, could hardly hope to control domestic politics in England the way it did in Geneva, and although it was rumored that France tried to stir up trouble in Ireland during the American war, there is no real evidence of French involvement there.[6] Nor is there any evidence that the French government ever protested or tried to influence the paper's coverage of British or Irish news.

The importance of the British political system in European political thought during the eighteenth century is well known. Voltaire and Montesquieu had contrasted English liberty with continental absolutism, and the latter's analysis of the system of checks and balances in the British constitution was one of the best-known features of his *Esprit des lois.* To be sure, there was another side to British political life: even Montesquieu had commented negatively on the restlessness, the tumult, and the disorder that characterized British elections and party controversies.[7] In describing British politics, the *Gazette de Leyde* embraced neither an Anglophile nor an Anglophobe interpretation of the British constitution. When Jean Luzac had taken over the editorship of the *Gazette de Leyde* in 1772, British politics appeared to be calming after a decade of intense parliamentary conflict and popular agitation. Throughout the 1760s, under Etienne Luzac's editorship, the paper had reported thoroughly and regularly on such controversies as the Wilkes agitation in 1763 and its sequel later in the decade. It had followed the various campaigns against different ministries, and it had documented the American colonies' noisy struggle against the Stamp Act. With regard to all these issues, the paper had followed its customary course of condemning extremism. It had not been particularly favorable to Wilkes: in 1768, its report on his speech thanking his electors had

6. R. B. McDowell, *Ireland in the Age of Imperialism and Reform, 1760–1801* (Oxford: Clarendon, 1979), 319.

7. Keith Baker, "Politics and Public Opinion," in Censer and Popkin, eds., *Press and Politics,* 214–21. There is a large literature on French views of the British constitution during the eighteenth century. See especially Gabriel Bonno, *La Constitution britannique devant l'opinion française de Montesquieu à Bonaparte* (Paris: Champion, 1931); Frances Acomb, *Anglophobia in France, 1763–1789* (Durham, N.C.: Duke University Press, 1950); and Josephine Grieder, *Anglomania in France (1740–1789)* (Geneva: Droz, 1985).

remarked that he used fine words, "but it is a shame that in the same representation that will show so many fine things to posterity, there will be so many broken windows," and it castigated "the most shameful disorders and excesses, committed in full view of the Magistrates, which, in degrading humanity, exhibit the most execrable anarchy."[8]

This distaste for Wilkes's rabble-rousing tactics by no means indicated any great sympathy with the existing Ministry. Commenting on a bill setting up new offices whose holders would be named by the king, the paper had written in 1768, "Every creation of new offices is an increase in the power of the Crown, something always to be feared in this country. The time may come when there will not be a George III on the throne."[9] If there was any English viewpoint the paper seemed to espouse, it was essentially that of Edmund Burke and the Rockingham Whigs: to defend British liberty, Parliament had to jealously guard its prerogatives against encroachments from the king, while at the same time rigorously eschewing any appeal to the mob "out of doors."

The *Gazette de Leyde*'s treatment of British affairs during the 1760s closely parallels the attitude it took later on political disorders in the Netherlands and then on the French Revolution. But in the 1770s and 1780s, Jean Luzac had to deal with quite a different set of issues in British politics. With the dissipation of the Wilkite agitation after 1771, popular agitation ceased to play a major role in British political life for nearly a decade. From 1770 to 1782, the Ministry remained firmly in the hands of Lord North; Burke and his coterie were equally firmly excluded from office. And the burning issue that concerned the *Gazette de Leyde* the most was not the balance of power within England, but the American war. Like many antiministerial figures in England itself, the paper had been critical of the various attempts to strengthen imperial authority in the North American colonies during the 1760s, and its reports noted early on the disagreement within the British government on how to deal with the intractable colonists. It was, characteristically, in favor of a middle course: "Too much weakness will cost us our superiority; and their [the colonists'] stubbornness tells us clearly what we can expect from a policy of rigor."[10] In criticizing harsh measures against the Americans, the paper only had to echo antiministerial voices in Britain itself. It repeatedly noted the extent of opposition to government measures in England and it printed the texts of speeches such as the Duke of Richmond's protest in late 1775 that "we cannot regard our fellow subjects in America from any other point of view than as free men forced to resist by acts of oppression and violence."[11] During this period,

8. *GL*, 12 Apr. 1768 (London, 1 Apr.).
9. Ibid., 22 Jan. 1768 (London, 12 Jan.).
10. Ibid., 29 Mar. 1774 (London, 18 Mar.).
11. Ibid., 14 Nov. 1775 (London, 3 and 7 Nov.).

then, the *Gazette de Leyde* identified itself fully with the parliamentary opposition to Lord North's Ministry, as did other international gazettes aiming at the French market.[12]

Although the paper's London correspondent clearly sided with the Opposition's criticism of North's war policy, Luzac's reporter was well informed and had no illusions about the chances of North's being ousted by domestic opposition. At the beginning of 1777, the *Gazette de Leyde* told readers not to be overly impressed with the Opposition's noisy denunciation of the unexpectedly high cost of the war: the English people would continue to pay what they were asked.[13] Although the American victory at Saratoga and the looming threat of French intervention in early 1778 forced Lord North to make "many painful admissions, that . . . contrast strangely with the language that the Ministerials used not only in 1775 and 1776 but even in the first weeks of the present session," North's majority remained solid.[14] The acquittal in 1779 of Admiral Augustus Keppel after a sensational trial in which he was accused of letting the French fleet escape was another blow to North, but once again the paper explicitly reported that his hold on Parliament was in no danger.[15]

A real threat to North arose only with the beginning of extraparliamentary agitation in Ireland and England. A dispatch from Dublin, dated 18 October 1779, brought news of demands for the restoration of the Irish Parliament's independence of the British legislature and added that "the enthusiasm for forming militia associations has spread everywhere in Ireland, and every citizen, regardless of his rank, who is not dressed in some sort of uniform, is looked on as useless to the community."[16] This report was the prelude to five years of intermittent coverage of Irish affairs. The Irish movement, which looked at the time like the beginning of a second war of independence, coincided with the rise of agitation in England.[17] In April 1780, the *Gazette de Leyde* reported that North had not only been defeated on a bill demanding a stricter account of the distribution of government pensions, but that resolutions against him had been passed by assemblies of freeholders at Westminster and Middlesex.[18] The Gordon Riots two months later briefly diverted attention from this more middle-class opposition movement, but the paper never expected this lower-class violence to have political results. The paper's hope for real change in British politics rose in the

12. Jack R. Censer, "English Politics in the *Courrier d'Avignon*," in Censer and Popkin, *Press and Politics,* 184–85.

13. *GL,* 7 Feb. 1777 (London, 31 Jan.).

14. Ibid., 27 Feb. 1778 (London, 20 Feb.).

15. Ibid., 26 Mar. 1779 (London, 19 Mar.).

16. Ibid., 9 Nov. 1779 (Dublin, 18 Oct.).

17. Ibid., 26 Nov. 1779 (Dublin, 10 Nov.).

18. Ibid., 18 Apr. 1780 (London, 11 Apr.).

spring of 1781 when Burke, speaking for the Rockingham fraction in Parliament, revived his Bill for Economical Reform.[19] But this attack on the Ministry also guttered out, and the paper turned its attention primarily to the course of the war for the rest of 1781.

What finally brought the North Ministry down was the news of decisive defeat in America. The *Gazette de Leyde* was slow to underline the significance of the several close votes that marked the erosion of North's majority in February and March 1782, but its correspondent was pleasantly surprised when North finally resigned.[20] The *Gazette de Leyde* immediately stepped up the volume of its English news coverage, supplemented by reports on the agitation in Ireland, and it warmly welcomed the new Rockingham-dominated Ministry, remarking that "it is natural for the nation to expect the greatest advantages from a completely popular administration, which has fought the vices of the preceding administration with so much vigor and energy." Its reporter anticipated that the new Ministry would rebuild the navy, carry out the plans for economy that Burke had proposed in 1780, and work to diminish the crown's influence.[21] The London correspondent's close identification with the moderate reforming plans of the Rockingham faction, which he had expressed only in muted form during North's tenure, thus became clear.

Like many of the new Ministry's own supporters and like most of the French-language press, however, the *Gazette de Leyde* soon became disillusioned as the divisions in the new governing coalition revealed themselves.[22] It accurately reported that Charles James Fox had failed to give William Pitt's parliamentary reform bill sufficient support, and anticipated that the Ministry would have to call new elections to get any of its measures passed.[23] After Rockingham's sudden death in July, the paper's correspondent reported that the surviving ministers were hopelessly split, since the Whig members would not accept the former Tory Lord Shelburne as their leader.[24] As the government tottered onward, the paper could still revert to the tones of classic Country ideology, as when it prefaced a discussion of measures intended to reduce the London crime rate with the reflection that "the corruption of morals is the surest means to establish the arbitrary power of a single man on the

19. Ibid., 9 Mar. 1781 (London, 2 Mar.).
20. Ibid., 29 Mar. 1782 (London, 19 and 22 Mar.).
21. Ibid., 5 Apr. 1782 (London, 29 Mar.).
22. On the French-language press's treatment of British politics in this period, see Richard M. Leighton, "The Tradition of the English Constitution in France on the Eve of the Revolution" (Ph.D. diss., Cornell University, 1941), 521–90.
23. *GL*, 17 May 1782 (London, 10 May).
24. Ibid., 12 July 1782 (London, 5 July). On the details of British parliamentary politics from 1782 to 1784, see John Cannon, *The Fox-North Coalition* (London: Cambridge University Press, 1969).

ruins of true liberty, by reducing the citizenry to indigence and fashioning them for servitude."[25] But its correspondence reflected a growing awareness that the hopes for reform were dwindling and that England's political problems could no longer be analyzed simply in terms of a conflict between arbitrary power and defenders of the people.

The political confusion that characterized the end of 1782 became even more acute in the following two years, as England experienced the most serious parliamentary crisis it had endured since 1715. Lord Shelburne found himself unable to build a successful coalition, but the other groupings in Parliament seemed equally unable to put together a majority.[26] The *Gazette de Leyde*'s correspondent reported the steps by which George III found himself compelled to accept for the first time a Ministry one of whose principal members—Fox—he had been determined to resist.[27] The Fox-North government faced heavy opposition from the outset, and by the end of the year Fox, defeated in the House of Lords over his bill to reform the East India Company, had been driven to making what the *Gazette de Leyde*'s correspondent interpreted as an almost revolutionary claim. Despite the House of Lords' opposition, Fox asserted that he held his post by the will of the English people and he would not quit it. The paper wondered how George III could tolerate "the threats of an administration, one of whose principal leaders publicly declares that he owes his position to the people, not to the sovereign."[28] Faced with such a direct assertion of popular sovereignty, the paper abandoned its customary suspicion of the crown and aligned itself with the forces it had traditionally distrusted the most.

In the first weeks of 1784, George III turned to the young William Pitt to bring down the Fox-North government, and the paper had to try to clarify for continental readers the intricacies of a parliamentary crisis of almost overwhelming complexity. As the paper put it, both the traditional English parties were split down the middle, the two Houses of Parliament were at loggerheads, the majority of the House of Commons was in opposition to Pitt, and the majority of the English people was in opposition to the majority of the Commons, while the king "is reduced to being the passive witness of all these intrigues."[29] The *Gazette de Leyde*, traditionally sympathetic to those who defended the rights of Parliament and the people against the crown, was now convinced that Fox was nothing more than "an ambitious leader without principles" whose administration had lost all real popularity.[30] It underlined "the unusual

25. *GL*, 12 Nov. 1782 (London, 1 Nov.).
26. Ibid., 14 Mar. 1783 (London, 28 Feb., 4 and 7 Mar.).
27. Ibid., 18 Mar. 1783 (London, 7 Mar.); and 21 Mar. 1783 (London, 14 Mar.).
28. Ibid., 30 Dec. 1783 (London, 19 Dec.).
29. Ibid., 10 Feb. 1784 (London, 27 Jan.).
30. Ibid., 26 Mar. 1784 (London, 12, 16, and 19 Mar.).

situation of the nation being in direct contradiction to its representatives, and these representatives nonetheless taking advantage of their
position to force the King, his ministers, and the Lords to submit to their
wishes."[31] It was with great relief that the paper reported the Fox-North
forces' final acceptance of their defeat three weeks later.

In the midst of the unruly struggles during the previous two years, the
traditional distinctions between the Ministry, allied with the crown, and
the Opposition, speaking for the interests of the people, had broken
down. The Fox government provided a warning of how far even such a
traditional body as the House of Commons could extend its claims if it
were allowed to bill itself as the embodiment of popular sovereignty.
Unable to make this unprecedented situation fit its traditional model,
based on the civic humanist ideal of a constitution with a balance between independent forces, the *Gazette de Leyde* followed much of British
public opinion in welcoming Pitt's electoral victory in 1784 and accepting the extinction of the movement for reform for which it had had such
high hopes just two years earlier.

The crisis of 1783–84 convinced the *Gazette de Leyde*'s correspondent
that the traditional commonwealth or Country paradigm of British
politics had collapsed. One result was that the paper lost most of its
interest in British affairs. The paper's disillusionment with England was
clearly stated during the Regency crisis of 1788, when George III became ill. The paper's reports made the significance of the Parliament's
assertion of its constitutional right to determine the conditions of any
regency clear. This was a crucial step forward in extending that body's
prerogatives at the expense of the crown's, but the *Gazette de Leyde*'s
correspondent concluded that the crisis had simply shown the importance of parties: "Although it is disagreeable to think that the heart of
the matter is nothing but the issue of determining who will have power
in his hands, the group behind Mr. Pitt or that behind Mr. Fox, one can
comfort oneself by recalling that, in most political controversies that
trouble the domestic tranquillity of peoples, selfish interest is the driving
principle."[32] This bleak view showed how completely the paper had
ceased to consider British political debates after 1784 as true struggles
for liberty.

The British parliamentary crisis of 1782–84, which had stripped the
island's politics of its status as a paradigm of the struggle for liberty, had
coincided with a second insular crisis, the high point of the Irish Volunteer movement.[33] The Irish movement for greater independence from

---

31. Ibid., 5 Mar. 1784 (London, 27 Feb.).
32. Ibid., 6 Jan. 1789 (London, 23 Dec.).
33. On the Irish movement, see McDowell, *Ireland*, 256–319; and Palmer, *Democratic Revolution*, 1:285–94.

Britain, which surfaced in 1779, had briefly threatened to follow the path of the American colonial movement. The *Gazette de Leyde*'s coverage expressed sympathy with Irish moderates who sought to find a compromise between submission to the British Parliament's authority and a demand for independence.[34] When the British proved able to keep a loyal majority in the Irish Parliament, the more radical Volunteer groups called for the convening of a National Convention in late 1783, and by the summer of 1784, Ireland seemed poised on the brink of open violence.

By this point, the reports in the *Gazette de Leyde* expressed the utmost apprehension at the way events seemed to be heading. "Everything here gives the most alarming impression of a determination to throw off every vestige of England's authority," the paper wrote in July 1784, noting with disapproval the extent of popular support for such a policy.[35] By now, the paper had abandoned all sympathy with anti-English protests and gave its editorial support to "the real patriots . . . those whose zeal for the public good is guided by disinterestedness and uprightness," and who supported a continuing connection with Britain.[36] It was with evident relief that the paper's Irish correspondent finally reported that "the most respectable portion of the citizenry has begun to oppose the project of a national congress. . . . They feel that the principles of pure democracy, on which the convocation of such an assembly would have to be based, are repugnant to the British constitution."[37] As in the case of Geneva, the *Gazette de Leyde* had condemned a movement for constitutional change as soon as its activities raised the possibility of an appeal to popular sovereignty or to violence. What could be tolerated across the Atlantic could not be endorsed in the European world itself.

Luzac and the Dutch Patriot Movement

By 1784, the predominant tone in the *Gazette de Leyde*'s news coverage had become one of concern that movements ostensibly aimed at consolidating liberty could easily degenerate into populist violence and anarchy. Even as his paper criticized the Genevan Représentants, the Foxites, and the Irish Volunteers, however, Jean Luzac was himself involved in a movement in his native Netherlands that seemed to be adopting very similar principles. Since the outbreak of the Fourth Anglo-Dutch War in December 1780, Luzac had become a prominent member of the

34. *GL*, 13 June 1780 (Dublin, 23 May).
35. Ibid., 6 July 1784 (Dublin, 18 June).
36. Ibid., 27 Aug. 1784 (Dublin, 5 Aug.).
37. Ibid., 29 Oct. 1784 (Dublin, 8 Oct.).

Dutch Patriots, who blamed the pro-British stadholder for permitting Britain's devastating preemptive strike against the Dutch fleet with which the war had started.[38] He used the *Gazette de Leyde* to try to keep up Dutch morale by suggesting—in the face of overwhelming evidence to the contrary—that the Netherlands had good chances of gaining effective foreign support against the British.[39] And he threw both his paper and his personal energies into the campaign for a diplomatic counterstroke against the British, in the form of Dutch recognition of American independence.

The success of this campaign, both in Leiden and at the national level, inspired the Patriots to turn their attention to political reform in the Netherlands itself.[40] They accused William V of undermining the "true liberty" of the Republic by using his patronage powers to build up a network of clients in local governments, and they blamed him for incompetent administration that had led to the overwhelming British victory in the war. Although the Patriots had no shortage of Dutch-language newspapers to promote their cause, they also published numerous reports in the *Gazette de Leyde*. Luzac could count on a network of pro-Patriot friends such as his cousin Johan Valckenaer, a young law professor at the Frisian University of Franeker, to keep him supplied with material.[41] A typical news item reported on the final vindication of the Patriot hero Joan Dirk Van der Capellen tot den Poll, the "Batavian Wilkes," in his four-year struggle with the Orangist members of the Estates of Overijssel. The openly partisan report concluded that the outcome proved "that an honest and virtuous Regent can always count on support from a nation which has not entirely lost the patriotic energy of its ancestors."[42]

News reports like these may have had little impact in the Netherlands itself, but the Patriots imagined that they were the most effective way in which they could publicize their cause to the outside world. Unlike the Americans, the Dutch Patriots sensed that much of the rest of Europe opposed their cause, and with good reason. An article in the *Gazette de*

38. According to the Dutch Patriot "archivist" Dumont-Pigalle, Luzac edited one of the innumerable pamphlets blaming the stadholder for the sorry condition of Dutch forces in 1780, *Verzameling van Stukken, betreffende de Augmentatie der Land- en Zee-Magt der Republieq* (Holland: n.p., 1782). On the general subject of Dutch involvement in the American Revolution, see Schulte Nordholt, *The Dutch Republic and American Independence*.

39. *GL*, 3 Apr. 1781 (Leiden, 1 Apr.).

40. For overall accounts of the Dutch Patriot movement, see Simon Schama, *Patriots and Liberators* (New York: Knopf, 1977), 64–135; Pieter Geyl, *La Révolution batave* (1783–98), J. Godard, trans. (Paris: Société des études robespierristes, 1971); and De Wit, *De Nederlandse Revolutie van de Achttiende Eeuw 1780–1787*.

41. For Valckenaer's activities in supplying the paper with news from Friesland, see his letters to Jean Luzac of 18 Feb. 1782, 15 Mar. 1782, and 12 Apr. 1782, in LUL, BPL 1030.

42. *GL*, 8 Nov. 1782 (Zwolle, 3 Nov.). On the significance of Van der Capellen's readmission to the Estates, see Murk de Jong Hendrikszoon, *Joan Derk van der Capellen* (Groningen: Wolters, 1921), 494–505.

Leyde in 1785 explicitly justified the space given to Dutch affairs in the paper by reference to the false reports circulating abroad: "In the outside world, above all in Germany, the idea that disorder and anarchy reign in the Republic is widespread."[43] This impression of foreign press hostility was accurate. The English papers denigrated the Patriots, the leading German journalists were hostile and the non-Dutch-based French-language press tended to be pro-Orangist as well.[44] Journals set up expressly for the purpose of enlightening the European world about the justice of the Patriot cause, such as Antoine-Marie Cerisier's *Politique hollandois*, were some comfort, but their reputation was slight and their audience small.

The *Gazette de Leyde*, with its immense prestige abroad, offered the Patriots a unique opportunity to state their case. The impact of the paper's efforts was limited by the length and obscurity of the addresses and resolutions that it translated into French, and by Luzac's refusal to impose clear names and labels on the Dutch Patriot factions as he would later do for the French revolutionaries. As propagandists, the Dutch Patriots were far less efficient than their French successors: whereas the French revolutionaries would later sum up the principles they were defending in the seventeen short articles of the Declaration of the Rights of Man, the never-completed Dutch Patriot manifesto, the *Grondwettige Herstelling*, took up two good-sized volumes.[45] But the *Gazette de Leyde* did what it could to further the Patriot cause. For example, it praised the citizen militia groups or *Vrijcorps*, similar to the Irish Volunteers, which Patriot activists sought to create in all the major towns. It is true that the terms of Luzac's endorsement show the fears that the ongoing political agitation begun in 1781 was beginning to arouse in him: he hailed the *Vrijcorps* as a defense against "the populace, in case of a riot," and as a bulwark of "the legitimate sovereign authority and those who represent it," by which he meant the regents of the various cities. The lower classes, he was sure, were "the blind instrument of those who claim to be friends of the Stadholder's dynasty."[46]

By 1784, Luzac was not just using his newspaper to publicize the

43. *GL*, 29 Apr. 1785 (The Hague, 27 Apr.).

44. The two most influential political magazines in Germany, Schirach's *Politische Journal* and Schlözer's *Stats-Anzeigen*, were bitter opponents of the Patriots. Schlözer helped launch another journal, the *Hollandische Stats-Anzeigen*, devoted exclusively to pro-Orangist propaganda. Schlözer to R. M. Van Goens (a prominent Orangist propagandist), 21 Sept. 1783, in KB, Ms. 130 D 15, K 11. Among the French-language publications, Linguet's widely circulated *Annales politiques* and Manzon's *Courier du Bas-Rhin* were outspokenly anti-Patriot.

45. *Grondwettige Herstelling, van Nederlands Staatswezen zo voor het algemeen Bondgenoot-schap, als voor het bestuur van elke byzondere Provincie*, 2 vols. (Amsterdam: J. Allart, 1784 and 1786). The work called for a reform of the traditional Dutch federal constitution as well as reforms in each separate province. Only two of the seven promised provincial sections appeared before the collapse of the Patriot movement.

46. *GL*, 6 Apr. 1784 (Leiden, 5 Apr.).

Patriots: he had also become one of the leading figures in the movement. Already in 1780 he had gained notoriety when one of the most outspoken of the Patriots, the Baptist minister Francis Adrian Van der Kemp, had been put on trial in Leiden for circulating a poem against the stadholder. Luzac had stepped forward to defend his friend and eventually won dismissal of the charges.[47] By 1782, John Adams recorded in his diary that Luzac had become the most respected political figure in Leiden, where he was said to be "universally beloved."[48] In 1784, Luzac served as defense counsel in an even more widely publicized political trial in which a prominent woman from Leiden stood accused of having tried to recruit her servants to assassinate the stadholder. This Vandermeulan case became a cause célèbre throughout the Netherlands. Luzac turned it into an occasion for a ringing defense of freedom of speech. Drawing on a well-known passage from Montesquieu's *Esprit des Lois*, he argued that if the servants' undocumented accusations were allowed to stand as evidence, "then any words, despite the absence of deeds, can give grounds for a criminal prosecution. . . . Are we going to erect an inquisition, to investigate and to determine what a citizen can say? . . . Then truly . . . no one is safe. Then fear and terror will take the place of patriotic outspokenness . . . then all civil freedom would be abolished."[49] The combination of Luzac's pro-Patriot tilt in the *Gazette de Leyde* and his personal activism made him a major target for the Orangist press. From its safe location in Prussian territory, Manzon's *Courier du Bas-Rhin*, the most virulent anti-Patriot organ and one of the *Gazette de Leyde*'s main rivals, honored Luzac with a satirical poem, and his distant cousin Elie Luzac, an Orangist propagandist in addition to his activities as a publisher and bookseller, printed a thirty-page diatribe against him.[50] While Luzac himself became increasingly prominent as a Patriot spokesman, the *Gazette de Leyde* became a major rallying point for the

47. Fairchild, ed., *Francis Adrian Van der Kemp*, 49.

48. L. H. Butterfield, ed., *Diary and Autobiography of John Adams* (Cambridge: Harvard University Press, 1961), 3:19 (entry for 10 Oct. 1782).

49. Jean Luzac, "Memorie van Suggestie," in *Verzameling van Stukken, betreffende de valsche beschuldiging tegens Catharina Taan, Wed. Vandermeulan, nevens een kort verslag van de uitkomst derzelve zaak* (Leyden: Herdingh, 1786), 26–27. Luzac referred explicitly to Montesquieu's condemnation of prosecutions against words unaccompanied by actions in his chapter on "Des paroles indiscrètes," in Book XII of the *Esprit des Lois*. Ironically, despite his modern-sounding defense of freedom of speech, Luzac made no objection to the use of the threat of torture to force his client's main accuser to recant his testimony. On the background of this case, see H. A. Höweler, "Een moordplan tegen Willem V?" *Leidsche Jaarboekje* (1964), 103–24. Luzac's role in the case was extensively publicized in an anonymous Patriot pamphlet attributed to him (incorrectly, in my opinion): *Défense des Belges confédérés, des Souverains respectifs de leurs provinces, et de leurs respectables et zélés Magistrats, contre l'Oracle des politiques étrangers, le "Courier du Bas-Rhin."* ("Holland": n.p., 1784), 136–57.

50. *Courier du Bas-Rhin*, 31 Dec. 1783; *Vaderlandsche Staatsbeschouwers* 1:529–59 (March 1785).

Patriot party. From the beginning of 1783, the Prussian ambassador to The Hague, Friedrich Wilhelm von Thulemeyer, had made a stream of complaints about Luzac's coverage. Prussia was embroiled in Dutch affairs on the Orangist side because the stadholder's wife, Princess Wilhelmina, was the niece of Frederic the Great. Thulemeyer saw Patriot bias in every reference the *Gazette de Leyde* made to Prussian démarches in favor of the stadholder's rights, and he delivered the customary ambassadorial threats to retaliate against the paper to back up his protests.[51] Luzac responded in a most uncustomary fashion, however. Breaking with the ordinary conventions of his type of journalism, he asserted that "the duties of a faithful citizen" required him to refute Prussian assertions.[52] The infuriated Prussian ambassador replied that "you have come up with an inflated and totally false notion of your duties." He rejected the radical notion that a newsman could have obligations to his home country: "I have no reason to believe that the Estates [of Holland] have commissioned you to direct public opinion."[53]

Luzac refused to back down. He went over the ambassador's head and tried to get the Prussian foreign minister Ewald Friedrich von Hertzberg to restrain him, but when this did not work, he took his case to the Leiden city council and the Estates of Holland, urging them to make the paper's cause part of the defense of the Republic's independence from foreign interference. If the city council and the provincial Estates followed their normal procedure of responding to Thulemeyer's complaints by issuing a warning to the paper, Luzac expostulated, the Dutch press would be silenced on affairs of national importance while "the agent of darkness in Cleves [the *Courier du Bas-Rhin*] would continue to mislead foreigners, indeed all of Europe, about the affairs of our country."[54] The city council, packed with Luzac's friends, took up this invitation to strike a blow for the Patriot cause, informing the provincial Estates that it found "nothing blamable" in the articles Thulemeyer had complained about.[55] As if this defiance of a great power's ambassador was not revolutionary enough, Luzac published his correspondence with Thulemeyer and his ringing defense of his editorial decisions in the *Politieke Kruyer,* one of the most widely circulated Patriot weeklies, where the affair occupied three consecutive issues.[56] By making his quarrel with the Prussian ambassador public, Jean Luzac had forced the Leiden city government to take a stand in favor of his right to defy foreign governments, and by publishing Thulemeyer's letters, Luzac treated at

51. Thulemeyer to Jean Luzac, 1 Feb. 1783, in LGA-VH, Z(2), no. 47.
52. Jean Luzac to Thulemeyer, 4 Feb. 1783, ibid., no. 48.
53. Thulemeyer to Jean Luzac, 6 Feb. 1783, ibid., no. 49.
54. Jean Luzac to Leiden city council, 24 May 1784, ibid., no. 69.
55. Leiden Burgemeesters to Estates of Holland, 24 May 1784, ibid., no. 68.
56. *Politieke Kruyer,* nos. 156–58 (1784).

least the Dutch public to the spectacle of a newspaperman elevating himself to the equal of a major government. As a result of its quarrel with the Prussians, the *Gazette de Leyde* seemed to be rewriting the rules for European international journalism, and Luzac had become a public personage, combining journalism and political activism in a way that anticipated the behavior of the journalist-politicians of the French Revolution.

At the end of 1784, Jean Luzac seemed poised to take a leading position in the Patriot movement against the Prince of Orange, and the *Gazette de Leyde* had become not only the most authoritative source of news about Dutch events for readers outside the country but also the acknowledged spokesman for the Dutch national cause. The French diplomatic representatives in The Hague recognized the paper's symbolic importance to the Patriots, and when it was unexpectedly banned in France in March 1785, they warned Versailles that it risked alienating the entire Patriot movement by attacking Luzac.[57] The paper continued to represent national opinion in the crisis between the Republic and Austria that broke out in late 1784 when Joseph II decided to take advantage of the chaos in the Dutch Republic to try to reopen the Scheldt River and revive the commercial fortunes of Antwerp. The Dutch decision to oppose him, reported in the *Gazette de Leyde* on 15 October 1784, threatened to provoke a war and the crisis immediately became "the principal, if not the only, object occupying the public's attention."[58] Just as the French Girondins later hoped to use a foreign war to unite their countrymen, the Dutch Patriots saw the potential conflict as a possible solution to the country's internal disputes. The crisis with Vienna overshadowed the Dutch Republic's internal political divisions, and the *Gazette de Leyde* took on the appearance of an official gazette as it conscientiously published statements from The Hague and sought to put the best face on the Dutch position, declaring, "Whatever happens, the Dutch nation will be safe from the reproach of having provoked this evil."[59]

The Dutch Republic, just defeated at sea by the British, had no better hope against the Habsburg empire in a land conflict. Dutch chances in an armed confrontation depended on outside support: with Britain and Prussia both backing the stadholder, Dutch resistance to Austria depended on French support. This put the *Gazette de Leyde* in a strategic but delicate position: it had to slant its articles to put the Dutch case in the most persuasive light, and to encourage patriotic spirit at home, but it

57. Vérac, French ambassador to The Hague, to Rayneval, 11 Mar. 1785, in MAE, Corr. Pol.—Hollande, 562.
58. *GL*, 19 Oct. 1784 (Leiden, 17 Oct.).
59. Ibid., 5 Nov. 1784 (Leiden, 3 Nov.).

had to avoid appearing to push the French government to commit itself. Matters were complicated by the fact that the French representatives in the Netherlands were prepared to go considerably further in supporting the Patriots than Versailles was.[60] Furthermore, the paper had to think of its own interests. The Austrians, taking advantage of Marie-Antoinette's influence, succeeded in having the gazette banned in France in early 1785; when this measure proved ephemeral, Joseph II punished Luzac by authorizing a reprint edition of the paper in Vienna, thereby cutting into its sales.[61]

The paper's Paris correspondent reported that the pros and cons of intervention were being carefully weighed in Versailles. "Its interests with regard to the European system, and what it owes to its honor and dignity," inclined France toward intervention, but "the desire to preserve the peace for the good of the nation and the benefit of its finances" pointed the other way.[62] Subsequent reports strained to give the impression of impending French action. Vergennes had supposedly told the royal council that "the honor of the King, the glory of France, the interests of the Kingdom, the state of affairs in Europe, all, in a word, required that the Dutch not be abandoned to the arbitrary laws or the superiority of the forces of a neighbor, whose preponderance in the general system of affairs was too obvious to be ignored."[63] In fact, Vergennes had no intention of being dragged into a war with France's main ally on behalf of the Dutch; he worked vigorously and ultimately successfully to mediate the dispute.[64] The *Gazette de Leyde*, whose coverage can most plausibly be interpreted as an attempt to rouse Dutch patriotic ardor by putting the most favorable light on French intentions, might have lost a crucial part of its credibility by stretching the evidence, but both Dutch and European events proceeded too rapidly to allow criticism to hurt the paper.

The Scheldt River crisis gradually petered out in the early months of 1785, but the stormiest year in Jean Luzac's life was just beginning. The *Gazette de Leyde* of 1 March 1785 carried a story that marked the paper's

60. Alfred Cobban, *Ambassadors and Secret Agents* (London: Jonathan Cape, 1954), 37–40.

61. On the reasons for the ban in France, see the note to the French ambassador in The Hague dated 17 Mar. 1785, in MAE, Corr. Pol.—Hollande, 562, indicating that Louis XVI had imposed this measure against the will of Vergennes and the French foreign policy establishment. Other documents in this volume indicate that the Austrian ambassador Count F.-C. de Mercy-Argenteau and the queen had taken special interest in French policy toward the Netherlands, although there is no explicit indication that they had lobbied for the ban on the paper. On the Vienna reprint edition, see Etienne Luzac to Dutch States-General, 1786, in LGA-VH, Z(2), no. 77.

62. *GL*, 29 Oct. 1784 (Paris, 22 Oct.).

63. Ibid., 7 Dec. 1784 (Paris, 26 Nov.).

64. Murphy, *Vergennes*, 408–13.

single most important intervention in the entire Patriot crisis of 1781–
87. It was a report, datelined Leiden, denouncing a supposed correspondence between certain politicians in The Hague and the exiled
Duke Louis of Brunswick, the German prince who had served as William V's "prime minister" until Patriot agitation had forced his dismissal
in 1781. The insinuation that the much-maligned duke was still directing the Orangist cause from his exile in Aachen, near the Dutch border,
later led to a bungling Patriot attempt to purloin the duke's papers,
which made the issue an international one because of the Dutch agents'
violation of German territory. In the face of this outrage, August Ludwig von Schlözer, the most prominent German political journalist of the
period, denounced the *Gazette de Leyde* and the Dutch Patriot press for
"unprecedented indecency" in "attacking the honor of Duke Louis in
the face of all Europe."[65] The *Gazette de Leyde* was dragged into a
journalistic brawl with its main rival, the outspokenly Orangist *Courier
du Bas-Rhin*, which had been showering Luzac and his journal with
abuse for several years.[66] And it was just at this point that the French
government suddenly banned the Leiden paper's circulation, for reasons that mystified Luzac and the *nouvellistes* in the French capital.[67]

   At this tense moment, Luzac decided to cut back sharply on his own
and the paper's involvement with Dutch politics. Despite his central
position in Patriot affairs, he was becoming increasingly unhappy with
the direction events were taking in his native Leiden. In April 1785 he
had accepted an appointment as professor of ancient languages and
modern Dutch history at Leiden University. According to the frustrated
Patriot Dumont-Pigalle, Luzac had refused to respond to Manzon once
he had become a university professor because "the position he now
holds does not allow him to compromise himself any further with any
other writer."[68] Alert readers learned of a major change in Luzac's
connection with the *Gazette de Leyde* on 15 April 1785, when the signature at the bottom of the paper, which had read "At Leiden, by Jean and
Etienne Luzac" ever since the two sons of Jean Luzac had officially
replaced their uncle as holders of the paper's privilege in April 1783,

65. August Ludwig von Schlözer, *Ludwig Ernst, Herzog zu Braunschweig und Luneburg*
(Göttingen: Vandenhoeck, 1786), 574.

66. Luzac had permitted himself occasional outbursts against Manzon, such as the
signed letter he printed in the *Gazette de Leyde* on 10 August 1784, denying one of Manzon's
charges and calling him "this vile and cowardly assassin of other people's reputations," but
he had largely resisted the temptation to engage in the kind of polemics common in the
English and American press of the period, as well as in the Dutch-language journals of the
Patriottentijd.

67. Jean Luzac to Vérac, 10 Mar. 1785, in MAE, Corr. Pol.—Hollande, 562; [Pidansat
de Mairobert, attrib.], *Mémoires secrets*, 28:166 (8 Mar. 1785); Lescure, ed., *Correspondance
secrète*, 1:546 (17 Mar. 1785).

68. Dumont-Pigalle, "Contre Luzac," in AR, DP, carton 59.

was suddenly altered to read "At Leiden, by Etienne Luzac." Jean Luzac had followed the pattern of so many other owners of French-language gazettes in the Netherlands: he had hired an editor to do his work.

The Dutch Patriots should have had reason to be pleased with Jean Luzac's replacement, Antoine-Marie Cerisier. A native Frenchman who had settled in the Netherlands in the 1760s or 1770s, Cerisier was one of those cosmopolitan supporters of movements for liberty who devoted his life to publicizing republican principles.[69] He admired the Dutch, and his *Tableau de l'histoire générale des Provinces unies*, which had begun to appear in 1777, gave the international reading public a history of the Netherlands from an anti-Orangist perspective. His numerous pamphlets in favor of the American Revolution were probably inspired by the French government, but they went beyond official French policy: he dreamed of creating a French-speaking republic alongside the liberated American states, "led by the voice of a Rousseau, a Mably, a Lauraguais, a Raynal, a Mercier."[70] His pro-American works brought him into contact with John Adams, who contributed to Cerisier's journal, the *Politique hollandois*, and recommended him for membership in the Massachusetts Academy of Arts and Sciences as "one of the greatest Wits, and Historians in Europe, and the best grounded in the American Principles of any man I have found in Europe."[71] The *Politique hollandois*, originally devoted primarily to American affairs, had evolved into a leading Dutch Patriot organ, carrying articles and reprints of pamphlets too long to be inserted in the newspapers. Cerisier's views thus seemed to be almost identical to Jean Luzac's, and his journalistic style was more openly polemical: he might have been expected to make the *Gazette de Leyde* even more vehement in the Patriot cause.

Instead, the paper under Cerisier's editorship virtually ceased to report on the Dutch Patriot movement. Members of the circle of French-speaking Patriot insiders had no doubt that this silence was the result of Luzac's decisions, rather than Cerisier's own inclinations. Johan Valckenaer, Luzac's cousin and a fiery Patriot agitator, accused Luzac of

69. On Cerisier, see Jeremy D. Popkin, "From Dutch Republican to French Monarchist: Antoine-Marie Cerisier and the Age of Revolution," in *Tijdschrift voor Geschiedenis* (1989) (forthcoming). Cerisier was born in France in 1749, and had originally come to the Netherlands as a member of the French diplomatic service. He was related to an Amsterdam chocolate-maker of the same name who advertised in the *Gazette de Leyde* in the 1780s and who was still in business in 1816, when Cerisier sent his son from France to undertake an apprenticeship. (Cerisier to P. H. Marron, letter of 15 Apr. 1816, in Amsterdam University Library, Ms. 41 Ci.)

70. A.-M. Cerisier, "Lettre écrite à un Ami sur la guerre présente entre l'Angleterre et l'Amérique," in William Barrow, *Histoire de la fondation des colonies des anciennes républiques, adaptée à la dispute présente de la Grande Bretagne avec ses colonies américaines* (A.-M. Cerisier, trans.) (Utrecht: Schoonhoven, 1778), 176. Lauraguais was a prominent French pamphleteer of the period, known for his opposition to the Maupeou "coup" of 1771.

71. Adams, letter of 3 Feb. 1782, in Adams Papers microfilms, r. 102.

EN HOLLANDE,
M. DCC LXXXIV.

Luzac's enemy: Dutch Patriot caricature of Jean Manzon, the Orangist editor of the *Courier du Bas-Rhin*, 1784. He is shown with a money-bag on his desk and copies of the works of Hobbes and Machiavelli on the floor next to his chair. Courtesy of the Harvard College Library.

preferring to make money by using the paper's scarce news space for "silly stories like that of the [Diamond] necklace," and the would-be Patriot mastermind Pierre-Alexandre Dumont-Pigalle, like Cerisier a Frenchman who had embraced the Dutch republican cause, blamed Luzac for keeping the French from appreciating the necessity of supporting the Patriot cause: "His silence made the French think nothing was happening, or that he did not dare refute Manzon, because the latter was right. That is what the Patriots owe to Maitre Jean, whose paper was the only one that might have enlightened the French."[72] Luzac's Patriot critics were particularly frustrated because they knew he had material in hand that would have been quite damaging to their bête noire, Jean Manzon: the latter, after a lengthy correspondence with Luzac, had been forced to concede that he had tried to extort money from the Duke of Brunswick in 1781, and had pleaded with Luzac not to expose him.[73] But Luzac decided against using the columns of his own paper to pursue the issue, and until the fall of 1786, the *Gazette de Leyde* was, as Dumont-Pigalle and Valckenaer charged, almost silent on Dutch affairs.

The Crisis of 1785 and the Defeat of the Patriots

As Jean Luzac exchanged the editorship of the *Gazette de Leyde* for a professorship, the Dutch Patriots were beginning to disagree among themselves about what sort of polity the United Provinces should be. Originally, the Patriot movement had been a protest against the supposedly excessive power of the stadholder, led by wealthy regents from the leading Dutch cities. By the end of 1784, these regents were finding themselves under increasing pressure from more radical Patriots, who wanted to reform not only the stadholderate but also the system by which small oligarchies ruled the cities and, through them, the provincial Estates and the States-General. And these "original Patriots," who were often regents themselves, were in turn being pushed by an even more radical current that wanted the total abolition of the stadholderate and of "aristocracies of all sorts."[74] Jean Luzac's native Leiden was one of the main battlegrounds between moderate and radical Patriots, and his

72. "Contre Luzac," in AR, DP, carton 59.

73. The *Gazette de Leyde* had mentioned this accusation briefly in its issue of 19 August 1785, provoking Manzon to demand a retraction. When Luzac responded with a private letter to Manzon listing the documents he had that backed up the accusation, Manzon abjectly confessed that the charges were true, but begged not to be forced into printing a public confession that he, at least, believed would ruin his career. Apparently Luzac decided to let the matter rest. Copies of the correspondence between Manzon and Luzac are in AR, DP, carton 50, "Procès de Manzon." Dumont-Pigalle, frustrated because Luzac would not allow the publication of the incriminating documents in the *Gazette de Leyde*, eventually inserted them in one of his pamphlets: P. A. Dumont-Pigalle, *Esquisse d'un grand tableau, ou Mémoires pour servir à l'histoire des Provinces-Unies des Pays-Bas* ("Hollande": n.p., 1786), 403–22.

74. Antoine B. Caillard, "Mémoire sur la Révolution de Hollande," in Louis Ségur, *Tableau historique et politique de l'Europe, depuis 1786 jusqu'en 1796, ou l'An IV* (Paris: Buisson, 1801), 1:292–94. Caillard's distinction between traditional regents, reforming regents, and "democrats" seems to fit the facts better than the bipartite schema of conservative and democratic factions adopted in modern works such as Palmer's and De Wit's.

involvement in the struggle there was undoubtedly the single most important event in his political life, confirming his rigid personal beliefs and setting the course for the rest of his career.

Luzac was not a member of the regent class. As a descendant of Huguenot immigrants, he was outside the network of interrelated families whose members filled the forty seats of the *Vroedschap* or council, from which the *Burgemeesters* and the city's deputies to the provincial Estates were chosen. It would not have been surprising if he had sided with the radicals who, drawing their inspiration from the maverick aristocrat Van der Capellen tot den Pol's anonymous pamphlet of 1781, *Aan het Volk van Nederland*, were demanding an opening up of the traditional city governments. Several members of Luzac's immediate milieu, including his brother-in-law Wybo Fijnje, publisher of the Dutch-language *Hollandsche Historische Courant* in nearby Delft, and his cousin Johan Valckenaer, the son of his beloved mentor L. C. Valckenaer, took this course.

Jean Luzac, however, emerged as one of the most outspoken leaders of the moderate wing of the Patriots, defenders of the regents' traditional privileges. In the crisis year of 1785, the most troubled moment in Leiden's internal politics, he took the lead in opposing the local radicals' key demand, that the debates and votes of the city council members be made public so that they could be held responsible to the citizenry. In a statement he wrote on behalf of the council's moderate members, Luzac warned against demagogues who would claim to speak for the people, and called for ordinary citizens to rally behind the regents to oppose their only real enemy, the stadholder.[75] Alarmed by the increasing role of crowd pressure in Dutch politics, he wrote a lengthy and widely read article, under the pseudonym "Sincerus Atticus," condemning the rise of mobocracy, which his brother-in-law Fijnje consented to publish in his *Hollandsche Historische Courant*. And he devoted his inaugural university lecture to denouncing the excesses of democracy in terms whose reference to immediate events were unmistakable.

The result of this outspoken engagement in Dutch politics was to make Luzac a marked man. Letters to the Patriot press condemned "the all too passionate and partial *Sincerus Atticus*."[76] An angry polemical pamphlet accused him of having abandoned his political beliefs "out of jealousy, out of envy, out of evil-heartedness."[77] His apparent desertion of the Patriot cause baffled even those who knew him well. In his notes

75. Jean Luzac, *Contra-Aanteekeningen van Negentien Leden van de Vroedschap der Stad Leyden; betreklyk tot het Adres, in Maart 1785, aan dezelve Vroedschap ingeleverd* . . . (Leiden: Herdingh, 1785), iii, vi.

76. *Hollandsche Historische Courant*, 30 Aug. 1785 (letter from Zwolle, 27 Aug.).

77. *Eerkrans voor den steller van het Rapport omtrend de Leydsche Propositie van Geheimhouding, den Hooggeleerden Heer Mr. Jan Luzac, Grieksche Hoogleeraar te Leyden* (n.p., n.d.), 17n.

for a pamphlet against Luzac that was never completed, Dumont-Pigalle returned repeatedly to the notion that there had been a close connection between Luzac's appointment to the professorship at Leiden in April 1785 and his apparent change of political heart. Was the professorship—an appointment that had had to be approved by the regents of the province—a reward for Luzac's agreeing to defend the Leiden oligarchy? Was Luzac, who the antidemocratic regents had also appointed as the city council's legal consultant, aiming at obtaining regent status for himself?

The notion that Luzac was swayed by the possibility of personal advancement may be partially true. His share of the profits from the *Gazette de Leyde* made him one of the wealthier individuals in Leiden, and he had additional income from his legal work and, after 1785, from his professorship. Thanks to his control of the newspaper, he was a much more influential man than most of the Leiden regents. But, as Dumont-Pigalle observed in many of his other notes on Luzac, his decision to defend the regents was also consistent with his basic principles. Luzac had never been a democrat or an enthusiast for revolution: the Leiden crisis of 1785 simply revealed the implications of the principles he had held all along.

The events of 1785 provoked Luzac into making his political ideas public for the first time. In his inaugural lecture and his "Sincerus Atticus" article, he revealed himself as a consistent proponent of mixed government. His ideal was "a tempered Aristo-Democracy" in which "on the one hand, the people have neither any part in the making of day-to-day decisions, nor any influence on the administration of justice, and, on the other hand, the naming of magistrates is not made completely independent of the citizens' voice."[78] Luzac's views placed him in the long tradition of Renaissance civic humanism. His inaugural lecture stressed the necessity of virtue and education to make a good citizen, and cited Cicero and other authors who had long been incorporated into this tradition. In the classic Aristotelian tradition, he put mixed government above pure democracy, and in the classic Dutch regent tradition, he saw the existing constitution of the Republic as a model of civic-humanist principles, needing to be defended against all alterations rather than reformed.

Luzac's more polemical article in his brother-in-law's *Hollandsche Historische Courant* made the relationship between his civic-humanist commonplaces and the immediate Dutch context more evident. It was in-

---

78. Jean Luzac, *Redevoering van Mr. Johan Luzac, ten betooge, dat de Geleerdheid de voedster is der Burger-Deugd, vooral in een Vry Gemeenebest . . .*, Jan de Kruyff, trans. (Leyden: Mostert, 1786), 54–55. As was customary, Luzac had given his inaugural lecture in Latin, but he arranged for its translation into Dutch.

spired by events in Utrecht, a stronghold of the radical Patriots, where an organized crowd had pressured the city council into expelling an unpopular member. This expulsion without a fair hearing violated "the first rule of justice . . . in taking from someone, without a hearing, by arbitrary power, his position in society, and his honor and dignity," Luzac complained. The Utrecht Patriots justified their action by claiming that the people held "the supreme power, the essential sovereignty" and were therefore free to dismiss any magistrate from office. Luzac admitted that "the original sovereignty, or *Majestis realis*, comes from the people. But I refuse to admit that the people can carry out actions of government." In defense of his position, he cited the names of John Locke and Algernon Sydney, but his argument much more closely resembled Burke's defense of the independence of members of Parliament, which Luzac proceeded to paraphrase. The people, having chosen representatives, were obligated to leave them the power to run the government without interference. Direct democracy would lead to an unheard-of tyranny; Luzac wound up his argument with a citation from the "immortal Montesquieu" on the dangers of direct popular influence on government.[79]

Luzac's advocacy of mixed government and his distrust of democracy recalled the political views of his American friend John Adams. As in Adams's case, Luzac's views reflected a bleak view of human nature. The French-born radical Patriot Dumont-Pigalle, who had known Luzac well before they split over Leiden politics in 1785, wrote in his notes on the *Gazette de Leyde*'s publisher that Luzac did not believe that fundamental reforms guided by abstract political ideas could be carried out. For Luzac, according to Dumont-Pigalle, "principles are nothing but a theory whose practice is not possible." The ultimate reason why high-sounding principles could not be implemented in practice was rooted in human nature: "Luzac told Cerisier that . . . all of his ideas of improvement and reform are mirages, impractical platonic ideas—that Cerisier did not know the human heart."[80]

The context for Luzac's abandonment of faith in the possibility of reform was Leiden city politics in 1785. By the middle of that year, tension in the town had reached a peak. The formation of a Patriot-dominated *Vrijcorps* in 1783 had led to an outbreak of rioting by lower-class supporters of the stadholder in June 1784. This Orangist riot was put down, and the radically minded *Vrijcorps* members exerted increasing pressure on the city council, itself already divided internally, to carry out reforms. In March 1785, the *Vrijcorps* touched off a constitutional crisis within the city by sending a mass petition directly to the provincial

79. "Sincerus Atticus" [Jean Luzac], "Brief aan den Eigenaar deezer Courant in dato 17 August 1785," *Hollandsche Historische Courant* (Delft), 20 and 23 Aug. 1785.
80. Citations from Dumont-Pigalle, "Contre Luzac," in AR, DP, carton 59.

Estates, bypassing the established city government and raising the specter of "dual power" in the city. When the council condemned this action, the radicals launched further protests. In response, Luzac drafted a memorandum for the conservative faction of the council, defending the secrecy of that body's proceedings.

Luzac saw that publicity would amount to giving the broader citizenry power over the councilmen: if they knew how each individual council member had voted, the people would be in a position to reward and punish them accordingly. If the council was to be able to fulfill its proper function in a system of mixed government and act independently of the populace, it therefore had to be able to keep its proceedings secret.[81] As the author of a pamphlet against Luzac put it, "according to him everything that a people does either by itself, or through its chosen representatives, for the restoration of its old rights or the prevention of possible . . . violations of them, is abusive." Luzac had tried to justify his position by citing the practice of the British Parliament, where speeches were public but votes were not: his critic pointed out the irony of Luzac, "who has ladled out to us the best English news for so many years in his French gazette," now asserting that political decisions had to be taken in secret.[82]

In the course of long-drawn-out maneuvers extending through 1785, the faction favoring publicity for city council debates finally won out.[83] Luzac was promptly dismissed from his position as legal consultant to the council, and in fact withdrew from municipal politics altogether. As the more radical Patriots maliciously noted, the Orangist press, which had previously attacked him as one of the leaders of the antistadholder movement, now came to his defense: the semiofficial Orangist organ, Pierre Frédéric Gosse's *s'Gravenhaagse Courant*, printed an article commending his stand against public proceedings.[84] Dutch-language Patriot periodicals that had earlier defended the *Gazette de Leyde* against Orangist attacks now lamented that "a man with so much credit and influence on so many men who govern the city and the province has adopted such sentiments."[85] Estranged from his Patriot friends and relatives, unwilling to embrace the Orangists, and embroiled in political disputes with his university colleagues, Jean Luzac found himself in unhappy isolation as the radical Patriots seized the ascendancy not only in Leiden but in other cities in Holland and the neighboring province of Utrecht.[86]

81. *Contra-Aantekeningen*. Luzac was generally acknowledged to have drafted the introductory statement to this pamphlet, although he was not a member of the council.

82. *Eerkrans*, 14n, 27–29n.

83. Blok, *Geschiedenis*, 3:363.

84. *s'Gravenhaagse Courant*, 22 Feb. 1786.

85. *Politieke Kruyer*, no. 310 (letter of 19 Jan. 1786).

86. On Luzac's quarrel with his Orangist colleague Adriaan Kluit, see Vrij, "Collegegeschil," 121–41. Luzac was not completely alone in breaking with the Patriot move-

Luzac's losing battle with the radicals in Leiden had no visible impact on the *Gazette de Leyde*, which printed very little Dutch news in the second half of 1785 and the first eight months of 1786. After the final defeat of the Patriot movement in September 1787, Dumont-Pigalle and other former Patriots blamed Luzac's silence during the debacle. They had to admit that in late 1786, the paper had resumed extensive coverage of the Patriot struggle, although they attributed this decision to "interested motives" on Luzac's part, alleging that his foreign subscribers had complained about his silence. But they claimed that "he was careful to support the cause of patriotism very feebly; he never stopped supporting the aristocrats [that is, the regents]."[87]

In reality, when the paper reentered the Dutch arena, it did so emphatically. In late 1785 and the first half of 1786, the radical Patriots had seemed to be succeeding despite Luzac's silence. The stadholder had abandoned The Hague, and his opponents were free to indulge in their own internal struggle over the extent of popular participation proper for a reformed constitution. In August 1786, however, Orangist troops occupied two pro-Patriot villages, Elburg and Hattem, in the province of Gelderland, demonstrating that the menace of stadholderian despotism was far from destroyed. As Simon Schama has written, "The attack on Hattem and Elburg . . . was taken by the Patriots as a virtual declaration of civil war." The crisis "galvanised [the Patriots] into urgent measures for their collective defense and rather tardily brought a measure of unity to the different factions."[88]

One sign of this revival of Patriot unity was the *Gazette de Leyde*'s sudden resumption of highly partisan coverage of Dutch politics. In the wake of the Hattem and Elburg affair, the paper defiantly proclaimed, "Regardless of the efforts of a despotism, all the more odious because its actions are aimed at increasing its own grandeur and power, and not at the public good, we can predict that it will not succeed. The nation's spirit has reached a degree of vigor and energy to which it would be hard to find an equal elsewhere."[89] The paper blamed the stadholder alone for this crisis, and it demanded that the public be allowed to know about his secret negotiations with foreign governments.[90] But, in an evolution from its stance in 1783 and 1784, the paper now called for specific

ment in 1785 and yet refusing to endorse Orangism. His friend Adrian Van der Kemp followed the same course. Harry F. Jackson, *Scholar in the Wilderness: Francis Adrian van der Kemp* (Syracuse, N.Y.: Syracuse University Press, 1963), 51–52.

87. [François Bernard], *Précis historique de la Révolution qui vient de s'opérer en Hollande* (Paris: Desenne and Volland, 1788), 66. Bernard had been editor of the French-language *Gazette d'Amsterdam* in 1786 and had corresponded regularly with Dumont-Pigalle about Luzac's shortcomings.

88. Schama, *Patriots and Liberators*, 108.

89. *GL*, 26 Sept. 1786 (Leiden, 24 Sept.).

90. Ibid., 5 Jan. 1787 (Leiden, 3 Jan.); and 16 Feb. 1787 (Leiden, 15 Feb.).

reforms in the traditional Dutch constitution. It praised the Estates of Holland for grappling with one of the most explosive issues raised during the Patriot period, by granting political rights to Catholics, which the paper called "a sure sign of the progress that the Dutch Nation has made in the understanding of the genuine rights of the citizen, and of liberty."[91] More broadly, the paper now acknowledged that the Republic had always suffered from an unstable balance of powers that permitted the stadholder to use "a blind and irritated populace" to make the country's constitution "monarchical despite the appearance of a republican administration."[92] To resolve this problem, the *Gazette de Leyde* endorsed a specific proposal first advanced by the city of Haarlem's representatives to the Estates of the province of Holland, calling for a mechanism to make that body responsible to the people.[93]

The mounting crisis in the Republic now led the *Gazette de Leyde* to endorse radical measures that it had often hesitated to approve in other countries. In April, it strongly approved the Amsterdam *Vrijcorps'* pressures on the city council to expel certain members who had entered into secret negotiations with the stadholder. The action had been carried out by "the part of the nation that one can regard as its soul and spirit, the class of honest, wealthy or industrious citizens," the paper asserted. It praised the orderly and nonviolent methods used, but it nevertheless had given its imprimatur to exactly the kind of revolutionary political tactics Luzac had combated so vigorously in Leiden less than two years earlier.[94] Even the outbreak of genuine violence in Utrecht shortly afterward did not drive the paper into its usual retreat toward moderation. Although it lamented the virtual civil war apparently raging in that city, the eight columns of detailed coverage in the issue of 15 May 1787 led to the editorial conclusion that "it is a matter of saving the whole Republic, Holland in particular, from the chains of slavery."[95]

The country was now virtually divided into two armed camps, and the paper had chosen a side. The gazette did condemn what it felt was excessive violence against the lower-class supporters of the stadholder in Amsterdam,[96] but it continued to urge the Patriots on and to complain when the Estates-General hesitated to act firmly against the stadholder.[97] Both the Patriots and the paper recognized that the success or failure of that movement might depend on the attitude of the Nether-

91. Ibid., 30 Jan. 1787 (The Hague, 27 Jan.).
92. Ibid., 6 Feb. 1787 (Leiden, 3 Feb.).
93. On the Haarlem plan, see Schama, *Patriots and Liberators*, 111; Geyl, *Révolution batave*, 80. For the paper's endorsement of it, see *GL*, 20 Feb. 1787 (Leiden, 18 Feb.).
94. *GL*, 27 Apr. 1787 (Leiden, 24 and 26 Apr.).
95. Ibid., 15 May 1787 (Leiden, 14 May).
96. Ibid., 1 June 1787 (Amsterdam, 30 May).
97. Ibid., 22 June 1787 (Leiden, 21 June).

lands' foreign neighbors; the paper sought to keep up morale by playing up reports that the English, who supported the stadholder, would not intervene, and by raising hopes that the French, who favored the Patriots, would.[98] And the *Gazette de Leyde* devoted more and more energy to countering unfavorable articles in other journals, particularly the Orangists' leading French-language outlet, the *Courier du Bas-Rhin*, which it denounced in almost every issue as a "receptacle of slanders and lies."[99] The traditionally impassive and understated *Gazette de Leyde* took on more and more of the characteristics of the "party press" in the English-speaking world: it became as vociferous as any of the Dutch-language Patriot organs in trying to direct events as well as describing them. Although the general body of the paper continued to fit the mold of the cautiously impartial international press, the columns devoted to Dutch affairs—close to 10 percent of the paper's overall content from January to September 1787—had taken on the tone of an ideologically motivated revolutionary journal.

This vehemently pro-Patriot tone and activist stance went well beyond Jean Luzac's personal position. In private letters, he was deeply troubled by the violence of those Patriots who wanted to convert the oligarchical city-republics of the United Provinces into genuine representative governments, or what Luzac dismissed as "complete democracy." In view of his strong reservations about democratic government, he must have been particularly pained to read in the *Courier du Bas-Rhin* that "Mr. J. L. jurisconsulte" was trying to indoctrinate the Dutch with the idea that "the magistrates and the Regents who think they govern us, are no more than our humble valets and representatives. . . . We can change them every day like our shirts."[100] Luzac also had to suffer the effects of a family quarrel about ownership of the *Gazette de Leyde* in which his leading opponent was Wybo Fijnje, a militant radical Patriot and publisher of the Dutch-language paper in nearby Delft, who was also the husband of Luzac's sister Emilie. The elder Etienne Luzac had died in January 1787. Under the terms of the contract he had made with his two nephews in 1783, ownership of the *Gazette de Leyde* went exclusively to them, with his two nieces receiving no share in it. Fijnje protested violently against this injustice to his wife, which deprived him of a chance of influencing the paper's editorial policy: in a letter written some years later, Jean Luzac told a family friend that during the argument Fijnje "attacked me in my own house with a knife in his hand."[101]

98. Ibid., 26 June 1787 (London, 19 June); and 7 Aug. 1787 (The Hague, 5 Aug.).
99. Ibid., 4 Sept. 1787 (Leiden, 3 Sept.).
100. "Premier dialogue entre un voiageur et un patriote Hollandois," in *Courier du Bas-Rhin*, 19 May 1787 (Cleves, 19 May).
101. Luzac to Cornelius de Gyzelaer, 11 Dec. 1796, in LUL, Luzac, carton 29. The incident is referred to more vaguely in Emilie Luzac's letter to her brother, 22 Aug. 1787,

Despite his private reservations about the radicals, when he was forced to choose between alliance with the democrats or alliance with the stadholder, Luzac reluctantly came down on the side of the former. He wrote to one friend that "there are circumstances in politics in which one must overlook certain irregularities in order to forestall yet greater evils. We find ourselves today in that most unhappy situation."[102] Luzac did not really share the rosy optimism about the Patriots' prospects that his paper propagated. According to Dumont-Pigalle, Luzac had never believed that the French would intervene to support the Patriots: he repeatedly told his friends that "the French Court had always been the most deceitful and the most perfidious that ever existed. That history was full of its betrayals." And, according to Dumont-Pigalle's note, he cited France's refusal to support Poland against Russia and its separate peace with Britain in 1783, which had left the Dutch to negotiate with the British on their own.[103] Cerisier, who continued to be the nominal editor during these months, was more wholeheartedly committed to the Patriot cause, but Luzac was most dissatisfied with his employee's performance. He complained of "the oversights, the negligence . . . that I had to correct in your work every day."[104]

The differences between Luzac's and Cerisier's personal views were not the reason for the *Gazette de Leyde*'s failure to reflect Luzac's own doubts and hesitations, however. Whatever his private misgivings about the Patriots' chances, Luzac was caught in the logic of public journalistic partisanship. Had the paper accurately reflected his own agonizing, it would have contributed to the weakening of whatever chances the Patriots possessed. If it had admitted to any doubts about the rightness or the chances of the Patriots' cause, the Orangist press would have been quick to trumpet the fact. Having decided to commit the paper to supporting what he personally felt was in the last analysis the correct side in the Dutch conflict, Luzac had to allow it to publish material that would favor that party's success, not its failure.

On 13 September 1787, Prussian troops entered the Dutch Republic's territory to put down the Patriot movement and restore the powers of the stadholder. The *Gazette de Leyde* bravely proclaimed that "the entire nation is rising in arms," but in fact the Patriots put up minimal resistance.[105] As the Prussians advanced, most people who had been active

---

ibid., and it is not entirely clear whether Luzac's statement about Fijnje's attack was meant literally or metaphorically.

102. Luzac to unnamed correspondent (apparently a Leiden regent), in LUL, Luzac, carton 28, nos. 35 and 36.

103. "Contre Luzac," in AR, DP, carton 59.

104. Luzac to Cerisier, n.d. but shortly after the Prussian intervention of September 1787, in LGA-VH, Z(2), no. 146.

105. *GL*, 14 Sept. 1787 (The Hague, 12 Sept.).

in the Patriot cause fled the country. Among the refugees were not only the *Gazette de Leyde*'s editor, Cerisier, and other French activists such as Dumont-Pigalle and François Bernard, but also Luzac's Patriot relatives Johan Valckenaer and Wybo Fijnje with his wife, Luzac's beloved sister Emilie. Luzac himself, as well as his brother Etienne, somehow escaped the dragnet. An English agent complained that while all the other "infernal gazettes, which vomitted fire and flame, are suppressed," Luzac, "who cunningly distilled poison, still goes on in the same way."[106] Luzac's moderation in Leiden's internal affairs in 1785 probably guaranteed him some protection and his paper's great prestige may have played a role as well. To be sure, the paper virtually ceased coverage of Dutch politics and returned to its pattern of before 1781, omitting almost all reference to its home country. Even so, on occasion Luzac's anti-Orangist sentiments did slip through. The Orangists might have overlooked his comparison of the virtues of the American constitution to the defects of the Dutch,[107] but they could not have missed Luzac's reprint of his former friend Pieter Paulus's speech protesting his dismissal from office in 1788 because of his Patriot views.[108] Nevertheless, the paper continued to publish without interruption; indeed, with the growing crisis in France to fill its columns, the enterprise was prospering as never before.

The survival and even the increasing prosperity of his newspaper did little to console Jean Luzac for the defeat of the antistadholderian cause. He remained estranged from the former friends and the close relatives with whom he had broken two years earlier. They blamed him for betraying the Patriot movement, whereas he blamed them for "the change of system, which began to take place in early 1785" and led to the Patriots' failure.[109] When the Batavian Revolution of 1795 finally allowed the exiled Patriots to return, the quarrel begun in Leiden ten years earlier resumed more violently than ever. Luzac was particularly angry at the criticism he received from the exiled Patriots because he had run considerable risks after September 1787 to assist friends and university colleagues facing Orangist persecution. He courageously took the lead in defending Bavius Voorda, a pro-Patriot professor dismissed after the Prussian occupation in 1787.[110] And, despite his strong feelings about his exiled relatives' role in the Patriot catastrophe in 1787, Luzac nevertheless assumed the burden of looking after their affairs. He

106. Archibald Maclaine to Sir Joseph Yorke (British ambassador to The Hague in the 1770s), 16 Oct. 1787, in A. Aspinall, ed., *The Later Correspondence of George III* (Cambridge: Cambridge University Press, 1966), 1:347.
107. *GL*, 6 Nov. 1787 (Leiden, 6 Nov.).
108. Ibid., 4 Mar. 1788 (Leiden, 3 Mar.).
109. Luzac to unknown correspondent, n.d., in LUL, Luzac, carton 28, no. 34.
110. Matthijs Siegenbeek, *Geschiedenis der Leidsche Hoogeschool* (Leiden: Luchtmans, 1829–32), 1:323.

tried to negotiate the sale of Wybo and Emilie Fijnje's journalistic property, the *Hollandsche Historische Courant*, in Delft, and to mediate between
his brother Etienne and the latter's brother-in-law Johan Valckenaer,
who had fled to France and now complained that Etienne was not
sending him enough financial support.[111] He sought to assure Valckenaer that the republican cause would rise again, that "times will not
remain this way forever," but he saw no immediate hope for the overthrow of "those who cling to slavish principles."[112] When Valckenaer
apparently reproached him for not doing enough to oppose the restored Orangists, however, Luzac responded with a bleak description of
his personal isolation. "All that I hear or read about public affairs is sad
and bitter. . . . Those who support Caesar [that is, the Orangists] abhor
me; those of Pompey's party [the Patriots] have either taken flight . . . or
now try to curry favor with the rulers. None of them talk to me, nor I to
them, and all that pertains to the fate of our country is concealed from
me."[113] The collapse of the Dutch Patriot movement left Luzac disillusioned and depressed: whatever hopes he had held for the triumph of a
reasoned republican liberty in the Old World had been crushed.

The Dutch Patriot movement's failure also marked the end of the
Gazette de Leyde's most significant experience as a party journal, directly
involved in attempting to influence the events it reported. Although the
paper took a clear position on many other political movements of the
time, it had never been so directly involved in any of them, and this
involvement had forced the paper to obey imperatives different from
those that normally governed its operations. Having decided to commit
the paper to a partisan cause, Jean Luzac had to allow it to speak in a
positive, affirmative tone to avoid harming the cause he had chosen. He
stopped short of adopting the violent, abusive language of the Dutch-
language party press or the hated *Courier du Bas-Rhin*, but he had to
abandon the pretense of impartial narration that normally served to
authenticate the paper's reports. The partisan environment of the *Patriottentijd* led the *Gazette de Leyde* to anticipate the press of the French
Revolution: Luzac learned firsthand the impossibility of standing aloof
from political passions during a revolutionary crisis. The experience
went contrary to his deeply held conviction that political passion and
extremism were inherently destructive. When the Revolution did break
out in France two years later, his sad experience of the mid-1780s would
make Jean Luzac regard the turmoil as a threat to both the republican
virtues he believed in and the very existence of newspapers like his own.

111. Emilie Luzac to Jean Luzac, 2 Jan. 1788, in LUL, Luzac, carton 29; Luzac to Johan
Valckenaer, n.d. but 1787 or early 1788, in ibid., carton 28, no. 62.
112. Luzac to Valckenaer, 21 Nov. 1787, in LUL, Ms. BPL 1030.
113. Ibid., 27 May 1788, in LUL, Ms. BPL 531. I thank my colleague David Olster for
assistance in translating this Latin passage.

[9]

The Challenge
of the French
Revolution

One of the ironies of the *Gazette de Leyde*'s situation during the last years of the Patriot struggle in the Netherlands was that the paper, despite the bitter quarrels in which its publisher was involved, was prospering as never before. The 90 percent of his news space that Jean Luzac did not devote to Dutch politics went to coverage of increasingly dramatic events elsewhere, and although the final collapse of the Patriots in September 1787 was a tragedy for Luzac himself, it freed his newspaper to concentrate even more heavily on other stories. Some of these events in the larger world seemed at first to offer more reasons for hope than the sorry outcome of the Dutch imbroglio; others at least presented opportunities to expand the sales of the *Gazette de Leyde*.

The Patriots' defeat forced the paper's editor Cerisier to flee to France, and Jean Luzac resumed editing the paper himself. Of the stories that occupied him during the later 1780s, the one that received the least space may well have occupied first place in his heart. The colonies' achievement of independence in 1783 had led to a drastic reduction in the paper's American coverage. But throughout the rest of his tenure as the paper's editor, he continued to print occasional pieces about the United States that demonstrated his concern for the success of the American experiment. In the face of hostile or skeptical reports, not only in the British press but in some continental journals, such as Schirach's *Politische Journal*, the *Gazette de Leyde* sought to put the best face on the new republic's problems and to advertise its successes. The fledgling American government could count on Luzac's paper to relay whatever public responses it wanted to make to European critics, as when an anonymous spokesman—probably John Adams—used it to deny rumors that the United States had approached the French philosophe Gabriel Bonnot de Mably for advice about its constitution.[1] On the other hand, the paper deliberately did not reproduce early reports concerning the Order of the Cincinnati, a proposal to grant special status to veterans of the war for independence which many European supporters of America feared would lead to the growth of a privileged caste in the new republic. Luzac waited until he had grounds to argue that the proposed organization had never had any official backing, explaining that "we put off mentioning this report, which seemed unlikely to us, because the equality of all citizens, which is the essence of a democratic constitution, would hardly permit the creation of such an Order in a republic like America."[2]

The *Gazette de Leyde*'s most significant service to the new American republic was the publicity it gave to the drafting of the Federal Constitution adopted in 1787. The difficulties that led to the decision to replace the Articles of Confederation had encouraged a number of European critics to pronounce the American experiment a failure. The Leiden paper gave the Americans a chance to defend themselves and to argue that the decision to draw up a new plan was not an admission of defeat:

> Even those political constitutions drafted with the greatest wisdom cannot, immediately after their creation, have a stability which comes from veneration and habit, and consequently comes only with time. It cannot be surprising, then, if the new American Republic experiences a few tremors before achieving such stability. The new state of things resulting from its independence, the large number of former friends of England, who remain within it, and the impossibility of rooting out the old prejudices that dominate them, must necessarily cause it some trouble at the outset.[3]

The paper was unable to report the debates leading to the new constitutional plan, since they were kept secret, but it welcomed the completed draft and made immediate plans to publish it, despite its length, since "it cannot fail to interest all those readers who have witnessed the misfortunes that the lack of such a constitution, fixed and determined in all respects, has just caused to one of the most flourishing of Republics in Europe."[4] This direct reference to Luzac's own country, where Prussian

1. *GL*, 23 Sept. 1783.

2. Ibid., 2 Jan. 1784 (Leiden, 2 Jan.). The *Gazette de France* had reported on the plans for the Order of the Cincinnati in its issue of 23 Dec. 1783, apparently the first European mention of the matter.

3. *GL*, 2 Jan. 1787 (New York, 28 Oct. 1786).

4. Ibid., 6 Nov. 1787 (Leiden, 6 Nov.). The paper began publication of the text of the Constitution on 13 November 1787, thus preceding the version in the *Journal politique de Bruxelles* on 17 November 1787 which Durand Echeverria has cited as the earliest French translation of the document. Echeverria, *Mirage in the West* (Princeton, N.J.: Princeton University Press, 1957), 162.

intervention had just quashed the Patriot movement two months earlier, made it clear that Luzac embraced the view of his American correspondents that the American experience had lessons for the Old Continent, views stated emphatically in a letter written for publication in the paper by the American agent Dumas in The Hague, a few months later:

> Thus, in combining constancy and sagacity with moderation and patience, in preferring mild methods and persuasion to force and constraint, in banishing from public councils the spirit of faction and selfishness, in spurning the ideas of restless and turbulent men, the American Confederation has brought its Republican System to the greatest degree of perfection that the human condition allows. It has achieved all the possible advantages of the Federative System, while avoiding its vices and defects. Thus the New World will have given the Old an example, which will be regarded fondly in Europe, but which no one will dare to imitate.[5]

The *Gazette de Leyde*'s interest in the American Constitution did not end with the publication of its text in November 1787. The paper enthusiastically advocated the ratification of the new document, downplaying the reports of opposition to it in some of the smaller states.[6] It showed little concern about the Virginia proposal to make ratification dependent on the adoption of a Bill of Rights, because it seemed likely that the other states would accept the idea.[7] When the *Gazette de France* told readers that the United States might break up because of opposition to the Constitution, the *Gazette de Leyde* promptly countered with reports on the broad support for it.[8] Later, Luzac published a series of "Letters from an American Merchant," actually written by Dumas, designed to diminish the impact of opposition to the Constitution.[9] Dumas praised the new Constitution because, among other things, it strictly limited the power of the people to intervene in political affairs, an attitude fully consonant with Luzac's own distrust of democracy.[10] Once the Constitution was in effect, the paper reported how many who had originally opposed it had now changed their minds, and it praised the *Federalist Papers*, "an excellent periodical work."[11]

5. *GL*, 29 Jan. 1788 (New York [*sic*], 6 Dec. 1787). Dumas identified himself as the author of this piece in a letter to Thomas Jefferson, 5 Feb. 1788, in Boyd, ed., *Jefferson*, 12:562–63.

6. *GL*, 15 Jan. 1788 (New York, 20 Nov. 1787).

7. Ibid., 29 Feb. 1788 (Philadelphia, 10 Jan.).

8. Ibid., 4 July 1788 (New York, 24 Apr., and Charlestown, 27 Apr.). Dumas had specifically requested publication of these reports to counter the effect of the *Gazette de Leyde*'s earlier mention of unfavorable accounts taken from the *Gazette de France*. Dumas to Jefferson, 24 July 1788, in Boyd, ed., *Jefferson*, 13:407.

9. Boyd, ed., *Jefferson*, 14:348–49n.

10. *GL*, 12 Dec. 1788.

11. Ibid., 13 Oct. 1789 (New York, 25 July); and 17 Nov. 1789 (New York, 30 Sept.).

By the time these last two articles appeared in the fall of 1789, American news had virtually vanished from the paper because of the avalanche of reports from France. Although the United States had ceased to be a major topic in the paper's columns, however, it reappeared from time to time as a happy alternative to the chaos into which not only France but all of Europe seemed to be descending. A dispatch datelined Philadelphia in 1791 boasted, "While Europe is prey to Cabinet intrigues, foreign wars, civil dissensions, the effects of ambition, jealousy and hatred," the United States "enjoys calm and happiness. . . . There is no nation under the sun, which enjoys greater prosperity and rosier prospects for its future welfare."[12] When the French revolutionary government's agent Edmond Genêt tried to rouse American opinion against Washington's policies, the paper documented American countermeasures to disabuse European opinion of any notion that the Americans were eager to follow the French example.[13] As Luzac became more and more despondent about events in France, America appeared ever more impressive: one of his editorial notes in 1794 remarked, "While Europe at the end of the eighteenth century offers the philanthropist the saddest prospect, . . . the New World seems to have been reserved to console him . . . America is an example of a truly just and moderate government."[14] Of course, the very success of the American system kept Luzac from devoting much space to it: "Lucky in its well-tempered liberty, it enjoys that quiet, which renders the Annals of a Nation the more sterile as its welfare becomes invulnerable to any disturbance."[15]

To the end of his editorship of the paper, the American example demonstrated to Luzac that a well-tempered republic was a genuine possibility. The success of the Americans, which his paper attributed to the good sense of the people, the wisdom of their leaders, and the excellence of their political institutions, contrasted sadly with the failure of all the movements for greater freedom that the *Gazette de Leyde* reported on in Europe, both before and after the French Revolution. The European experiences fit in with the generally pessimistic spirit of the civic-humanist tradition out of which Luzac came: on the whole, Luzac and his readers did not expect virtue to triumph in this fallen world. But the ongoing theme of American virtue and success served an essential purpose in the overall economy of the *Gazette de Leyde*'s reporting on the world: it provided the assurance that the cause of liberty was not a chimera.

Meanwhile, the troubles that broke out in 1786 in the Austrian Neth-

12. Ibid., 12 July 1791 (Philadelphia, 13 May).
13. Ibid., 20 Dec. 1793.
14. Ibid., 7 Feb. 1794 (Leiden, 7 Feb.).
15. Ibid., 3 Feb. 1795 (Leiden, 3 Feb.).

erlands, just south of the United Provinces, offered the *Gazette de Leyde* a chance to exploit a lucrative market. Superficially, the Belgian resistance to Joseph II's rationalizing reforms resembled the Dutch Patriot agitation: in both cases, traditional local bodies resisted an accretion of centralized power. Indeed, Luzac initially drew an explicit parallel between the two movements, when he urged the stadholder to follow the example Joseph II had set by agreeing to listen to his subjects' protests.[16] The Estates of the "Belgian nation" were doing nothing more than taking "respectful but firm and well-thought-out steps . . . to defend the constitution" and the *Gazette de Leyde* expressed satisfaction when the emperor and his subjects seemed to have settled their differences through negotiation.[17]

The Prussian intervention soon ended any hopes that the Dutch troubles could be resolved along the lines followed in Belgium, but by the end of 1787, it was also clear that matters in the emperor's domains were not yet settled. Rioting in Brussels in January 1788 cost several lives. Luzac attributed this outbreak to the uneducated lower classes, but it destroyed any sympathy he felt for the Belgian protesters. Furthermore, the central issue in the continuing protests was Joseph II's attempt to bring Catholic education under state control, and Luzac, who failed to distinguish between the conservative Catholic followers of Henri van der Noot and the more liberal supporters of Jean François Vonck, was not about to lend his support to a movement whose members were not only Catholics but also opponents of the Jansenists with whom the *Gazette de Leyde* had always sided.[18] By the fall of 1789, when the troubles in Belgium were being strongly affected by the revolution in neighboring France, he characterized the Belgian demands as "prejudices that more instruction among the people would remove."[19]

At the end of December 1789, a successful revolutionary movement overthrew the Austrian authorities altogether. The *Gazette de Leyde*'s extensive coverage of events gave a full picture of what had happened and conceded that "no event of this kind was ever accompanied by less disorder," but it warned that the rebels had opened a Pandora's box: since "sovereignty has been returned to the people," there would be disagreement about who should now have power. Some would "object to the very distinction of social orders," but others would insist that power now rested with the traditional Estates, dominated by aristocrats and clergy. The prospect for any peaceful resolution of the crisis was

16. Ibid., 8 May 1787 (Leiden, 7 May).
17. Ibid., 25 May 1787 (Leiden, 24 May); and 12 June 1787 (Leiden, 10 June).
18. Ibid., 29 Jan. 1788 (Brussels, 24 Jan.); 8 Feb. 1788 (Brussels, 3 Feb.). For the Belgian unrest in the 1780s see Janet L. Polasky, *Revolution in Brussels* (Hanover, N.H.: University Press of New England, 1987).
19. *GL*, 25 Aug. 1789 (Leiden, 24 Aug.).

slight.[20] The paper's editorial sympathies were now entirely with the Austrian authorities, who returned and suppressed the Belgian revolution by force at the end of 1790. Luzac rejoiced at this conclusion, condemning "the fanaticism . . . that the leaders of the Belgian insurrection have resorted to to keep it alive. . . . If the Belgian nation's complaints against the suppression of its constitutional rights by the late Emperor were not totally unfounded, it is a shame that this people, in defending its rights, has covered itself with shame and opprobrium," he editorialized.[21]

The Belgian movement did nothing to quell Luzac's misgivings about attempts to apply the theory of popular sovereignty in the Old World. But his paper's coverage of the Belgian controversies undoubtedly served to boost sales. The *Gazette de Leyde* functioned with respect to the Belgian upheaval in the same way that its enemy the *Courier du Bas-Rhin* had with respect to the Dutch troubles: it gave the opponents of a broad-based popular movement an outlet for their views that was out of the reach of the protesters. Certainly the Austrian government appreciated the paper's support: in January 1791, Leopold II, Joseph II's successor, offered Luzac a medal, and Luzac was able to use this opening to resolve his long-standing grievance against the government-protected reprint of his paper in Vienna.[22]

The *Gazette de Leyde* and the Prerevolutionary Crisis in France

American and Belgian news, together with the first reports of the new surge of reform activity that began in 1788 in Poland, gave the *Gazette de Leyde* more than enough news to cover when Luzac could not or would not print reports about the Netherlands. But throughout the second half of the 1780s, these stories were overshadowed by occurrences in the country that was at once the continent's major power and the paper's major market. Although it never became the newspaper's sole concern, the course of events in France came to dominate the paper by 1787; this remained the paper's main story throughout the following decade. Luzac at first welcomed the French movement for reform, but, as in the Dutch and Belgian cases, he soon came to have grave reservations about it. As revolutionary enthusiasm mounted in France, it faded in Leiden. By the time the troops of the French Republic occupied the Netherlands

20. Ibid., 1 Jan. 1790 (Ghent, 27 Dec. 1789).
21. Ibid., 26 Nov. 1790 (Leiden, 24 Nov.). Interestingly, the paper distinguished between the movement in the Belgian provinces and the insurrection against the Catholic bishop of Liège which occurred at the same time. Ibid., 26 Oct. 1790 (Leiden, 25 Oct.).
22. LGA-VH, Z(2), no. 79.

in January 1795, Luzac and the paper had become firmly identified with opposition to the new French regime, and in the wake of the Batavian Revolution, he found himself fighting an uphill battle to keep his paper from being destroyed by the consequences of its most important news story.

At the time Jean Luzac had hired Antoine-Marie Cerisier to edit the *Gazette de Leyde*, the paper's coverage of France was just beginning to expand again after a period of quiescence due to pressure from Versailles. The new finance minister, Calonne, who now dominated policymaking, was a far more controversial figure than Necker's immediate successor, the colorless Joly de Fleury, and he had to face the debt crisis resulting from Necker's borrowing during the American war. His efforts to resolve these debts were bound to bring him into conflict with the sworn enemies of all tax increases, the judges of the parlements. As early as 1784, the *Gazette de Leyde* began to reprint parlementary remonstrances, those formal expressions of dissent that had been absent from its pages since 1777.[23] In the early months of 1785, the paper publicized the former minister Necker's work, *De l'administration des finances*, which was, among other things, a thinly veiled attack on Calonne.[24] The paper's coverage was not particularly hostile to Calonne: indeed, it defended him more often than it sided with critics. But by mid-1785, the number of articles about Calonne's various financial projects was sufficient to indicate to the most obtuse that major controversies were shaking France's political and financial elites.

The story that really freed the *Gazette de Leyde* from the last remaining shackles on coverage of France had no direct link to the financial crisis, however. It was the celebrated affair of the Diamond Necklace, which became public with the arrest of Cardinal de Rohan, a peer of the realm, on 15 August 1785. Here was a scandal that would have whetted the appetite of journalists of any age, involving allegations of the queen's adultery and other scandals in high places. Initially, the *Gazette de Leyde* was one of the French court's chosen vehicles for publicizing its own version of the affair. Its first stories were strongly unfavorable to the accused cardinal and particularly insistent on clearing the queen's name. In an extraordinary departure from Old Regime journalistic practice, the paper even furnished the purported transcript of the conversation in which Louis XVI and Marie-Antoinette had supposedly confronted Rohan with their accusations. No journalist, least of all the cautious Jean

23. *GL*, 18 May 1784 (Bordeaux, 3 May); 21 and 28 Sept. 1784 (Parlement of Paris, remonstrance of 31 Aug. 1784). For a more detailed account of the paper's coverage of French politics from 1784 to 1789, see Jeremy Popkin, "The *Gazette de Leyde* and French Politics under Louis XVI," in Censer and Popkin, eds., *Press and Politics*, 96–127.

24. *GL*, 7 Jan. 1785 (Paris, 31 Dec. 1784); 11 Jan. 1785 (Paris, 3 Jan.).

Luzac, would have quoted a reigning monarch and his wife directly without specific instructions.[25]

Before long, however, the *Gazette de Leyde* went over to the cardinal's side in reporting the case. Although the revelations of Rohan's involvement with the charlatan Cagliostro and the adventuress Madame de la Motte did nothing to make him more presentable, the cardinal and his supporters were adept at publicity and at exploiting the fissures in France's ruling circles. Rohan hired as his lawyer Guy-Baptiste Target, one of the heroes of the parlementary-Jansenist resistance to the Maupeou "coup" in 1771, and the cardinal defied Church discipline by choosing to have his case tried by the Parlement of Paris. This endorsement of their view of the primacy of civil over ecclesiastical authority made the dissolute cardinal a Jansenist political hero. The *Gazette de Leyde*'s Parisian news coverage showed the results: the paper soon concluded that "His Eminence is not guilty of any wrongdoing . . . ; he was misled by his excessive credulity and his excessive trust in others."[26] After nine months of intense publicity, the Parlement of Paris finally decided in the cardinal's favor, absolving Rohan of all wrongdoing. The *Gazette de Leyde* published a complete roll call of the judges' votes, and added its own comment: "If one of the most pleasant duties of the reporter is to render justice to the truth, he cannot remain indifferent when he sees oppressed innocence triumph over fraud, artifice, imposture, and ingratitude all combined together."[27]

Since the French domestic press had not been permitted to report on the Diamond Necklace affair at all, and the French-government-controlled papers such as the *Courrier de l'Europe* had been forced to be very discreet, the case allowed the *Gazette de Leyde* to reestablish its role in the kingdom's affairs after the dull years from 1777 to 1784. And even after the cardinal's acquittal, there was no lack of news to report. Barely six months after the Rohan verdict, Calonne, the controller-general, took the extraordinary step of announcing that the government faced a severe financial crisis and summoning an Assembly of Notables to consider measures to deal with it. For the next two years, the capacity of France's traditional institutions to deal with such a crisis was put to the ultimate test: the result of their failure was the French Revolution.

Its coverage of the prerevolutionary crisis in France was the *Gazette de Leyde*'s finest journalistic hour. From January 1787 to the end of June

25. Ibid., 30 Aug. 1785 (Paris, 22 Aug.); also in *Gazette de Cologne*, 2 Sept. 1785, and *Hamburg Correspondent*, 31 Aug. 1785. The same text was subsequently incorporated into the apocryphal memoirs of Madame de Campan, Marie-Antoinette's lady-in-waiting, with one alteration to make it even more damaging to the cardinal. Jeanne-Louise Genet de Campan [*sic*], *Memoirs of the Court of Marie-Antoinette* (London, 1851), 2:21–22.

26. *GL*, 9 Sept. 1785 (Paris, 2 Sept.).

27. Ibid., 9 June 1786 (Leiden, 7 June).

1789, the paper gave a better-informed and more extensively documented narrative of French events than any other contemporary source. During these years, France was inundated with pamphlets that gave more details about specific events than the *Gazette de Leyde*, but the domestic periodical press remained muzzled until the convocation of the Estates-General in 1789, and readers still needed a chronological account of the news to make sense of the flood of polemical literature. The Leiden paper's Paris correspondent, Pascal Boyer, continued to furnish Luzac with his basic account of French affairs, but Luzac supplemented Boyer's bulletins, which also appeared in the rival *Courier du Bas-Rhin*, with correspondence from key cities in the French provinces and with reams of documents that were rarely printed in full in any rival newspapers. During this period, the paper published sixty-seven remonstrances from various parlements; it published the resolutions of the various *bureaux* into which Calonne's Assembly of Notables was divided; and it gave the texts of manifestoes from a variety of bodies opposing the policies of Louis XVI's successive ministers as the French government stumbled down the road that led to the convening of the Estates-General.

Luzac's intention in publishing these reports was not to promote a revolutionary upheaval in France. Much of his French news, such as the official *procès-verbal* of the first Assembly of Notables,[28] was in fact furnished by the French government. The crown's traditional institutional opponents, the parlements, were another major source. Since 1751, the paper had seen these aristocratic bodies as the country's main defense against the threat of despotism. In May 1788, when Calonne's successor Loménie de Brienne, in a desperate bid to force through urgent tax reforms, followed the precedent of the Maupeou "coup" in 1771 and tried to abolish these refractory sovereign courts, the *Gazette de Leyde* behaved as it had in the 1750s and in 1770–71: it publicized the parlements' protests and it emphasized the parallels to the Maupeou experience. "The terrible conflict that has arisen between the royal power and the magistrature, reminding France of the shock she experienced eighteen years ago through a revolution of the same sort, has deeply saddened all friends of the public good," the paper's Paris report intoned.[29] As in 1771, the paper expressed the conviction that the attack

---

28. Old Regime assemblies regularly made a record of the topics they discussed and the resolutions they passed, although they omitted the substance of debates; speeches by the king and the ministers were normally included as well. These *procès-verbaux* were destined for eventual publication, but the *Gazette de Leyde*'s version, which was not published in the French domestic press, preceded the official publication of the *Procès-Verbal de l'Assemblée des notables tenue à Versailles, en l'année 1787* (Paris, 1788) by more than a year.

29. *GL*, 16 May 1788 (Paris, 9 May).

on the traditional court system would fail; it voiced this judgment at a time when experienced diplomatic observers still believed the plan would be carried through.[30] And, as in the Maupeou period, the paper persevered in its editorial policy despite French government pressures, which culminated in a ban on its circulation in France at the end of July 1788.[31]

The paper's bulletins purported to be an objective record of these controversial events, but in fact the *Gazette de Leyde* was serving as a partisan paper: readers who compared Luzac's Paris bulletins with those in the *Courier du Bas-Rhin* discovered that Jean Manzon had decided to unmask Boyer's one-sided reporting by peppering it with polemical footnotes supporting the "bold but . . . absolutely indispensable project" Brienne had undertaken "to level the robinocratic aristocracy" of the parlements.[32] As in the case of the Dutch Patriot troubles, Jean Luzac was finding that it was impossible to print news about the increasingly controversial events without making his paper part of the controversy.

But the paper's support for the parlements during the crisis of 1788 did not mean that it opposed fundamental constitutional reform in France. From the moment when Calonne had summoned the first Assembly of Notables at the beginning of 1787, the *Gazette de Leyde*'s articles had expressed the hope that events would "lead the ministry to a further stage, closer to the ancient constitution of national assemblies."[33] The wording of this statement would have conveyed an unmistakable message to anyone who had followed French political discourse since the 1750s: the "national assemblies" that were supposedly a part of the "ancient constitution" were the Estates-General, in which, according to the pro-parlementary "patriot" pamphleteers who had denounced Maupeou's reforms in 1771, the French nation had exercised its rights.[34] In the summer of 1787, when the Paris Parlement itself refused to register new taxes and called for the convocation of the Estates-General, the paper's Paris correspondent interpreted its action as the triumph of these "patriot" principles:

30. Ibid., 1 July 1788 (Paris, 23 June); compare the British ambassador Dorset's dispatch of 2 July 1788 in Oscar Browning, ed., *Despatches from Paris, 1784–1790* (London: Camden Society, 1909–10), 2:72–73.

31. The *Gazette de Leyde* was banned after the arrival of its issue of 22 July 1788, according to a letter of Thomas Jefferson, then the American ambassador (Boyd, ed., *Papers of Jefferson*, 13:467). Jefferson and other members of the diplomatic corps continued to receive copies by private mail. By 27 August 1788, Luzac's friend Caillard, the secretary of the French embassy in The Hague, was able to report that Foreign Ministry officials had been able to have the ban lifted. Caillard to Luzac, 27 Aug. 1788, in LUL, Luzac, carton 29.

32. *Courier du Bas-Rhin*, 29 June 1788.

33. *GL*, 30 Jan. 1787 (Paris, 22 Jan.).

34. On the evolution of pro-parlementary political arguments in the 1770s and 1780s, see Dale Van Kley, "The Jansenist Constitutional Legacy in the French Prerevolution 1750–1789," *Historical Reflections/Réflexions historiques* 13 (1986), 393–453.

It is good to see the parlement now recognizing this grand principle. Less than twenty years ago, the very mention of the Estates-General was too much for it, as it has been for all the ministers since Cardinal Richelieu. Times have certainly changed. The parlement no longer claims to be a "miniature Estates-General. . . ." It will leave to the assembled nation the right to examine and pass taxes, and it will no longer incur the criticism it has sometimes received of having sacrificed the interests of the population. Here is, without a doubt, the most complete proof that the parlement has given up all its old prejudices: that it is far from resisting royal authority for the sole pleasure of showing its power and that it deserves, more than ever, the confidence and the gratitude of the nation for its attachment to the old constitutions of the kingdom.[35]

This praise of the parlements for declaring their own incompetence to represent the nation came from the paper's Paris correspondent, as the printing of this bulletin in the rival *Courier du Bas-Rhin* shows. But the sentiments were also those of Luzac himself. In a letter to a French friend, drafted just before the collapse of Brienne's effort to abolish the parlements in 1788, Luzac disavowed any sympathy with the parlements in and of themselves. "What you say, sir, about the real motives of this senseless opposition to the government's plans on the part of some of your fellow countrymen is all too true. I myself have seen, in my own country, vanity, ambition, and personal interest take the place of love of the public good. I can judge the pretended patriotism of aristocrats, whether they are republicans here or *parlementaires* in France." He denied that his paper's articles had been influenced by "a penchant for the parlementary cause, of which I am in no way a partisan." But the parlements' obstruction of ministerial measures was merely a sign of a deeper evil: "The disorder in the finances preceded the parlementary crisis . . . is it necessary to say it, sir? The wars were part of the cause, but even more the waste, the sad fruit of intrigues, of favors given to those who merited them the least . . . of this waste that a Turgot, a Necker vainly sought to oppose at the price of their position."[36]

Luzac, like the "patriot" party that had emerged during the Maupeou crisis, thus saw France's problems as essentially the result of moral and financial corruption at court. The solution, in his view, was the creation of some form of constitutional representation for the nation. To be sure, his personal sympathy went to those who thought reform could be carried out peacefully, without resort to violence. In the letter just cited,

35. *GL*, 31 July 1787 (Paris, 23 July); also in *Courier du Bas-Rhin*, 1 Aug. 1787.
36. Luzac, draft of letter to unnamed correspondent, probably Caillard, who had blamed the parlements for precipitating the financial crisis in a letter to Luzac of 27 Aug. 1788 (LUL, Luzac, carton 29). Luzac's draft is undated but a postscript at the end mentions that he had just learned of Necker's reappointment as controller-general (25 Aug. 1788). Letter in ibid., carton 28, no. 75.

he reiterated his conviction that "truth is in the middle" and that extremism was inherently evil. The appointment of the cautious reformer Necker as Brienne's successor in August 1788 stirred Luzac to do something not at all customary for him: he drafted a personal note of support to the new minister, praising both his political skills and the sentiments he had expressed in his work on *Des opinions religieuses*, published earlier that year.[37] Throughout the fall of 1788, the *Gazette de Leyde* put Necker's actions in the best possible light. It was no doubt the minister himself who authorized the paper to publish a remark he was said to have made to his intimates to the effect that "everything will go well, if everyone will just agree, if harmony prevails; the French will not be as obligated to me as they imagine."[38]

The switch from opposing Brienne to praising Necker did not mean that the *Gazette de Leyde* had simply changed from what the British would have labeled an opposition paper to a ministerial one. The paper's Paris bulletins criticized Necker for not acting swiftly to deal with pressing problems, and when Necker failed to put forward a genuine reform program of his own, the paper lent its endorsement to the suggestions of the reformers in Dauphiné, led by Joseph Mounier, who had resisted the abolition of their provincial parlement by summoning a provincial assembly at the town of Romans.[39] The *Gazette de Leyde* praised and reprinted the various proclamations issued by the Dauphiné reformers and lauded the talents of their author, Mounier. The Dauphiné program for the creation of both local and national representative assemblies, with double representation of the Third Estate and deputies voting in common, seemed to the paper to be the best answer to France's needs. The *Gazette de Leyde* defended this suggestion against traditionalists who opposed the dilution of the privileged orders' preponderance that it entailed, asserting that "enlightenment . . . has spread in the last hundred years [and] had created too much difference between the century of Louis XIII and that of Louis XVI for one to believe that the two first orders of the state . . . will refuse to see the obvious."[40] But it also defended the Dauphiné plan against radicals who objected that it gave the privileged orders too much of a role: "It is part of the essence of a monarchy that there be gradations between the different classes of civil society."[41] The paper's preference for moderate reform inspired criticism even from Luzac's friend Caillard, the secretary of the French embassy in The Hague. He tried to win Luzac over to "the sublime idea

37. Luzac to Necker, n.d. but 1788, ibid., carton 28, no. 26.
38. *GL*, 31 Oct. 1788 (Paris, 20 and 24 Oct.).
39. On Mounier and the Dauphiné movement, see Jean Egret, *La Révolution des notables: Mounier et les monarchiens* (Paris: Armand Colin, 1950).
40. *GL*, 31 Oct. 1788 (Paris, 20 and 24 Oct.).
41. Ibid., 25 Nov. 1788 (Paris, 17 Nov.).

of Turgot," who had wanted France to have assemblies "composed of property-owners without any distinction of orders," and he tried unsuccessfully to get the *Gazette de Leyde* to endorse the proposals of the abbé Sieyès, which called for the abolition of the traditional system of orders.[42]

Luzac, however, clung to his hopes for the triumph of moderation. As the year 1789 began in France, the *Gazette de Leyde* looked on events there with a mixture of hope and apprehension. The Estates-General had been summoned, but the rising political excitement threatened any orderly process of reform. When violence broke out in Brittany between partisans of the Third Estate and defenders of the nobility, the paper's report warned that the commoners' "pretensions are pushed to an extreme."[43] Alarmed by the sweeping demands contained in some of the *cahiers de doléances* drafted for the Estates-General, the paper criticized Frenchmen "who believed that all ecclesiastical, political, and economic reforms should be carried out by the very first assembly of the nation."[44] The paper's underlying attitude was summed up in an article covering the first elections for deputies, which stated, "The way to obtain nothing in civil contestations is to demand everything, and the public good has never resulted from the complete victory of one party or another."[45] And when the Estates-General finally convened and quickly became deadlocked because of the privileged orders' resistance to meeting and voting in common, the paper condemned both sides' intransigence, urging that "one . . . know how to put limits on the dangerous *desire to change*, which is not always the desire to improve and which, even when the intention is good, is often deceived in the means to carry it out, and, on the other hand, that one . . . make a distinction between sound and healthy principles, and the stubbornness of trying to pass off as fundamental rights what was originally simply an abuse . . . incompatible with the present state of the government and the people."[46]

As a result of its detailed coverage of the French prerevolutionary crisis, the *Gazette de Leyde* consolidated its position as Europe's preeminent newspaper. No other European periodical carried as much serious news about French affairs prior to the storming of the Bastille. The *Hamburg Correspondent*, the best of the German papers, gave French events about half as much space as the *Gazette de Leyde* did; the London

42. Caillard to Luzac, 27 Aug. 1788, n.d. but between Oct. 1788 and Feb. 1789, in LUL, Luzac, carton 29. The paper recommended numerous pamphlets during the prerevolutionary crisis, but its only reference to Sieyès was a passing mention of his *Qu'est-ce que le Tiers Etat?* toward the end of March 1789, long after the work had made its major impact.
43. *GL*, 3 Feb. 1789 (Rennes, 20 Jan.).
44. Ibid., 31 Mar. 1789 (Paris, 23 Mar.).
45. Ibid., 24 Mar. 1789 (Paris, 15 Mar.).
46. Ibid., 12 June 1789 (Leiden).

Times, despite a boast about "the acknowledged superiority of our Foreign Intelligence,"[47] did not even have a correspondent of its own in the
French capital until mid-June of 1789. The French domestic papers
could not compete effectively with Luzac's; the first uncensored dailies
only began to appear toward the end of June 1789, and initially their
summaries of the debates in the newly baptized National Assembly were
less complete than Luzac's. The public rewarded Luzac handsomely for
the quality of his coverage: the paper's profits soared from 22,900
gulden in 1787 to an all-time high of 29,400 gulden in 1789.[48]

The *Gazette de Leyde*'s reputation and influence in France reached a
peak during the prerevolutionary crisis as well. On behalf of the French
embassy, Caillard complained to Luzac about the increasing number of
French subjects who sent letters to the paper, motivated "by the hope of
being published and making a splash in your journal."[49] The ultimate
consecration of the paper's role in French political life at the end of the
Old Regime came with the French nobility's last effort to maintain its
political prerogatives. On 24 June 1789, the deputies of the nobility
assembled for their final meeting, before bowing to the king's instructions and joining the other orders in the merged sessions of what was
now the National Assembly. The major speaker was the longtime parle-
mentaire firebrand, Jacques Duval d'Eprémesnil, now converted by
events from a challenger of ministerial authority to a defender of a dying
cause. As he saw the last remnants of the nobility's power slipping away,
d'Eprémesnil chose to devote his speech not to denouncing the triumphant radicals of the Third Estate or even to opposing the liberal nobles
who had joined them, but to "long complaints about some articles from
the *Gazette de Leyde*."[50] There could have been no better recognition of
how central the *Gazette de Leyde* had been in the dramatic events that led
to the French Revolution.

A Revolution in Journalism

As soon as the French government suspended censorship of domestic
newspapers in June 1789, Jean Luzac realized that his publication faced
a new and unprecedented situation in the country that had always
represented his largest market. Publications in Paris were now free to
give direct reports about the events there, rival representations of political reality that reached Parisian readers on the same day as the occur-

47. *Times*, 30 June 1789.
48. LGA-VH, Z(2), no. 119.
49. Caillard to Luzac, 22 July 1788, in LUL, Luzac, carton 29.
50. *GL*, 7 July 1789 (Paris, 29 June, reporting session of the nobility on 24 June).

rences they reported and arrived in the French provinces long before the *Gazette de Leyde*'s copies did. Furthermore, these French papers soon were able to claim that they enjoyed greater freedom and hence greater credibility than the extraterritorial gazettes: after the National Assembly passed the Declaration of the Rights of Man, French journalists enjoyed a clear constitutional protection that the extraterritorial papers had never possessed. The victory of the forces of reform that the *Gazette de Leyde* had cautiously but firmly supported meant the sudden end of the situation that had permitted the Leiden paper to flourish as France's most important political newspaper.

The main threat to the *Gazette de Leyde*'s position came from the rapid growth of new journals in France itself. Even before the Estates-General met, it had been clear that the French public would demand published accounts of its sessions, and the *directeur-général de la librairie* had been besieged with requests for permission to publish the debates.[51] Although the government fought a rearguard action against unauthorized newspapers, temporarily shutting down Mirabeau's *Etats-généraux* in May 1789, it soon had to agree to put out an official bulletin as a supplement to the *Gazette de France*. In announcing the appearance of this new publication, the *Gazette de Leyde* sought to persuade its French readers that they would still detect "a little more freedom" in its own accounts than they could hope to find in an authorized newspaper.[52] But by the beginning of July 1789, French readers could find as much freedom as they wanted in the new unauthorized publications that sprang up, sponsored by Mirabeau and other ambitious politicians or by profit-minded publishers. The earliest of these revolutionary newspapers were skimpy summaries of the newly renamed National Assembly's proceedings, such as Bertrand Barère's *Point du Jour*, whose first number reported the session of 19 June. Until after the storming of the Bastille, the *Gazette de Leyde*'s reporting of the National Assembly's debates was probably still the most complete account available, but for French readers the paper had lost its timeliness: they already knew the essential news before Luzac's paper arrived. Even outside of France, new publications devoted exclusively to French events made the Leiden paper out of date by the time it arrived.[53]

The first of the new French revolutionary newspapers were hastily improvised, badly printed responses to a crisis whose duration could not be foreseen. The *Gazette de Leyde* commented disapprovingly about their

51. There were at least nine such petitions in the period from January to May 1789. AN, V(1), 549.

52. *GL*, 9 June 1789.

53. An example is the *Bulletin de Versailles* found in the collection of the Newberry Library (call no. FRC 5.161.1), which appears to have been published in Brussels.

mixture of reporting and heated opinion and remarked that they "give false impressions of everything that has happened."[54] The gazette maintained that readers accustomed to the Leiden paper's quality of coverage would not turn to sources with such evident partisan opinions. But by the fall of 1789, French readers began to find professional news reporting equal to that of the *Gazette de Leyde* in a number of domestic papers, such as Panckoucke's *Moniteur*, which quickly supplanted the foreign press as the Revolution's own "journal of record." One damaging blow to the *Gazette de Leyde* came from its own Paris correspondent, Boyer, who decided to take advantage of the new journalistic opportunities the Revolution had created. He began by retailing his bulletins to new customers; Luzac was soon complaining that "our correspondent, whom we pay very well for an exclusive personal correspondence, has now reached the point of sending us an engraved bulletin that facilitates the multiplication of copies."[55] But Boyer soon founded his own newspaper, the *Gazette universelle*, with none other than Luzac's own former editor, Antoine-Marie Cerisier, as his collaborator.

Boyer and Cerisier took direct aim at their former employer's publication, pointing out in their prospectus that the *Gazette universelle* would "always be ahead of the foreign papers, particularly that of Leiden, the most widely read of all, and it will not cost extra, although it will appear every day."[56] Rather than emulating the highly partisan tone of many of the new revolutionary papers, the *Gazette universelle* copied the *Gazette de Leyde*'s unemotional style. "We are not, and we do not wish to be, anything but historians," Boyer and Cerisier assured their readers. "The truthful and exact account of the facts, above all of those that affect the lives of peoples, and the welfare of men, that is the glory to which we aspire."[57] They offered excellent foreign coverage as well as reports about the French National Assembly, and they clearly aimed their paper at the sophisticated cosmopolitan readership that had previously subscribed to the foreign gazettes. For the *Gazette de Leyde*, the *Gazette universelle* was the most dangerous kind of competition: a paper run by insiders who knew exactly how the Leiden journal achieved its effects, but published on the scene of the continent's major news event.

Replacing Boyer as a correspondent was not difficult. Luzac's friends Johan Valckenaer and Filippo Mazzei, both of them in the French capital in 1789, were violently critical of Boyer's rather negative reports on the National Assembly and were only too happy to recruit substitutes for him. By early 1790, the paper was receiving its reports from two

54. *GL*, 7 July 1789 (Paris, 29 June).
55. Luzac to Johan Valckenaer, 6 Oct. 1789, in LUL, Ms. BPL 1030.
56. *Gazette universelle*, 15 Dec. 1789.
57. Ibid., 1 Dec. 1789.

journalistic unknowns, Louis Joseph Faure and Gauvin Gallois. "They furnish very good materials for the National Assembly," Luzac wrote to Valckenaer in January of that year. "I hope that in time they will also be able to keep up with the other news of the day."[58] But the *Gazette de Leyde* simply could not compete with the resources of the successful new Paris dailies: its two part-time correspondents could not possibly run down as much news as papers located on the scene, which were often blessed with connections to political insiders as well. The Paris dailies had far more space to devote to revolutionary events, and they got the news out much faster.

The Paris papers were able to afford different methods of production as well. The *Gazette de Leyde* tried to cope with the flood of news generated by the Revolution using the same technical means it had always employed. The only physical change in the paper up to 1795 was the appearance of occasional four-page "second supplements" to accommodate the burgeoning amount of information. These extra sheets, included with the issues of the paper for which four days of production time was available, brought the amount of information the paper could carry per week up to almost the level of a typical Paris daily, since most Paris papers printed seven half-sheet issues a week but used larger type. The *Gazette de Leyde* was still only distributed twice a week, however, and the time lag between the arrival of information in Leiden and its appearance in print remained considerable. The Paris papers, operating on a larger scale and not having to include in their purchase price as heavy a charge for delivery as Luzac did, could afford more compositors and pressmen for night work. The most important political papers in Paris throughout the Revolution were morning dailies; thanks to their new methods of production, they could give readers at least a partial summary of the previous afternoon's assembly debates less than twenty-four hours after they had happened.

As the Revolution progressed, the *Gazette de Leyde* faced additional problems in maintaining its place in the newspaper market. Other governments' reactions to events in France threatened any chance of finding alternative outlets. The Spanish government, which had forbidden the *Gaçeta de Madrid* to mention the troubles in France, banned all foreign newspapers at the end of December 1789,[59] and in the years that followed, numerous other European governments took similar measures. Such bans rarely succeeded in practice, but they did disrupt

58. Luzac to Johan Valckenaer, 12 Jan. 1790, in LUL, Ms. BPL 1030. Faure and Gallois were French lawyers and friends of Mazzei's who had been part of the circle of men interested in political reform that gathered around Thomas Jefferson during his service as American ambassador to Paris in the late 1780s. Edoardo Tortarola, *Illuminismo e Rivoluzioni. Biografia politica di Filippo Mazzei* (Milan: Franco Angeli, 1986), 104, 160.

59. *GL*, 2 Feb. 1790 (Madrid, 12 Jan.).

normal service to subscribers. The troubles of the revolutionary era also affected the transmission of information to Leiden. Throughout the period from 1772 to 1789, the only reason the paper had occasionally failed to receive its normal news bulletins on schedule had been bad weather. But as early as November 1789, Luzac had to inform readers that political turmoil in Brussels had cut off the mail from Paris.[60] The outbreak of the war between France and Austria in 1792 meant that the paper was separated from Paris by an active battlefront. On many subsequent occasions, the paper had to tell readers that it had not been able to obtain any news from Paris; its first report on Robespierre's fall in 1794 reached Leiden by a roundabout route through Mannheim.[61]

An even more serious problem was the impossibility of maintaining the paper's lofty reputation for political impartiality. The *Gazette de Leyde* in fact had never been without opinions about French politics, but in the highly charged atmosphere after 1789, there was no longer any consensus about political values in France itself. From the outset of the Revolution, the *Gazette de Leyde* suffered repeated attacks because of its supposed bias. Luzac continued to maintain that his paper's coverage was in accordance with the eternal rules of political wisdom, but to most French readers it seemed suspiciously partisan. As the Revolution became increasingly radical, Luzac made his own distaste for it less and less secret. In doing so, he was not only following his own penchants, but he was copying the example of the Paris papers, all of them highly partisan. But, although he refused to acknowledge the fact, the result was that his paper had no special claim to be an "impartial narrator" anymore: it had joined the revolutionary fray.

The *Gazette de Leyde* had been uneasy about the rising tide of political violence in France even before the Estates-General met. Its account of the Reveillon riot on 28 April 1789, in which Paris workers sacked a wealthy manufacturer's house, used language that foreshadowed typical counterrevolutionary views of the Revolution: "The rioters, drunk on wine and liquor they had plundered . . . , pushed their excesses to the most outrageous extent."[62] In its coverage of the Estates-General's sessions in May and early June, the paper condemned both the intransigence of those who opposed all reforms and the impatience of those who wanted to move too quickly. The *Gazette de Leyde*'s sympathies lay with the liberal nobles, a minority in their own chamber, who favored common meetings with the deputies of the other two orders. When the king finally yielded to the demands of the newly proclaimed National Assembly and directed the nobles and clergy to join its sessions, the

60. Ibid., 20 Nov. 1789 (Leiden, 19 Nov.).
61. Ibid., 15 Aug. 1794 (Mannheim, 5 Aug.).
62. Ibid., 8 May 1789 (Paris, 30 Apr.).

paper expressed profound relief that a peaceful accommodation had been reached. "We have just escaped from a most disquieting situation," it reported.[63]

In private, Jean Luzac expressed the opinion that both the revolutionary party and its opponents were running the risk of plunging the country into disaster. In response to his cousin Johan Valckenaer's enthusiastic letters from Paris, Luzac acknowledged that his paper was attracting criticism in France, "since the suspicions and the partiality of those who are dragged into the whirlpool of civil conflicts stifles all sentiment of fairness." For his part, he was still certain that "the truth is always found in the middle . . . equally distant from one side of the circle and the other, and the spirit of party rarely recognizes this point, so visible but so small." He took satisfaction in noting that "your popular enthusiasts find our reports too favorable to the opposing party, and the chief of that party, the agitator d'Epr[émesnil] denounces us as enemies of the aristocracy." Like many modern journalists, he cited this two-sided criticism to show that his paper's coverage was essentially balanced. He continued to place his personal faith in Necker: "I regard those who try to topple him as enemies of France."[64] In print, he conceded that there had been some inaccuracies in the paper's reports. "It is hard to be sufficiently careful in discussing affairs as complicated as those of France have now become. . . . Although guided by principles of moderation and peace, we fear we have often fallen short."[65]

The *Gazette de Leyde*'s articles during the two weeks between the reunion of the three orders and the sudden dismissal of Necker reflected more fear of revolutionary excesses than of counterrevolutionary plots. "The events which we have just witnessed these last few days have given further proof of how close the greatest evil is to the greatest good and how easily the restoration of national liberty can lead to anarchy, if the people do not have enough virtue to limit their desires," one dispatch warned.[66] Subsequent articles justified the summoning of additional troops to Paris. Even though the paper was exceptionally well informed about the plans for a counterrevolutionary coup that culminated in Necker's dismissal, it continued to address its admonitions primarily to the people of Paris, urging them not to "trouble the work of their

63. Ibid., 3 July 1789 (Paris, 25 June).

64. Luzac to Valckenaer, 7 July 1789, in LUL, Ms. BPL 1030. Valckenaer was favorably impressed with the determination of the French reformers, as compared with the incapacity the Dutch Patriots had demonstrated, but during the crisis leading to the storming of the Bastille, even he worried that "democratic principles are being taken a bit too far." Cited in Jerome A. Sillem, *Het Leven van Mr. Valckenaer (1759–1821)* (Amsterdam: Van Kampen, 1883), 1:146.

65. *GL*, 21 July 1789 (Leiden, 20 July). Luzac had just received his first confused reports of the storming of the Bastille when he wrote this.

66. Ibid., 10 July 1789 (Paris, 2 July).

representatives, the confidence of their king, and the perspective of the common happiness."[67]

On the same day that this article appeared in Leiden, the Paris crowd stormed the Bastille. The paper greeted this event cautiously, holding back the first reports it received in hope that their depiction of "blood spilled by troops in the middle of the capital and all the horrors that announce a civil war" would turn out to be exaggerated.[68] The next number brought readers a full narrative of the revolutionary *journée*, but it put the events in a strange light, claiming that the bourgeoisie had been forced to take arms against "the populace, eager to take advantage of public calamities either by abusing the pretext of liberty or by serving as the instrument of despotism in giving itself over to pillage." Whereas the *Courier du Bas-Rhin*, after publishing the same report, concluded, "Posterity may be inclined to excuse the Parisians . . . they fought today only for their liberty," the *Gazette de Leyde* offered this more cautious judgment: "It is is thus that good results from the midst of the most extreme evils."[69] For once, Luzac's private opinions were somewhat more radical than the text of his paper: although he wrote to Valckenaer that he trusted that the French people would "exploit this triumph with moderation and wisdom," he went on to say he hoped that "this moderation will not prevent it from banishing from the vicinity of the throne those vermin whose perfidious counsels have exposed the kingdom to turmoil and the most complete disintegration."[70]

Like many other foreign observers, as well as many in France itself, Luzac was shaken by the lynching of the commander of the Bastille, Delauney, and of several other prominent royal officials which followed the storming of the fortress. The 28 July issue carried a letter from Foulon, a member of the Conseil d'Etat, denying that he had participated in the counterrevolutionary plot that had led to Necker's dismissal; the next issue of the paper brought the news that Foulon had been killed by the mob on 23 July. Luzac exclaimed, "It is time that the friends of true liberty recognize . . . that unrestrained license often overturns it at the moment of its establishment. The arbitrary power of the mob [is] far more dangerous to it than that of despotism itself."[71] Whether incorporated in Boyer's dispatches from Paris or added as editorial comments in Leiden, these expressions of fear of the mob as an agent of despotism echoed Luzac's interpretation of events in the Netherlands during the Patriot period, when the urban crowd had served as

67. Ibid., 14 July 1789 (Paris, 4 July).
68. Ibid., 21 July 1789 (Leiden, 20 July).
69. Ibid., 24 July 1789 (Paris, 17 July); CBR, 25 July 1789.
70. Luzac to Valckenaer, 21 July 1789, in LUL, Ms. BPL 1030.
71. *GL*, 31 July 1789.

an Orangist instrument against the middle classes. The Dutch experience made Luzac only too apprehensive about the direction French events were taking.

The Revolution and the New Constitution

The violence accompanying the storming of the Bastille preoccupied Jean Luzac, but the *Gazette de Leyde* could not dwell indefinitely on the events of the fourteenth of July 1789. The exigencies of the news business forced the paper to concentrate on the ongoing flow of events, and indeed, over the following two years, Luzac's worst fears about France were not realized. The reports in his paper continued to favor the moderate members of the National Assembly whom it had already praised before the crisis of July, particularly Mounier and Trophime-Gérard Lally-Tollendal, who "distinguished themselves by the wisdom and moderation of their opinions. . . ."[72] The paper was taken by surprise by the sweeping abolition of special privileges on the night of 4 August, and commented that if it had not witnessed the scene, "we would scarcely believe that the representatives of the nation, animated by a patriotic enthusiasm superior to all particular interests, could have carried out a revolution affecting the rights and privileges of the different orders, corporations and provinces, that one would hardly dared to have expected from the most violent clash of opinions, or even from a civil war."[73] The *Gazette de Leyde* quickly reprinted the text of the Declaration of the Rights of Man; its rather lukewarm enthusiasm for the document was consistent with the reaction of the rest of the non-French press.[74]

The apparent success of the reform process after July 1789 offered the paper some hope that the French Revolution might yet result in the framing of an acceptable constitution, despite the unhealthy level of popular violence. The paper's correspondent summed up this dual attitude of hope and fear in a lengthy comment at the end of August 1789:

> The truth is that our national reform is bought at the price of violent shake-ups, and if the demonstrations of courage, disinterestedness, and true patriotism have been multiplied, on the other hand we have experienced all the disadvantages that necessarily accompany a general fermen-

72. Ibid., 31 July 1789 (Paris, 24 July).
73. Ibid., 14 Aug. 1789 (Paris, 7 Aug.).
74. Jean-Pierre Allinne, "La Déclaration des Droits de l'Homme et les aspirations libérales en Europe. Le témoignage de la presse," *Annales historiques de la Révolution française*, no. 262 (1985), 434.

tation, however salutary its effects. Among these disadvantages is the
desire to make the change from evil to good too quickly.

The paper mentioned the intrigues of groups that wanted to prevent
significant reform altogether, but its main concern was the struggle
within the National Assembly between two parties, "one guided by the
partisans of the system that grants the most to the People, the other
formed by a sort of coalition among the clergy, the nobility and 130 to
140 members of the Third Estate," who had joined together to oppose
extremism.[75] Subsequent articles conducted a regular partisan attack
against the unnamed members of the "Palais-Royal faction . . . the left
side of the hall" in the Assembly, and detailed some of the tactics by
which they stirred up the populace in Paris.[76] The paper put its hopes in
the moderates, who seemed to be in the majority in the Assembly for the
moment,[77] and it welcomed Mirabeau's great speech on finances of 26
September 1789 as evidence that he "deserved . . . a distinguished place
among the Orators of Europe, or rather among the small number of
individuals, as dangerous as they are useful, who Nature has created to
dominate the public assemblies of Nations," although it lamented his
failure to give Necker firmer support.[78]

Whatever hopes the *Gazette de Leyde* had that the Revolution would
now remain free from violence were dashed by the *journée* of 5–6
October 1789. The paper's first printed report on the events, written
from Versailles between 7 and 9 P.M. on 5 October, was uncharac-
teristically dramatic: it captured the tension at the court as troops prepared to meet the rumored march from Paris, and conveyed a vivid
sense of the uncertainty of the outcome of the crisis.[79] The three days
between this and the next issue of the paper allowed the *Gazette de Leyde*
to assemble a detailed and fairly unemotional narrative of the *journée*,
but Luzac must have been frustrated not to be able to inform his readers
sooner about the outcome of events constituting "if not a second revolution, at least the completion of that which began to change the state of
affairs in this Kingdom in July."[80]

Nevertheless, the overall tone of the paper's coverage of France did
not change radically as a result of this new outbreak of violence. It
continued to fear that the leadership of the movement had fallen into
the hands of unprincipled extremists: it lamented Mounier's decision to
go into exile rather than continue a hopeless struggle against a hostile

75. *GL*, 8 Sept. 1789 (Paris, 31 Aug.).
76. Ibid., 11 Sept. 1789 (Paris, 4 Sept.).
77. Ibid., 15 Sept. 1789 (Paris, 7 Sept).
78. Ibid., 9 Oct. 1789 (Versailles, 1 Oct.).
79. Ibid., 13 Oct. 1789 (Versailles, 5 Oct.).
80. Ibid., 16 Oct. 1789 (Paris, 8 Oct.).

public opinion,[81] and it regretted the decision to abolish property qualifications for members of future Assemblies, pointing out that "Athens
dated the corruption of its government . . . from the moment when those
who, having no property to lose, but something to gain from public
disorders, were admitted into the Republic's Councils."[82] But, unlike the
diehard opponents of the Revolution in France, the *Gazette de Leyde* had
by no means written off the entire revolutionary experiment as hopeless. Indeed, by the end of November, it was sufficiently impressed to
state, "The work of the constitution is making great strides, and the
foundations have been laid so well, that this consideration alone suffices
to give reasons for optimism about the regeneration of French power."[83] This change of tone may simply reflect the employment of a new
correspondent—it was about this time that the paper gave up on Boyer,
who was just about to launch his own *Gazette universelle*—but it also
reflected a fundamental tension in the *Gazette de Leyde*'s thinking about
the French Revolution: the paper had no serious theoretical objection to
the constitutional arrangements worked out by the National Assembly,
or to its claim to have the authority to make a new constitution. Its
objections were entirely to the behavior of the Assembly's members and
the amount of violence that accompanied the revolutionary process.

The paper's coverage of French politics in 1790 and 1791 continued
to reflect this basic split between distaste for the revolutionary process
and acceptance of its results. The paper lamented the development of
parties, particularly the Jacobins, whom it denounced in January 1790
for "fomenting the spirit of discord, of suspicion, of reciprocal animosity
and the desire for vengeance," and it continued to denounce popular
unrest. The revolutionary press that did so much to incite this disorder
was another frequent subject of criticism; the paper disliked "the blameworthy license with which a horde of periodical writers and others
strive . . . to maintain among the multitude dispositions so dangerous for
France," and it condemned Marat by name.[84]

French supporters of the Revolution clearly sensed that the paper was
not on their side. The *Révolutions de Paris*, one of the most important
revolutionary journals, complained that "a gazetteer in Leiden collects
idiocies and popular rumors here and presents these absurdities to all of
Europe as important and mysterious truths," and Brissot's *Patriote françois* wrote, "When one lives right here and can testify to the calm that
prevails, shouldn't one be revolted to see a foreign journalist . . . reproach the people of Paris for its 'bloodthirsty disposition' and for 'the

81. Ibid., 30 Oct. 1789 (Paris, 22 Oct.).
82. Ibid., 10 Nov. 1789 (Paris, 1 Nov.).
83. Ibid., 4 Dec. 1789 (Paris, 26 Nov.).
84. Ibid., 29 Jan. 1790 (Paris, 22 Jan.).

most violent agitation'?"[85] From Paris, Luzac's friends Valckenaer and Mazzei waged a concerted campaign to persuade Luzac to publish more favorable reports. In a lengthy missive reviewing the entire course of French politics since 1774, Mazzei wrote, "The more I think about the circumstances, the more I am persuaded that it would have been impossible to proceed with moderation. I admire how many good things have already been accomplished, and I am amazed at the small number of mistakes." He was delighted when Luzac's correspondent Boyer was replaced, and promised that "the friends of truth and accuracy will be much more content with your paper."[86]

Luzac's friend Caillard, still at the French embassy in The Hague, added his voice to this chorus of critics. He deplored the violence that had accompanied the Revolution, but maintained that it was the fault of the privileged orders: "To find the real cause of all the evils that have occurred, it is necessary to go back to the obstinacy of these groups." Their provocation of the common people had created the crisis: "Who should be blamed for the devastations of the tiger? The tiger himself, or those who broke his chains and forced him to leave his cage?"[87] This pressure from trusted friends could not have made his journalistic work pleasant for Luzac. In early 1791, Bavius Voorda, a faculty friend in Leiden, described him as ill, hopelessly overworked, embroiled in disputes with the other professors, and overburdened with the newspaper, "which is like a constantly moving treadmill with no vacation." Voorda lamented that Luzac distrusted his brother Etienne too much to leave the running of the paper to him, and he hoped that Luzac would consent to hire an assistant.[88] Luzac did briefly hire a certain Brahain Du Cange, a former French embassy employee, but the man found the paper too antirevolutionary and returned to France by late 1792.[89]

Perhaps partly as a result of these various pressures, the *Gazette de Leyde*'s coverage of the French Revolution in 1790 and 1791 became less critical than in 1789. Indeed, on some points the paper expressed unqualified enthusiasm about the National Assembly's achievements. The paper hailed the granting of civic and political rights to non-Catholics

85. *Révolutions de Paris*, no. 11 (27 Sept. 1789), 17–18; *Patriote françois*, 25 Aug. 1789.
86. Mazzei to Luzac, 22 Mar. 1790, in LUL, Luzac, carton 29.
87. Caillard to Luzac, 27 Nov. 1789, ibid.
88. Voorda to Cornelius van Gyzelaer, letters of 21 Feb. 1791, and 14 May 1791, ibid.
89. Johan Valckenaer to Etienne Luzac, 21 Jan. 1793, in LUL, Ms. BPL 1036X; Sillem, *Valckenaer*, 1:179. Du Cange was a Frenchman who had worked as a journalist in the Netherlands during the Patriot troubles, writing first for the Orangists and later for the Patriot side. Expelled in 1787, he frequented Dutch radical circles in Paris during the Revolution. Jean Alexandre and Marie-Rose Perrin-Chevrier, "Un gentilhomme paisible, le 'Batave' Jacobus Blaauw," *Annales historiques de la Révolution française*, no. 261 (1985), 342n. The *Journal de la Montagne* of 3 germinal, An II, refers to a discussion about him at the Jacobin club two days earlier.

and strongly supported the expropriation of Church property in 1789 and the Civil Constitution of the Clergy issued in 1790; it refused to admit that this latter measure had strengthened opposition to the Revolution and called the successful election of new bishops in March 1791 proof that "spirits were much more prepared for this revolution of the religious system than many people believed."[90] Although the *Gazette de Leyde* said that any continuation of slavery in the French colonies would "contradict . . . the general principles consecrated by the Revolution", it praised the gradualist compromise voted by the Assembly.[91]

As the members of the National Assembly themselves became somewhat more conservative in the face of mounting difficulties in 1791, the paper congratulated them for trying to limit subversive agitation. It strongly endorsed the Le Chapelier law against associations, which it interpreted not as a measure against incipient trade unions but as a barrier to political agitation in the streets. The law "sets the proper limits of liberty in a state, where good order should not contradict the rights of citizens."[92] And as the Assembly, now firmly dominated by its more conservative members, finished its "revision" of the draft constitution in 1791, the *Gazette de Leyde* hailed its members for "manifesting the intention that the completion of the Constitution be the completion of the Revolution."[93]

This generally favorable attitude toward the completed Constitution of 1791 and a number of its key provisions did not mean that the paper had abandoned all its worries about the outcome of the Revolution. It balanced its praise of some of the National Assembly's decisions with criticism of others. Although the paper had consistently supported demands for political representation for the Third Estate throughout the prerevolutionary crisis, it was alarmed when titles of nobility were finally abolished in 1790: "Such a sudden, radical change, so opposed to ideas that have been accepted in Europe for a thousand or twelve hundred years, seemed disproportionate for a state, that has declared it wants to remain a monarchy."[94] The paper was particularly indignant about the legislation against emigrés, calling it a result of "a patriotism which, by its exaggeration, contradicts its own principles."[95] But the *Gazette de Leyde* found less to criticize in the Assembly's laws than in the men who made them. It lambasted the selfish ambition of the deputies who forced the dismissal of the Ministry in late 1790,[96] and condemned Mirabeau

90. *GL*, 5 Jan. 1790 (Paris, 28 Dec. 1789); and 29 Mar. 1791 (Paris, 21 Mar.).
91. Ibid., 24 May 1791 (Paris, 16 May).
92. Ibid., 24 May 1791 (Paris, 13 May).
93. Ibid., 16 Sept 1791 (Paris, 9 Sept.).
94. Ibid., 9 July 1790 (Paris, 2 July).
95. Ibid., 1 Apr. 1791 (Paris, 25 March).
96. Ibid., 26 Oct. 1790 (Paris, 18 Oct.).

for reappearing at the Jacobin club after quitting it for a while, warning him that "it is almost always necessary to choose between the maxims of the Man of the People and the wise man."[97] But if the new constitution could be implemented and the unrest accompanying its elaboration stilled, the paper remained convinced that France would be saved.

For the *Gazette de Leyde*, as for many in France, the royal family's abortive flight to Varennes threw into doubt the possibility that the carefully balanced constitution worked out by the National Assembly could really be implemented. Because of the paper's location, the *Gazette de Leyde* actually reported the capture of the king before it had received the news of his escape from Paris: its first news bulletin was dated June 26 and based on a report from Brussels dated the day before. A supplement to the same June 28 issue of the paper reported further rumors, including a claim that the queen had evaded arrest, and included a summary of events in Paris up to 6 P.M. on 21 June, the day on which the royal family had fled the city.[98] The paper, though closely linked to the moderates in the National Assembly, did not participate in their effort to pretend that the king's departure had been involuntary: it labeled the flight an "escape" and blamed it on the king's reactionary advisors, who had tried to convince him "that the French people secretly detested the Constitution."[99] Thus the *Gazette de Leyde* clung to its conviction that the Constitution was the key issue, and that all opposition to it, whether from counterrevolutionaries or radicals, was to be condemned. The same issue of the paper which contained this passage also contained a supplement in which readers were reminded that the new constitution promised to be "a *juste milieu* traced between the arbitrary power of monarchy and the anarchic licence of democracy," and it concluded, "Let us hope that after such a great storm France will soon enjoy . . . a free but effective constitution, with the sincere and unanimous endorsement of the King and the Nation."[100]

But would the new constitution work? The final sessions of the National Assembly, in which moderate deputies galvanized by the crisis sparked by the king's flight had "revised" the draft constitution in a conservative direction, had momentarily raised the paper's hopes that France might find stability after all. The gazette's first reactions to the results of the elections for the new Legislative Assembly that met in October 1791 were positive, although it issued warnings about the influence of Danton and of the republicans Condorcet and Brissot, "declared enemies of constitutional monarchy."[101] "The most important point for

97. Ibid., 4 Jan. 1791 (Paris, 27 Dec. 1790).
98. Ibid., 28 June 1791 (Leiden, 26 and 27 June, and Paris, 21 June).
99. Ibid., 1 July 1791 (Paris, 24 June).
100. Ibid., 2 July 1791 (Leiden, 2 July).
101. Ibid., 20 Sept. 1791 (Paris, 12 Sept); and 7 Oct. 1791 (Paris, 30 Sept.).

the people's welfare and the lasting solidity of the Constitution, will be to strengthen the harmony between the legislature and the executive power," the paper adjured the new deputies.[102] But the Legislative Assembly's first sessions quickly showed that "the fears that the true friends of liberty and of good order had conceived, in examining the majority of choices for the present legislature . . . are now amply confirmed."[103] The next issue of the paper outlined the already evident party divisions in the new Legislative Assembly, stating that it was divided between 150 Jacobins, a group of moderates, and the majority of the deputies, who refused to adhere to any faction.[104] Although the Jacobin radicals were in the minority in the Assembly, the paper noted with alarm their steadily increasing influence in the streets of Paris. By the end of the year, the paper was printing outspoken denunciations of the Assembly, whose goal was now stated to be "to perpetuate the disorder, to destroy all the mechanisms of government, to harass, indeed to destroy the Executive Power."[105] Readers of the *Gazette de Leyde* were left in little doubt: the implementation of the Constitution of 1791 had not ended the chaos in France.

102. Ibid., 11 Oct. 1791 (Paris, 3 Oct.).
103. Ibid., 14 Oct. 1791 (Paris, 7 Oct.).
104. Ibid., 18 Oct. 1791 (Paris, 10 Oct.).
105. Ibid., 16 Dec. 1791 (Madrid, 21 Nov.).

An Old Regime Gazette
in the Revolutionary
Maelstrom

The *Gazette de Leyde*'s French news coverage from 1789 to 1791 was thorough and generally critical of the French Revolution, although the paper's opposition was not as extreme as that voiced by the royalist press in Paris or by Edmund Burke in London. Readers in the Netherlands and northern Europe continued to regard Luzac's paper as a dependable source of information about France. But the emergence of an unfettered press in France itself meant that the paper largely lost its relevance for readers there. The paper's location outside of France, which before the Revolution had served as an implicit guarantee of its independence, now branded it as a possible agent of counterrevolutionary forces. The revolutionary papers in Paris condemned it as an organ of international reaction. In 1792, when Austrian emperor Francis II finally revoked the privilege Joseph II had granted in 1786 for a reprint edition of the paper in Vienna, the *Chronique de Paris* claimed that the move was payment for "the position Luzac has taken relative to France, that is, for having become an aristocrat."[1]

So long as the Revolution remained a domestic French event, the *Gazette de Leyde* seemed to have lost its journalistic raison d'être. The paper continued to have a small number of French subscribers: some of the early Jacobin clubs included it among the journals they furnished to their members, and the better-appointed Paris reading rooms made it

---

1. *Chronique de Paris*, 28 July 1792. In fact, Francis's predecessor Leopold II, grateful for the paper's attitude toward the Belgian revolt of 1789–90, had already decided to restore good relations with the paper in January 1791, long before a Franco-Austrian war had become likely. Hoppé, secretary of the Austrian embassy in Brussels, to Luzac, 30 Jan. 1791, in LGA-VH, Z(2), no. 79.

one of their few foreign titles.[2] On the eve of the *journée* of 10 August 1792, a Jacobin deputy in the Legislative Assembly cited the paper's claim that the moderates still had a majority in that body as evidence of the need to depose the king: clearly, the *Gazette de Leyde* had come to be regarded as a counterrevolutionary organ.[3] Undoubtedly it was sought after primarily for its news of other countries: few of the Paris papers devoted much space to foreign affairs during the first years of the Revolution. As noted earlier, the paper's loss of its French market led to a steep decline in its profits.[4]

By mid-1791, however, the French Revolution was rapidly ceasing to be an exclusively French concern. On 19 July 1791, the *Gazette de Leyde* carried the text of a Spanish diplomatic note to France demanding that Louis XVI's freedom be restored to him, and the paper added, "We believe we can firmly issue an assurance that the other European powers will adopt the same policy."[5] The Revolution now faced the threat of foreign intervention. To Luzac, who had so recently lived through the Prussian occupation of the Netherlands, there was nothing unrealistic about this prospect: unlike observers inside France, he was not under the illusion that the French could expect to settle their own affairs in complete isolation from the rest of Europe.

The emergence of the possibility of foreign intervention in France, and eventually of a pan-European war, altered the nature of the Revolution as a news story in the *Gazette de Leyde* and offered the paper the possibility of regaining some of the uniqueness as a news source that it had lost in 1789. Although the Leiden paper was remote from Paris, it was well placed to gather information from the other capitals of Europe, where it had long cultivated authoritative sources. The vast majority of the new Paris newspapers founded after 1789 had only rudimentary foreign correspondence, and to the extent that they identified with the Revolution, they faced a major obstacle in gaining sympathetic informants close to the rulers of those states whose decisions were to determine whether there would be a foreign attack on France. The *Gazette de Leyde* was thus in a position to offer an excellent account of the diplomacy that led to war in 1792. At the same time, the paper, which had lost all influence on French domestic politics, could hope to exert at least a modicum of influence on this diplomatic process. If it was no longer widely read in Paris, it was certainly still attended to in Vienna, Berlin,

2. Michael L. Kennedy, *The Jacobin Clubs in the French Revolution: The First Years* (Princeton, N.J.: Princeton University Press, 1982), Appendix E; prospectuses for the Cabinet littéraire national and the Chambre patriotique et littéraire from 1791.

3. Legislative Assembly session of 9 Aug. 1792, as reported in *Journal de Perlet*, 10 Aug. 1792; and *Chronique de Paris*, 10 Aug. 1792.

4. LGA-VH, Z(2), no. 119.

5. *GL*, 19 July 1791 (Leiden, 17 July).

Stockholm, and other European capitals. It also influenced the reporting of many Paris newspapers, which lacked sources of their own in other European capitals.[6] The special virtues of an Old Regime international gazette came into play for almost the last time as Luzac set out to report and guide the diplomatic intrigues that now unfolded across Europe.

In its news about the diplomatic crisis, the paper was careful to avoid overemphasizing the role of the French emigrés, as most of the French press did. The paper had defended the right of French citizens to leave their country, and there is no doubt that it had found an important audience among the French expatriates in the Austrian Netherlands and the Rhineland. But the emigrés were like all other private political groupings as far as the paper was concerned: their agitation might occasionally be commented upon, but they were not a constituted government, and the paper acted as if their activities could not decisively affect public affairs. An article in September 1791 mentioned that the emigrés in Germany were spreading rumors of an impending Austrian attack on France, but the paper, probably at the Viennese government's instigation, stated flatly that Austria was making no war preparations and claimed that the emigré comte d'Artois had arrived in the Imperial capital without an invitation.[7] Two weeks later, the paper had a similar item from Berlin, maintaining that there would be no attack on France, "in view of the uncertainty of events, the difficulty of the enterprise and its dangers, even in case of success."[8] As far as the *Gazette de Leyde* was concerned, the question of war or peace would be decided by what the sovereign rulers of Europe did, not by the wishes of disaffected French aristocrats.

Despite its distaste for the course of the French Revolution, the paper's purpose in reporting on foreign courts' deliberations about France was not to encourage intervention or war but to do everything possible to avoid such an outcome. Luzac aimed to reassure the French that foreign menaces were less dangerous than they seemed, while persuading other governments that an armed attack on France would be counterproductive. By defusing the increasingly tense atmosphere, he hoped to give moderate forces in France a chance to assert themselves. He therefore lent himself to maneuvers, many of them no doubt suggested by officials in the foreign ministries of the major powers, to undermine the effect of seemingly bellicose measures against France, while exhort-

6. Georges Michon, *Le rôle de la presse en 1791–1792. La déclaration de Pillnitz et la guerre* (Paris: T.E.P.A.C., 1941), 11.

7. *GL*, 6 Sept. 1791 (Leiden, 4 Sept.). The consensus of modern historians is that Austria's Leopold II did not take the decision to prepare for war with France until the end of December 1791.

8. Ibid., 20 Sept. 1791 (Berlin, n.d.).

ing all parties to work for a peaceful solution. At the same time, however, his vocation as a reporter did not allow him to gloss over the unmistakable evidence of a drift toward war.

The paper's commentary on the Austro-Prussian Pillnitz declaration, which it printed in its issue of 27 September 1791, exemplifies its approach to the war crisis. Whereas many Frenchmen interpreted this expression of support for Louis XVI as a virtual declaration of war against the Revolution, Luzac correctly pointed to its highly qualified nature:

> One must have little insight into the present situation of Europe, and above all into the way the most enlightened portions of nations think, to persuade oneself that, after Louis XVI's acceptance [of the new French constitution], there could possibly be a crusade of the Sovereigns against the French constitution. One must have little acquaintance with the language of diplomacy, to see in the Declaration of the Emperor and the King of Prussia a commitment for the near future, or even a definite commitment to take the risk of an enterprise of this nature, the reaction to which might produce incalculable effects in other countries.[9]

A subsequent issue elaborated on the contents of the various Austro-Prussian agreements at Pillnitz, showing that they were not at all concentrated on action against France and that indeed much of their substance concerned affairs in Poland and eastern Europe.[10] An issue in mid-October claimed that Spain could not afford an intervention in France even if it wanted to, and the next paper carried items about the Imperial government's measures to restrict emigré activities in Belgium and stated that Sweden, whose king Gustav III was one of the main agitators for strong action to save Louis XVI's authority, would not push the matter.[11] The paper thus used its prestige in an effort to persuade thinking people throughout Europe that foreign governments had no intention of attacking France.

Within a few weeks of this round of denials, however, the paper began to detect a different note in the actions of at least some European courts. It became clear to Luzac that at least Russia and Sweden wanted to see some sort of action against the Revolution, although many of the paper's articles continued to stress the unlikelihood of the unanimity needed to make Austria and Prussia carry out their vague promises at Pillnitz.[12] But as the new year dawned, another story emphasizing the German

9. Ibid., 27 Sept. 1791 (Leiden, 24 Sept.).
10. Ibid., 7 Oct. 1791 (Frankfurt, 30 Sept.).
11. Ibid., 14 Oct. 1791 (Madrid, 23 Sept. 1791); and 18 Oct. 1791 (Leiden, 16 Oct. and Stockholm, 30 Sept.).
12. Ibid., 29 Nov. 1791 (Warsaw, 11 Sept. [sic], and Coblentz, 22 Nov.).

princes' willingness to curb the activities of the emigrés was followed almost immediately by a report that the Austrian army was ready to march.[13] The *Gazette de Leyde*'s initial assumption that the threats against France, couched in the cautious, conditional language of Old Regime diplomacy, would be as inoperative as so many other Old Regime diplomatic manifestoes was proving to be false.

As 1792 began, the *Gazette de Leyde*'s most pressing concern was the French reaction to the foreign princes' menacing moves. While admitting that the Powers' declarations naturally alarmed the French, the paper was pained to see "with what determination, what malice, what blind fury a certain party seeks to drive France into a war, whose outcome no human foresight can calculate."[14] A story a month later conceded that counterrevolutionary aristocrats and Jacobins alike were pushing for war, and noted how the war fever was promoting domestic radicalism, such as the Paris Commune's decision to arm citizens too poor to qualify for the National Guard.[15] The politicians who had gained control of the Legislative Assembly struck the paper as fanatics as dangerous as the religious fanatics they were seeking to combat. "The opinions of most of the men who enjoy the people's favor are so exaggerated that . . . one cannot help fearing the most unfortunate events in the future," the paper wrote on the eve of the war. But its condemnation of the Jacobins did not lead it to support the rival Feuillant faction, "for whom patriotism most often means only not being Jacobin, to judge by the reception of certain members noted for their antipatriotism."[16] Like Jean Luzac in the party quarrels among the Dutch Patriots in 1785–87, the paper thus separated itself from all the contending factions in France, at the price of being unable to suggest any practical policy that might ward off the disaster it foresaw.

The actual declaration of war on 20 April 1792 was thus no surprise to the *Gazette de Leyde*, which admitted that the decision fulfilled "the wish of all who identify with patriotism in France," while pointing out once again that "it was no less desired by the leaders of the emigrés."[17] The *Gazette de Leyde*'s clear-eyed account of the events that led to the war of 1792 had been in the best tradition of its diplomatic news gathering. Separated from the party quarrels of Paris, which led the papers there to place undue blame on the emigrés and to exaggerate news favorable to their faction's hopes, the Leiden paper had been able to make a more objective assessment of the international situation. It was one of the last

13. Ibid., 6 Jan. 1792 (Frankfurt, 29 Dec. 1791); and 20 Jan. 1792 (Frankfurt, 6 Jan.).
14. Ibid., 20 Jan. 1792 (Paris, 13 Jan.). The reference was of course to Brissot's faction of the Jacobins.
15. Ibid., 24 Feb. 1792 (Paris, 14 Feb.).
16. Ibid., 17 Apr. 1792 (Paris, 9 Apr.).
17. Ibid., 27 Apr. 1792 (Paris, 20 Apr.).

times Luzac's publication would outdo all other European newspapers in covering a major story.

The *Gazette de Leyde* and the Radical Revolution

War news had always taken priority over all other subjects in the *Gazette de Leyde*, and Luzac initially expected military operations to render French domestic politics less newsworthy, but the paper recognized from the start that this conflict might differ considerably from previous wars. The French had launched their campaign by translating the Declaration of the Rights of Man and their new Constitution into German as propaganda weapons; the paper opined, "They will not be the least dangerous weapons the enemies of France will have to fear."[18] But events in Paris itself took such a sensational course that the paper continued to be compelled to cover them in detail.

The *journée* of 20 June 1792, during which an angry crowd invaded the Tuileries palace and held Louis XVI captive, inspired Luzac to write one of his most outspoken editorial statements. Comparing the bitter conflicts in France with the patriotic unity of the Poles in the face of foreign pressure, he charged that in France,

> the spirit of anarchy and licentiousness respects neither law nor King, and seems to think that the salvation of the state can only come from the most complete confusion. . . . It appears that Providence has employed the Polish Revolution to refute the calumnies of the supporters of Despotism, who use the example of the French Revolution to prove their thesis, that true liberty is not made for the human race, and that Sovereigns have an interest in severely punishing all those peoples, who dare to aspire to it."[19]

Luzac still refused to renounce the cause of liberty and join the conservative camp, but he had abandoned any hope that good could still emerge from the chaos in Paris.

In view of the events leading up to it, the paper was hardly surprised when the *journée* of 10 August 1792 finally toppled the French monarchy, but it had largely exhausted its vocabulary of shock and horror at "the criminal boldness of the Jacobin Party" even before the fatal event occurred.[20] The paper castigated the new rulers of France for buying the support of the peasants by hasty decrees abolishing various compensation payments established in 1789, and it carefully noted that many departments had not welcomed the overthrow of the king.[21] The Sep-

18. Ibid., 1 May 1792 (Paris, 23 Apr.).
19. Ibid., 29 June 1792 (Leiden, 27 June).
20. Ibid., 14 Aug. 1792 (Paris, 5 Aug.).
21. Ibid., 24 Aug. 1792 (Paris, 17 Aug.); and 28 Aug. 1792 (Paris, 20 Aug.).

tember massacres of suspected counterrevolutionaries in the Paris prisons only served to underline the depth to which France had fallen: "The French have covered themselves with an opprobrium that centuries will not efface."[22]

The paper's coverage of these dramatic events was more extensive and, of course, more critical than what was now printed in the Paris press: those papers that did not support the radical regime, including Boyer and Cerisier's *Gazette universelle*, had been suppressed. Indeed, other papers outside France asserted that it was the *Gazette de Leyde*'s hostile articles that led the Paris revolutionaries to ban the circulation of foreign papers in the country.[23] But the *Gazette de Leyde*'s reports, detailed as they were, were not as complete as those in certain other foreign papers. Their tone, for all their condemnation of revolutionary excesses, was relatively impersonal and lacked the freshness of the coverage in the German-language *Hamburg Correspondent*, which had at least two informants on the scene in Paris, one of whom had actually marched with his battalion in the attack against the Tuileries on 10 August.[24] The German paper was no more favorable to the "cannibal horde"[25] on the banks of the Seine than the *Gazette de Leyde*, but it had been able maintain better contacts in the French capital. Luzac's inability to guarantee the most accurate and most up-to-date news coverage, even when the Paris papers had been reduced to silence about some of the most significant events in their own country, was a sign of the decline in the *Gazette de Leyde*'s journalistic fortunes. The paper, the last significant representative of the prerevolutionary international press, was no longer able to take advantage of controls being imposed on newspapers in other countries.[26]

The practical difficulties facing his newspaper made less impression on Jean Luzac than the political disasters sweeping the continent. Caught between the forces of revolutionary violence and conservative reaction, the cause of a measured liberty seemed hopeless. "Why must it be," Luzac asked one corrrespondent, "that the cause of liberty . . . has become today a shameful one, unless one is willing to be the partisan of an empty slogan and the apologist of popular tyranny, and of all the cruelties, all the vile tricks, all the impostures, frauds, and injustices that go along with it?" Those who had tried to bring reform to France were

22. Ibid., 11 Sept. 1792 (Leiden, 8 Sept.).

23. J. W. Berkelbach van der Sprenkel, "De Fransche Revolutie in de contemporaine Hollandsche couranten," *De Gids* (1939), 348.

24. *Hamburg Correspondent*, 21 Aug. 1792 (Paris, 13 Aug.).

25. Ibid., 15 Sept. 1792 (Paris, 4 Sept.).

26. Of the other major prerevolutionary gazettes, the *Courrier de l'Europe* had ceased publication in 1791 and the *Courrier d'Avignon* had been transformed into a pro-revolutionary provincial paper. The other Dutch French-language gazettes and the *Courier du Bas-Rhin* continued to publish, but seem to have had little importance compared to the Paris papers and the new papers founded outside of France by the French emigrés.

guilty of "having followed principles, true in themselves, but inapplicable in [France]."[27] Luzac continued his task of chronicler, but he no longer had any hope that his efforts would help bring about positive results.

The autumn of 1792 was a full of practical difficulties for Luzac. The onset of actual fighting in the war gave the paper more news to cover, but it also interfered with the regular flow of dispatches. Because the armies in Belgium disrupted communications between Luzac and his correspondents in Paris, it was difficult to follow the progress of the main Austro-Prussian advance into Champagne. The Paris press might be subject to increasingly stringent controls, but it received a steady flow of government-furnished information from the armies at the front, and on the other side the Austrian and Prussian armies gave German-language newspapers official reports on their progress, but Luzac had to scramble to obtain what crumbs of firsthand information he could.

It took the paper more than a month to secure a clear picture of the events at the crucial battle of Valmy. The first rumors of a French victory there had reached Leiden very quickly—they were reported on 25 September 1792—but claims from both sides contradicted each other and led Luzac to explain to his readers the difficulties he was having in obtaining reliable information: "In the midst of a war caused by the most violent, we might say the most atrocious, passions on both sides, it is hardly strange that these passions dictate the most exaggerated and contradictory reports, which are often known to be false even by those who are the first to spread them."[28] Only at the end of October, when it had been able to compare the official French and Austro-Prussian versions of events, was the paper prepared to state that Valmy had in fact been the decisive battle "and that the two French commanders showed that they were not inferior to the head of the allied forces in the art of choosing their positions, in preventing the enemy from occupying them, and in defending themselves."[29] The *Gazette de Leyde*'s caution in accepting suspect battle reports enabled it to avoid some of the hasty mistakes of the Paris papers, on the one hand, and the German press, on the other, but it must have put a severe strain on its readers' patience.

At the same time that the paper was piecing together the story of Valmy, it was also continuing to cover events in Paris, where the National Convention had now replaced the Legislative Assembly. The paper found this body no more to its liking than its predecessor; a typical

27. Luzac to William Short, American ambassador to the Netherlands, 14 Sept. 1792, in Ferdinand J. Dreer Collection, Pennsylvania Historical Society, Philadelphia. I thank my colleague Mark Summers for providing me with a copy of this letter.

28. *GL*, 9 Oct. 1792 (Leiden, 8 Oct.).

29. Ibid., 26 Oct. 1792 (Leiden, 25 Oct.).

report remarked, "There is hardly a session of the Convention, where one does not arrive at the greatest reciprocal insults."[30] The great issue dominating the debates was the trial of the king. The paper's stories sympathized with the deputies who opposed his trial and execution; they were praised as being "guided by knowledge of the human heart, and not only by respect for human weaknesses but also by political circumspection and foresight," which led them to believe that there would be "more undesirable than useful consequences from a rigorous resolution."[31] But there was no doubt about which way the wind was blowing in Paris. The paper's editorial adjuration to the French to heed "the shock, the universal cry of horror and indignation . . . that arises from one end of Europe to another,"[32] had no more impact on events than the equally outspoken statements in the several crypto-royalist papers that had managed to reestablish themselves in Paris in the late fall of 1792.[33]

On 29 January 1793, the *Gazette de Leyde* told readers, "A few more hours, and the good, the virtuous Louis XVI will have expired!"[34] The next issue included a sentimental eulogy of his virtues, and the text of his testament, which was to become a basic document of counterrevolutionary propaganda.[35] The paper's coverage of the king's trial enraged the Dutch exiles in Paris and widened the gulf between Jean Luzac and his former friends: a month after Louis XVI's execution, Valckenaer wrote to Etienne Luzac, "His honor the Professor Jean Luzac had better start to change the tone of his paper. Believe me, it is high time . . . I swear to you in all conscience that most of what he has said and written about the death of Louis XVI and the surrounding circumstances is completely false."[36] As the Revolution became more radical, the *Gazette de Leyde*, whose basic attitude toward the events in France had not changed since 1789, was coming to seem more and more counterrevolutionary.

The king's execution, dramatic as it was, did not occupy the paper's exclusive attention in the winter of 1793: Luzac also described the unexpected military expansion of France. In November and December 1792, the French armies occupied Belgium and the Rhineland, and pro-French radicals seized power in Geneva. The Jacobin press in Paris presented these events as proof of the Revolution's universal popularity; the *Gazette de Leyde* stressed instead the reluctance with which many of

30. Ibid., 13 Nov. 1792 (Paris, 5 Nov.).

31. Ibid., 27 Nov. 1792 (Paris, 19 Nov.).

32. Ibid., 4 Jan. 1793 (Leiden, 2 Jan.).

33. Jeremy D. Popkin, "The Royalist Press in the Reign of Terror," *Journal of Modern History* 51 (1979), 690–91.

34. *GL*, 29 Jan. 1793 (Paris, 21 Jan.).

35. Ibid., 1 Feb. 1793 (Paris, 25 Jan.).

36. Valckenaer to Etienne Luzac, 16 Feb. 1793, in LUL, Ms. BPL 1036X.

the "liberated" peoples accepted these changes. "A very respectable portion of our citizenry wants not the destruction of our old government, but its improvement," read a dispatch from Mainz after the French arrived, and the paper was particularly well informed about resistance to the French in the Belgian provinces, where an early dispatch accurately analyzed the revolutionaries' dilemma: "Before the Belgian Republic can be organized on the French system, we will have to overcome many obstacles from the Estates, the nobles and the clergy, who have the major part of the nation behind them. One will face the unpleasant alternative of either having to use force to impose this system, which is contrary to the principles of the French, or of having to fight continuously against the opposition of a numerous and determined party."[37] As it committed itself ever more firmly to the opponents of the French, the *Gazette de Leyde* was taking a definite risk: French units were advancing on the United Provinces themselves. In this conflict, Luzac made no pretense of impartiality, and when the Dutch unexpectedly halted the French invasion, he editorialized to the effect that if "big talk was part of the Dutch character," then the Dutch would have every right to boast of their success.[38]

While the Dutch were holding off this first French invasion, the party struggle between the Girondins and the Jacobins was reaching its peak in Paris. The articles in the *Gazette de Leyde* saw little to distinguish the two groups of revolutionaries, however, and gave the impression that France was already living under a severe dictatorship. When he learned that the Convention's committees were keeping the news of military defeats in Belgium secret from the population, Luzac wrote that "under a democratic government, the people knows no more about the real state of things than it did when those entrusted with royal authority made a state secret out of everything."[39] Given the paper's completely negative attitude toward every development in Paris after the execution of the king, it is not surprising that its account of the Montagnards' victory over Brissot and his colleagues on 31 May 1793 was relatively brief and undramatic; the paper simply saw it as further evidence for the proposition that throughout the French Revolution, "the constant struggle between two parties has always ended in the triumph of the more violent."[40] Subsequent issues brought news of the federalist revolt in Lyon and the uprising in the Vendée, but the paper neither endorsed these outbreaks nor did it seem to have much faith in their chances of success. It settled for the by now banal observation, "In a word, there is

37. *GL*, 30 Nov. 1792 (Mainz, 16 Nov.); and 7 Dec. 1792 (Brussels, 3 Dec.).
38. Ibid., 19 March 1793 (Leiden, 19 March).
39. Ibid., 2 Apr. 1793 (Leiden, 30 March).
40. Ibid., 14 June 1793 (Paris, 2 June).

the most terrible conflict throughout all of France."[41] Marat's assassination was categorized as "the loss of one of the leaders of the Parisian ochlocracy,"[42] as Luzac continued to apply labels derived from classical history to the events in France. The experiences of Greece and Rome assured him that the French democratic experiment could not last, but they gave few definite clues as to how it would collapse, and the paper's articles, though uniformly hostile to the Jacobins, had become a sterile narrative of public events in Paris, enlivened only by occasional critical remarks about the folly of revolutionary policies.

As the French Republic began its second year, the *Gazette de Leyde*'s Parisian reports gradually began to sound a new note. Whereas its coverage from 10 August 1792 until after the federalist revolts had contained little information that was not available in the better Paris papers, the Leiden paper's Paris newsletters now began to contain rumors about the internal divisions among the revolutionaries that did not find their way into print within France. An article dated 27 September 1793 gave an accurate assessment of political realities in the French capital, mentioning the continuation of party divisions within the Convention and adding, "All the authority of the present Government being concentrated in the Committee of Public Safety, all rivalries are naturally directed toward it."[43] Two weeks later, the paper referred to the "germ of discord" emerging between Robespierre and the Jacobins, on the one hand, and Danton and the Cordeliers, on the other.[44]

An even more informative letter a month later commented on the debate about the arrest of certain deputies implicated in financial scandals. It remarked that a resolution barring the arrest of deputies who had not been given a hearing in the Convention "was an attack on the supremacy of the Committees, or more precisely on the sovereignty of the sans-culottes, whose wishes the Committees carry out," and was therefore naturally defeated.[45] Another report interpreted Robespierre's speech to the Jacobin club on 28 November 1793 as a sign that "he is not undisturbed by the efforts of those who are jealous of him."[46] The Paris press of this period contained polemical exchanges that indicated how divided the triumphant revolutionaries remained, but none of these papers gave as clear an analysis of the sources of these conflicts and their potential implications as the *Gazette de Leyde*.[47] Its warning that

41. Ibid., 12 July 1793 (Paris, 3 July).
42. Ibid., 26 July 1793 (Paris, 16 July).
43. Ibid., 8 Oct. 1793 (Paris, 27 Sept.).
44. Ibid., 22 Oct. 1793 (Paris, 11 Oct.).
45. Ibid., 26 Nov. 1793 (Paris, 15 Nov.).
46. Ibid., 13 Dec. 1793 (Paris, 2 Dec.).
47. See particularly the account of the press controversies centering around Hébert's activities in Gérard Walter, *Hébert et le Père Duchesne* (Paris: Janin, 1946), 188.

"it is in the nature of things, that if the present Government does not degenerate into a kind of Protectorate, and if France does not have its own Cromwell, these all-powerful men will sooner or later tumble from the same precipice as their predecessors," was not simply an abstract prediction based on historical precedents but a reasonable extrapolation from the information contained in the paper's own reports.[48]

Poland and Thermidor

The outbreak of the war and the establishment of the Jacobin dictatorship, which limited press freedom inside France and thereby gave French-language papers outside the country a distinctive journalistic function again, both contributed to a marked restoration in the *Gazette de Leyde*'s profits. Despite the loss of the French market and competition from French-language newspapers founded by some of the French emigrés, such as Jean-Gabriel Peltier's *Correspondance politique*, published in London,[49] the *Gazette de Leyde*'s annual profits during the stormiest two years of the Revolution almost equaled the highest levels reached in the prerevolutionary period.[50] Indeed, by this time the Revolution had created a new market for the paper among the thousands of French emigrés who had fled the country. The displaced aristocrats and well-to-do bourgeois who made up the emigré colonies in towns and cities all over the continent were drawn from precisely those social groups that had always been most likely to read the paper, and their precarious situation made them more avid than ever for news, particularly reports untainted by publication in Paris. A pamphlet of the period described the typical emigré newshound: "He never comes up to you without having his pockets full of letters, gazettes, and clippings." The cafés and reading rooms that subscribed to the *Gazette de Leyde* and other European newspapers were centers of emigré sociability.[51] The radical phase of the Revolution thus meant good business for Jean Luzac.

Luzac's paper also continued to prosper during this period because it was not entirely devoted to French news. The Paris papers, hampered by revolutionary censorship after 10 August 1792, isolated by the war, and serving an audience whose main interest was domestic affairs, gave little space to events in the rest of the world. Above all, none of them provided such extensive coverage of the events in Poland from 1788 to

48. *GL*, 27 Dec. 1793 (Paris, 16 Dec.).
49. Hélène Maspéro-Clerc, *Un journaliste contre-révolutionnaire: Jean-Gabriel Peltier (1760–1825)* (Paris: Société des études robespierristes, 1973), 78–79.
50. LGA-VH, Z(2), no. 119.
51. *Portrait des émigrés d'après nature* (Paris: Desenne, [1795]), 29–30.

1794. After the end of the crisis of the First Partition in 1774, Poland dropped from the *Gazette de Leyde*'s sight for many years. The paper had not abandoned its sympathy for the Poles, but, as Luzac explained in 1776, he had to follow his sense of news, which at that point meant giving American reports precedence over Polish ones.[52] But during the early years of the French Revolution the drama of the Four-Year Diet and the subsequent revolution made Poland the paper's largest source of news not directly related to French affairs.

This second and far more significant cycle of attempted reform in Poland and foreign interference had begun in 1788. As the Diet prepared to convene, the paper set the scene for its readers: the three neighboring monarchies were raising claims again, and the Poles remained divided among themselves. Not only Luzac's paper but the European press in general sensed that important events were impending in Warsaw, and summaries of the Diet sessions appeared regularly in major German, French, and English papers. The Diet's proceedings soon began to move in unexpected directions. Stanislas-August's moderate reform efforts proved to have more support than anticipated.[53] Indeed, control of the Diet soon passed from the king to a group of reformers who called themselves the Patriots, and who were determined to recast Polish institutions in a fundamentally new way. By 1791, members of this group made contacts with the *Gazette de Leyde* and its Polish coverage for the remainder of the Four-Year Diet essentially reflected their views.[54]

The critical phase in the Diet's sessions came when it undertook the drafting of a new constitution, eventually promulgated in May 1791. The *Gazette de Leyde* followed this Polish constitution-making with great interest, particularly because of the parallels and contrasts it offered to the revolutionary process in France. From the outset, the paper's reports were emphatically in favor of reform, and considerably harsher toward its opponents than in the French case. On the crucial issue of the granting of political rights to non-nobles, the paper condemned Polish conservatives who opposed giving what the paper's correspondent called "the natural rights of Man, and those that distinguish the citizen from the slave" to commoners. "These being the sentiments of the majority of the Polish nobility," the correspondent reflected, "it is only too obvious that the base from which the new constitutional laws should be raised ... is slender and frail, at the mercy of ambition and intrigue, which are and inevitably must be the moving forces in an oligarchy."[55]

52. *GL*, 22 Oct. 1776 (Leiden, 21 Oct.).
53. Ibid., 11 Nov. 1788 (Warsaw, 25 Oct.).
54. Lojek, "International French Newspapers," 61–62.
55. *GL*, 12 Jan. 1790 (Warsaw, 26 Dec. 1789).

In view of the strength of this conservative opposition, the paper's correspondent had reason to wonder whether the Diet "is really animated by principles of independence and impartiality, such as are appropriate to the honor and the interests of a republican nation."[56]

The completion of the Constitution in 1791 stilled the *Gazette de Leyde*'s doubts. "Everyone recognizes the strength and, consequently, the real independence that the Polish Nation is going to acquire from the reunion of all its sections in a single body, which will no longer be divided by the opposing interests of two orders," the paper reported, and it praised the great nobles, the magnates, for "showing themselves above the prejudices and *amour-propre* of their birth."[57] It was not just the principles of the Constitution that the *Gazette de Leyde* celebrated, but the way it had been ratified. "Yesterday produced the most fortunate Revolution for Poland," one report on the events of 3 May 1791 began. "It did not cost a drop of blood, not a single soldier was employed, nor any weapon, and, without any violence, . . . all the legitimate rights of liberty are protected more than ever."[58] A second letter of the same date repeated the same points about the "miracle" of the day before, and went on to praise the Polish Constitution for guaranteeing the country against "an excessively democratic leveling" such as had occurred in France, while contrasting it favorably with the British system as well.[59] The sentiments expressed in the paper's Polish correspondence were those of Luzac's pro-Patriot correspondents and of Stanislas-August, who had now put himself at the head of the reform movement, but they were undoubtedly those of Luzac himself as well. With the exception of the American Constitution, he had never committed his paper so enthusiastically to the celebration of such a movement, and he hastened to print the main clauses of the new document.

Alas, neither the Polish Constitution nor the *Gazette de Leyde*'s satisfaction that liberty had finally scored a triumph on the European continent were destined to last. Stanislas-August's enemies accused him of conspiring with the French, and he soon had to employ the paper's good offices to publish an official denial.[60] Poland's powerful neighbors had no intention of letting the Constitution succeed. When war broke out between France and Austria and Prussia, Russia prepared to exploit the situation to send troops into Poland. The Poles were forced to undertake "a war . . . for the defense of a truly free and independent Constitu-

56. Ibid., 11 Jan. 1791 (Warsaw, 25 Dec. 1790).
57. Ibid., 6 May 1791 (Warsaw, 20 Apr.).
58. Ibid., 20 May 1791 (Warsaw, 4 May).
59. Ibid. This article's frequent laudatory references to Stanislas-August and its extravagant praise for his conduct in comparison with Louis XVI's leave little doubt that it was inspired by the Polish king himself.
60. *GL*, 22 July 1791 (Leiden, 20 July; Warsaw, 2 July).

tion,"[61] the only kind of war Luzac was prepared to endorse, but the combat was a hopeless one, especially after Stanislas-August abandoned the Patriot cause at Targowice. The year 1793 brought the Second Partition, which the paper's dispatches from Russia now blamed, in familiar fashion, on the unhappy country's own disunity: "Those who understand the workings of human affairs ought to have expected that civil discord would lead [Poland] to new losses, but no one could have imagined that the second Partition would be so great."[62]

The meeting of the remains of the Polish Diet at Grodno in August 1793 gave the paper the chance to report a last flicker of old-style Polish patriotism. Whereas the paper's coverage of the Constitution of 1791 had had little potential impact in Poland, since the Patriot movement had generated an extensive domestic press of its own,[63] the Polish Patriots were now muzzled in their own country and sent their bulletins to the *Gazette de Leyde* in the explicit hope that "the sensation caused in Europe by the proceedings at Grodno will finally produce some movement in their favor."[64] The orators at this last session of the Diet certainly supplied the paper with ringing cries for patriotic self-sacrifice: Luzac chose to print particularly long extracts from the speech of a certain Kinbar, who urged his compatriots to brave exile to Siberia rather than accepting the terms of the Second Partition. "Suffering means nothing to virtue," Kinbar exclaimed. "Let us go to Siberia then! . . . Her deserts will become a paradise for us, because everything, even our shadows, everything will remind us of our virtue, our devotion to the Fatherland."[65]

Luzac was at home with these sentiments of exalted stoicism in the civic-humanist style, but for all his pro-Polish sympathies, he felt little kinship with the more vigorous activism of the Kosciusko rebellion the following spring. With the horrors of the French Revolution dominating the paper's pages—the arrest of the Dantonists had just been decreed—the *Gazette de Leyde*'s first dispatch about the Polish insurrection stated, "Poland . . . is about to offer a new example of a country which throws itself into all the horrors of the most bloody excess, because it could never settle on a reasonable liberty. Nothing is left to it now but the fury of Jacobinism or a complete submission to foreign domination."[66] These initial sentiments, which probably corresponded to those of one of the partitioning powers' ambassadors in the Polish capital,[67] gave way for a

---

61. Ibid., 22 June 1792 (Warsaw, 6 June).
62. Ibid., 30 Apr. 1793 (Petersburg, 2 Apr.).
63. Grossbart, "Presse polonaise," part 1, 145–46.
64. *GL*, 20 Aug. 1793 (Warsaw, 3 Aug.).
65. Ibid., 23 Aug. 1793 (Leiden, 23 Aug.).
66. Ibid., 15 Apr. 1794 (Warsaw, 29 Mar.).
67. Ibid. The tone of these dispatches is very similar to that of later stories in the paper, datelined Berlin, which consistently denigrated the movement.

few issues to more positive reports which stressed the strong popular support for the movement and its determination to avoid French-style extremism.[68] But the revolutionaries' decision to execute four prominent supporters of the Russians led the paper to "the most sinister auguries" concerning the future of their movement.[69] The *Gazette de Leyde*'s coverage of the revolt, much more extensive than that in the Paris press, certainly lacked the unqualified enthusiasm of the bulletins in the *Journal de la Montagne*, which greeted these executions by exclaiming, "That's the way! Courage, brave Poles, and *ça ira* better and better."[70] Even as the Russian armies were on the march, the *Gazette de Leyde* still fretted about Polish extremism and praised the revolutionary government in Warsaw for punishing troublemakers who tried to stir up the people.[71]

The *Gazette de Leyde*'s coverage of Poland thus followed the same curve as its coverage of France: support for the patriotic movement as long as it continued to appeal to Old Regime constitutional traditions, followed by condemnation when reform turned to radicalism and violence. Just as the rise of radicalism in Poland had convinced Luzac that the Polish cause was doomed, he foretold the collapse of the Jacobin regime in France. When the demagogic journalist Jacques-René Hébert was finally arrested in March 1794, Luzac felt justified in observing, "Those who, from the outset of the French Revolution, have observed with reflection the views, the conduct, and the character of the men who have raised themselves up, by crimes and bloodshed, from the lowest and most corrupt scum of the nation to the highest degree of power, have never ceased to foresee and to foretell that these same men . . . would end up destroying each other . . . and from this, after the greatest suffering, there will finally come about, through exhaustion from so many disorders and horrors, the reestablishment of the laws and a generally recognized authority."[72] Subsequent events seemed to confirm Luzac's predictions. After the arrest and execution of Danton, the paper reported that "Robespierre cleverly profited from the division that reigned among his enemies, to destroy them by using them against each other."[73] Although the Committee of Public Safety was now "more powerful . . . than the King under the old regime,"[74] the paper was on the alert for signs that its long-awaited fall was coming, and it correctly

68. *GL*, 25 Apr. 1794 (Warsaw, 9 Apr.); and 20 May 1794 (Leiden, 20 May).
69. Ibid., 27 May 1794 (Leiden, 27 May).
70. *Journal de la Montagne*, 23 prairial, An II. The *Journal de la Montagne* was the Jacobin club's official paper.
71. *GL*, 29 Aug. 1794 (Warsaw, 11 Aug.).
72. Ibid., 28 Mar. 1794 (Leiden, 27 March).
73. Ibid., 25 Apr 1794 (Paris, 14 Apr.).
74. Ibid., 23 May 1794 (Paris, 12 May).

saw a favorable signal in the unexpected fact that several deputies who had spoken publicly against the decree of 22 prairial, An II, which gave the Committee of Public Safety the right to order the arrest of Convention deputies without any formalities, had not been arrested.[75]

The *Gazette de Leyde*'s readers were thus well prepared for the issue of 15 August 1794, which brought a quick synopsis of the drama of 9 thermidor, An II. This "extract of the reports from Paris" referred back to the debate about the prairial law and identified the speakers in it, Bourdon de l'Oise and Tallien, as leaders of the group that had overthrown the Incorruptible; it also publicized the three-way division within the Committee of Public Safety, identifying Collot d'Herbois, Barère, and Billaud-Varenne as having joined the thermidorian plot and Carnot, Jean-Bon St. André, Prieur, and Lindet as having refused to take sides. Particularly compared to the limited news reports in the Paris papers, which aimed at vilifying Robespierre while concealing the mechanics of the plot that had brought him down, the *Gazette de Leyde*'s news bulletins were on a par with its best reporting at the outset of the Revolution; they constituted as full an "instant history" as could be expected of such complex and controversial events.

Unlike the thermidorian press that promptly emerged in Paris, however, the *Gazette de Leyde* reserved judgment on the men who had displaced Robespierre. It was well aware that they were not moderates, and Luzac concluded pessimistically that the debates about the proper role of the Jacobin club two months after Robespierre's overthrow indicated that "those who want to maintain the revolutionary government in all its rigor still have the advantage over the moderate system."[76] Gradually, the paper took into account the growing evidence of a reaction against the Terror, and by February 1795, the paper's Paris bulletin asserted that "the revolutionary government . . . is on its way out, and its termination is loudly demanded."[77]

The way back to sanity and moderation was not easy, of course. In the spring of 1795, the paper had to report the two sans-culotte attacks on the Convention known as the *journées* of germinal and prairial, which, though unsuccessful, demonstrated the depth of popular discontent as prices mounted and bread became ever more scarce. The paper's Paris correspondent lamented that "it is beyond human ability to predict when this violent and uncertain state will finally give way to a stable and orderly condition."[78] But the paper, following the progress of the mod-

75. Ibid., 27 June 1794 (Paris, 16 June). An article about this debate in a Paris paper marked the first public evidence of the developing thermidorian conspiracy in Paris.
76. Ibid., 3 Oct. 1794 (Leiden, 2 Oct.).
77. Ibid., 27 Feb. 1795 (Paris, 16 Feb.).
78. Ibid., 29 May 1795 (Paris, 22 May).

erates in the Convention at home and the peace negotiations with Prussia abroad, was basically optimistic. "The progress the Convention is making toward the final goal of its work, the establishment of a regulated government on the double basis of good order at home and peace abroad, has been very remarkable," it asserted in April 1795.[79] The prairial riot gave the paper a last bad scare, as well as a chance to demonstrate the increased speed of communications resulting from the French revolutionaries' innovations: it received word of the *journée* via the French command in Utrecht, which in turn had learned of it sooner than normal thanks to the semaphore telegraph which now ran from Paris to the Belgian border.[80] But this final explosion of popular discontent marked the last challenge to the thermidorians from below. With its failure, they and the *Gazette de Leyde*'s Paris correspondent could breathe more easily.

The French Invasion and the Batavian Revolution

Even before the thermidorian Republic had fended off the last sans-culotte uprisings, the victorious French armies had surged through Belgium and occupied the territory of the Dutch Republic. As the French advanced, the stadholder and his supporters fled, and the former supporters of the Patriot movement took power in the bloodless Batavian Revolution. Jean Luzac and the *Gazette de Leyde*, which had reported the French and Polish revolutions from a safe distance, were now in the middle of a revolutionary situation. The conflict between Luzac and the political radicalism that had expressed itself first in the Dutch Patriot movement of the 1780s and then far more forcefully in the French Revolution now came to a head. For the next three and a half years, Luzac struggled to defend the political and journalistic ideals to which he had devoted his life, but he and his paper were too much a part of the world of prerevolutionary Europe to survive in the new atmosphere resulting from the Batavian Revolution.

From the moment the French Revolution broke out, the former leaders of the Dutch Patriot movement had anticipated that the changes taking place in France would some day permit them to take power in their own country. Just after the fall of the Bastille, Jean Luzac's cousin Johan Valckenaer, exiled to France after September 1787, wrote to Luzac asking him whether the French Revolution might provoke a similar movement in the United Provinces. Luzac replied in the negative: "Without organization, without unity, without recognized leaders

79. Ibid., 21 Apr. 1795 (Paris, 13 Apr.).
80. Ibid., 2 June 1795 (Leiden, n.d.).

who could constitute a center of direction, what chance is there of making the slightest movement with success?"[81] But Valckenaer and the other Dutch exiles in France did not give up. And, despite their difficulties with Jean Luzac during the 1780s, they initially expected that he would join with them in working to change the hated Orangist regime that had been restored in 1787. Luzac continued to suffer slights at the hands of the Orangists, particularly in connection with his post at the university, but he showed no interest in the exiles' schemes. He declined to participate in a plan put forward in 1792 by his old friend Pieter Paulus, Valckenaer, and others to offer the stadholder the status of a genuine constitutional monarch in exchange for a constitution that would break the power of the Regent class, even though "the plan of some great rank was held out to him."[82]

Around this time, Valckenaer, who had emerged as one of the leaders of the radical Dutch exiles in France, made a trip to Leiden during which he tried to buy control of the *Gazette de Leyde*. His motive was political, but his approach was to win over his sister's husband, Jean Luzac's brother Etienne, the co-owner of the paper. The result was to revive the poisonous civil war within the extended Luzac family that dated back to the disputes of 1785–87. The differences in personality and political principles between Luzac and Valckenaer were reflected even in the two men's handwriting: Luzac's small, precise, always running in ruler-straight lines across the page, Valckenaer's a bold, slanting scrawl. Exiled in France, Valckenaer had embraced the vigorous radicalism of the men of 1789 and even, to some extent, those of 1793; Luzac, as we have seen, held ever more strongly to the political ideals associated with Holland's venerable city-republics. The breach opened between the two in 1792 never healed: even after Jean Luzac's death in 1807, Johan Valckenaer still wrote to Etienne Luzac recalling the "hate-filled letters" his brother had written to him.[83]

Although Luzac had refused to involve himself in the Patriot exiles' schemes to profit from the opportunity created by the French Revolution, he had not succeeded in isolating himself from the rising political tension events in France generated in the Netherlands. He warded off

81. Luzac to Johan Valckenaer, 21 Aug. 1789, in LUL, Ms. BPL 1030.

82. William Vans Murray, diary entry, 19 Oct. 1798 (record of a conversation with Luzac), in LC, William Vans Murray papers.

83. Valckenaer to Etienne Luzac, 6 July 1807, in ibid., Ms. BPL 531. The rupture in 1792 is described, from Jean Luzac's point of view, in a subsequent letter of 11 Dec. 1796, written to his friend Cornelius de Gyzelaer in LUL, Luzac, carton 29, no. 1. Although the political differences between Valckenaer and Luzac had been clear earlier, it was evidently the 1792 visit that turned them into genuine personal enemies. Luzac's letters to Valckenaer just before the visit were still warm and personal in tone; afterward, direct correspondence between them seems to have ceased. Letters of 20 Mar. 1792, and 6 Apr. 1792, in LGA-VH, BB (1).

Valckenaer's designs on the *Gazette de Leyde* in 1792, but his academic post involved him in other political disputes related to the Revolution. In 1794, after having been passed over several times because of his anti-Orangist reputation,[84] he was elected to the post of *Rector Magnificus*, making him the official representative of the university. He spent his entire 1794–95 term in a series of frantic efforts to defend the university's complex web of special privileges in an increasingly hostile environment. The most serious affair grew directly out of the French Revolution's repercussions in Holland: a political dispute between some Orangist military officers and some revolutionary-minded students led to the killing of a student named Schaak. It fell on Luzac, as university rector, to try to ensure that justice was done. His outspoken protests against the Orangist authorities' protection of the guilty officer demonstrated both his personal outrage at the case and his determination to uphold the right of university members not to be restricted in the free expression of their opinions, but the infuriated students attacked him for being too moderate and the case led to a barrage of pamphlets, many of them sharply critical of Luzac.[85] This case was followed by yet another crisis, when the stadholder's police arrested a certain Pieter Jan Marcus, a former Patriot who had enrolled as a student after 1787 in order to gain the benefit of the university's academic immunity. This affair, in which Luzac once again saw the threat of a tyrannical authority violating the rights of citizens and traditional corporate institutions, generated reams of paper and called heavily on Luzac's legal skills.[86]

The Marcus affair was still dragging on when the French suddenly arrived, and the hard-working rector had to defend the university's complex system of corporate privileges to the armed representatives of a republic that had long since decided to dispense with such things. Luzac pointed out that the university had originally been founded "to reward the patriotic valor with which this city defended itself against the Spanish tyranny," and argued that the professors' immunities, of which the freedom from the quartering of soldiers was the most salient at the moment of his writing, had been granted by the Dutch people's legitimate representatives.[87] Meanwhile, the faculty had not received their salaries for three months, and Luzac even had to obtain firewood to warm the students who had begun doing patriotic guard duty at night. By the end of his twelve-month term, Luzac certainly had good reason to

---

84. Luzac, letter to J. C. v. d. Kemp, n.d., in LUL, Luzac, carton 28, no. 85.

85. The *mémoires* Luzac drafted to send to the stadholder on 21 Mar. 1794 and 16 June 1794 are in LUL, Luzac, carton 25. See also Siegenbeek, *Geschiedenis*, 1:329–30, and [Broerius Broes], *Aan den Lasteraar van Mr. Johan Luzac, thans rector magnificus van Hollands Hooge Schoole te Leyden* (n.p, n.d. but 1794), a response to pamphlets against Luzac.

86. Documents in LUL, Luzac, carton 25, dated 1 Dec. 1794 and afterward.

87. "Mémoire aux représentants du Peuple Français," in ibid., Feb. 1795.

believe that he had experienced the full weight of the French occupation and the Batavian Revolution.

As he worked to defend the university's interests, Luzac also had to decide how to treat the Batavian Revolution in his paper. The issue of 20 January 1795 informed readers that the stadholder had resigned his posts and fled, the Patriot leaders of 1787 had regained control of Leiden and the French had reached Amsterdam. Luzac's priority was to stress the peacefulness and moderation of the process: "The Revolution is taking place in the main cities of Holland without anyone having to suffer and without any violence. There is every reason to hope that, after such a fortunate beginning, the same spirit will continue to animate the Nation."[88] His intention was transparent: to strengthen those who wanted to forestall any French-style revolutionizing in the Netherlands.

The obvious dangers of the new political situation led to rumors that the *Gazette de Leyde* would relocate to a country outside the French sphere of influence.[89] But Luzac quickly convinced himself that he could still speak his mind freely in the Netherlands. He wrote to one of his foreign correspondents, "You have good reason to congratulate us on the peaceful way in which events here worked out. It surpassed our hopes, and as for me, it turned out that the serpent of calumny could only break its teeth when it bit on iron."[90] He soon went beyond reporting the news to take a distinct editorial stand. "We remarked seven years ago . . . that 'every revolution carried out by force and maintained by constraint or vengeance carried within it the germ of its own destruction,'" Luzac editorialized. "We will dare to predict that the revolution which has just taken place in our republic will be more long-lasting if it follows the principles which have guided it up to now." He went on to oppose any retaliation against supporters of the fallen Orangist regime, urging the Batavian revolutionaries to "be magnanimous and generous with regard to the past."[91] In the context of Dutch politics, where radicals such as Valckenaer, newly returned from France, were calling for a thoroughgoing purge of the Orangists, this was a highly partisan position.

As if his newspaper articles had not made his position sufficiently clear, Luzac used the occasion of his official rectorial lecture at the university in February 1795 to announce his hostility to the new French principles being applied in the Batavian Republic. He entitled his

88. *GL*, 23 Jan. 1795 (Leiden, 21 Jan.).
89. The London *Morning Chronicle* of 8 Jan. 1795 claimed that the Luzacs had obtained permission to move to the Danish free city of Altona. There is no indication in the archival sources that Luzac ever considered such a project.
90. Jean Luzac to [Baudus], n.d. but prob. Apr. 1795, in LUL, Luzac, carton 28, no. 41.
91. *GL*, 20 Feb. 1795 (Leiden, 19 Feb.).

speech, delivered to an audience that including leading members of the provincial government, "Socrates as Citizen," and used it to contrast the political wisdom of the classical republican tradition to the errors of democratic radicalism. He drew on the classic discussions of mixed government in Aristotle and Polybius, calling the latter's writings "the most broad-ranging, the most thorough and the best known in all of antiquity concerning the different forms of government."[92] In spite of the arrival of the French, he repeated the condemnation of direct democracy he had made in 1785: "I hold a country, where the will of the people is the highest law in everyday administration, the most unhappy." He repeated that a country could only be free when its citizens were prepared to put aside personal interests in their dedication to freedom, and when they were virtuous in their private lives as well as their public ones. Such citizens would be willing to entrust the administration of public affairs to the best among them, and he unhesitatingly proclaimed himself an adherent of "aristocracy" in this sense.[93] In glorifying the martyrdom of Socrates at the hands of an unrestrained democracy, Luzac was explicitly referring to himself: as he wrote, he had given his life to the cause of "freedom and independence," and he, too, had been punished for doing so.[94]

Lest anyone in the province of Holland miss the point of his challenge to the revolutionaries, Luzac himself translated his Latin oration into Dutch and mailed copies to friends all over the Netherlands and as far away as America, with cover letters amplifying his criticisms of political democracy and of the new Dutch government. Nor did the supporters of the Batavian Republic mistake his message: his oration became one of the main pieces of evidence the Dutch radicals used in their long campaign against the man they now labeled "Jean Socrates." In a letter to Valckenaer, then still in Paris, Etienne Luzac, himself a member of the provisional city government just elected to implement the Batavian Revolution, said the speech had shown that "our fatherland will get no service from his outstanding talents. No one, I fear, will seek him out, and he cannot put himself forward."[95]

For a time, Jean Luzac's outspoken opposition to revolutionary radicalism had no direct consequences for him, and he continued to voice muted but distinct criticism of the new Batavian regime in the columns of the *Gazette de Leyde*. Luzac did perform some useful services for the new government, such as publishing an indignant response to rumors that the French had made a secret agreement with Prussia providing for

92. Jean Luzac, *Socrates als burger beschouwd* 2d ed. (Leyden: Honkoop, 1797), 159.
93. Ibid., xxxiii, vi, 18, xxvii.
94. Ibid., vii–viii.
95. Etienne Luzac to Valckenaer, 16 Mar. 1795, in LUL, Ms. BPL 1036X.

the restoration of the stadholder.[96] But the paper made it obvious that it was not in sympathy with the Batavian radicals who wanted to replace the traditional decentralized Dutch polity with a unified republic modeled after France. An article in October 1795 gave a fair-minded summary of the arguments being made for and against the summoning of a national convention to draw up a new constitution for the country, but readers could sense that the author sided with those who the article said "have been struck by the French example. . . . They have feared the abuse of unlimited powers; they saw in it a confusion of powers, which, being exercised in the name of the *Sovereignty of the People*, necessarily ended up becoming arbitrary and producing tyranny."[97] But this cautious defense of the old Dutch constitution was a rearguard action. The Dutch radicals who favored a convention and a unitary, as opposed to a federalist, constitution were not prepared to tolerate Luzac's opposition.

The Struggle

In January 1796, the storm that had been brewing since the arrival of the French finally burst over Luzac and the paper. By this time, Luzac's brother-in-law Wybo Fijnje and his cousin Johan Valckenaer had both returned from France. They now occupied key positions in the provisional republican government, and they decided to strike at their incorrigible relative on two fronts. On 8 January 1796, the Batavian Republic's Committee of Public Safety, Wybo Fijnje presiding, wrote to Etienne Luzac, in his capacity as the *Gazette de Leyde*'s printer, informing him that the French government had complained about an article in one of the paper's recent issues, concerning the Tuscan ambassador Count François-Xavier Carletti's dispute with the French Directory. Etienne Luzac was directed to come up with "a different editor, loyal to the republican form of government" within eight days.[98] In fact, it was Valckenaer who had solicited the complaint from the French, via his friend Jacobus Blaauw, the Batavian Republic's ambassador in Paris. As Valckenaer explained to his sister Johanna Suzanne, wife of Etienne Luzac, it would be embarrassing for him to take over the paper personally, but "I have three persons in mind for the editorship."[99] The complaint itself was obviously trumped up: Jean Luzac had no difficulty demonstrating that the offending article had also appeared in the

96. *GL*, 7 July 1795 (Leiden, 7 July).
97. Ibid., 20 Oct. 1795 (The Hague, 18 Oct.).
98. Jean Luzac, *Verzameling van Stukken, betreffende het gedrag der Curateuren van Holland's Universiteit te Leyden, in de jaaren 1796. en 1797. Bijzonder in de zaak van Mr. Johan Luzac . . .*, (Leiden: Honkoop, 1797), 1–2.
99. Valckenaer to Johanna Suzanne Luzac, n.d. but Jan. 1796, in LGA-VH, B(2).

Dutch-language press in the Netherlands and in papers published in Paris and other cities in French territory.[100]

Jean Luzac's initial reaction to this attack was to abandon the paper. He had already been forced into virtual silence on Dutch politics, and he told his brother Etienne, "as far as I am concerned, I would prefer to let them prohibit the paper, rather than having to edit it under the control and inspection of someone else." If Etienne wished to keep the enterprise operating, that was his business: "I cannot and will not make dispositions concerning your choices, your interests, your honor."[101] Indeed, he asserted that "the paper has long been a burden to me that embittered my life," and he saw no reason why he should fight to hang on to it and thereby jeopardize the position of his brother and the "poor workers" whose income depended on the enterprise.[102] Etienne Luzac accordingly set out to recruit a replacement for his brother, turning first to a journalist from Paris who found the salary offered too low,[103] and then to the paper's longtime correspondent in Hamburg, Jean-Louis Baudus, who initially agreed to take the position but then changed his mind.[104] The upshot was that Jean Luzac continued to edit the paper; he assumed that Valckenaer abandoned his attack on it for fear of ruining the property on which his sister's family's income depended.[105]

Meanwhile, Fijnje and Valckenaer had attacked Jean Luzac from another direction. On 2 February 1796, the Provisional Assembly of the Province of Holland, under their guidance, directed the curators of the Leiden University to look into the advisability of keeping a notorious counterrevolutionary on their teaching staff.[106] The curators, moving with a haste notably absent in most academic proceedings, replied to the Provisional Assembly six days later to the effect that they, too, had noticed "the aristocratic sentiments, and the outlook unfavorable to the French and Batavian revolutions" that characterized the *Gazette de Leyde*, and they accordingly deprived Luzac of his appointment to teach modern Dutch history, while permitting him to continue as professor of classical languages.[107] Luzac's initial reaction, just as in the case of his editorship, was to quit his post altogether rather than accept a humiliating compromise.[108] But in this case, too, he soon changed his mind and

100. Ibid., Z(2), nos. 81–83 (copies of the *Hollandsche Courant* of Leiden, the *Courrier universel du Citoyen Husson* of Paris, and the *Courier Belgique*).

101. Jean Luzac to Etienne Luzac, 14 Jan. 1796, ibid., no. 88.

102. Jean Luzac to Etienne Luzac, 19 Jan. 1796, ibid., no. 92.

103. C. Appia to Etienne Luzac, 30 nivose, An IV, in LUL, Luzac, carton 26.

104. Baudus to Etienne Luzac, 2 Feb. 1796, Z(2), no. 95.

105. Jean Luzac to Cornelius de Gyzelaer, 11 Dec. 1796, in LUL, Luzac, carton 29.

106. Valckenaer's letter to his sister, cited in note 99, shows that he had advance knowledge of this maneuver.

107. Luzac, *Verzameling . . . zaak van Mr. Johan Luzac*, 4–7.

108. Luzac, letter of 26 Feb. 1796, ibid., 11–19. On Luzac's ouster from the university, see Schöffer, "Leids Hoogleraar."

decided to make a fight. Friends urged him to stand up for freedom of thought and make his case public.[109] Driven both by his personal convictions and his furious resentment at the way Valckenaer and Fijnje, both of whom he had helped during their years in exile, were treating him, Jean Luzac undertook to turn his case into a national cause célèbre that would not only enable him to keep control of his newspaper but that would expose the radicals for what they were.

For the next two years, Jean Luzac called on every resource at his disposal to fight the radicals. He mailed out copies of the Dutch version of his "Socrates as Citizen" speech to numerous deputies in the Provincial Assembly of Holland, where the moderate federalist faction was stronger than in the National Assembly in The Hague, and urged them to overrule the university curators.[110] In a strongly worded petition to the Provincial Assembly, he warned that if his dismissal from the university was upheld, Holland's revolutionary government would have been turned into a tyranny, and he defended the *Gazette de Leyde*'s portrayal of the Jacobin phase of the French Revolution. If his conviction that "the most esteemed, the most honorable, the most respectable, in a word, the best inhabitants of a free state" should be charged with governing it was proof of aristocratic sentiments, then the current French government of the Directory, with its strict property qualifications for voting, was an aristocracy.[111] He published letters in the Dutch-language press stating his case,[112] and organized articles favorable to himself in the Paris press, where the *Nouvelles politiques*, the successor to Boyer and Cerisier's *Gazette universelle*, praised the "services his gazette . . . rendered for so many years to the progress of the real principles of social regeneration."[113] Finally, when the curators refused to accept the Provincial Assembly's instructions to reinstate him, he used the documentary techniques that had been the mainstay of his paper's reputation and published all the petitions and memoranda he had compiled in his defense as a *Collection of Documents, concerning the Action of the Leiden University Curators*, so that if he could not regain his post, he would at least have proved that "Batavian freedom was an Asiatic despotism."[114]

The one resource Luzac did not have at his disposal in this struggle was the *Gazette de Leyde* itself. Luzac had never used the paper to fight his

---

109. Gyzelaer to unknown correspondent, 13 Apr. 1796, in LUL, Luzac, carton 29.

110. Letters of 1796 to H. C. Cras, M. Temminck, Hartman, Kantelaer, van den Spuyt, Beelde, van Maanen, Simon Styl, Adrian van der Kemp, all in ibid., carton 28.

111. Jean Luzac, "Memorie" to Provincial Assembly, in *Verzameling . . . zaak van Mr. Johan Luzac*, 47.

112. Letter to *Leydsche Courant*, 18 Jan. 1797, in *Verzameling . . . zaak van Mr. Johan Luzac*, 149–53.

113. *Nouvelles politiques* (Paris), 18 germinal, An V. This short article did not satisfy Luzac, who wrote to P. H. Marron, another French friend, urging him to insert a longer piece in another Paris paper. Luzac to Marron, 1797, in LUL, Luzac, carton 28, no. 30.

114. Jean Luzac, *Verzameling . . . zaak van Mr. Johan Luzac*, 303–4.

battles in Dutch politics in the 1780s, but he could not have called on it in the 1790s because of his conflict with his brother Etienne, the co-owner, who now emerged for the first time as a major influence on the paper's content. Etienne, born in 1756, was eight years younger than his brother, and considerably closer in age to his brother-in-law, the redoubtable Johan Valckenaer, whose sister he had married in 1783. Like Jean, Etienne had attended Leiden University and graduated in 1781 with a degree in law, and he had been active in the Patriot movement of the 1780s.[115] The contract drawn up in 1783 between the elder Etienne Luzac and his two nephews clearly put Jean Luzac in a stronger position to control the family newspaper, however. Although the brothers were to split the paper's profits equally, Jean Luzac was guaranteed an additional 2,000 gulden for his work as editor, whereas Etienne received no separate salary as printer. He had the distinctly less glamorous job of handling the paper's bookkeeping, and the contract provided that if he engaged in any other business ventures, his brother would be entitled to half of the resulting profits.[116]

Jean Luzac's younger brother must have been aware that his older sibling held a patronizing view of him. In a letter from the late 1780s, Jean Luzac had written, "I know my brother; I know his faults perfectly well, or better, his weaknesses, but I also know his good qualities." He criticized Etienne's meanness in money matters and some of his principles, concluding that in contrast to his younger brother, "I think that man is not in the world just for oneself and to show off in one's own small circle."[117] It was not Etienne who received correspondence from famous men abroad and visits from them when they stopped in Leiden, nor did he enjoy the prestige of an academic appointment. It was the Batavian Revolution that first permitted Etienne to cut a figure in public affairs. Unlike his older brother, he supported the overthrow of the traditional Dutch government, and he was named to the provisional city council established in Leiden after the arrival of the French in 1795, though he soon stepped down.[118] But Etienne's political ideas were vague, consisting essentially of a generalized hope that things would work out for the best, coupled with fears "that that happy time is farther off than it seems."[119]

The well-meaning but indecisive Etienne now found himself caught between two much stronger personalities, his brother Jean and his

115. LGA-VH, Q (papers concerning Etienne Luzac, 1756–1827).
116. Articles 5, 8, 9, 13 of contract, dated 18 Feb. 1783, in ibid., Z(2), no. 51.
117. Jean Luzac to Johan Valckenaer, n.d. but after Sept. 1787, in LUL, Luzac, carton 28, no. 62.
118. Etienne Luzac to Johan Valckenaer, letters of 12 Feb. 1795 and 10 March 1795, in LUL, Ms. BPL 1036X.
119. Etienne Luzac to Johan Valckenaer, 27 May 1794, in ibid.

brother-in-law Johan Valckenaer. By the middle of 1796, as Jean Luzac embarked on his campaign against the Batavian radicals, relations between the two brothers had reached the breaking point. Johan Valckenaer, accused of complicity in an unsuccessful protest against the moderates in the provisional Batavian government, had just been hustled off, somewhat against his will, to serve as the Dutch ambassador to Spain. From Paris, he wrote to Etienne Luzac asking that the *Gazette de Leyde* publish a defense of his conduct.[120] Etienne complied: with the paper's printing equipment in his house, he was in a position to have the last word about its contents. Jean Luzac was furious. In a letter to his brother, he demanded to know "why must it be the so decried *aristocratic* paper of J. Luzac that defends him [Valckenaer] in the eyes of the world?" He continued bitterly, "But what am I saying? the paper of J. Luzac? Because of his influence and interference, I hear myself from your own mouth called your writer and your employee."[121] Eventually, the conflict led to a complete break between the two brothers. The rupture pained Etienne, who wrote to Valckenaer, "You know my heart, you know that I have a horror of every sort of dissension and disagreement, and here for the past eighteen months a quarrel has divided me from a man who is estimable in many ways and who is dear to me."[122]

Meanwhile, the paper, reduced to virtual silence about Dutch politics, continued to report on events outside the Netherlands. Jean Luzac was not a man to be reduced easily to compliance with a party line, and the *Gazette de Leyde*'s coverage of France had continued to have a certain critical tone to it. When the Convention's decision to force the French voters to reelect two-thirds of its members to the legislative councils of the new Directory led to the counterrevolutionary vendémiaire uprising in Paris in October 1795, the paper assessed the Convention's reliance on the army to put down the revolt as a sign of weakness.[123] But as Luzac became increasingly entangled in his struggle with the Batavian Republic after 1795, the paper's French coverage became less and less interesting. The Paris papers, often delayed in reaching the Netherlands between 1792 and 1795, were now easily available again; the Dutch-language press chronicled both French and Dutch events adequately; and the emigré papers published in countries outside the French sphere of influence, like the *Journal de Francfort*, were livelier.

120. Valckenaer to Etienne Luzac, 19 June 1796, in ibid. On the Amsterdam cannoniers' revolt that Valckenaer was accused of backing, see Sillem, *Valckenaer*, 1:323–27.

121. Jean Luzac to Etienne Luzac, n.d. but 1796, in LUL, Luzac, carton 28, no. 22.

122. Etienne Luzac to Valckenaer, 5 July 1798, in LUL, Ms. BPL 1036X.

123. *GL*, 16 Oct. 1795 (Paris, 5 Oct.). The vendémiaire revolt also led to the interruption of regular mail service from Paris for several days, which gave Luzac some anxious moments. He had to rely on unconfirmed reports and private letters for two consecutive issues after receiving the first word of the event. *GL*, 16 Oct. 1795 (Leiden, 14 and 15 Oct.).

The *Gazette de Leyde*'s news coverage of France became increasingly
derivative, drawn primarily from the *Moniteur* and, after the first shock
of the French occupation, from the moderate right-wing papers in
Paris.[124] Since the Paris press was enjoying its greatest degree of freedom since the days of 1789 to 1792, the *Gazette de Leyde* no longer had
any chance to publish news that could not be published in France itself,
and its comments on events there held no special interest. Indeed, the
paper professed to find the details of the Directory's parliamentary
politics rather boring. "The constantly changing show that the French
Republic, Paris especially, offers each day to the eyes of the attentive
world," one article remarked, "eventually wears out even the most dis-
passionate spectator by its rapid and varied movement."[125]

These difficulties reduced the *Gazette de Leyde*'s circulation to a level
well below what it had reached in the late 1780s, but the paper's sales
were fairly stable at this lower level until Jean Luzac finally lost control of
it in 1798.[126] The declining profit figures did not result entirely from a
fall in sales: the revolutionary upheavals also complicated the collection
of payments from foreign subscribers. When the French occupied the
Netherlands in early 1795, Luzac's brother Etienne wrote anxiously to
Valckenaer to see if there was any chance to recover monies owed him by
the prerevolutionary *Bureau des gazettes étrangères*, and he rejoiced when
the Peace of Basel between France and Prussia allowed him to resume
shipments to northern Germany.[127] French authorities continued to
mention the paper's circulation, particularly in the newly annexed Belgian departments whose loyalty to the French republic was considered
shaky.[128] The paper continued to command respect. A German journalist who reviewed the bound volume of its 1796 issues as a book concluded, "If the essence of a newspaper is a synchronic account of simul-
taneous events in different places, the forty-eighth volume of these
reports . . . still fulfills this goal most completely." Even this reviewer had
to admit, however, that "because of political conditions in the Netherlands, it has lost some of its outspokenness, and because of the [British]

124. On the rise of the *Journal de Francfort* at the *Gazette de Leyde*'s expense, see *Allgemeiner Literaturzeitung*, 14 Mar. 1796. On the Paris press in this period, see Jeremy D.
Popkin, *The Right-Wing Press in France, 1792–1800* (Chapel Hill: University of North
Carolina Press, 1980), and "Les journaux républicains," *Revue d'histoire moderne et contemporaine* 31 (1984), 143–57.
125. *GL*, 7 Feb. 1797 (Paris, 1 Feb.).
126. Figures for monthly payments to the Dutch post office for 1795 through 1798 and
annual profit figures both confirm this. Postal payments totalled 315 gulden for the period
May to December 1795 (an annual rate of approximately 540 gulden), 486 gulden for
1796, 562 gulden for 1797, and 338 gulden for 1798. (AR, Derde Afdeling, Commis-
sarisen der Posterijen, inv. no. 284). For profits see Table 3 and LGA-VH, Z(2), no. 119.
127. Etienne Luzac to Valckenaer, 16 Mar. 1795, in LUL, Ms. BPL 1036X; Valckenaer
to Etienne Luzac, 7 May 1795, ibid.
128. Police reports in AN, F 7 3451.

naval blockade of the Netherlands, some of the freshness of its reports."[129] Nevertheless, the paper had clearly lost the commanding
position it had once held in the international press market.

The one domain in which the *Gazette de Leyde* could still offer original
news coverage was the ongoing continental war. Unlike the Paris papers, even the flourishing counterrevolutionary ones, the Leiden paper
felt free to draw primarily on non-French sources for its news about the
campaigns of 1796 and 1797, and to convey the sentiments of the
governments and populations overwhelmed by the French rather than
the obligatory enthusiasm the French papers purveyed. Luzac's military
bulletins, ordinarily dry and technical, suited to the deliberate nature of
Old Regime warfare, reflected the shock and amazement caused by the
sudden French crossing of the Rhine in September 1795: it was "one of
those events that marks a turning point in history." Luzac also chronicled the extensive destruction resulting from the new style of warfare.[130] When Napoleon led his troops to the rapid conquest of northern
Italy in 1796, the paper's newsletters described the panic in Milan, as the
Austrian officials fled, and the disarray in Vienna, where rival parties
tried to pin the blame on different generals.[131] A Viennese dispatch
from the following year expressed a discouragement that certainly was
not to be found in the Austrian press: "The failure of our plans in Italy
seems pre-ordained."[132]

Luzac also took advantage of the relative editorial freedom he continued to enjoy in 1797 to print news critical of pro-revolutionary movements throughout Europe. A dispatch from Bologna, capital of the
short-lived Cispadane Republic, commented acidly that the French-
sponsored constitutions being created throughout the peninsula invariably brought with them higher taxes and "the evil of internal dissensions,
hatred, vengeances, even civil war."[133] The paper's limited reporting on
Britain emphasized the threat of radicalism there and condemned Fox
and his followers for stirring up agitation against the Pitt government,
"despite the risk of overturning the state and putting a system they
inwardly disavow into power."[134] The paper naturally rejoiced at the
success of the French moderates in the legislative elections of April 1797,
but any hope Luzac may have entertained for a general roll-back of
revolutionary principles dissolved with the coup d'état of 18 fructidor,
An V (4 September 1797) in Paris, in which the more radical members of
the Directory rid themselves of their moderate colleagues and purged

129. *Allgemeiner Literaturzeitung*, 3 April 1797.
130. *GL*, 18 Sept. 1795 (Cologne, 11 Sept.); and 6 Oct. 1795 (Coblentz, 20 Sept.).
131. Ibid., 31 May 1796 (several Italian reports); and 3 June 1796 (Vienna, 18 May).
132. Ibid., 10 Feb. 1797 (Vienna, 25 Jan.).
133. Ibid., 18 Apr. 1797 (Bologna, 20 Mar.).
134. Ibid., 9 June 1797 (London, 31 May).

the legislative councils. The *Gazette de Leyde* provided full details about the coup, but no reflections on its significance. Before Jean Luzac could test the limits of his freedom to comment on French and European affairs after the fructidor coup, however, a coup of 22 January 1798 brought the Dutch radicals to power in the Netherlands and set the stage for Luzac's final ouster from the editorship.

Even from faraway Spain, Johan Valckenaer had continued to peruse Jean Luzac's news articles with a jaundiced eye. After the fructidor coup, he wrote to his sister, telling her that whatever difficulties her family had experienced were all due to "your evil brother[-in-law], Citizen Jean Socrates. . . . That citizen should consider himself lucky that he doesn't write his paper on French soil."[135] The coup of 22 January 1798 put the Dutch radicals in a position to win their long-drawn-out battle with the troublesome editor. The coup unchained the Dutch radical press: its editorialists set up a cry for appropriate punishment of the "unworthy Professor Luzac."[136] And Luzac's radical brother-in-law Wybo Fijnje was now one of the members of the Batavian Republic's governing Directory.

With Fijnje in the government, Valckenaer on his way back to the Netherlands, and the paper's one-time hired editor Brahain Du Cange, who had in the intervening years defrauded both Etienne Luzac and Johan Valckenaer, now in the Netherlands and intriguing against the paper,[137] Jean Luzac's position had become hopeless. Even before the coup, Luzac had rejected the most favorable settlement of the university dispute his friends in the Provincial Assembly of Holland had succeeded in obtaining for him: he had been offered a pension equivalent to his faculty salary, but he refused to accept money he had not earned.[138] On 10 April 1798, the Department of General Police informed the paper that it had once again received a complaint from the French government, and on 5 May 1798 the Dutch government forbade further publication of the *Gazette de Leyde*.[139] For the first time in 121 years, the paper was silenced.

Neither the ban on the paper nor the government which banned it lasted long. But in both cases, short-lived measures had enduring effects. The radical Dutch unitarists were ousted from power in yet an-

135. Valckenaer to Johanna Suzanne Luzac, 18 Nov. 1797, in LGA-VH, B(2).

136. *Politieke Blixem*, 30 Jan. 1798.

137. Etienne Luzac had complained to Valckenaer about Du Cange's dishonesty in a letter of 20 July 1795, in LUL, Ms. BPL 1036X. He complained about Du Cange's apparent influence with the French authorities in The Hague in a subsequent letter of 8 May 1798, in ibid.

138. Jean Luzac to Committé-Provinciaal van Holland, 14 Jan. 1798, printed copy tipped in at back of copy of Anon., *Advisien van Mr. Matthias Temminck, Mr. Hendrick Vollenhoven, en Jacob van Halmael over het rapport van Dirk Hoitsma en J. Nolet, in de Zaak van Mr. J. Luzac* (1798), in LGA.

139. LGA-VH, Z(2), nos. 104–5.

other French-sponsored coup on 13 June 1798, but by then they had made permanent changes in the nation's political institutions, ending forever the autonomy of the Dutch cities and provinces and laying the foundations for a strong central government. The ban on the *Gazette de Leyde* was lifted three days after the coup of 13 June 1798,[140] but Jean Luzac was no longer in control of the paper he had made famous. It was Etienne Luzac who had taken steps to be allowed to resume publication. He had been as outraged as his brother at the prohibition of the paper in May 1798. As he wrote to Valckenaer, who, to his disappointment, had been sent back to Spain, "My paper, for which I had so much love and tenderness, and which was said to be esteemed by so many, has been suppressed on orders of the Executive Council, and I have been deprived of a very respectable existence . . . I know well that the paper was not written in the current fashion, but I also know that as long as one only recounts the facts and makes no reflections about them, that one ought to be able to count on being protected."[141] But Etienne Luzac had quickly understood what was necessary to get the paper back in business. He had made the rounds of the French and Dutch authorities in The Hague without results. "In the meantime, the young man whose name is now on the paper arrived; we talked, we arranged things with my co-owner [Jean Luzac], and a few days later the first number of the *Nouvelles politiques* appeared." Etienne Luzac still resented the handling of the matter, but he concluded, "I think things may turn out less disagreeably for me than I had supposed."[142]

Etienne Luzac, in his own way as dedicated to maintaining the paper as his stubborn brother, had bowed to the realities of life in French-dominated Europe: he had recognized that there was no place left for a newspaper that insisted on its right to depict political affairs as its editor saw fit, without regard for the wishes of the triumphant revolutionaries. It remained merely to work out proper compensation for his brother Jean, who remained the legal co-owner of the paper. But the fight had finally gone out of Jean Luzac. By a contract signed 20 August 1798, he separated himself permanently from the editorship of the paper, turning it over to Abraham Blussé, Junior, the scion of a publishing family in nearby Delft.[143] Jean Luzac made this arrangement without his brother's knowledge, and the two continued to fight over the financial management of the paper for nearly two years, until Etienne Luzac finally agreed to approve Jean Luzac's outright sale of his half-interest in the enterprise to Blussé.[144]

140. Ibid., no. 106.
141. Etienne Luzac to Valckenaer, 8 May 1798, in LUL, Ms. BPL 1036X.
142. Ibid., 17 May 1798.
143. Contract dated 20 Aug. 1798, in LGA-VH, Z(2), no. 108.
144. Etienne Luzac to Jean Luzac, 9 May 1800, ibid., no. 111.

An Epilogue

And so, under the title of *Nouvelles politiques*, the *Gazette de Leyde* lived on into the Napoleonic era, a shadow of its former self but still not entirely dead. Profits even rose slightly, thanks to readers' thirst for news about the Napoleonic campaigns, although even in the best year, 1804, they never reached the level of 10,000 gulden again. Despite the acrimonious terms under which he had abandoned the paper, Jean Luzac even continued to take some interest in its affairs. Friends in the diplomatic community still forwarded to him items they wanted included in the paper,[145] and the news of his hero George Washington's death led him to draft an article which he sent to his successor as a signed letter to the editor, not without a covering letter referring the sympathy Washington had expressed for "the multiple wrongs, the sustained injustices that I have had to endure . . . in my relations with your paper."[146]

For both the *Gazette de Leyde* and Jean Luzac, however, the events of 1798 had marked the real end of an era. The paper's modest prosperity in the first half-decade of the Napoleonic era was only temporary. In 1806, Napoleon installed his brother Louis as king of the Netherlands. Louis took a genuine interest in his Dutch subjects—so much so that in 1810 his annoyed brother abolished his kingdom and annexed its territory directly to France—but Louis also completed the process of converting the *Gazette de Leyde* into a servile government organ, purchasing it outright from Etienne Luzac in 1807 for the price of 16,000 gulden.[147] Under royal ownership, the paper quickly sank into complete insignificance. A French police report of 1811 concluded, "There is no need to discuss the *Journal politique* of Leiden. . . . It sells only 400 copies," and the French prefect who inherited responsibility for it after the annexation complained that it lost money.[148]

Conditions in the Napoleonic era were somewhat kinder to the Luzac brothers than to their once-famous newspaper. Etienne Luzac became one of the prosperous bourgeois notables who dominated local affairs after the Batavian Republic had been remodeled along the lines of Consular France in 1801. Like many of his counterparts in France during the same period, he moved effortlessly from loyalty to one regime to loyalty to the next, holding local offices and judgeships under the conservative republican regime from 1801 to 1806, the Bonapartist kingdom from 1806 to 1810, and again after the creation of the King-

---

145. William Vans Murray to Jean Luzac, 1 Feb. 1800, in Huntington Library, Rufus King papers, RK 471.
146. *GL*, 11 Feb. 1800, and cover letter in LGA-VH, P(7).
147. Documents concerning the sale are in ibid., Z(2), nos. 118, 119, 121, 124.
148. AN, F 7 3459; prefect's note in list of papers in annexed territories in F 18 24A.

dom of the Netherlands in 1813. He died quietly in 1827, leaving an estate of more than 150,000 gulden.[149]

Jean Luzac, too, made his peace with the conservative republic installed under the patronage of Napoleon in 1801. Financially, he complained that he had been ruined by the revolutionary decade: by 1799, he had lost his income from the paper, his faculty salary, and the better part of the investments he had made over the years in foreign governments' bonds, now rendered almost worthless by the consequences of the Revolution.[150] But after 1801, things took a better turn. He escaped from his political quarantine and even served as a member of the consultative committee chosen to draft a new constitution, which lasted until the installation of Louis as king in 1806.[151] He had been restored to his professorship in 1802, and he remained devoted to the university: his last intervention in public affairs was a long memorandum for Louis Bonaparte's government, defending its traditional corporate privileges against "an exaggerated system of equality" which "has made people try to level down all the privileges and destroy all the benefits that devotion to the sciences and the arts procure to those who make them the difficult occupation of their life."[152]

It was only after his dismissal as editor in 1798 that Luzac really devoted himself to classical scholarship. He edited several ancient texts for publication, and he told a correspondent that he was now "entirely given over to the study of literature and antiquity."[153] He was still sought out by distinguished visitors, such as the abbé Barruel, author of one of the best-known denunciations of the French Revolution.[154] Had it not been for his failing health and the death of his beloved wife in 1806, he might have been reasonably content. Unfortunately, Barruel's visit found him "in a state of the greatest affliction." He was losing his sight and was no longer able to go on with his scholarly work.[155]

The end came suddenly for Jean Luzac on 12 January 1807. As he was taking a morning stroll along the Rapenburg, the tree-lined canal where he had owned a house for many years, a barge loaded with gunpowder exploded: it was the greatest disaster Leiden had suffered in centuries. Among the victims was the former editor of the *Gazette de Leyde*, whose body was found floating in the canal. It was perhaps appropriate that Jean Luzac died in an accident resulting from his country's forced

149. LGA-VH, Q; settlement of estate, 20 Nov. 1827.
150. Luzac to G. J. Gérard, 9 Aug. 1799, in LUL, Luzac, carton 28.
151. Luzac to unknown correspondent, 1802–3, ibid., no. 56.
152. "Mémoire succinct sur la Constitution actuelle de l'Université de Leide," in ibid., carton 24.
153. Jean Luzac to Baron de Loë, 1 Jan. 1805, in LUL, Ms. BPL 1886.
154. Ste. Croix to Luzac, 25 May 1806, in LUL, Luzac, carton 29.
155. Luzac to M. de Ste. Croix, 4 July 1806, in BN, Ms. N.a.f. 501, f. 119.

participation in the aftermath of the French Revolution, the same event that had also crushed the life of his beloved newspaper. His friends erected a monument to him that still stands in Leiden's largest church, the Pieterskerk. Its inscription reads, "To our friend Mr. Jean Luzac, professor. He was the terror of oppressors, the comfort of the oppressed." For many years, it was the only memorial to the famous editor. The Orangist Kingdom of the Netherlands saw no need to honor one of the stadholder's most dedicated opponents, nor did nineteenth-century liberals see their principles foreshadowed in Luzac's devotion to the institutions of the Dutch Old Regime. Only the citizens of the American republic in which Jean Luzac had invested so many of his hopes saw fit to remember him: in 1909, the members of the Netherlands Society of Philadelphia donated the plaque that can still be seen on the front of Luzac's house at number 112, Rapenburg, recalling the "champion of truth and righteousness and of the cause of the United States of America in the Leyden Gazette 1772–1785."

[11]

The *Gazette de Leyde*,
Politics, and Journalism

Both Jean Luzac and the *Gazette de Leyde* expired as the European news industry was standing on the threshold of a great period of expansion. The events of the French Revolution, which had finally overwhelmed the *Gazette de Leyde*, had given a lasting stimulus to public interest in political affairs; the innovations of the Industrial Revolution soon provided the means to satisfy the growing demand for news in ways Jean Luzac had never dreamed of. In 1814, as the Napoleonic wars were coming to an end, the London *Times* put into operation the first power-driven newspaper printing press: its use allowed the *Times* and the other newspapers that followed its lead to increase their press runs to unheard-of levels, and also to expand the size of their papers and the amount of news and information they carried. The press run of the *Gazette de Leyde* in 1772, when Jean Luzac took on the editorship, was probably no more than twice that of the most successful European newspapers a hundred years earlier. A century later, the circulation of the most successful French-language newspaper, the *Petit Journal*, had reached a level almost a hundred times greater than the *Gazette de Leyde*'s best achievements.[1] In the same period, the invention of the electric telegraph had made the transmission of news almost instantaneous. Modern methods of transportation allowed the mass press of the nineteenth century to reach its readers in hours rather than days, and increased literacy permitted newspapers to reach most of the adult population of Western nations. Newspapers, even elite organs such as

1. The *Petit Journal*'s daily press run averaged 523,000 in 1878 and had climbed to 825,000 by 1884. Bellanger et al., *Histoire générale de la presse française*, 3:221.

the London *Times*, became great business enterprises, generating as much revenue in a day as Luzac's paper had in a year.

Not only did the Industrial Revolution transform the technological basis of the news industry, the political revolutions Jean Luzac had chronicled in the last decades of the eighteenth century set the stage for a transformation of the press's political significance. Indeed, the *Gazette de Leyde* itself had for a time evolved in the direction of overt partisanship, during the troubled years of the Dutch *Patriottentijd*. The Patriots' defeat in 1787 caused the paper to retreat to more traditional patterns, but the vehemently partisan newspapers of the French Revolution soon went even further in this direction. These papers themselves were ephemeral, but the new role they created for the newspaper press as the spokesman for the sovereign people endured. The great newspapers of the nineteenth century—the London *Times*, the Paris *Journal des Débats* and the *Constitutionnel*, and their myriad competitors throughout the continent—openly combined political advocacy and reporting in a manner that Jean Luzac would have neither understood nor approved.

The particular circumstances that led to Jean Luzac's departure from the *Gazette de Leyde* in 1798 and the paper's cessation of publication a few years later were less to blame for the publication's disappearance than the great changes taking place in the world around it. The *Gazette de Leyde* had been part of the Old Regime and it was fated to disappear along with the conditions that had permitted it to flourish. Before they disappeared, however, *Gazette de Leyde* and the other newspapers of the eighteenth century helped produce the new world that made them obsolete, and, like the Old Regime itself, they left behind a legacy that continued to influence their successors, often in unrecognized ways.

The Elite Press of the Late Eighteenth Century

The international French-language gazettes of the late eighteenth century were the elite press of their era, serious, well-documented newspapers designed for those readers with enough wealth, education, and leisure to demand the best available political information. Of the dozen or so papers of this sort available in the 1770s and 1780s, the *Gazette de Leyde* was clearly the most respected, even if it did not necessarily have the widest circulation. To be sure, like all European newspapers of the eighteenth century, the *Gazette de Leyde* existed within the framework of political institutions that gave rulers the right to determine what news their subjects received. Even in Great Britain, the only country where censorship had been formally abolished, Parliament only conceded the press's right to report its deliberations in 1771, and newspaper editors and publishers could still be tried for printing criticism of the government.[2] Everywhere else in the European world, including the Netherlands, the very right to publish a newspaper, as well as the determination of what it could print, depended on privileges granted by the sovereign authority. Enlightened rulers might permit wide-ranging press freedom, but, as August Ludwig von Schlözer noted, where freedom of the press depended on the sovereign, it could be taken away as easily as it was granted.[3]

The laws granting rulers absolute authority over the press were not an accurate representation of the reality of eighteenth-century life, however. By Jean Luzac's day, most educated Europeans considered that they had a right, established by custom, to a basic minimum of news concerning public events: wars, treaties between states, changes of rulers, even great natural disasters. In a civilization based on individual private property, too many of the subjects' practical interests were bound up with such public events for them to be considered exclusively the ruler's concern. But it was not merely the selfish concerns of diplomats, bond holders, and military officers that created a demand for access to news of public affairs. The growing public of educated men and women across Europe was increasingly ready to claim a moral right to know what their rulers were doing and to judge their actions. Only in exceptional circumstances, such as the radical phase of the Dutch Patriot movement and the French Revolution, did this claim become a demand that the public should choose its rulers. But the identification of secretive government with despotism, and of openness with legitimacy, made it increasingly difficult for European rulers to keep their subjects totally in the dark about political events. "One of the principles of the despotic form of government is to keep the people in ignorance of events in the world in general, and above all of those around them," the *Gazette de Leyde*'s Constantinople correspondent wrote in 1784, contrasting the Turkish prohibition on newspapers with the situation in Europe, where "in most monarchies there is at least a public journal, which keeps the nation informed about current events from the government's point of view."[4] As Gottlob Benedikt von Schirach, another of the leading journalists of Jean Luzac's generation, argued, this concession to the public's

2. Peter Thomas, "The Beginning of Parliamentary Reporting in Newspapers, 1768–1774," *English Historical Review* 74 (1959), 625–32; on prosecutions for seditious libel, see Levy, *Emergence*, and Black, *English Press*, 135–96.

3. Schlözer, in *Stats-Anzeigen* 8 (1785), no. 31, p. 292, cited in Franz Schneider, *Pressefreiheit und politische Oeffentlichkeit* (Neuwied: Luchterhand, 1966), 156.

4. *GL*, 5 Oct. 1784 (Constantinople, 27 Aug.).

right to know was actually useful to rulers: "Everywhere there has been an increase in publicity about politics, a result of the enlightenment of our age ... and governments enjoy increasing trust as they become more open."[5]

European states responded to this demand for news by sponsoring their own newspapers. But from the time newspapers first appeared, the official press had had to coexist with other publications that were not directly government-sponsored. These ostensibly independent news publications were often influenced and manipulated behind the scenes, as the *Gazette de Leyde* was, but their content never became identical to that of the official press. At a minimum, they put articles from the authorized papers of different states side by side, but in general they went further: as the elder Etienne Luzac indignantly complained to the French ambassador in the Hague in 1772, if he could only print what was already in the official press, "what esteem would you have for my paper?"[6] And in reality, this partial independence of the unauthorized press served an essential function for even the absolutist regimes of the period: it served to legitimate their actions by proving that they were not afraid to permit the European public at large to examine and to judge them.

Etienne Luzac's retort to the French in 1772 pointed up the inescapable paradox built in to this system, however: independent newspapers could only serve their legitimating function for the governments which connived at their activities if they were permitted to publish information not contained in the avowedly official press. Indeed, their credibility could only be sustained if they were allowed to publish at least some material genuinely critical of governments and ministers. European governments struggled against this fact of life, but they could not escape from it. The French government in the 1770s came up with a very elaborate scheme to bring the independent press under control when it subsidized the *Courrier de l'Europe*, an ostensibly independent gazette published in London but actually for much of its life printed on French soil. But so long as readers could compare this ingenious simulacrum of an independent newspaper with the *Gazette de Leyde*, the *Courrier*'s reputation could only be maintained by allowing it to print what Jean Luzac printed. For all its pains, the French ministry ended up paying lavishly to find itself in the same situation it had been in before the *Courrier* was created.

The existence of privately owned newspapers not under direct gov-

5. Gottlob Benedikt von Schirach, introduction to Johann Hermann Stoever, *Historisch-statistische Beschreibung der Staaten des teutschen Reichs* (Hamburg: B. G. Hoffmann, 1785), xi.

6. Etienne Luzac to Desnoyers, French ambassador to The Hague, 5 July 1772, in LGA-VH, Z(1), no. 34.

ernment control thus created a narrow but significant zone in which political information that went beyond what established governments would have wished to make public could circulate. European governments frequently found this situation to their advantage, and they were expert at manipulating it to serve their short-term goals. They could, if they wished—and they often did—exert sufficient pressure on particular editors to dissuade them from publishing unwanted reports, and they could even ban offending papers. But governments could not dismantle the system as a whole. Indeed, before 1789, none of the French-language international gazettes was ever permanently suppressed. Far more stable than the unregulated and vigorously competitive London papers, the *Gazette de Leyde* and its colleagues bent before storms, but always righted themselves when the weather cleared. Even when they were most subdued, their mere existence continued to remind subscribers that there was a realm of news beyond what their rulers were willing to provide. The eighteenth-century continental newspapers brought forward no practicing newsman who was also a forthright spokesman for the freedom of the press. But in their own way, they helped make freedom of information a part of European civilization.

The most profound effect of the prerevolutionary European press, then, was the institutionalization of practices that made it difficult for governments to withhold significant political information from the public. Certainly, it is a long step from publicizing government actions to governments conceding a need for public approval of their actions. But it was only because the periodical news press could be depended on for reliable information that meaningful public discussion of politics could take place. The newspapers of the eighteenth century were not and did not claim to be spokesmen for the public. As the German press historian Franz Schneider has put it, "Through their informational content, they were catalysts and instigators of discussions about public affairs, but not yet the vehicles for that discussion. They were reporters of news, but not yet representatives of public opinion."[7] But without their presence, no significant debate about politics would have been possible.

For continental Europe's political elites at the end of the Old Regime, the international gazettes, of which the *Gazette de Leyde* was the most reputable, thus performed what modern students of the press have called an agenda-setting function: they told their readers "what to think *about*."[8] Circulating to readers all over the civilized world, the French-

7. Schneider, *Pressefreiheit,* 77.
8. Maxwell E. McCombs and Donald L. Shaw, "The Agenda-Setting Function of the Press," in Doris A. Graber, ed., *Media Power in Politics* (Washington, D.C.: Congressional Quarterly, 1984), 66.

language international press served to unify its diverse public and to give them a common political culture. It also gave them a sense of historical time. The philosophers of the age agreed that the notion of time was a human construct, derived from the experience of a succession of events: "There would be no *time* without real and successive creations, arranged in a continuous series."[9] The newspaper press, more than any other eighteenth-century medium, established a common perception of historical time: in its pages, political events succeeded one another in orderly sequences, so that the process of converting the chaos of occurrences into the orderly human construct of history could take place.[10]

The Old Regime newspapers were thus essential agents in the creation of a common political culture. They offered their readers material on which to base critical discussions of the political world, and gave those discussions a regular rhythm and a common focus. And the process of discussion these newspapers fostered had radical implications for the world of which these newspapers were an integral part. The readers who participated in the endless flow of talk inspired by the press eventually demanded that their own opinions about politics become the sovereign authority for political action.[11] When the French revolutionary Jacques-Pierre Brissot, writing in 1789, demanded freedom for the periodical press because only through the medium of newspapers could one "teach the same truth at the same moment to millions of men" in such a way that they could "discuss it without tumult, decide calmly and give their opinion,"[12] he was calling for a press quite different from that of the Old Regime, but he was extrapolating from the experience of the Old Regime press itself, which had already demonstrated the power of periodicals in framing public debate. The elite newspapers of prerevolutionary Europe, such as the *Gazette de Leyde*, were among the building blocks out of which the structure of modern political systems based on the representation of public opinion—political systems antithetical both to the narrow world of Dutch republicanism that nurtured the *Gazette de Leyde* and to the wider world of absolutist monarchies in which the paper circulated—was created.

9. Samuel Formey, "Tems," in Diderot and d'Alembert, eds., *Encyclopédie*, 16:95.

10. Rétat, "Les gazettes: De l'événement à l'histoire," 34, 37. On the role of periodicals in structuring the sense of time, see also Joël Saugnieux, "Le temps, l'espace et la presse au siècle des Lumières," *Cahiers d'histoire* 23 (1978), 313–34.

11. For the process by which rational public discussion led to the subverting of traditional forms of political authority, see Reinhart Koselleck, *Kritik und Krise* (Frankfurt: Suhrkamp, 1973 [orig. 1959]), which heavily influenced the better-known exposition in Jürgen Habermas's *Strukturwandel der Oeffentlichkeit*.

12. Jacques-Pierre Brissot de Warville, *Mémoire aux Etats-Généraux: Sur la nécessité de rendre dès ce moment la presse libre, et surtout pour les journaux politiques* (Paris: 1789), 10.

The *Gazette de Leyde*'s Impact in the Age of Revolution

The European press, particularly the international gazettes, created the public space in which a politics based on public opinion could emerge, and gave political elites a common base of political information. But specific newspapers such as the *Gazette de Leyde* strove to do more than that: they also sought to guide events in a certain direction. The tensions of the revolutionary period, however, made it increasingly difficult for any periodical to do this and still fulfill the unifying function that the international gazettes, particularly Luzac's, had previously performed. The outbreak of the French Revolution finally destroyed the cohesive international public that had been the prerequisite for the existence of the Old Regime's elite press.

As we have seen, Jean Luzac, even while clinging to the notion of the gazetteer as an impartial recorder of events, had committed himself to the support of certain political causes, and he was certain that his paper in fact had some measurable effect on the direction of events during the revolutionary era. The causes he espoused had in common their connection with the eighteenth century's notion of constitutional liberty: a liberty based not on abstract, universal human rights but on the thicket of historical privileges unique to each state. This idealized constitutionalism, with its accompanying demand for citizens who would put the defense of their country's constitutional structure above their selfish private interests, expressed itself in "patriot" movements as diverse as the American revolt against British rule and the Polish resistance to the partitions. Luzac, imbued with the spirit of classical republicanism, of Calvinist suspicion of monarchy, and of Dutch civic and provincial self-government, allied himself with kindred souls in all the countries his newspaper covered. His international newspaper was a living embodiment of the connections between the scattered movements for political change that R. R. Palmer has called "the democratic revolution of the eighteenth century." And the paper had considerable impact on these movements, even though its editor frequently had personal reservations about their goals.

Despite its cautious and moderate language, the *Gazette de Leyde* was a partisan newspaper long before the French Revolution created an explicitly partisan press in Europe. Furthermore, the *Gazette de Leyde*'s ideological consistency made it a standard against which critical readers could measure the positions taken by rival publications whose editors' opinions were for sale, such as Jean Manzon of the *Courier du Bas-Rhin*. In its lofty disdain for anecdotes and slander, Jean Luzac's paper represented all European political contestations as clashes of principles. Even as it operated in the Old Regime world of amoral *raison d'état*, the *Gazette de Leyde* accustomed the European public to judge the political world according to moral and ideological values.

Had he been asked to sum up the practical effect of his nearly thirty years of editorial work, Jean Luzac would probably have been proudest of what he saw as his contribution to the success of the American war for independence from Britain. He claimed credit for having alerted even the officials of the French government to the significance of the colonists' spirit of rebellion as early as 1774, and his American friends were unstinting in their praise of the role his newspaper played in influencing European public opinion. To be sure, it was not public enthusiasm but American military success and French naval and economic aid that determined the outcome of the American war. The *Gazette de Leyde* did not win independence for the colonists, nor can it be asserted that the French government could not have given aid to the Americans in the absence of a favorable climate of opinion. But there is no doubt that French intervention was made easier because of that climate of opinion, and that Dutch recognition of the American republic, an important step in the consolidation of American success, was facilitated by a successful public relations campaign there. And unquestionably the *Gazette de Leyde* was one of the most important forces in shaping French, Dutch, and general European opinion about both the merits of the American case and the chances of the American cause throughout the 1770s and 1780s. The plaque that grateful Americans placed on Jean Luzac's house in Leiden in 1909 was well deserved.

In generously and effectively supporting the Americans, Luzac never recognized that they were in the process of creating a polity that went beyond the classical paradigm of mixed republican government. Influenced, no doubt, by his close relationship with John Adams, the American revolutionary leader most devoted to the classical paradigm, Luzac chose to overlook the radical implications of the American enunciation of the doctrine of popular sovereignty: for Luzac, the American Revolution created the last of the classical civic republics, not the first of the modern democracies. Neither he nor Adams recognized that, in a modern historian's words, "Americans had retained the forms of the Aristotelian schemes of government but had eliminated the substance."[13] The *Gazette de Leyde* helped consolidate the success of the American experiment without recognizing its true significance.

The *Gazette de Leyde*'s impact on the principal European events it covered during Jean Luzac's editorship is harder to assess, but its judgment of their ideological significance was clearer. The paper favored the losing side in the Dutch Patriot struggle, the Polish reform movement,

13. Gordon S. Wood, *The Creation of the American Republic* (New York: Norton, 1972), 604.

and ultimately in the French Revolution; whatever concrete influence it may have had in these cases was outweighed by the strength of contrary forces. Embittered Dutch radicals like Dumont-Pigalle blamed Luzac's refusal to put the paper at their disposition for the failure of the Patriot movement in the 1780s, but they did the *Gazette de Leyde* too much honor: the real reasons for the Patriots' collapse were the internal divisions in the movement and the French government's unwillingness to provide military and diplomatic support against the British and the Prussians. The *Gazette de Leyde* undoubtedly helped promote sympathy with the Patriot cause outside of the Netherlands, however: in the face of a press in other countries that was generally hostile or at best indifferent to the Dutch troubles, Luzac's paper served as the main spokesman for the movement. Arthur Young, traveling in France in 1787, found considerable sentiment for a war with Britain on behalf of the Dutch.[14] It can hardly be doubted that many of these French armchair warriors had followed the development of the Dutch crisis in the *Gazette de Leyde*.

Although his paper supported the Patriot movement in 1783–84 and in 1786–87, Luzac himself hesitated to endorse the direction that movement took after early 1785 because he saw clearly for the first time the danger that a reform movement originally dedicated to the restoration of an idealized mixed polity supposed to have existed in the past might instead end up demanding a government in which the voice of one element in the republic—the people—would have an absolute predominance. He had only to look at what happened to the rest of the Dutch press to see what the fate of the *Gazette de Leyde* would be if the radical Patriots triumphed. Luzac found himself nevertheless forced to choose among what he considered unacceptable alternatives and to commit the paper to the Patriot side in 1787, but the Prussian intervention spared him from having to deal with a triumphant democratic government— for a time.

For the Poles, the *Gazette de Leyde* was able to do even less. The cabinets of Berlin, St. Petersburg, and Vienna were far less susceptible to the pressure of public opinion than that of Versailles, and those cabinets' decisions determined the fate of their helpless neighbor. Nevertheless, Luzac's paper ensured that Poland's fate did not go unnoticed. The Polish king and the Patriot leaders certainly thought it was worth their while to arrange favorable coverage in the paper. More than any other periodical at the time, the *Gazette de Leyde* publicized the valiant efforts at reform that culminated in the liberal constitution of May 1791, and thus preserved for posterity proof that Poland's fate was not wholly due to internal weaknesses and divisions. The *Gazette de Leyde*'s coverage was one link in the chain of publicity that kept sympathy for Polish indepen-

14. Arthur Young, *Travels in France during the Years 1787, 1788 and 1789* (Cambridge: Cambridge University Press, 1950), 75–76.

dence alive in western Europe throughout the nineteenth century and made some contribution to the eventual reemergence of an independent Polish state after the First World War.

The French government's efforts to court the *Gazette de Leyde*, through its embassy in The Hague, and to suppress it when it became too outspoken in 1788, testify to the paper's influence in the prerevolutionary crisis. So long as France's politics was an affair of a relatively small elite working within traditional institutions, the paper remained a genuine force. After the events of 1789, however, the situation changed: the *Gazette de Leyde* rapidly lost whatever direct impact it had enjoyed inside France. Furthermore, no generally recognized "newspaper of record" arose to take its place. In the fiery crucible of revolutionary politics, no journalistic representation of events, not even a literal transcript of debates in the French assemblies, could impose itself as unbiased and win universal acceptance. Newspapers such as Boyer and Cerisier's *Gazette universelle*, which consciously set out to emulate the *Gazette de Leyde*, found themselves regarded as partisan publications and soon came to behave accordingly.[15] Revolutionary newspapers varied in their quality as sources of information, but the acknowledged elite press, the prerevolutionary international gazettes, ceased to exist after 1789.

Although the *Gazette de Leyde*'s impact on French affairs virtually disappeared after 1789, Luzac's assessment of the issues at stake in the Revolution was more accurate than his judgment of any previous political crisis. His vision sharpened by the Dutch experience of a few years earlier, he condemned the radicalism and violence of the French movement. The paper remained an important participant in the Europe-wide debate about the significance of the Revolution, and its cautious and generally critical attitude toward that movement, even in its early reforming phase, helped shape educated readers' views of French events. Along with other widely circulated newspapers that took a similar view, the *Gazette de Leyde* offered a more detached representation of the Revolution than the French domestic press, and this skepticism about the Revolution, rather than genuine enthusiasm, was probably the most common attitude among the Dutch, German, and Swiss upper-class readers who made up the Leiden paper's audience after 1789. There were, of course, other reasons why such people frequently came to oppose the French Revolution when it arrived in their countries, but it would be surprising if the consistently critical reports in the continent's most respected news periodical had made no impact on the climate of European opinion. But this role as one of many partisan participants in the Europe-wide debate about the Revolution was far different from the part the paper had played in prerevolutionary politics.

15. Jeremy D. Popkin, "The Elite Press in the French Revolution: the *Gazette de Leyde* and the *Gazette universelle*," in *Studies on Voltaire and the Eighteenth Century* (forthcoming).

However diminished the practical impact of the *Gazette de Leyde*'s representation of political reality in the revolutionary years may have been, the paper remained an irritant to the supporters of the French Revolution. For the revolutionaries, a political news organ that rejected popular sovereignty, even in the name of a lofty notion of civic virtue, was not an impartial newspaper: it was an instrument of counterrevolution. As such, it could not be tolerated. The struggle between Jean Luzac and Johan Valckenaer was a microcosm of the struggle between two conceptions of liberty, one rooted in Europe's classical and city-state traditions, the other growing out of Rousseau's passionate critique of the doctrine of mixed government. The Batavian revolutionaries who condemned Luzac's "aristocratic thinking" mislabeled their opponent, but they were correct in seeing that he was their enemy. In a purely practical sense, the Batavian republicans, supported by the French army, could undoubtedly have spared themselves the effort of forcing Jean Luzac to abandon his newspaper. But in a symbolic sense, the silencing of a newspaper that claimed the right to judge a popular government on the basis of principles derived from the past was a necessary part of the revolutionary destruction of the Dutch and the European Old Regime.

The *Gazette de Leyde* had never dictated opinions to its educated, cosmopolitan audience the way the London *Times* is said to have done in England fifty years later. Luzac's paper never dominated the market the way the *Times* did in the first part of the nineteenth century. It initiated no crusades and stirred no mass movements. Indeed, the paper set itself to combat two of the most powerful historical forces of its time: the growing power of democracy in western Europe and the increasing strength of authoritarian government in eastern and central Europe. Jean Luzac's little printed sheets of paper failed to stop either of these tendencies. But they had their influence on the climate of European political opinion. That influence was often ineffectual in the short run, but the *Gazette de Leyde* was one of the many channels through which the spirit of early modern European republicanism, opposed to the excesses of both democracy and authoritarianism, remained a vital part of the European political tradition and influenced the political thought of the nineteenth century and beyond.[16]

The *Gazette de Leyde* and Elite Journalism

The *Gazette de Leyde* was important in its own day because it helped create and structure a realm of informed public discussion about politics and because it promoted a particular set of attitudes toward the major

16. On the influence of this republican heritage, see Yves Durand, *Les républiques au temps des monarchies* (Paris: Presses universitaires de France, 1973), 202–4.

political crises of its day. But it is of greatest interest to the modern world because its story exemplifies many of the problems and possibilities of the elite press whose existence is bound up with the prospects for freedom and intelligent decision making in the modern world. Indeed, the cosmopolitan eighteenth-century European press has much in common with the increasingly internationalized news media of the end of the twentieth century. Like the elite newspapers of the Western world today, Jean Luzac's *Gazette de Leyde* served as the standard by which the independence and responsibility of all other newspapers in its time could be measured. Jean Luzac's paper strove to embody the qualities of freshness, accuracy, and impartiality that readers and journalists agreed a newspaper ought to have, but which have always been rare.

To be sure, the *Gazette de Leyde*'s independence was not absolute. It depended heavily on information furnished by various governments, and it depended on their permission to circulate. But one of the inherent paradoxes of political journalism is that a newspaper can only obtain the highest quality of information if the political elites whose actions make up the news trust the paper and confide in it. As a modern political scientist has written, any newspaper that "stands out as an organ of elite opinion" on the basis of the quality of its news must be "intimate with the government,"[17] and people in power do not voluntarily furnish information to newspapers openly hostile to them. Despite constitutional protections that the *Gazette de Leyde* never enjoyed, eminent newspapers such as the London *Times* of the nineteenth century and the *New York Times* of the twentieth have been closely tied to the political elites of their respective countries. *New York Times* reporter Harrison Salisbury, a thoroughgoing admirer of his own newspaper, has described the publication of the Pentagon Papers in 1971 as its *first* serious open defiance of the American government's wishes with respect to a major story concerning foreign policy.[18]

It is one of the inherent tensions in the Western journalistic tradition, however, that elite newspapers are valued not only for the completeness of the information they contain but also for the quality of their commitment to certain ideals. The virtues that are expected of elite newspapers, and that they ascribe to themselves, have changed remarkably little since the time of Jean Luzac. In 1896, when he took over the *New York Times*, Adolph Ochs promised that his paper would "give the news, all the news, in concise and attractive form, in language that is parliamentary in good society, and give it as early, if not earlier, than it can be learned

17. Ithiel de Sola Pool, cited in Bernard C. Cohen, *The Press and Foreign Policy* (Princeton, N.J.: Princeton University Press, 1963), 136.
18. Harrison E. Salisbury, *Without Fear or Favor* (New York: Ballantine Books, 1980), 12, 14.

through any other reliable medium; to give the news impartially, without fear or favor, regardless of any party, sect or interest involved." His statement could have served as a statement of Jean Luzac's intentions, and so could *Le Monde*'s declaration in 1944 that "its highest goal is to assure readers of clear, accurate, and, as much as possible, rapid and complete reports."[19]

The commitment elite newspapers make to honesty and impartiality in presenting the news is, of course, a moral commitment: elite newspapers promise to put aside the selfish motives that incline most newspapers, like most individuals, to think only of what is to their particular advantage. But the idealism that the public expects of elite newspapers is not merely a selfless devotion to precise accuracy: they are expected to support those actors on the historical stage who behave in accordance with the selflessness and devotion to the general welfare that is demanded of the newspaper itself. In the *Federalist Papers* (no. 51), James Madison, one of Jean Luzac's contemporaries, wrote that "if men were angels, no government would be necessary. If angels were to govern men, neither external nor internal controls on government would be necessary." But a less than perfect world requires both government and a news press, and the latter is expected to resist temptation sufficiently to serve as one of the controls on the virtue of the former.

As we have seen, Luzac believed that it was a journalist's moral duty to be accurate and impartial, but he did not believe "that impartiality consists in a cold refusal to choose between right and wrong."[20] And, as we have seen, he identified right and justice with those historical actors of his own day who exemplified republican virtue: the French *patriotes* who sought to temper the arbitrary power of the crown, the American revolutionaries, the Dutch Patriots, the Polish reformers. Deeply committed to the virtues of classical mixed government, Luzac could not be brought to sympathize with those who sought to give too much power to any one of the three groups whose interests the classical theory of mixed constitutions sought to balance. He was unyielding in his detestation of monarchs who acted despotically, but he was equally condemnatory of aristocrats who sought to maintain a monopoly on power and of radicals who would unbalance a constitution in the direction of democratic rule.

Luzac wrote little of the content of his *Gazette de Leyde*. But he chose its correspondents, he selected the documents it would republish, he decided which events it would single out for extensive coverage, and he did

19. Adolph Ochs, statement of principles, 19 Aug. 1896, cited in Meyer Berger, *The Story of the "New York Times," 1851–1951* (New York: Simon and Schuster, 1951), 107. *Le Monde,* 19 Dec. 1944, cited in Jean-Noel Jeanneney and Jacques Juilliard, *"Le Monde" de Beuve-Mery* (Paris: Seuil, 1979), 303.

20. Luzac to Hertzberg, 21 Mar. 1783, in LGA-VH, Z(2), no. 54.

pen the short but often crucial comments that framed and interpreted this news coverage for his readers. His paper's high reputation was based not only on the factual accuracy of its reports and its reputation for refusing direct subsidies but on the consistent quality of its moral commitment to political virtue. In this, the *Gazette de Leyde* resembled the elite newspapers of later eras: they, too, have been voices for causes. As John Merrill, the leading student of the modern elite press, has written, "A quality paper . . . must judge events and not simply report them, and have definite opinions and express them courageously."[21]

However respected their professional work is, journalists who express opinions know that they will be accused of partiality. Living in a revolutionary era, Jean Luzac confronted this dilemma in all its force. His devotion to the ideal of a pure and perfect form of mixed government distanced him from all existing European governments and from all but a handful of would-be reformers: neither governments nor reform movements ever succeeded in exemplifying perfect virtue. Luzac's devotion to a high ideal provided him with a vantage point from which he could maintain a critical perspective toward all aspects of European political reality and therefore sustain his inner conviction that he was indeed impartial. Since most of the European states in which the *Gazette de Leyde* circulated, including France, propagated an image of themselves as mixed polities—in contrast to the absolute monarchies of eastern Europe in which, as we have seen, the paper's influence was limited—Luzac and his newspaper functioned as gadflies calling on both rulers and would-be reformers to live up to their own professed ideals.

The French Revolution, as is well known, introduced both legal guarantees of press freedom and ideological restrictions more stringent than those of the Old Regime. Despite the revolutionaries' failure to live up to their initial promises, the Revolution did contribute to establishing the modern principles of press freedom. But something was lost for many years in the process: the willingness to tolerate an authoritative elite newspaper such as the *Gazette de Leyde*. Those revolutionary newspapers that aspired to such a status found themselves either sucked into the whirlpool of partisan controversy and destroyed, like Boyer and Cerisier's *Gazette universelle*, or discredited by their open willingness to serve whatever faction held power, like Panckoucke's *Moniteur*.

Happily, the end of the *Gazette de Leyde* was not the end of the ideal of journalistic independence. The demand for news has remained a central aspect of Western civilization, and there has always been a place in the press market for high-quality newspapers independent of ruling authorities. Jean Luzac's *Gazette de Leyde* takes its place in the honor roll of

21. Merrill, *Elite Press*, 8.

distinguished newspapers that also includes such papers as the London *Times*, the *Augsburger Allgemeine Zeitung*, the *New York Times*, and *Le Monde*. The fate of the *Gazette de Leyde* during the French Revolution is a reminder, however, that journalistic independence is a fragile thing. Whatever the laws may say, independent newspapers can thrive only when open discussion among the citizens does not automatically undermine the legitimacy of the rulers. In Britain since the early nineteenth century and in the United States this has usually been the case, and students of the Anglo-American press have taken this situation to be the norm. But in a wider perspective, the Anglo-American situation has been more an exception than a rule. There are no other major European countries where governments have not, at one time or another, rejected the principle of freedom of information in the name of some assertedly higher value: the sovereignty of the people, the defense of the nation, the interests of the proletariat or of the *Volk*. The existence of newspapers filling the role once held by the *Gazette de Leyde* is not to be taken for granted.

Despite the fact that freedom of information has always been under threat in most of continental Europe, the story of the *Gazette de Leyde* demonstrates that the ideal of independent reporting has deep historical roots outside the Anglo-American world. Those roots go back beyond the French Revolution, which first made press freedom a constitutional principle in Europe: they grow out of the humanist tradition of republican liberty based on virtue. The ethical demand that the journalist hold up the mirror of truth to a reality which too often shows rulers failing to meet standards of morality is no modern demand: it is an inheritance from an earlier epoch of Western civilization. Even in democratic countries, this journalistic ideal survives in uneasy juxtaposition with other demands on journalists and the news media: that they should promote efficient and effective government, guide and educate their readers rather than merely informing them, and produce maximum profits for their owners.

Jean Luzac's struggle to provide readers with what he regarded as the truth about their world is thus emblematic of the situation of would-be independent journalists in the world today. And when we recognize that the ideal of independent and honest news reporting is not a product of the modern era, as theorists of the press, such as John Merrill, and practicing journalists, such as Harrison Salisbury, have claimed, but that it has its origins in concepts of freedom and virtue that date to the Renaissance and before, we may also recognize that the threats to freedom of information do not come only from such modern evils as capitalist greed and totalitarian lust for power. In all ages, devotion to journalistic honesty has required an unusual degree of idealism and commitment.

The story of Jean Luzac and the *Gazette de Leyde* illuminates not only the way in which the forces operating in the revolutionary era at the end of the eighteenth century threatened a certain ideal of journalism: it is a graphic reminder of the difficulty even the most honest and dedicated journalists face in living up to that ideal today.

A Farewell to Jean Luzac

In the course of this study, we have seen that the *Gazette de Leyde* came to be what it was for many reasons. It responded to a real need of European political culture in the late eighteenth century, meeting the demands of both rulers and educated elites for a reliable representation of the political events of the day. But its ability to fill this need was severely circumscribed by the nature of the society in which it functioned. The paper was limited by technology of the preindustrial period, and restrained by the political structures of the Old Regime. Jean Luzac himself had no illusions about the extent of his ability to rise above these limitations: he described himself as simply trying to do the best job he could within them.

Nevertheless, one cannot examine the documents we have about Jean Luzac's life and read the copies of the *Gazette de Leyde* without sensing the force of his strong personality in the apparently impersonal content of the paper. One has only to compare the tone of the *Gazette de Leyde* with that of its rival, Jean Manzon's *Courier du Bas-Rhin*, to see how different individuals, working with the same materials, could produce very different results. The sober, serious, principled language that characterized the *Gazette de Leyde* was a natural expression of the hard-working Calvinist citizen of eighteenth-century Leiden who edited the paper.

Luzac certainly was not the most original or creative journalist of his age. His hated rival Manzon produced a livelier paper within the constraints of Old Regime journalism. Contemporaries, such as Linguet and the great journalistic writers of the French Revolution—Desmoulins, Marat, and Brissot—broke those constraints and created a journalism whose rhetorical power is still astonishing today. The publishers of the English press showed that the newspaper could serve a whole gamut of social and economic needs beyond those that interested Luzac.

Nor was Jean Luzac a wholly admirable character. The self-righteousness that so many of his close acquaintances denounced in him is only too apparent in his private letters; it poisoned friendships and family relations and contributed to the destruction of his beloved newspaper. Luzac's intellectual limitations are painfully evident in his published works: his devotion to liberty was genuine, but his liberty was a cramped ideal, fettered by dogmatic assumptions inherited from antiquity and from the course of Dutch history. He was unable to see any way to combine freedom with democracy, and he could not overcome the rigid social prejudices that caused him to fear the common men and women whose hard labor made possible the comfortable life he and his readers enjoyed. Even the admiration that one naturally feels for a man who fought so valiantly to defend what he believed in should be tempered by a recognition that Luzac led a very sheltered life. Compared to the misfortunes of his Paris correspondent Pascal Boyer, who had been in the Bastille under the Old Regime and ended up on the guillotine under the new, Luzac's long war with the Dutch radicals was a combat with only minor risks. Throughout his journalistic career, the good burgher of Leiden never had to leave the comforts of his home; he risked neither his life nor even any considerable part of his property in his struggle for freedom to publish what he chose.

Nevertheless there is something heroic about the figure of Jean Luzac. The ideal he devoted himself to—accuracy and honesty in reporting the news, combined with a disinterested devotion to freedom—is one that still has meaning today. Our definition of freedom is different, but we can still recognize in Jean Luzac one of the great embodiments of liberal journalism. Imperfect though he was as a human being, he succeeded better than most in living a life of high principle and thereby providing a genuine service to the world around him. If unpolluted news is essential to the life of any society worthy of respect, Jean Luzac stands as an example of the virtues we require even today from our journalists.

Sources and
Bibliography

Manuscript Sources

The two main collections of manuscript sources dealing with Jean Luzac and the *Gazette de Leyde* are the Luzac Family Archive, in the Leiden University Library, and the Luzac papers in the Van Heukelom Family Archive, housed in the Leiden Gemeentearchief. The former contains personal correspondence to and from Jean Luzac, mostly for the period after 1785, and a variety of related documents; the latter has the surviving papers concerning the *Gazette de Leyde* itself. Both these collections were employed by the nineteenth-century Dutch scholar W. P. Sautijn Kluit in his monograph "Fransche Leidsche Courant," but he excerpted only a fraction of the documentation available about the paper and its editor. I have cited from the original manuscript sources wherever possible.

In addition to these two main bodies of archival material, I have used a variety of other manuscript sources. The Leiden University Library has documents concerning Luzac not housed in the Luzac Family Archive, including correspondence among Jean Luzac and his brother Etienne and the latter's brother-in-law Johan Valckenaer. In the Dumont-Pigalle papers in the Algemeen Rijksarchief of The Hague, the basic source for the history of the Dutch Patriot movement, is a large dossier labeled "Contre Luzac," containing gossip and information about Jean Luzac collected from his circle of French-speaking acquaintances. Other volumes of the Dumont-Pigalle collection also contain relevant information. Also in the Algemeen Rijksarchief are the papers of the American representative in the Netherlands, Charles Dumas, which include a

[267]

number of letters to Luzac and references to the *Gazette de Leyde*, and documents from the Dutch postal service and the provincial government of Holland with information about the paper. There are a handful of Luzac letters in other Dutch libraries, including the Amsterdam University Library and the Koninklijk Bibliotheek of The Hague, and in libraries in other countries, such as the Bibliothèque nationale and the Huntington Library. Letters to and from Jean Luzac are found in the papers of John Adams, and numerous references to the paper appear in the published correspondence of Thomas Jefferson. Documents concerning the French government's relations with the paper are scattered through the French Ministry of Foreign Affairs series "Correspondance politique—Hollande."

PRINTED SOURCES

Works of Jean Luzac (by date)

Specimen Academicum, exhibens observationes nonnullas apologeticas pro Jurisconsultis Romanis, ad locum Ciceronis in Oratione pro Murena Capp. XI–XIII princ. Leiden: Luzac, 1768.

Aantwoord van Mr. Johan Luzac, aan den Wel. Ed. Heer Mr. Elias Luzac. Leiden: n.p., 1775.

Verzameling van Stukken, betreffende de Augmentatie der Land-en Zee-Magt der Republieq. Holland: n.p., 1782.

Contra-Aanteekeningen van Negentien Leden van de Vroedschap der Stad Leyden; betreklyk tot het Adres, in Maart 1785, aan dezelve Vroedschap ingeleverd . . . Leiden: Herdingh, 1785.

Redevoering van Mr. Johan Luzac, ten betooge, dat de Geleerdheid de voedster is der Burger-Deugd, vooral in een Vry Gemeenebest . . . Jan de Kruyff, trans. Leiden: Mostert, 1786.

Verzameling van Stukken, betreffende de valsche beschuldiging tegens Catharina Taan, Wed. Vandermeulan, nevens een kort verslag van de uitkomst derzelve zaak. Leiden: Herdingh, 1786.

Socrates als burger beschouwd. 2d ed. Jean Luzac, trans. Leiden: Honkoop, 1797.

Verzameling van Stukken, betreffende het gedrag der Curateuren van Holland's Universiteit te Leyden, in de jaaren 1796. en 1797. Bijzonder in de zaak van Mr. Johan Luzac . . . Leiden: Honkoop, 1797.

W. P. C. Knuttel's *Catalogus van de pamflettenverzameling berustende in de Koninklijke Bibliotheek*, a standard reference, also attributes to Jean Luzac two pamphlets in French, *Mémoire juridique, où l'on examine impartialement jusqu'à quel point sont fondé les plaintes du Roi de la Grande-Bretagne, sur la secrète correspondance entre la Ville d'Amsterdam et les Colonies Angloises dans l'Amerique* (1781), and *Défense des Belges confédérés* (1784). The *Mémoire juridique*, a condemnation of Dutch supporters of the American Revolution, can hardly have been written by Luzac. The *Défense des Belges confédérés*, a pamphlet defending the Dutch Patriots, criticizes the Dutch republican constitution for being insufficiently democratic; because of this and because of its style, it seems more likely to have been written by one of the French supporters of the Dutch Patriot movement, perhaps Dumont-Pigalle, than by Luzac himself.

Pamphlets concerning Jean Luzac

Advisen van Mr. Matthias Temminck, Mr. Hendrik Vollenhoven, en Jacob van Halmael . . . over het rapport van Dirk Hoitsma en J. Nolet, in de Zaak van Mr. J. Luzac. N.p., 1798.

[Broes, Broerius]. *Aan den lasteraar van Mr. Johan Luzac, thans rector magnificus van Hollands Hooge Schoole te Leyden.* Leiden, n.d. [1794].

Eerkrans voor den steller van het Rapport omtrend de Leydsche Propositie van Geheim-houding; den Hooggeleerden Heer Mr. Jan Luzac, Grieksch Hoogleeraar te Leyden. N.p., n.d.

Historisch Verhaal van het Gepasseerde te Leyden, met de Propositie van Geheimhouding. Leiden: Heyligert, van Tiffelen and Onnekink, 1786.

Luzac, Elie. *Aantekeningen op het Antwoord van Mr. Johan Luzac, aan den Wel.-Ed. Heer Mr. Elias Luzac.* Leiden: n.p., 1775.

Copies of the *Gazette de Leyde* consulted

Nearly all citations of the *Gazette de Leyde*, or, to give it its official title, the *Nouvelles extraordinaires de divers Endroits*, are drawn from the set of presentation copies for the years 1739 through 1809 now in the Regen-stein Library at the University of Chicago. Library records show that the University of Chicago acquired this set of the paper in 1902, but do not indicate its provenance. In consulting other copies of the paper, I have found minor typographical differences between the University of Chicago's copy and those in other libraries, but no differences in the text. Other copies consulted include those in the Leiden University Library, Bibliothèque nationale, Bibliothèque Mazarine, Library of Congress, Folger Library, Lilly Library (Indiana University), Newberry Library, and Huntington Library.

Other Eighteenth-Century Periodicals

Affaires de l'Angleterre et l'Amérique
Ami du Roi
Amsterdam [*Gazette d'Amsterdam*]
Annales patriotiques [Paris]
Annales politiques, civiles, et littéraires
Annonces, Affiches et Avis Divers pour la ville de Marseille
Annual Register
Berlinische Nachrichten
Braunschweigische Nachrichten

Briefwechsel meist historischen und politischen Inhalts
Bulletin de Versailles
Chronique de Paris
Correspondance de MM. les députés des communes de la province d'Angers, avec leurs
   commettants
Courier du Bas-Rhin
Courrier d'Avignon
Courrier de la Meuse
Courrier de l'Europe
Courrier de Versailles à Paris, et de Paris à Versailles
Eclair
Esprit des Gazettes, ou Recueil des Evénemens politiques et extraordinaires
Esprit des Journaux françois et étrangers
Etats Généraux. Bulletin de la correspondance de la députation du tiers état de la
   sénéchaussée de Brest
Etats Généraux. Correspondance de Bretagne
Gaçeta de Madrid
Gazette de Cologne
Gazette de France
Gazette de Hambourg [Warsaw]
Gazette de La Haye
Gazette d'Utrecht
Gazette Nationale, ou le Moniteur Universel
Gazette universelle [Paris]
Gazzetta di Parma
Hollandsche Historische Courant
Holländische Stats-Anzeigen
Holländische Zeitung
Journal de Francfort
Journal de la Montagne
Journal de Lyon
Journal de Paris
Journal des Etats Généraux
Journal des Etats Généraux tenu par la Députation du Dauphiné
Journal Général de France
Journal Général de l'Europe
Leydse Courant
Mercure de France
Morning Chronicle
Nieuwe Nederlandsche Jaarboek
Nouvelles de Versailles
Nouvelles Ecclésiastiques, ou Mémoires pour servir à l'histoire de la Constitution Uni-
   génitus
Nouvelles littéraires et politiques [Gazette des Deux-Ponts]
Nouvelles politiques [Paris]
Ouderwetsche Nederlandsche Patriot
Patriote françois

Point du Jour
Politieke Blixem
Politieke Kruyer
Politique hollandois
Politische Gespräche der Todten
Politische Journal
Post van der Neder-Rhijn
Révolutions de Paris
Schlesische Privilegirte Zeitung
Schwäbische Merkur
s'Gravenhaagse Courant
Staats- und Gelehrte Zeitung des Hamburgischen Unpartheyischen Correspondenten
Stats-Anzeigen
Times [London]
Vaderlandsche Staatsbeschouwers
Versailles et Paris
Zeitung fur Städte, Flecken und Dörfer [Wolfenbüttel]

Other Printed Primary Sources

Arneth, Alfred d', and Jules Flammermont, eds. *Correspondance secrète du Comte de Mercy-Argenteau avec l'Empereur Joseph II et le Prince de Kaunitz.* 2 vols. Paris: Imprimerie nationale, 1889.

Aspinall, Arthur, ed. *The Later Correspondence of George III.* 5 vols. Cambridge: Cambridge University Press, 1966.

Beaufort, W. H. de, ed. *Brieven van en aan Joan Derck van der Capellen tot den Poll.* Utrecht: Kemink, 1879.

Beaumarchais, Pierre Augustin Caron de. *Correspondance.* Brian M. Morton, ed. 4 vols. Paris: Nizet, 1969–78.

[Bernard, François]. *Précis historique de la Révolution qui vient de s'opérer en Hollande.* Paris: Desenne and Volland, 1788.

Bielfeld, Jacob Friedrich von. *Institutions politiques.* 2d ed. 3 vols. Leiden: Luchtmans, 1767–72.

Boulard, M. S. *Le manuel de l'imprimeur.* Paris: Boulard, 1791.

Boyd, Julian B., ed. *Papers of Thomas Jefferson.* 20 vols. Princeton, N.J.: Princeton University Press, 1950–.

Browning, Oscar, ed. *Despatches from Paris, 1784–1790.* 2 vols. London: Camden Society, 1909–10.

Butterfield, L. H., ed. *Diary and Autobiography of John Adams.* 4 vols. Cambridge, Mass: Harvard University Press, 1961.

Caraccioli, Louis-Antoine de. *Paris, le modèle des nations étrangères, ou l'Europe françoise.* Venice and Paris: Duchesne, 1777.

Cerisier, Antoine-Marie, trans. *Histoire de la fondation des colonies des anciennes républiques, adaptée à la dispute présente de la Grande-Bretagne avec ses colonies americaines.* Utrecht: Schoonhoven, 1778.

———. *Observations impartiales d'un vrai Hollandois, pour servir de Reponse au Discours d'un soi-disant bon Hollandois à ses compatriotes.* Arnhem: Nyhof, 1778.

————. *Suite des observations impartiales d'un vrai Hollandois, sur les intérêts et l'état présent des affaires politiques de la France, de l'Angleterre, des Provinces-Unies des Pays-Bas et des Etats-Unis de l'Amérique.* Arnhem: Nyhof, 1779.

————. *Tableau de l'histoire générale des Provinces unies.* 10 vols. Utrecht: Schoonhoven and Wild, 1777–84.

Charrière, Isabelle de. *Oeuvres complètes.* 10 vols. Amsterdam: Van Oorschot, 1979–81.

Collection complette de tous les ouvrages pour et contre M. Necker, avec des notes critiques, politiques et secrètes. Utrecht: n.p., 1781.

Correspondance politique et anecdotique sur les affaires de l'Europe, et particulièrement sur celles de l'Allemagne depuis l'année 1780 jusqu'à présent. 5 vols. N.p., 1789–90.

Défense des Belges confédérés, des Souverains respectifs de leurs provinces, et de leurs respectables et zélés Magistrats, contre l'Oracle des politiques étrangers, Le "Courier du Bas-Rhin". "Hollande," 1784.

Dumont-Pigalle, Pierre A. *Esquisse d'un grand tableau, ou Mémoires pour servir à l'histoire des Provinces-Unies des Pays-Bas.* "Hollande": n.p., 1786.

[Dumont-Pigalle, Pierre A.]. *Le diner du Lion d'Or, ou Aventures singulières arrivées en Juillet 1783, au Sr. Manzon, Alias, Fort-en-Gueule, redacteur de la Gazette intitulée, Le Courier du Bas-Rhin.* N.p, n.d.

Encyclopédie methodique ou par ordre de matières. Paris: Panckoucke, 1782–1828.

Fitzmaurice, Edmond, ed. *Lettres de l'abbé Morellet à Lord Shelburne.* Paris: Plon, 1898.

Forster, Georg. *Ansichten vom Niederrhein.* G. Steiner, ed. Berlin: Akademie-Verlag, 1958.

Fortescue, John, ed. *Correspondence of King George the Third.* 6 vols. London: Macmillan, 1928.

Fruin, Robert, ed. *Depeches van Thulemeyer, 1763–1788.* Amsterdam: J. Muller, 1912.

Grabner, J. *Briefe über der vereinigten Niederlände.* Gotha: Ettinger, 1792.

Hubert, Eugène, ed. *Correspondance des ministres de France accrédités à Bruxelles de 1780 à 1790.* 2 vols. Brussels: Kiesling, 1920–24.

Jacobi, Adam. *Vollständige Geschichte der siebenjährigen Verwirrungen und der Revolution in den vereinigten Niederlanden.* Halle: J. J. Gebauer, 1789.

Jakob, Ludwig Heinrich. [review of Luzac, *Socrates*] in *Annalen der Philosophie und des Philosophischen Geistes* 3 (1797), 179–81.

Janssen, Frans A., ed. *Zetten en Drukken in de achttiende Eeuw: David Wardenaar's Beschrijving der Boekdrukkunst (1801).* Haarlem: Enschedé, 1982.

Küttner, K. G. *Beyträge zur Kenntniss vorzüglich des gegenwärtigen Zustandes von Frankreich und Holland.* Leipzig: Dyckischen Buchhandlung, 1792.

Lescure, A., ed. *Correspondance secrète inédite sur Louis XVI, Marie-Antoinette, la cour et la ville de 1777 à 1792.* 2 vols. Paris: Plon, 1866.

Lettres de Philippe Mazzei et du roi Stanislas-Auguste de Pologne. Rome: Istituto storico italiano, 1982.

Lewis, W. S., ed. *Horace Walpole's Correspondence.* New Haven, Conn.: Yale University Press, 1960–.

Marshall, Joseph. *Travels Through Holland, Flanders, Germany, Denmark, Sweden, Lapland, Russia, the Ukraine and Poland, in the Years 1768, 1769, and 1770.* 3 vols. London: J. Almon, 1772.

Mazzei, Philip. *Memoirs of the Life and Peregrinations of the Florentine Philip Mazzei 1730–1816*. Howard R. Marraro, trans. New York: Columbia University Press, 1942.

Mémoires justificatifs de la Comtesse de Valois de la Motte, écrit par elle-même. London: n.p., 1789.

Mercier, Louis-Sébastien. *Les entretiens du Palais-Royal de Paris*. Paris: Buisson, 1786.

———. *Tableau de Paris*. "Nouvelle édition." 12 vols. Amsterdam, 1782–88.

[Métra]. *Correspondance secrète, politique et littéraire*. 18 vols. London: John Adamson, 1787–90.

Mieris, Frans van, and Daniel van Alphen. *Beschryving der Stad Leyden*. Leiden: Heyligert and Honkoop, 1784.

Naemwijzer, waer in gevonden worden de Naemen van de Ed. Groot Achtb. Heeren Regenten der Stad Leyden. Leiden: Honkoop, 1790.

Necker, Jacques. *De l'administration des finances de la France*. 3 vols. N.p., 1785.

Pestel, Friedrich Wilhelm. *Vollständige Nachrichten von der Republik Holland aus authentischen Quellen gesammelt*. Berlin: Buchhandlung der Realschule, 1784.

[Pidansat de Mairobert, attrib.]. *Journal historique de la Révolution opérée dans la Constitution de la Monarchie françoise, par M. de Maupeou, Chancelier de France*. 7 vols. "Nouvelle édition, revue, corrigée & augmentée." London: John Adamson, 1776.

[Pidansat de Mairobert, attrib.]. *L'espion anglois, ou Correspondance secrète entre Milord All'Eye et Milord All'Ear*. 10 vols. "Nouvelle édition, revue, corrigée et considerablement augmentée." London: John Adamson, 1784–85.

[Pidansat de Mairobert, attrib.]. *Mémoires secrets pour servir à l'histoire de la république des lettres en France, depuis MDCCLXII jusqu'à nos jours*. 36 vols. London: John Adamson, 1777–89.

Portrait des émigrés d'après nature. Paris: Desenne, [1795].

Rélation de la conjuration contre le gouvernement et le magistrat de Genève qui à éclaté le 8 Avril 1782. N.p., n.d.

Schirach, Gottlob Benedikt von. "Einleitung." In Johann Hermann Stoever, *Historisch-statistische Beschreibung der Staaten des teutschen Reichs*. Hamburg: Hoffmann, 1785, ix–xxx.

Schlözer, August Ludwig von. *Ludwig Ernst, Herzog zu Braunschweig und Luneburg*. Göttingen: Vandenhoeck, 1786.

Segur, Louis P., ainé. *Tableau historique et politique de l'Europe, depuis 1786 jusqu'en 1796, ou l'An IV*. 2d ed. 3 vols. Paris: Buisson, 1801.

Storch, Heinrich. *Schetsen, Tooneelen, en Waarneemingen, verzameld op eene reize door Frankryk*. Leiden: Trap, 1792.

Varin, A. L. A. *Chambre patriotique et littéraire: Pour la lecture des meilleurs ouvrages et de tous les papiers publics*. Paris: J. B. Chemin, 1791.

Vaufleury. *Cabinet littéraire nationale, au Palais Royal*. Paris: L. Potier de Lille, 1791.

Voltaire, F. M. A. *Voltaire's Correspondence*. T. Besterman, ed. 101 vols. Geneva: Institut Voltaire, 1953–77.

Watson, Elkanah. *Tour in Holland in 1784*. Worcester, Mass.: Thomas, 1790.

Wendeborn, Gebhard F. A. *D. Gebh. Fr. Aug. Wendeborn's Erinnerungen aus seinem Leben*. Hamburg: Bohn, 1813.

Wharton, Francis, ed. *The Revolutionary Diplomatic Correspondence of the United States*. 6 vols. Washington, D.C.: Government Printing Office, 1889.

Young, Arthur. *Travels in France during the Years 1787, 1788 and 1789*. Cambridge: Cambridge University Press, 1950.

Yvernois, François d'. *Précis historique de la dernière Révolution de Genève, et en particulier de la Réforme que le Souverain de cette République a faite dans les Conseils Administrateurs*. N.p., n.d.

SELECT BIBLIOGRAPHY OF SECONDARY SOURCES

The following is restricted to books and articles containing information about (a) the life of Jean Luzac; (b) the city of Leiden and the Netherlands during Luzac's career as editor; and (c) the history of printing, the eighteenth-century press and the growth of public opinion. Citations to works consulted only for information on the political events dealt with in the *Gazette de Leyde* will be found in the notes.

The Life of Jean Luzac

[Baudus, Jean]. "Notice sur M. Luzac, mort au désastre de Leyde." *Journal de l'Empire*. 22 Dec. 1807.

Bilderdijk, Willem, and Matthijs Siegenbeek. *Leidens Ramp*. Amsterdam: Allart and Ruis, 1838.

Duvyerman, J. P. "Jean Luzac, vroegtijdige grondrechten-publikatie." *Nederlands Juristenblad*, 29 May 1965, 453–55.

Galerie historique des contemporains ou nouvelle biographie. 8 vols. Brussels: Wahlen, 1817–20.

Knappert, L. "Een gedenksteen voor Professor Jean Luzac." *Leidse Jaarbookje* 7 (1910), 112–22.

Schöffer, Ivo. "Een Leids Hoogleeraar in politieke moeilijkheden. Het ontslag van Johan Luzac in 1796." In J. F. Heijbroek, A. Lammers, and A. P. G. Jos van der Linde, eds., *Geen Schepsel Wordt Vergeten*. Amsterdam and Zutphen: Trouw, 1985, 61–80.

Vrij, E. J. "Het collegegeschil tussen de hoogleeraren Adriaan Kluit en Jean Luzac." *Jaarboekje voor geschiedenis en oudheidkunde van Leiden en omstreken* 63 (1971), 121–42.

History of Leiden and the Netherlands

Alexandre, Jean, and Marie-Rose Perrin-Chevrier. "Un gentilhomme paisible, le 'Batave' Jacobus Blaauw." *Annales historiques de la Révolution française*, no. 261 (1985), 335–52.

Algemene Geschiedenis der Nederlanden. 10 vols. Haarlem: Fibula Reeks, 1980.

Blok, Petrus H. *Geschiedenis eener Hollandsche Stad*. 4 vols. The Hague: Nijhoff, 1910–18.

Buijnsters, P. J. *Wolff en Dekken. Een biografie*. Leiden: Nijhoff, 1984.

Cobban, Alfred. *Ambassadors and Secret Agents*. London: Jonathan Cape, 1954.

Colenbrander, Herman T. *De Patriottentijd*. 3 vols. The Hague: Nijhoff, 1897–99.

De Jonge, J. C. *Nederland en Venetie*. The Hague: Van Cleef, 1852.

De Vries, Jan. "Barges and Capitalism: Passenger Transportation in the Dutch Economy, 1632–1839." *Afdeling Agrarische Geschiedenis Landbouwhogeschool Waginingen* 21 (1978), 33–398.

De Vries, Johannes. *De economische Achteruitgang der Republiek in de Achttiende Eeuw*. 2d ed. Leiden: Stenfert Kroese, 1968.

———. "The Population and Economy of the Preindustrial Netherlands." *Journal of Interdisciplinary History* 15 (1985), 661–82.

De Wit, Cornelius. *De Nederlandse Revolutie van de Achttiende Eeuw 1780–1787*. Oirsbeek: n.p., 1974.

Edler, F. *The Dutch Republic and the American Revolution*. Baltimore: Johns Hopkins University Press, 1911.

Fairchild, Helen Lincklaen, ed. *Francis Adrian van der Kemp, 1752–1829. An Autobiography*. New York: Putnam, 1903.

Frijhoff, Wilhelm. *La Société néerlandaise et ses gradués, 1575–1814*. Amsterdam: APA-Holland University Press, 1981.

Geyl, Pieter. *La Révolution batave (1783–98)*. J. Godard, trans. Paris: Société des études robespierristes, 1971.

Hart, Simon. *Geschrift en Getal*. Dordrecht: Historische Vereniging Holland, 1976.

Hendrikszoon, Murk de Jong. *Joan Derk van der Capellen*. Groningen: Wolters, 1921.

Höweler, H. A. "Een moordplan tegen Willem V?" *Leidsche Jaarboekje* (1964), 103–24.

Jackson, Harry. *Scholar in the Wilderness: Francis Adrian van der Kemp*. Syracuse, N.Y.: Syracuse University Press, 1963.

Kemper, I. J. de Bosch. *Letterkundige Aanteekeningen betreffende de Geschiedenis van het Nederlandsche Staatsleven en Staatsregt*. Amsterdam: 1871.

Knuttel, W. P. C. *Catalogus van de pamflettenverzameling berustende in de Koninklijke Bibliotheek*. 7 vols. The Hague: 1889–1920.

Kossmann, E. H. *Politieke Theorie in het zeventiende-eeuwse Nederland*. Amsterdam: N. V. Noord-Hollandsche Uitgevers, 1960.

———. *Verlicht Conservatisme: Over Elie Luzac*. Groningen: Wolters, 1966.

Kroes-Ligtenberg, Christine. *Dr. Wybo Fijnje*. Assen: Van Gorcum, 1957.

Leeb, I. Leonard. *The Ideological Origins of the Batavian Revolution*. The Hague: Nijhoff, 1973.

Marx, Jacques. "Elie Luzac et la pensée éclairée." *Documentatieblad 18. Eeuw* 11–12 (1971), 74–105.

Nijhoff, Dirk C. *De Hertog van Brunswijk*. The Hague: Nijhoff, 1889.

Overvoorde, J. C. *Geschiedenis van het postwezen in Nederland vòòr 1795*. Leiden: Sijthoff, 1902.

Popkin, Jeremy D. "From Dutch Republican to French Monarchist: Antoine-Marie Cerisier and the Age of Revolution." *Tijdschrift voor Geschiedenis* (forthcoming 1989).

————. "Print Culture in the Netherlands on the Eve of Revolution." In Margaret Jacob and Willem Mijnhardt, eds. *Decline, Enlightenment and Revolution: The Dutch Republic in the Eighteenth Century* (forthcoming).

Prak, Maarten R. *Gezeten Burgers. De Elite in een Hollandse Stad: Leiden 1700–1780.* The Hague: Hollandse Historische Reeks, 1985.

Riley, James C. *International Government Finance and the Amsterdam Capital Market, 1740–1815.* New York: Cambridge University Press, 1980.

Schama, Simon. "The Enlightenment in the Netherlands." In Roy Porter and Mikulas Teich, eds., *The Enlightenment in National Context.* Cambridge: Cambridge University Press, 1981, 54–71.

————. *Patriots and Liberators.* New York: Knopf, 1977.

Schilling, Heinz. "Die Geschichte der nordlichen Niederlände und die Modernisierungstheorie." *Geschichte und Gesellschaft* 8 (1982), 475–517.

Schulte Nordholt, Jan Willem. *The Dutch Republic and American Independence.* Herbert H. Rowen, trans. Chapel Hill: University of North Carolina Press, 1982.

Siegenbeek, Matthijs. *Geschiedenis der Leidsche Hoogeschool.* 2 vols. Leiden: Luchtmans, 1829–32.

Sillem, Jerome A. *Het Leven van Mr. Johan Valckenaer (1759–1821).* 2 vols. Amsterdam: Van Kampen, 1883.

Van Dijk, E. A., and J. Trijsburg, W. F. Wertheim, and A. H. Wertheim-Gijse Weenink, eds. *De Wekker van de Nederlandse Natie. Joan Derk van der Capellen 1741–1784.* Zwolle: Waanders, 1984.

Woltjer, J. J. *De Leidse Universiteit in verleden en heden.* Leiden: Universitaire Pers Leiden, 1965.

Zwager, H. H. *Nederland en de Verlichting.* 2d ed. Haarlem: Fibula-Van Dishoeck, 1980.

Secondary Literature on the History of the Press, Publishing, and Public Opinion

The extensive literature dealing exclusively with the French domestic press during the revolutionary period has been omitted. For bibliography of works in this field, see Bellanger et al., *Histoire générale de la presse française*, vol. 1, and Jeremy D. Popkin, *The Right-Wing Press in France, 1792–1800* (Chapel Hill: University of North Carolina Press, 1980).

Acomb, Frances. *Mallet du Pan (1749–1800).* Durham: Duke University Press, 1973.

Albaric, Michel. "Un page d'histoire de la presse clandestine: 'Les Nouvelles Ecclésiastiques,' 1728–1803." *Revue française d'histoire du livre* 10 (1980) 319–32.

Allinne, Jean-Pierre. "La Déclaration des Droits de l'Homme et les aspirations libérales en Europe. Le témoignage de la presse." *Annales historiques de la Révolution française*, no. 262 (1985), 426–45.

Andriessen, Simon. "Johan Luzac, zijn 'Gazette de Leide' en de Amerikaanse onafhankelijkheidsoorlog." Unpubl. ms., Leiden, 1977.

Ascoli, Peter. "American Propaganda in the French Language Press during the American Revolution." In *La Révolution américaine et l'Europe* (Colloque de Toulouse, 1978). Paris: Centre national de la recherche scientifique, 1979. 291–305.

———. "The French Press and the American Revolution: The Battle of Saratoga." *Proceedings of the 5th Annual Meeting of the Western Society for French History* (1977), 46–55.

Aspinall, Arthur. *Politics and the Press.* London: Home and Van Thal, 1949.

———. "The Reporting and Publishing of the House of Commons' Debates 1771–1834." In Richard Pares and A. J. P. Taylor, eds., *Essays Presented to Sir Lewis Namier.* London: St. Martins, 1956, 227–57.

———. "The Social Status of Journalists at the Beginning of the Nineteenth Century." *Review of English Studies* (July 1945), 216–32.

Azam, Denise Aimé. "Le ministère des affaires étrangères et la presse à la fin de l'ancien régime." *Cahiers de la presse* 1 (1938), 428–38.

Bailyn, Bernard, and John B. Hench, eds. *The Press and the American Revolution.* Worcester, Mass: American Antiquarian Society, 1980.

Bellanger, Claude, et al. *Histoire générale de la presse française.* 5 vols. Paris: Presses universitaires de France, 1969–74.

Bénétruy, J. *L'atelier de Mirabeau.* Geneva: Jullien, 1962.

Berger, Meyer. *The Story of the "New York Times," 1851–1951.* New York: Simon and Schuster, 1951.

Berkelbach van der Sprenkel, J. W. "De Fransche Revolutie in de contemporaine Hollandsche couranten." *De Gids* (1939), 323–57.

Birn, Raymond. *Pierre Rousseau and the "Philosophes" of Bouillon.* Geneva: Institut Voltaire, 1964.

Black, Jeremy. *The English Press in the Eighteenth Century.* Philadelphia: University of Pennsylvania Press, 1987.

Black, Jeremy, and Pat Rogers. "Oldmixon Incurs 'The Displeasure of the Most Honourable House of Peers.'" *Factotum* [Newsletter of the Eighteenth-Century Short Title Catalogue], no. 24 (Aug. 1987), 5–9.

Blanc-Rouquette, Marie-Thérèse. *La presse et l'information à Toulouse, des origines à 1789.* Toulouse: Association des Publications de la Faculté des Lettres et Sciences Humaines de Toulouse, 1967.

Blühm, Elgar, and Rolf Engelsing, eds. *Die Zeitung.* Bremen: Schünemann, 1967.

Bödeker, Hans-Erich. "Zur Rezeption der französischen Menschen-und Burgerrechtserklärung von 1789/1791 in der deutschen Aufklärungsgesellschaft." In *Grund- und Freiheitsrechte im Wandel von Gesellschaft und Geschichte.* Göttingen: Vandenhoeck and Ruprecht, 1981, 258–86.

Bodel Nyenhuis, Johannes T. *De Wetgeving op de drukpers en boekhandel in de Nederlanden tot in het begin van de 19e eeuw.* Amsterdam: Van Kampen, 1892.

Bond, Donovan H., and W. Reynolds McLeod, eds. *Newsletters to Newspapers: Eighteenth-Century Journalism.* Morgantown, W.V.: School of Journalism, 1977.

Botein, Stephen. "'Meer Mechanics' and an Open Press: The Business and Political Strategies of Colonial American Printers." *Perspectives in History* 9 (1975), 127–225.

Botein, Stephen, Jack R. Censer, and Harriet Ritvo. "The Periodical Press in Eighteenth-Century English and French Society: A Cross-Cultural Approach." *Comparative Studies in Society and History* 23 (1981), 464–90.

Bots, Hans, ed. *La diffusion et la lecture des journaux de langue française sous l'ancien régime*. Amsterdam and Maarssen: APA-Holland University Press, 1988.

Boulay, Helga. "La chute de la monarchie vue par trois périodiques de Hambourg." *Annales historiques de la Révolution française*, no. 255–56 (1984), 204–28.

Boulay, Helga. "La presse à Hambourg et Altona et la Révolution française." *Les genres et l'histoire au XVIIIe et XIXe siècles*, 2 vols. Besançon: Annales littéraires de l'Université de Besançon, 1983.

Carey, James W. "The Problem of Journalism History." *Journalism History* 1 (1974), 3–5, 27.

Castronovo, Valerio, Giuseppe Ricuperati, and Carlo Capra. *La stampa italiana dal cinquecento all'ottocento*. Bari: Laterza, 1976.

Censer, Jack R. "Die Presse des Ancien Régime im Uebergang—Eine Skizze." In Reinhart Koselleck and Rolf Reichardt, eds., *Die Französische Revolution als Bruch des gesellschaftlichen Bewusstseins*. Munich: Beck, 1988, 127–52.

Censer, Jack R., and Jeremy D. Popkin, eds. *Press and Politics in Pre-Revolutionary France*. Berkeley: University of California Press, 1987.

Chartier, Roger. *Lectures et lecteurs dans la France d'ancien régime*. Paris: Seuil, 1987.

Chartier, Roger, Henri-Jean Martin, and Jean-Pierre Vivet, eds. *Histoire de l'edition française*. 4 vols. Paris: Promodis, 1983–85.

Cohen, Bernard C. *The Press and Foreign Policy*. Princeton, N.J.: Princeton University Press, 1963.

Conti Odorisio, Ginevra. *S. N. H. Linguet dall'ancien regime alla rivoluzione*. Rome: Giuffrè, 1976.

Couperus, Marianne, ed. *L'étude des périodiques anciens*. Colloque d'Utrecht. Paris: Nizet, 1972.

Couvée, D. H. "The Administration of the 'Oprechte Haarlemse Courant' 1738–42." *Gazette* 4 (1958), 91–110.

Dahl, Folke. *Dutch Corantos 1618–1650: A Bibliography*. The Hague: Nijhoff, 1946.

Dann, Otto, ed. *Lesegesellschaften und bürgerliche Emanzipation*. Munich: Beck, 1981.

Darnton, Robert. *The Business of Enlightenment*. Cambridge, Mass.: Harvard University Press, 1979.

———. "L'imprimerie de Panckoucke en l'an II." *Revue française d'histoire du livre* 9 (1979), 359–69.

———. *The Literary Underground of the Old Regime*. Cambridge: Harvard University Press, 1982.

———. "Writing News and Telling Stories." *Daedalus* no. 104/2 (1975), 175–94.

Desmond, Robert W. *The Information Process: World News Reporting to the Twentieth Century*. Iowa City: University of Iowa Press, 1978.

Douxchamps-Lefèvre, Cécile. "Un magazine de la Cour de France au début du règne de Louis XVI." *Revue historique*, no. 549 (1984), 95–108.

Dubosq, Yves-Z. *Le livre français et son commerce en Hollande de 1750 à 1780.* Amsterdam: H. J. Paris, 1925.

Dumont, Franz. "La déclaration des droits de l'homme et du citoyen en Allemagne." *Annales historiques de la Révolution française* 50 (1978), 220–42.

Echeverria, Durand. "French Publications of the Declaration of Independence and the American Constitutions, 1776–1783." *Papers of the Bibliographical Society of America* 47 (1953), 313–38.

Edroiu, Nicolai. *Horea's Uprising: European Echoes.* Bucharest: Academiei Republicii Socialiste Romania, 1984.

Eeghen, Isabella H. van. "De Amsterdamsche Courant in de Achttiende Eeuw." *Jaarboek Amstelodamum* 44 (1950) 31–58.

Eisenstein, Elizabeth. "On Revolution and the Printed Word." In Roy Porter and Mikulas Teich, eds., *Revolution and History.* Cambridge: Cambridge University Press, 1986, 186–205.

———. *The Printing Press as an Agent of Change.* 2 vols. New York: Cambridge University Press, 1979.

Elben, Otto. *Geschichte des Schwäbischen Merkurs 1785–1885.* Stuttgart: Verlag des Schwäbischen Merkurs, 1885.

Engelsing, Rolf. *Der Burger als Leser. Lesergeschichte in Deutschland 1500–1800.* Stuttgart: Metzler, 1974.

Ester, Karl d'. *Das politische Elysium oder die Gespräche der Todten am Rhein.* Neuwied: Strüdersche Buchdruckerei, 1936–37.

Everth, Erich. *Die Offentlichkeit in der Aussenpolitik von Karl V. bis Napoleon.* Jena: Fischer, 1931.

Faÿ, Bernard. *L'esprit révolutionnaire en France et aux Etats-Unis à la fin du XVIIIe siècle.* Paris: Champion, 1925.

Feyel, Gilles. *La "Gazette" en province à travers ses réimpressions, 1631–1752.* Amsterdam and Maarssen: APA-Holland University Press, 1982.

———. "La presse provinciale au XVIIIe siècle: Géographie d'un reseau." *Revue historique,* no. 552 (1984), 353–74.

Fishman, Mark. *Manufacturing the News.* Austin: University of Texas Press, 1980.

Fontius, Martin. "Mettra und seine Korrespondenzen." *Romanische Forschungen* 76 (1964), 405–21.

Funck-Brentano, Frantz. *Figaro et ses devanciers.* Paris: Hachette, 1909.

———. *Les nouvellistes.* 2d ed. Paris: Hachette, 1905.

Galtung, Johan, and Mari Holmboe Ruge. "The Structure of Foreign News." In Jeremy Tunstall, ed., *Media Sociology.* Urbana: University of Illinois Press, 1970, 259–98.

Gans, Herbert J. *Deciding What's News.* New York: Vintage, 1980.

Gaskell, Paul. *A New Introduction to Bibliography.* Oxford: Clarendon, 1972.

Gelbart, Nina R. *Feminine and Opposition Journalism in Old Regime France.* Berkeley: University of California Press, 1987.

Gibbs, Graham C. "The Role of the Dutch Republic as the Intellectual Entrepôt of Europe in the 17th and 18th Centuries." *Bijdragen en Mededelingen betreffende de Geschiedenis der Nederlanden* 86 (1971), 323–49.

Godechot, Jacques. "L'expansion de la déclaration des droits de l'homme de 1789 dans le monde." *Annales historiques de la Révolution française* 50 (1978), 201–213.

————. *La Grande Nation.* 2d ed. Paris: Aubier, 1983.

Graff, Harvey J. *The Legacies of Literacy.* Bloomington: Indiana University Press, 1987.

Grossbart, Julien. "La presse polonaise et la Révolution française 1789–94." *Annales historiques de la Révolution française* 14 (1937), 127–50, 241–56, and 15 (1938), 234–66.

Groth, Otto. *Die Zeitung,* 4 vols. Mannheim: J. Bensheimer, 1928.

————. *Geschichte der deutschen Zeitungswissenschaft.* Munich: Weinmayer, 1948.

Guinard, Paul-J. *La presse espagnole de 1737 à 1791.* Paris: Centre de recherches hispaniques, 1973.

Haacke, Wilmont. *Die Politische Zeitschrift 1665–1965.* Stuttgart: Koehler, 1968.

Habermas, Jürgen. *Strukturwandel der Offentlichkeit.* Berlin: Luchterhand, 1962.

Harris, Michael. "The Management of the London Newspaper Press during the Eighteenth Century." *Publishing History* 4 (1978), 95–112.

Hatin, Eugène. *Bibliographie historique et critique de la presse périodique française.* Paris: Didot, 1866.

————. *Les gazettes de Hollande et la presse clandestine aux XVIIe et XVIIIe siècles.* Paris: Pincebourde, 1865.

————. *Histoire politique et littéraire de la presse en France.* 8 vols. Paris: Poulet-Massis, 1859–61.

Hermann-Mascard, Nicole. *La censure des livres à Paris à la fin de l'ancien régime (1750–1789).* Paris: Presses universitaires de France, 1968.

Hinds, Charles F. "The *Courrier d'Avignon* in the Reign of Louis XVI." M.A. thesis, University of Kentucky, 1958.

Hutson, James W. "Letters from a Distinguished American. The American Revolution in Foreign Newspapers." *Quarterly Journal of the Library of Congress* 34 (1977), 292–305.

Inglis, Brian. *Freedom of the Press in Ireland, 1784–1841.* 1954.

Jansen, Paule, et al. *L'année 1778 à travers la presse traitée par ordinateur.* Paris: Presses universitaires de France, 1982.

Jeanneney, Jean-Noel, and Jacques Juilliard. *"Le Monde" de Beuve-Mery.* Paris: Seuil, 1979.

Jentsch, Irene. *Zur Geschichte des Zeitungslesens in Deutschland am Ende des 18. Jahrhunderts.* Ph.D. Diss., Leipzig, 1937.

Klaits, Joseph. *Printed Propaganda under Louis XIV.* Princeton, N.J.: Princeton University Press, 1976.

Kluit, Willem P. Sautijn. "De Fransche Leidsche Courant." *Handelingen en Mededeelingen van de Maatschappij der Nederlandsche Letterkunde te Leiden* (1869–70), 3–183.

————. "Delfsche Couranten." *Handelingen en Mededeelingen van de Maatschappij der Nederlandsche Letterkunde te Leiden* (1872) 25–88.

————. "De Hollandsche Leidsche Courant." *Mededeelingen gedaan in de Vergaderingen van de Maatschappij der Nederlandsche Letterkunde te Leiden* (1870–71), 3–86.

————. "De Rotterdamsche Courant." *Mededeelingen van de Maatschappij der Nederlandsche Letterkunde te Leiden* (1877–78), 1–92.

————. *De s'Gravenhaagsche Courant.* Leiden: Brill, 1875.

————. "Geschiedenis der Nederlandsche Dagbladpers tot 1813." *Bijdragen tot de Geschiedenis van den Nederlandschen Boekhandel* 7 (1896) 87–284.

————. "Hollandsche en Fransche Utrechtse Couranten." *Bijdragen en Mededeelingen van het Historisch Genootschap, gevestigd te Utrecht* 1 (1878), 26–168.

————. *Le politique hollandois*. Leiden, 1882.

Koselleck, Reinhart. *Kritik und Krise*. Frankfurt: Suhrkamp, 1973 (orig. 1959).

Labrosse, Claude, and Pierre Rétat. *L'instrument périodique*. Lyon: Presses universitaires de Lyon, 1985.

Lebrun, François. "Une source d'histoire sociale: La presse provinciale à la fin de l'ancien régime. Les 'Affiches d'Angers' (1773–1789)." *Mouvement social*, no. 40 (1962), 56–73.

Leonard, Thomas C. *The Power of the Press: The Birth of American Political Reporting*. New York: Oxford University Press, 1986.

Levy, Darline Gay. *The Ideas and Careers of Simon-Henri-Nicolas Linguet*. Urbana: University of Illinois Press, 1980.

Levy, Leonard W. *Emergence of a Free Press*. New York: Oxford University Press, 1985.

Lindemann, Margot. *Deutsche Presse bis 1815*. Berlin: Colloquium, 1969.

Lippmann, Walter. *Public Opinion*. New York: Free Press, 1965. (orig. 1922).

Lojek, Jerzy. "Gazettes internationales de langue française dans la seconde moitié du XVIIIe siècle." In *Modèles et moyens de la réflexion politique au XVIIIe siècle*. 3 vols. Lille: Presses universitaires de Lille, 1977, 1:369–82.

————. "International French Newspapers and Their Role in Polish Affairs during the Second Half of the Eighteenth Century." *East Central Europe* (1974), 54–64.

————. *Polska inspiracja prasowa w Holandii i Niemczech wczasach Stanislawa Augusta*. Warsaw: Panstwowe Wydawnictwo Nankowe, 1969. [Notes and summary in French.]

Lüsebrink, Hans-Jürgen, and Rolf Reichardt. "La prise de la Bastille comme 'événement total.' Jalons pour une théorie historique de l'événement à l'époque moderne." In *L'evénement* (Colloque d'Aix-en-Provence, 1983). Marseille: Laffitte, 1986, 77–102.

Lutnick, Solomon. *The American Revolution and the British Press 1775–1783*. Columbia: University of Missouri Press, 1967.

McKenzie, D. F. "Printers of the Mind: Some Notes on Bibliographical Theories and Printing-House Practices." *Studies in Bibliography* 22 (1969), 1–75.

Mantoux, Paul. *Notes sur les comptes rendu des séances du Parliament anglais au XVIIIe siècle conservés aux Archives du Ministère des Affaires étrangères*. Paris: Giard and Briere, 1906.

Manuel, Pierre. *La police de Paris dévoilée*. 2 vols. Paris: Garnéry, 1791.

Marker, Gary. *Publishing, Printing, and the Origins of Intellectual Life in Russia, 1700–1800*. Princeton, N.J.: Princeton University Press, 1985.

Maspéro-Clerc, Hélène. "Une 'gazette anglo-française' pendant la guerre d'Amérique: Le 'Courier de l'Europe (1776–1788).'" *Annales historiques de la Révolution française*, no. 227 (1976), 572–94.

————. *Un journaliste contre-révolutionnaire: Jean-Gabriel Peltier (1760–1825)*. Paris: Société des études robespierristes, 1973.

————. "Samuel Swinton, éditeur du Courier de l'Europe à Boulogne-sur-Mer (1778–1783) et agent secret du gouvernement britannique." *Annales historiques de la Révolution française*, no. 262 (1985), 527–31.

Merrill, John C. *The Elite Press*. New York: Pitman, 1968.

Michon, Georges. *Le rôle de la presse en 1791–1792. La déclaration de Pillnitz et la guerre*. Paris: T.E.P.A.C., 1941.

Money, John. "Taverns, Coffeehouses and Clubs: Local Politics and Popular Articulacy in the Birmingham Area in the Age of the American Revolution." *Historical Journal* 14 (1971), 15–47.

Moran, Daniel J. "Cotta and Napoleon: The French Pursuit of the *Allgemeine Zeitung*." *Central European History* 14 (1981), 91–109.

————. "The Cotta Press in the Reform Era, 1794–1819." Ph.D. diss., Stanford University, 1982.

Morelli Timpanaro, Maria Augusta. "Legge sulla stampa e attivita editoriale a Firenze nel secondo Settecento." *Rassegna degli archivi di stato* 29 (1969), 613–700.

————. "Persone e Momenti del giornalismo politico a Firenze dal 1766 a 1799." *Rassegna degli archivi di stato* 31 (1971), 400–73.

Morineau, Michel. *Incroyables gazettes et fabuleux métaux: Les retours des trésors Americains d'après les gazettes hollandaises*. Cambridge: Cambridge University Press, 1985.

Morison, Stanley. *The English Newspaper*. Cambridge: Cambridge University Press, 1932.

[Morison, Stanley, et al.] *History of the "Times."* 5 vols. New York: Macmillan, 1935–53.

Moulinas, René. *L'imprimerie, la librairie et la presse à Avignon au XVIIIe siècle*. Grenoble: Presses universitaires de Grenoble, 1974.

Moureau, François. "La presse allemande de langue française (1686–1790). Etude statistique et thématique." *Aufklärungen* 1 (1985), 243–52.

————. "Lumières et libertés vues de Clèves en 1768 par le Courier du Bas-Rhin." In *Le concept de la liberté dans l'espace rhénan* (Colloque de Mulhouse, 1974). Gap: Faculté des lettres de Mulhouse, 1976, 77–86.

Olivier, Louis. "Bachaumont the Chronicler: A Doubtful Renown." *Studies on Voltaire and the Eighteenth Century* 143 (1975), 161–79.

Palmer, Robert R. *The Age of the Democratic Revolution*. 2 vols. Princeton, N.J.: Princeton University Press, 1959–64.

Pollak, Michael. "The Performance of the Wooden Printing Press." *Library Quarterly* 42 (1972), 218–64.

Popkin, Jeremy D. "International Gazettes and Politics of Europe in the Revolutionary Period." *Journalism Quarterly* 62 (1985), 482–88.

————. "Pamphlet Journalism at the End of the Old Regime." *Eighteenth-Century Studies* 22 (forthcoming 1989).

————. "Political Communication in the *Aufklärungsgesellschaft:* Gottlob Benedikt von Schirach's *Politische Journal*," In Hans-Ulrich Bödeker, ed., *Aufklärungsgesellschaft als Kommunikationssystem*. Göttingen: forthcoming.

Printing the Times since 1785. London: Printing House Square, 1953.

Prüsener, Marlies. "Lesegesellschaften im 18. Jahrhundert." *Archiv für Geschichte des Buchwesens* 13 (1972), 369–594.

Puttemans, André. *La censure dans les Pays-Bas autrichiens.* Brussels: Palais des Académies, 1935.

Quéniairt, Jean. *Culture et sociétés urbaines dans la France de l'ouest au XVIIIe siècle.* Paris: Klincksieck, 1978.

Réau, Louis. *L'Europe française au siècle des lumières.* Paris: Albin Michel, 1938.

Rétat, Pierre. "Les gazettes: De l'événement à l'histoire." In Henri Duranton et al., eds., *Etudes sur la presse* 3 (1978), 23–38.

Rétat, Pierre, ed. *L'attentat de Damiens.* Paris: Centre national de la recherche scientifique, 1979.

Rétat, Pierre, ed. *Le journalisme d'ancien régime.* Lyon: Presses universitaires de Lyon, 1982.

Robiquet, Paul. *Théveneau de Morande.* Paris: Quantin, 1882.

Rychner, Jacques. "A l'ombre des Lumières: Coup d'oeil sur la main d'oeuvre de quelques imprimeurs du XVIIIe siècle." *Studies on Voltaire and the Eighteenth Century* 155 (1976), 1925–56.

———. "Running a Printing House in Eighteenth- Century Switzerland: The Workshop of the Société Typographique de Neuchâtel." *The Library*, 6th ser., 1 (1979), 1–24.

Salisbury, Harrison E. *Without Fear or Favor.* New York: Ballantine, 1980.

Saugnieux, Joel. "Le temps, l'espace et la presse au siècle des Lumières." *Cahiers d'histoire* 23 (1978), 313–34.

Schneider, Franz. *Pressefreiheit und politische Oeffentlichkeit.* Neuwied: Luchterhand, 1966.

Schneider, Maarten, and Joan Hemels. *De Nederlandse Krant 1618–1978.* 4th ed. Baarn: Het Wereldvenster, 1978.

Schudson, Michael. *Discovering the News.* New York: Basic Books, 1978.

Schwarzkopf, Joachim von. [series of articles about newspapers in different countries], in *Allgemeiner Litterarischer Anzeiger* (1800), 41–47 (Denmark); 49–56 (Sweden and Russia); 65–68 (Turkey); 1449–56 (North America); 1457–62 (Spain and colonies); 1473–80 (Netherlands); 1481–86 and 1489–95 (Switzerland); 1633–36 (Poland); 1641–46, 1649–54 and 1657–61 (Italy); and (1801); 324–26 (Portugal); 329–33 (India and China); 337–41 (European colonies); 345–51, 353–60, and 361–68 (Prussia). Promised articles on the French and British papers never appeared.

———. *Ueber Zeitungen: Ein Beytrag zur Staatswissenschaft.* Frankfurt: Varrentrapp, 1795.

Schweitzer, K., and R. Klein. "The French Revolution and Developments in the London Daily Press to 1793." *Publishing History* 18 (1985), 85–97.

Sgard, Jean. "Journale und Journalisten im Zeitalter der Aufklärung." In Hans-Ulrich Gumbrecht, Rolf Reichardt, and Thomas Schleich, eds., *Sozialgeschichte der Aufklärung in Frankreich.* 2 vols. Munich: R. Oldenbourg, 1981, 2:3–33.

———. *Les trente récits de la journée des Tuiles.* Grenoble: Presses universitaires de Grenoble, 1988.

Sgard, Jean, ed. *Dictionnaire des journalistes.* Grenoble: Presses universitaires de Grenoble, 1976.

———. *Presse et histoire au XVIIIe siècle: L'année 1734.* Paris: Centre national de la recherche scientifique, 1978.

———. *La presse provinciale au XVIIIe siècle.* Grenoble: Centre de recherches sur les sensibilités, 1983.

Smith, Anthony. *The Newspaper: An International History.* London: Thames and Hudson, 1979.

Solomon, Harold M. *Public Welfare, Science, and Propaganda in Seventeenth-Century France.* Princeton, N.J.: Princeton University Press, 1972.

Stockum, W. P. van. *La librairie, l'imprimerie et la presse en Hollande à travers quatre siècles.* The Hague: Mouton, 1910.

Strasser, Kurt. *Die Wiener Presse in der josephinischen Zeit.* Vienna: Notring, 1962.

Tate, Robert S., Jr. "Petit de Bachaumont: His Circle and the Mémoires secrets." Geneva: Institut Voltaire, 1968.

Thiry, Louis. "La petite histoire. Un précurseur de la Révolution au pays de Liège, les archives de la Société typographique de Herve." *La Vie Wallonne* 14 (1933–34), 375–92 and 15 (1934–35), 11–28, 43–54, 80–93.

Thomas, Peter. "The Beginning of Parliamentary Reporting in Newspapers, 1768–1774." *English Historical Review* 74 (1959), 623–36.

Tuchman, Gaye. *Making News.* New York: Free Press, 1978.

———. "Objectivity as a Strategic Ritual: An Examination of Newsmen's Notions of Objectivity." *American Journal of Sociology* 77 (1972), 660–79.

Tucoo-Chala, Suzanne. *Charles-Joseph Panckoucke et la libraire française 1736–1798.* Pau: Marrimpouey, 1977.

Vaillé, Eugène. *Histoire générale des postes françaises.* 6 vols. Paris: Presses universitaires de France, 1952–55.

Vanderscheuren, B. "Les premières années du Journal Général de l'Europe." *La Vie Wallonne* 34 (1960), 245–82.

———. "Pierre Lebrun et la révolution brabançonne." *La Vie Wallonne* 34 (1960), 114–38.

———. "Pierre Lebrun et la révolution liègeoise." *La Vie Wallonne* 35 (1961), 243–67.

Varin d'Ainville, Marie. *La presse en France, génèse et évolution de ses fonctions psychosociales.* Paris: Presses universitaires de France, 1965.

Varloot, Jean, and Paule Jansen, eds. *L'année 1768 à travers la presse traitée par ordinateur.* Paris: Centre national de la recherche scientifique, 1981.

Ventre, Madeleine. *L'imprimerie et la librairie en Languedoc au dernier siècle de l'Ancien Régime 1700–1789.* Paris: Mouton, 1958.

Venturi, Franco. *Settecento riformatore.* 5 vols. Turin: Einaudi, 1976–84.

Vercruysse, Jeroom. "Journalistes et Journaux à Bruxelles au XVIIIe siècle." *Etudes sur le XVIIIe siècle* 4 (1977), 117–27.

Versprille, Annie. "Oordeel over de Gazette de Leyde." *Jaarboekje voor Geschiedenis en Oudheidskunde van Leiden en Omstreken* 52 (1960), 160–61.

Weigelt, Carl. *150 Jahre Schlesische Zeitung im Verlag von Wilh. Gottl. Korn in Breslau.* Breslau: Korn, 1892.

Welke, Martin. "Die Legende vom 'unpolitischen Deutschen.' Zeitungslesen im 18. Jahrhundert als Spiegel des politischen Interesses." *Jahrbuch der Wittheit zu Bremen* 25 (1981), 161–88.

Werkmeister, Lucyle. *The London Daily Press 1772–1792.* Lincoln: University of Nebraska Press, 1963.

White, David M. "The 'Gate Keeper': A Case Study in the Selection of News." *Journalism Quarterly* 27 (1950), 383–90.

Wiles, Roy. *Freshest Advices: Early Provincial Newspapers in England.* Columbus: Ohio State University Press, 1965.

Wilke, Jürgen. "Auslandsberichterstattung und internationaler Nachrichtenfluss im Wandel." *Publizistik* 31 (1986), 53–90.

———. *Nachrichtenauswahl und Medienrealität in vier Jahrhunderten.* Berlin: De Gruyter, 1984.

Index

Library of Congress Cataloging-in-Publication Data

Popkin, Jeremy D., 1948–
    News and politics in the age of revolution : Jean Luzac's Gazette de Leyde /
Jeremy D. Popkin.
        p. cm.
    Bibliography: p.
    Includes index.
    ISBN 0-8014-2301-5 (alk. paper)
    1. Nouvelles extraordinaires de divers endroits. 2. Press and politics—
Europe—History—18th century. 3. Europe—Politics and government—18th
century. I. Title.
PN5259.L453N687   1989   302.23'22'09409033—dc20   89-31379